God's
Inerrant
Word

God's Inerrant Word:

An International Symposium
On The Trustworthiness
Of Scripture

Edited by
John Warwick Montgomery

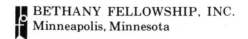 BETHANY FELLOWSHIP, INC.
Minneapolis, Minnesota

Library of Congress Cataloging in Publication Data

Montgomery, John Warwick.
God's Inerrant Word
Conference on the Inspiration and Authority of Scripture,
Ligonier, Pa., 1973.
1. Bible—Evidences, authority, etc.—Congresses.
2. Bible—Inspiration—Congresses.
I. Montgomery, John Warwick, 1931- ed.
II. Title.
BS480.C623 1973
220.1
74-4100
ISBN 0-87123-179-4

Printed in U.S.A.

Within that awful volume lies
The mystery of mysteries!
Happiest they of human race,
To whom God has granted grace
To read, to fear, to hope, to pray,
To lift the latch, and force the way;
And better had they ne'er been born,
Who read to doubt, or read to scorn.

—Sir Walter Scott on the Holy Scriptures

THE LIGONIER STATEMENT

We believe the Holy Scriptures of the Old and New Testaments to be the inspired and inerrant Word of God: We hold the Bible, as originally given through human agents of revelation, to be infallible and see this as a crucial article of faith with implications for the entire life and practice of all Christian people. With the great fathers of Christian history we declare our confidence in the total trustworthiness of the Scriptures, urging that any view which imputes to them a lesser degree of inerrancy than total, is in conflict with the Bible's self-testimony in general and with the teaching of Jesus Christ in particular. Out of obedience to the Lord of the Church we submit ourselves unreservedly to his authoritative view of Holy Writ.

John M. Frame

John H. Gerstner

Peter R. Jones

John Warwick Montgomery

James I. Packer

Clark H. Pinnock

R. C. Sproul

FOREWORD

At the turn of the century, Abraham Kuyper warned of the possibility that developing trends in the higher criticism of the Christian Scriptures could become an exercise in "Biblical vandalism." That warning is no longer a future possibility but a *fait accompli.* More and more Biblical criticism comes from a context of anti-historical and anti-revelational ideologies. The result has been confusion, skepticism, and despair. Church communities have opted for pluralistic and relativistic theology in order to accommodate the loss of authority. "Studied ambiguity" is the hallmark of modern confessional statements. In a word, the foundations of the church have been rudely shaken.

Each generation of Christian believers must deal afresh with the question of authority. A mere restatement of former views without reference to contemporary issues is inadequate; a *de novo* statement divorced from all past reflection is irresponsible. Thus, this volume appears as a contemporary attempt to speak stereoscopically to the modern vacuum of authority—with one eye on contemporary issues and the other on the wisdom of the history of the church.

The essays in this book were written as research articles for delivery at the Conference on the Inspiration and Authority of Scripture, Ligonier, Pennsylvania, in the fall of 1973. The Conference was sponsored by the Ligonier Valley Study Center, a facility developed to make the resources of Christian scholarship available to today's laymen and pastors.

Ligonier, Pennsylvania   R. C. Sproul
26 October 1973   Convener,
                         Conference on the Inspiration and
                                 Authority of Scripture

* * *

The eleven essays comprising the text of this book were all publicly delivered at the Ligonier Conference. Appended is an additional paper which, though not presented at the Conference, the essayists deemed particularly germane to its stated objectives.

CONTENTS

1. Biblical Inerrancy: What Is at Stake?. 15
   John Warwick Montgomery

2. "Sola Scriptura" in History and Today. 43
   J. I. Packer

3. Lessons from Luther on the Inerrancy of Holy Writ 63
   John Warwick Montgomery

4. Calvin's View of Scripture 95
   J. I. Packer

5. Warfield's Case for Biblical Inerrancy 115
   John H. Gerstner

6. Limited Inerrancy: A Critical Appraisal and
   Constructive Alternative 143
   Clark H. Pinnock

7. God and Biblical Language: Transcendence and
   Immanence 159
   John M. Frame

8. Scripture Speaks for Itself 178
   John M. Frame

9. The Inspiration of Scripture and the Authority
   of Jesus Christ. 201
   Clark H. Pinnock

10. The Apostle Paul: Second Moses to the New
    Covenant Community 219
    Peter R. Jones

11. The Case for Inerrancy: A Methodological Analysis . . . 242
    R. C. Sproul

Appendix
The Approach of New Shape Roman
Catholicism to Scriptural Inerrancy: A Case Study. . . 263
John Warwick Montgomery

Contributors 282
Index   283

EDITOR'S INTRODUCTION

Contemporary evangelical Christianity has demonstrated great vitality both in its stress on an unchanging gospel and in its forthright proclamation of saving truth. Yet in spite of this (or perhaps because of it, since nothing maddens the Evil Foe like fidelity to God's will), the present evangelical situation is fraught with extreme peril. Opposition to unqualified biblical authority has begun to erode evangelical testimony from within the ranks, and the importation of Barthian dichotomies has reinforced the natural tendency of pietistic fundamentalism to sacrifice the objective truths of Scripture on the altar of subjective experience.

The cry of "paper pope" has been shouted at evangelical Protestants ever since the Reformation. Today, however, one observes with amazement and with sorrow that in the very orthodox circles where the 20th century battle for biblical authority has been most courageously fought, voices are being raised against the inerrancy of Holy Writ. In 1963, Dewey M. Beegle, of the late, great Biblical Seminary in New York, published his work, *The Inspiration of Scripture*, in which—having embraced neo-orthodox, dialectic presuppositions as to the nature of truth—he imposes them on Scripture, denies its inerrancy, and makes the incredible claim that evangelicals by a "mental readjustment" can now retain inspiration without inerrancy and thereby rejoin mainline Protestant ecumenical theology. North Park Seminary in Chicago, long known for its uncompromising free-church orthodoxy and piety, is now characterized by an anti-inerrancy approach to the Bible that finds scriptural truth-value not in any historical soundness or factual consistency possessed by the Word, but in its ability to trigger spiritual experience. Concordia Seminary, St. Louis, a bastion of biblical orthodoxy in the days of Theodore Engelder and W. F. Arndt, has in the last two decades weakened its stand appallingly; how much can be seen from the September, 1965, issue of the *Concordia Theological Monthly*, where arguments contra inerrancy once directed against the Church from outside (e.g., non-possession of the original autographs of the biblical books) are now advocated by faculty members themselves. And in many quarters of the American evangelical scene, from East coast to West, as well as in England and on the continent, theologians who should be testifying to Scripture's total truth are preferring to avoid the word "inerrancy," are making no efforts to explain apparent discrepancies in the Bible, and are re-defining "truth" so that the Scripture can—we are confidently told—retain its absolute revelational veracity without the necessity of factual accuracy.

The anti-inerrancy trend in evangelical Protestantism has the characteristics of Aristotle's classic tragedy: it has occurred in a remarkably short time, and it produces both pity and fear in the sensitive observer—pity that our theologians have learned so little from history (the United Presbyterian Confession of 1967 is the inevitable consequence of the deterioration of belief in biblical inerrancy in the Presbyterian Church U.S.A. in the 1920's), and fear that such naïveté will totally corrupt evangelical witness here and abroad.

The Ligonier Conference and the essays delivered at it were designed specifically to serve as an adrenal injection for the faint-of-heart who question the place of inerrancy in historic Christian theology or doubt that modern research is compatible with an errorless Bible. The essayists may differ from each other in a number of respects (their epistemologies, for example, stand in frequent tension), and they do not assume responsibility for the view of their colleagues; but, as the Ligonier Declaration makes crystal clear, they hold in common the historic Christian confidence in an entirely trustworthy Bible. They would impart that confidence to the readers of this volume, and they pray the Lord of the Church to use their efforts to that end. *Quod non est biblicum, non est theologicum,* is their motto, and it remains the only path to Reformation and renewal.

JOHN WARWICK MONTGOMERY

31 October 1973:
The Festival of the Reformation
and the Eve of All Saints' Day

1

BIBLICAL INERRANCY: WHAT IS AT STAKE

John Warwick Montgomery

A favorite preacher's text is I Corinthians 14:8: "If the trumpet give an uncertain sound, who shall prepare himself to the battle?" Those who quote the verse perceive that the contemporary church suffers from uncertainty as to its message. The problem, however, is a good deal more acute. In large regions of the ecclesiastical landscape, the warriors appear totally incapable of identifying the battlelines. The silence is ominous: hardly anyone seems to be able to find the trumpet, much less to play even uncertain sounds on it.

HAS ANYONE SEEN A TRUMPET?

This critical situation is most readily observable among practitioners of so-called "liberal" religion. While some are calling down fire from heaven and directly promoting the use of force to blast the establishment in favor of disenfranchised local minorities, and advocating the quick disposal of the unborn through unrestricted abortion, others in the same camp are pacifistically condemning any military opposition to totalitarian efforts that would swallow up minorities on the other side of the globe, and labeling western involvements as the imperialistic and wanton killing of defenseless children. One observes, to put it mildly, a certain lack of precise criteria of moral judgment.

But the clergyman of liberal persuasion is less often conspicuous for muddled activism than for sheer ineffectiveness: his archetype is the Rev. Mr. Eccles (note the play on "ecclesiastical") in John Updike's novel, *Rabbit, Run*, who feels deeply the needs of frustrated modern man, but is totally incapable of meeting those needs because he has no authoritative word of judgment or grace to offer. The one cleric described in Geoffrey Gorer's *Modern Types* (superlatively illustrated by Ronald Searle) is "Rev. Basil Lamb":

> The Reverend Basil Lamb's proudest boast is that when he is not dressed in canonicals, nobody takes him for a clergyman. "The dear fellows," he claims, "treat me as one of themselves. . . ."
> In the first years after demobilization, Basil Lamb was often able to be of use to the dear lads, and his Party was building the New Jerusalem zealously in the House of Commons. Subsequently Basil Lamb could not but note that far too few of the men, and far too many of their tiresome wives and mothers and aunts, sought his professional advice or attended his church, even though he kept his services as short as possible, and preached bright and simple sermons which dealt with practical matters, without any taint of mysticism or the supernatural. The supernatural, indeed, is a distressing idea to the Reverend Basil Lamb, and he would faint with surprise were he to witness a miracle. The one scriptural verse he quotes with any frequency deals with publicans and sinners; and he has little doubts that, by playing darts in an open-necked shirt, he is completely carrying out the injunctions of the Founder of Christianity.[1]

Confusion about—or rank skepticism toward—the "injunctions of the Founder of Christianity" is so widespread in ecclesiastical circles today that British pundit and recent Christian convert Malcolm Muggeridge can write: "In such circumstances it is not surprising that the ministry should attract crackpots, eccentrics, and oddities who in happier times would have appeared as characters in Waugh's earlier novels rather than as beneficed clergymen. Scarcely a day goes by but some buffoon in holy orders makes an exhibition of himself. . . . Can it be wondered at, then, that the church's voice, when heard, is more often than not greeted with derision or just ignored?"[2]

Failure on the trumpet, however, has by no means discouraged the would-be musicians of Protestant liberalism. Quite the contrary: they conceive their talent to lie particularly in full-scale ecumenical orchestrations. The result has been the expansion of off-key trumpet solos (often played on another instrument by mistake) to ear-shattering, full-bodied cacophony. University of Glasgow Professor Ian Henderson's study of the attempts of Anglican officialdom to absorb the Scottish Presbyterian church is a most sobering illustration. Theological considerations have been of minor consequence in what Henderson—though himself deeply influenced by German radical theology—calls "power without glory: a study in ecumenical politics." [3] The well-known Consultation on Church Union (COCU) has been so concerned to bring about organizational unity that it has advocated union first and the resolving of awkward diversities of belief afterwards.[4] Writes Charles Merrill Smith (author of *How to Become a Bishop Without Being Religious*) in his equally cynical sequel, *The Pearly Gates Syndicate*:[5]

> The Ecumenical Movement is presently embodied in an organization called Consultation on Church Union, or COCU for short (which is not the most fortunate acronym we ever heard). . . .
> The statement [COCU's *Principles of Church Union*] says that in the matter of creeds the new Christian Corporation will use the Apostles' Creed because it is "shaped by biblical language and resonant with biblical testimonies." It says that COCU will also use the Nicene creed because "through many critical periods it has successfully warned the Church against many deceptive distortions in its faith." The statement goes on to say that "the responsibility of the united Church as guardian of the apostolic testimony includes its obligation, from time to time, to confess and communicate its faith in new language and new formulations . . ."
> Here the untutored layman is likely to bog down completely. What is being said, though, is relatively simple. The correct reading is, "Some people like the sound of the Apostles' Creed, and others have a sense of being orthodox when they repeat the intricate verbosities of the Nicene Creed, so we will dish up both creeds in our services from time to time. On the other hand, since no sane man can affirm either of these creeds literally without compromising his conscience, we will write some new creeds which won't offend him. This way, maybe we can keep everybody happy." [6]

Such creedal confusion was the target of sociologist Pete Berger's address as keynote speaker at the October, 1971, meeting of COCU delegates in Denver, Colorado. Modern churchmen are making the great mistake of "listening to an entity known as 'modern man' in the expectation that thence will come the redemptive word." What is needed is "the stance of authority," so that the churchman can provide a clear answer to the question, "What does the church have to say to modern man?" The church will remain ineffective if it continues to have as spokesmen "the people who have been falling all over each other to be 'relevant' to moderr̄e⸍ man. Ages of faith are not marked by dialogue, but by proclamation." [7]

A commendable and perceptive analysis! Yet it does little more than expose the raw wound of the problem, for what modern churchman *is* confident of his proclamation? Who is sure of his authority? From how many pulpits and church conventions does one hear the words, "Thus saith the Lord"?

A natural reaction to this atmosphere of irrelevant relevance is to turn from liberal Protestantism to theological viewpoints more conducive to proclamation with authority. In Roman Catholicism, surely, one does not encounter the problem of the uncertain trumpet! Here religious authority has been clearly defined: in infallible Scripture guaranteed and interpreted by an infallible magisterium.

Such a description of the Roman Church could hardly be faulted historically, and may well be as accurate as it ever was officially. But the cracks in the ideological walls of Rome are today as evident as the cracks in the steps of the leaning tower of Pisa. Dominican Robert Campbell's book, *Spectrum of Catholic Attitudes*, shows that contemporary Catholics entertain widely divergent views on fundamental questions, including the issue of theological authority. Daniel Callahan says of papal infallibility that he does "not happen to believe it at present" and that "the doctrine is meant to function in some symbolic way; it is not to be taken literally." [8] Leslie Dewart, commenting on the inerrancy of the Bible, discards propositional truth for personal truth in turgid terms dear to the heart of any Protestant neo-orthodox: "To the degree that we become aware that beyond the adequation of the mind to reality, truth requires the ever more intense presence of the self to itself, inerrancy should become totally inadequate as a category expressing the relation between revelation and belief. Truth is not the adequacy of a representation, but the adequacy of existence. The ultimate truth is not the adequate representation of ultimate facts: it is the truth that decisively confers life, it is the truth that 'saves.' " [9]

Hans Küng, highly regarded in Protestant circles for his book, *Justification*, in which he argues the remarkable proposition that no contradiction exists on the doctrine of justification between the Canons and Decrees of the Council of Trent and Barth's *Church Dogmatics*, has more recently dealt with the issue of infallibility. In his work of that title he makes quite plain that the Roman Catholic world no longer possesses firm and mo-

nolithic confidence in assured ecclesiastical—or scriptural—
teaching:

> To which therefore does infallibility belong: to the
> Church or the Bible? As it does not belong to the Church,
> neither does it belong to the Bible. . . .
> As errors of natural science and history in one of
> Shakespeare's historical plays in certain circumstances
> can even help us to perceive, not worse but better, through
> all its temporal relativity, the intention and statement of
> the temporal relativity, the intention and statement of the
> drama, so too with errors of the Bible in natural science
> and history. . . .
> As the community of believers, the Church does not
> possess any propositional infallibility, but she certainly
> does have a fundamental indefectibility in the truth. Scrip-
> ture as the record of the original faith in Christ does not
> possess any inherent propositional inerrancy. . . .
> Scripture, which is by no means free from error, at-
> tests unrestrictedly *the* truth as the perpetual fidelity of
> God.[10]

In the face of such an analysis the obvious question arises
as to how one determines "the truth" which is "the perpetual
fidelity of God" if its propositional representations are erroneous. Surely some final authority must exist, and it would appear
that it now rests in the New Shape Roman theologian and his
community of like-minded souls. There is thus more than irony
in the definition of infallibility in Dominican Maurice Lelong's
"New Church Lexicon" (*Lexicon de l'Eglise Nouvelle*): "The
scandal of Vatican I. Infallibility can only be collective and popular" (*La honte de Vatican 1. L'infaillibilité ne peut être que
collective et populaire*).[11] Inerrancy can no longer focus on
one book or one man; it is now corporate and democratic! Does
this suggest the profound truth that no one ever dispenses with
authority—one only relocates it?

The failure of contemporary Roman Catholicism, no less than
Protestant liberalism, to provide assured religious authority
drives us to serious consideration of the Protestant evangelical
movement. Here, if anywhere, the trumpet should be heard
clearly, for no other theological orientation in Christendom has
so consistently stood for the historic Church's declaration of Sola
Scriptura. Unconvinced by church authority and unimpressed
by the chimerical standards of modern relevance, evangelicals
have simply "preached the Word": proclaimed God's judgment
and grace on the basis of unerring Scripture.

Or so we like to think. In point of fact, the history of evangelicalism displays an ambivalent attitude toward infallible biblical authority. One can distinguish, as Canadian historian Donald C. Masters has done, "conservative" and "liberal" evangelicals: both stress the vital importance of personal salvation through the gospel of Christ, but the former "adhere to the old idea of the total inspiration of the Scriptures" while the latter maintain that "the Scriptures not only contain the Word of God but . . . factual error." [12] Nineteenth century evangelicalism displayed such scholarly defenders of the inerrancy of Holy Writ as Gaussen (*Theopneustia*) and Warfield (*The Inspiration and Authority of the Bible*), but at the same time counted in her number leaders who would not affirm that the Bible was free of factual error (James Orr, Henry Drummond).[13] Today, entire evangelical faculties of theology line up on either side of the issue: Covenant, Dallas, Talbot, Trinity, Westminster, France's Faculté Libre de Théologie Réformée, Germany's Bibelschule Bergstrasse affirming the total reliability of Scripture; Asbury, Bethel, Fuller, North Park, the Free University of Amsterdam allowing the issue of biblical error to remain an open question. Respected evangelical scholars such as Berkouwer, F. F. Bruce, Daniel Fuller, and Bruce Metzger have expressly asserted that they do not consider the inspiration of Holy Writ to require the inerrancy of all the Bible's assertions. The issue is actively debated in the pages of evangelical publications such as the *Journal of the American Scientific Affiliation*, and entire evangelical denominations—the Southern Baptists and the Missouri Synod Lutherans immediately come to mind—are in the throes of civil war over the degree and extent of biblical authority.

This diversity on the Scripture issue among evangelicals should not be too surprising when we recall that evangelicalism is a relatively modern Christian movement, stemming from late 17th century pietism and more especially from 18th century English Methodism and 19th century American frontier revivalism. The evangelical movement thus came to birth simultaneously with and in part in reaction to the rise of modern secularism. Biblical criticism was already nascent, and evangelicals were prone from their earliest history to make the subjective experience of salvation, rather than the objective finality of Scripture, the primary weapon in their arsenal against unbelief. As we shall see later, in our essay concerning Luther's attitude toward the inerrancy of the Bible, it is necessary to cut back behind the modern secular era entirely—to the Reformation period and the era of Protestant Orthodoxy—in order to find unqualified and

universal subscription to total biblical authority. Father Burtchaell, a contemporary Roman Catholic scholar who does not
hold to the inerrancy of Scripture, describes the historical situation accurately when he writes in his valuable monograph,
Catholic Theories of Biblical Inspiration since 1810:

> Christians early inherited from the Jew the belief
> that the biblical writers were somehow possessed by God,
> who was thus to be reckoned the Bible's proper author.
> Since God could not conceivably be the agent of falsehood,
> the Bible must be guaranteed free from any error. For
> centuries this doctrine lay dormant, as doctrines will: ac-
> cepted by all, pondered by few. Not until the 16th century
> did inspiration and its corollary, inerrancy, come up for
> sustained review. The Reformers and Counter-Reformers
> were disputing whether all revealed truth was in Scripture
> alone, and whether it could dependably be interpreted by
> private or by official scrutiny. Despite a radical disagree-
> ment on these issues both groups persevered in receiving
> the Bible as a compendium of inerrant oracles dictated by
> the Spirit. Only in the 19th century did a succession of em-
> pirical disciplines newly come of age begin to put a succes-
> sion of inconvenient queries to exegetes. First, geology and
> paleontology discredited the view of the cosmos and the
> cosmogony of Genesis. Next, archeology suggested that
> there were serious historical discrepancies in the sacred
> narrative. Later, as parallel oriental literatures began
> to be recovered, much of Scripture lay under accusa-
> tion of plagiarism from pagan sources. Literary criti-
> cism of the text itself disclosed that the writers had freely
> tampered with their materials, and often escalated myth
> and legend into historical event. After all this, considerable
> dexterity was required of any theologian who was willing
> to take account of the accumulation of challenging evi-
> dence, yet continued to defend the Bible as the classic and
> inerrant Word of God.[14]

Evangelicals, with more than the average dose of anti-in-
tellectualism and a powerful tendency to overrate the heart while
underrating the head, have not always been able to marshal the
"dexterity" which is indeed necessary for defending the Bible's
total truth in an era of criticism and unbelief.

Granted, the vast majority of today's Protestant evangelicals—particularly on the grass roots level—*do* hold to the inerrancy of Scripture. It is of more than routine significance that
by far the most influential evangelical theological journal, *Christianity Today*, has consistently affirmed in no uncertain terms
its allegiance to an inerrant Bible.[15] The overwhelming success

of conservative evangelicals at the July, 1973, convention of the Lutheran Church-Missouri Synod attests the continuing power of the classic view of biblical authority in today's church.[16]

But no less apparent is the steady increase of the anti-inerrancy viewpoint among American clergy. Jeffrey K. Hadden, in his careful sociological study, *The Gathering Storm in the Churches* (1969), has shown not only that but a small proportion of clergy—whatever their denominational affiliation—hold to the inerrancy of Scripture, but that there is a direct correlation between age and belief in this doctrine. Consider Hadden's statistics:

PASTOR'S AGE AND BELIEF IN THE INERRANCY OF SCRIPTURE [17]

"Scriptures are the inspired and inerrant Word of God not only in matters of faith but also in historical, geographical, and other secular matters."	% Agreeing					
	Episcopalian	Methodist	Presbyterian	American Baptist	American Lutheran	Missouri Synod Lutheran
All	5	13	12	33	23	76
Under 35	4	8	6	17	6	63
35-44	2	12	9	30	26	74
45-54	9	15	17	41	32	85
Over 55	8	17	21	42	50	90

A necessary conclusion from these statistics is that—even in the most traditionally conservative of the church bodies surveyed—the trend to a non-inerrancy view of the Bible has been vigorously operative: the younger the clergyman, whether Methodist, Presbyterian, Baptist, or Lutheran, the less likely he will believe that the Bible is totally veracious.

But does it really make a difference: Liberal evangelicals are not in the least troubled by the deteriorating clerical willingness to affirm inerrancy—nor do they see anything particularly significant in the fact that this deterioration parallels a comparable decline in the belief of American pastors in such christological doctrines as the miracle of the Virgin Birth.[18] For the liberal evangelical, it is a prime article of faith that the "heart" of the Christian message—the gospel, Christ Himself, the personal experience of salvation—is in no sense dependent on biblical inerrancy. To the contrary: in the opinion of not a few liberal evangelicals, belief in the inerrancy of Scripture is a positive detriment to effective gospel proclamation, for it shifts the attention away from the "Living Word" (Christ) to the "written word" (the Bible). Cannot the central truths of Scripture be maintained—perhaps even raised to clearer focus—without asserting the reliability of the Bible in "historical, geographical, and other secular matters"? Cannot the "theological and moral infallibility" of Scripture stand even with de facto errors in its non-essentials? Does the trumpet of Christian proclamation have to make an uncertain sound just because the biblical orchestration is not free from discords?

Let us meet these fundamental questions head on by considering, first, the underlying logical issues at stake in the inerrancy dispute, and then proceed to what can only be described as the "errors of errancy."

LOGIC, ANYONE?

For convenience, we shall discuss the claims of liberal evangelicals relative to an errant Scripture under three heads, each representing a fundamental allegation. It is alleged, first, that the gospel and the spiritual content of the Bible can be affirmed without regarding the Scripture as inerrant; secondly, that Christ can be adequately preached without Scripture being inerrant; and thirdly, that one can sensibly affirm the infallibility of the Bible even though one does not agree to the veracity of all of its details. Our contention is that no one of these allegations can be sustained, for all three involve logical blunders fully capable of ruining not only one's bibliology but one's theology as a whole.

1. Inerrant gospel without inerrant Scripture? One of the most basic convictions of the non-inerrancy position on Scripture is that its theological and moral content can be unqualifiedly relied upon even though its historical, scientific, and other non-theological assertions reflect the fallible knowledge of the biblical writers' own time. Since the Bible was given by God for the salvation of men, it is argued that only the salvatory content of Scripture is consequential theologically, and nothing is lost if the Bible turns out to be fallible when it deals with matters irrelevant to redemptive truth and morality.

Those who argue in this vein do not all state their argument in precisely the same terms. Some—for example, Daniel Fuller—are much concerned to disaffirm "partial inerrancy": they hold that everything in the Bible can be regarded as "revelation," and insofar as every biblical statement functions revelationally, to that extent it is perfectly true. However, those who speak in these terms are no less concerned to establish two levels of "revelational propositions": those that are "directly revelational" and therefore unquestionably reliable, and those that only "facilitate the transmission of what is directly revelational" and which can therefore turn out to be erroneous. These latter Fuller also labels as "non-revelational" statements!

> The whole Bible is revelation. Most of its propositions are directly revelational, while others and certain aspects of some revelational propositions function to facilitate the transmission of what is directly revelational. . . .
> One misinterprets Scripture if he tries always to harmonize with science and history aspects of Biblical statements whose purpose is only to facilitate the communication of revelational truth. . . . Since such matters . . . are non-revelational, they lie outside the boundary of the Biblical writers' intention, and are therefore irrelevant to the question of Biblical inerrancy.[19]

Other liberal evangelicals more boldly state that the Bible's "inerrancy" applies to its "spiritual" dimension alone, and are not unhappy with such expressions as "partial inerrancy" or even "partial inspiration." Here the differences pertain chiefly to what one considers the *truly* "spiritual" or "redemptive" content of the Bible: the gospel only? all "doctrinal" assertions, but nothing else? doctrine plus ethics? Jesus' doctrine and ethics only? Jesus' teachings plus the apostolic witness? The entire corpus of New Testament teaching, but not all Old Testament teachings? etc.

Without entering into these many variations, we can note the common theme: one aspect of Scripture (or one way of looking at all of Scripture) is "spiritual," and another is "secular"; the former can be implicitly trusted, while the latter is subject to man's fallibility. Regardless of how carefully the viewpoint is stated, it *necessarily* involves a dualism between what is infallibly reliable in the Bible and what is not; this dualism cannot be escaped semantically (by more carefully stating the argument) since the point of the argument logically is to justify Scripture's authority (positively) while allowing for de facto errors in its content (negatively).

But precisely at this logical watershed the argument fails, and must always fail. From the incarnational perspective of the Bible itself, all dualisms of "spiritual" and "secular," however defined, are rejected. The epistemological theme of Scripture is not "the Word disembodied" or "the Word" (like Ivory Soap?) "floating "spiritually," but "the Word *made flesh*."

Not only does the Bible itself offer a monistic philosophy of knowledge, but this viewpoint is necessitated by the very nature of the fields of knowledge themselves. Only the naive specialist really believes that science is qualitatively different from geography, or geography from history, or history from ethics, or ethics from theology. "Homo sum," declared the Roman dramatist Terence,[20] "humani nihil a me alienum puto" (I am a man and I consider nothing human alien to me): all human knowledge is one and on this anvil all epistemological dualisms are broken. At the midpoint of the 19th century, when knowledge was expanding at an unprecedented rate, John Henry Cardinal Newman warned in his classic essay on the nature of the university:

> Summing up, Gentlemen, what I have said, I lay it down that all knowledge forms one whole, because its subject-matter is one; for the universe in its length and breadth is so intimately knit together, that we cannot separate off portion from portion, and operation from operation, except by a mental abstraction.... Next, sciences are the results of that mental abstraction, which I have spoken of, being the logical record of this or that aspect of the whole subject-matter of knowledge. As they all belong to one and the same circle of objects, they are one and all connected together; as they are but aspects of things, they are severally incomplete in their relation to the things themselves, though complete in their own idea and for their own respective purposes; on both accounts they at once need and subserve each other.[21]

Today, with a geometrical increase in knowledge unimagined by Newman, hyperspecialization has become a major cultural disease. C. P. Snow has eloquently reiterated Newman's point for our time in his *Two Cultures*, stressing the essential interrelationship between the sciences and the humanities.[22] Jacques Barzun, one of the finest minds of our day, argues in *The House of Intellect* that it is "a tacit denial of Intellect" itself that in human relationships one man "believes that his subject and his language cannot and should not be understood by the other." [23]

In the last half century the vast accumulation of knowledge and the proliferating specialized disciplines have led to important advances in general classification theory and documentation technique; these have invariably and necessarily recognized the essential unity of all knowledge and the arbitrary nature of all subject divisions. Writes the great classification theorist Henry Evelyn Bliss in his seminal work, *The Organization of Knowledge and the System of the Sciences*: "The data and the concepts of science in endless diversity are so interrelated that the system is indeed unitary; yet for convenience, for interests or purposes we define or delimit studies and branches of science, of technology, of history, or of philosophy." [24] Ernest Cushing Richardson, another great name in the same field, made the same point more popularly in his discussion of *Classification: Theoretical and Practical*:

> It is to be remembered all the time through this discussion that sciences are not separate things, but only divisions in the sense that a man's hands, feet, eyes, etc., are parts of a whole. Every man is a unity. A distinction between hand and wrist is practical and useful, but who shall say just where hand stops and wrist begins? So, too, of science and the "branches of knowledge" —who shall say where the trunk stops and the branches begin? [25]

The point does not require belaboring. For practical purposes we may—perhaps we must—distinguish between historical," "geographical," and "theological" statements in Holy Writ; but these distinctions are no more inherent to reality than the divisions between hand and wrist or trunk and branches. It is thus logically impossible to argue for an alleged perfection resident "spiritually" in Scripture while admitting imperfections in scriptural knowledge viewed from a "secular" standpoint. Fallibility in the latter necessitates fallibility in the former—and this leaves one incapable of affirming a single doctrinal or moral teaching of the Bible with finality.

Is it any wonder then that those, such as the Roman Catholic exegete Loisy, beginning with "relative inerrancy" (the Bible erroneous only in matters of science and history) and pursuing vigorously the implications of this viewpoint, ultimately conclude "that the principle of relative truth is in fact of universal application" [26]? Toward the end of his life Loisy could thus describe his developed view: "As far as I am concerned, the Bible, being a book written by men for men, does not escape the condition of every human book, and it could only be, even in matters of faith and morals, in complete rapport with the truth of a single epoch, that of its composition." [27] By the time he was excommunicated for these antiscriptural views by a pope considerably more orthodox than certain recent incumbents of the office, he had admitted privately that he had even lost his belief in God and could no longer believe in any spiritual reality whatever.[28]

Loisy's tragic mistake had been to think that the "religious" could be separated from the "non-religious" in the Bible, such that secular errors would not affect Scripture's fundamental teachings; when eventually the unity of the Bible overwhelmed him, as it always must, sooner or later, he was left with error everywhere and no faith at all. One thinks of Robert Pease's striking novel, *The Associate Professor*, which clinically tracks the psychic collapse of a physics professor who refuses to see the direct parallels between phenomena in his field of specialty and the characteristics of his personal life. Even when a visiting lecturer inadvertently draws the connection with utmost precision, the professor is incapable of responding.

> Knudsen's head snapped up. But no one seemed to notice that he had been asleep.
> "So just before I have to turn the lecture room over to Professor Knudsen, I'd like to step out of the realm of physics and leave you with a religious—or, if you will, a psychological—analogue.
> "Think of an accelerator which is unstable as a locked room, a closed circle of hostile people, a place of oppression or hatred. Think of the beam fluctuations which are amplified by the instability—as a human neurosis, maybe a person's fear he is being spied upon, or that he will be attacked. In that atmosphere the neurosis will grow. If a person is in that atmosphere for many time constants, he must either find grace or his neurosis will grow until he cannot control it, and it will destroy him. Thank you." [29]

Had Professor Knudsen not drawn hard lines between physics and religion, grace might have reached him. Had Loisy not first attempted to separate the non-religious from the religious in Scripture, grace might still have been available to him. Rec-

ognition of the unity of all of scriptural content is as essential
to theological sanity as realization of the unity of all knowledge
is necessary to genuine mental health.

2. *A saving Christ without an inerrant Scripture?* Since it
is the living Christ who saves and not a book, liberal evangelicals
consider axiomatic the conviction that an errant Bible is power-
less to detract from the heart of Christianity. Jesus will still
be the same, yesterday, today, and forever: still as much capable of saving men as He ever was. An evangelical is one
who preaches the "evangel," and the evangel is Christ—so why
should a good evangelical have to do more than preach Christ?
Is not the inerrancy of Scripture an albatross about the neck,
reducing the Christian's effectiveness in evangelism by forcing
him to defend Scripture when he should simply be proclaiming
God's love in Christ?

The preceding discussion concerning the necessary interrelationship of all fields of knowledge offers a response to this
fallacious reasoning as well. Christ's saving acts—upon which
all proclamation of the gospel depends—were as much historical
acts as theological or "spiritual" events. Thus an errancy view
of Scripture relative to its alleged "secular" contents will as
thoroughly undermine the portrait of Jesus as it will the general
theological or moral teachings of the Bible or the biblical gospel.
Indeed, since few would dispute that the theological, ethical,
and evangelical content of Scripture came to particular focus
in Jesus' earthly ministry, the reliability of the biblical message
of salvation is directly bound up with the historical reliability
of that ministry. There is no avoiding the issue of the "secular"
veracity of Scripture in the interests of the "spiritual": and
certainly not in the life of the biblical Savior, whose miraculous
birth took place in the days of Herod the King and whose death
and resurrection occurred under Pontius Pilate.

But if it is argued (as I believe one can) that the deity
of Christ and the saving core of His teachings can be established
by the general historical reliability of the New Testament
documents, why should it be necessary or even desirable to
go beyond this to an alleged inerrancy of Scripture, thereby
assuming responsibility for a host of problem-passages? First,
because otherwise the church is left with a minimalistic message—with a theology that is little more than a soteriology—and
the whole counsel of God is reduced virtually to a unitarianism
of the Second Person of the Trinity. But even more important
(if possible), Jesus' very deity would be imperiled, since, as
has been shown time and again, even the most cursory historical

examination of His attitude toward the Old Testament shows that He considered it inerrantly true.[30]

Logically, if the Bible is *not* inerrant, though Jesus thought it was, He can hardly be the incarnate God He claimed to be and for whom the same claims are made by His Apostles. Had He been mistaken on this point, the church could well ask whether any single teaching of Jesus on any subject (including the way of salvation) might not also reflect His sincere misunderstanding. A "God" of this kind (even if He were indeed divine) would do us no more good than a non-God, for in neither case could we ever confidently rely on his teachings.

If—to avoid the force of this argument—the liberal evangelical says that Jesus *did* know that the Bible wasn't inerrant, but dealt with it in terms of the mind-set of His day, "so as not to create unnecessary barriers to faith," we must emphasize that such a Jesus would be no more worthy of an attribution of deity than the Jesus who was mistaken about the Bible's reliability. For a Jesus who would let the end justify the means, allow His followers to be deceived on such a vital religious question (the extent of revelational reliability), and promote confusion and unnecessary strife in the subsequent history of the church through His equivocation, could hardly stand as a divine model for man's ethical emulation.

"Kenotic" (limitation) theories will not solve this dilemma. A meaningful incarnation demands an incarnate God who knows what He is doing—on earth as it is in heaven—and tells the truth—on earth as it is in heaven. This is precisely the Jesus of the Gospel accounts: the One who knows that He existed before Abraham, who condems lying as a mark of the devil, and who so unites reliability in "secular" matters with "theological" reliability that He can say to Nicodemus (and to us), "If I have told you earthly things, and ye believe not, how shall ye believe, if I tell you of heavenly things?" [31]

3. An infallible Bible in spite of errors? Sensing the uncomfortable implications of a partial inerrancy view that would focus only on the gospel or Jesus in Scripture, liberal evangelicals endeavor, as we have already observed, to hold to plenary inspiration while at the same time admitting to de facto biblical error. This is generally accomplished by claiming (a) that the Bible is always—plenarily—true in its divine intent, but (b) it does not necessarily intend to convey factually true information in non-revelatory matters. Let us hear again from Daniel Fuller.

A book is inerrant only against the criterion of its

writer's intention. Interpretation is not concerned with everything that was in an author's mind, but only with the meaning which he necessarily implied by what he intended to say. Consequently the Biblical writers are to be judged only on the terms of the revelational teachings they intended to communicate, for revelation concerns what eye cannot see or ear hear by itself.

Thus since the Bible declares that its purpose is to impart revelation, we run no risk of distorting its message as we credit its revelational teachings and admit the possibility that its non-revelational statements and implications are a reflection of the culture of the writer and his original readers. Such an approach is perfectly willing to let Biblical statements in the non-revelational areas of science and history be fully tested against what men can find out about such matters for themselves and in terms of the pedagogy the Biblical writers used to impart this revelation.[32]

Two crushing logical fallacies characterize this argumentation, one relating to the problem of "intent" (the intentional fallacy) and the other to the over-all meaningfulness of the claim to intentional reliability (technical nonsensicality). The "intentional fallacy" was isolated and refuted in a classic paper of that title by philosophers of art Wimsatt and Beardsley; in their words, "the design or intention of the author is neither available nor desirable as a standard for judging the success of a literary work of art." To understand the force of their position, listen to the excellent summary by Aldrich:

The question of meaning and the attempts to answer it have often featured the intention of the artist. In fact, some theorists have taken the statement of the artist's intention as an answer to the question. This supposition has been criticized and dubbed the intentionalist fallacy. It is a mistake to suppose that you discover the meaning of the work of art when you uncover what the artist intended to realize in it. As one may say something he did not intend to say, so may the artist fail. Not only this. Even after realizing the discrepancy between what his work "says" and what he intended to say, he may be unable to rectify it to square with his intention, if he is not master of the material of the art. Still more, he may think his intention has been adequately realized in the work, and be shown by objective criticism that it is not, or that a more adequate formulation is feasible by rectifying elements in the composition that "said" something he was not aware of and that negated what he did have in view. All this

could happen in language as well. For example, the favorite
English translation of Rabelais by Thomas Urquhart
simply spills over, beyond the original text, with what
Rabelais had in mind; thus it fulfills better the author's
intention than his own work did. Thus do the material
and the medium have their own powers of expression
which may run counter to the intention of the user, depending on how he deploys them.[33]

The point of this analysis is that the totality of any creative
or didactic work is the only proper basis for understanding
it. Since "the material and the medium have their own powers
of expression," one cannot isolate an alleged intention of the
author by which to create value-levels in his work ("revelational," "non-revelational"). Obviously, he intended to put everything in his work that is there, or it would not be there;
obviously also he intended (if he is a truthful person) to
convey no falsehoods and to be as accurate as possible. Neither
the human authors nor the divine Author of Scripture intended
to do other than they did in writing the Bible; or, putting it
more explicitly, if they did intend something else, we would
have no way of knowing it. The work itself—the entire biblical
text—is our only basis for saying anything about the author's
intent. Presumably, in the issue of inerrancy, the prime concern
is with the supervening "intent" of the divine Author, and the
incarnate Christ tells us simply, quoting the God of the Old
Testament, that "man shall not live by bread alone, but by
every word that proceedeth out of the mouth of God." One
must therefore operate with every word and consider every
word as significant. Had God "intended" otherwise, the text
would (by definition) be different from what it is! [34]

Embedded in the liberal evangelical's attempt to preserve
an infallible Bible in spite of errors is a further and even more
serious fallacy. We invariably find that the "non-revelational
areas" are the areas of "science and history"—the areas of
prime testability. Sometimes the critic of inerrancy reveals the
situation even more plainly, as when Fuller declares that "revelation concerns what the eye cannot see or ear hear by itself."
Evidently, the reason why Scripture can still remain totally
infallible while containing error is that its infallibility pertains
to "what eye cannot see by itself." In those areas where specific
testability is possible (science, history, etc.) the Bible can
turn out to be in error—but when this occurs, it makes no difference, since "eye can see by itself" in these cases and thus
the material is non-revelational. The result—if one carries this

line of reasoning to its logical conclusion[35]—is the following remarkable series of propositions: Where the Bible errs, it is non-revelatory; when it is capable of being tested by the "eye alone" (i.e., apart from faith) it is precariously revelatory—revelatory only until proven wrong; and where it cannot be tested it always remains revelatory and inerrant!

It should be perfectly plain that this approach to the Bible represents little more than an asylum of ignorance. The position, in fact, is technically (epistemologically) nonsensical and meaningless, since in principle no evidence is allowed to count against the claim to "revelational inerrancy." The moment one brings up a testable assertion of Scripture, it is potentially if not actually relegated to the non-revelational category. The Bible is held up as infallibly reliable precisely where it *cannot* be tested. This is just like believers in sea serpents claiming that they appear only when no scientists are present.

One cannot have it both ways: either the Bible contains errors and is therefore fallible, or it is infallibly free of mistakes. Both the human writers and the divine Author intended to write what they wrote, and if Jesus knew what He was talking about, the success was total and the resultant Scripture entirely reliable. To avoid blunders in thinking in this area as in all others, we cannot do better than to conform our perspective to that of Christ Himself.

THE ERRORS OF ERRANCY

The principal contentions of the liberal evangelical thus offer a singularly unsatisfactory approach to the question of biblical reliability. Quite clearly the advocate of this position is trying—without success, though with honorable motives—to eat his revelational cake while retaining the indigestible scriptural errors claimed by the secular critics.

But has not the liberal evangelical posed some insuperable objections for the believer in the Bible's inerrancy? What about the human factor: do not all of man's productions necessarily suffer from his fallibility, and must not the Bible be so regarded? And how about those missing autographs: is this not the conservative evangelical's own asylum of ignorance? What, finally, can be said of those who affirm the absolute truth of a book, when the sense experience necessary even to identify it as the Bible is subject to error? It is now our purpose to examine these three objections to scriptural inerrancy; and we shall find them (not inappropriately) erroneous.

1. Errare humanum est. One of the most consistent arguments delivered against the inerrancy doctrine by its opponents of every stripe—from secularists to mediating evangelicals—is the simple reminder that "to err is human." [36] Even if one holds that God is the "ultimate Author" of the Bible, the very fact that the Scriptures passed through human minds and hands necessitates (it is argued) a fallible result.

The stark phrase "to err is human" has been repeated so often and so uncritically through the centuries—and has seemed to be reinforced by so many and varied examples of human blunders and follies—that it has unjustifiably been raised to the level of a metaphysical principle. But a moment's reflection will show that, while man frequently errs, he does not err all the time, or in any given case *necessarily*. The directions for operating my washing machine, for example, are literally infallible: if I do just what they say, the machine will respond. Euclid's *Geometry* is a book of perfect internal consistency: grant the axioms and the proofs follow inexorably. From such examples (and they could readily be multiplied) we must conclude that human beings, though they often err, *need* not err in all particular instances. To be sure, the production over centuries of sixty-six inerrant and mutually consistent books by different authors is a tall order—and we cheerfully appeal to God's Spirit to achieve it—but the point remains that there is nothing metaphysically inhuman or against human nature in such a possibility. If there were, have we considered the implications for christology? The incarnate Christ, as a real man, would also have had to err; and we have already seen that error in His teachings would totally negate the revelational value of the incarnation, leaving man as much in the dark as to the meaning of life and salvation as if no incarnation had occurred at all.

The fallacy of "errare humanum est" derives not from the biblical picture of man as totally depraved (total moral self-centeredness is not synonymous with necessitarian erroneousness), but from world-views of a very different kind. In the East, the Buddhist insistence on incompleteness and Becoming as opposed to Being has important affinities with this viewpoint: the ideogram for the tea house can mean "abode of the A-Symmetrical," symbolizing the basic Zen insistence on endless process. "In the tea room (sukiya) or in the Japanese house the decorations are always off-center. . . . The challenge of the tea room is to build it of several seemingly incompatible materials. . . . It is not art, therefore, to paint a complete picture or

write a poem complete with dénouement. . . . A complete picture or a complete poem negates the Buddhist premise of Becoming." [37]

In the Western tradition, the metaphysical insistence that
man must err always and everywhere has its source in Platonic
rational idealism: the realm of forms or ideas or ideals is transcendent and can be represented only inadequately and fallibly
here on earth. This philosophy of the transcendent ideal com-
mendably recognized man's incapacity to save himself through
manipulation of his environment, and (as Augustine rightly saw)
could thus serve as a schoolmaster to bring men to Christ.
But, like the Old Testament law, it was capable of becoming
a most dangerous instrument when regarded as an end in itself.
The center and theme of Christian revelation is that the perfect
does come to earth: perfect God becomes perfect Man, with
no loss of Godhead. But the pagan Platonist—and the naive
Christian who has absorbed Platonic categories without realizing
it—will not permit unqualified perfection to come to earth even
when God Himself is responsible for it, as He is in the production
of inerrant Scripture.

Logically, if one becomes embroiled in the Platonic fallacy
of necessary metaphysical dualism, the only way to preserve
the revelatory truth of Scripture would be to hold that the book
really isn't of the earth at all. This is precisely the conclusion
to which certain Muslim theologians of the medieval period
were driven by the pressure of Neoplatonic thought: for the
Koran to be revelation, it must be literally uncreated! "Everything in the heavens and earth and what between them lies
is created, except God and the Koran," they cried. Comments
Islamic specialist A. J. Arberry:

> If the Koran were allowed to be created, the danger
> was great that it might next be alleged by those steeped
> in Neoplatonist thought that God's Word as revealed to
> Mohammed through the mediation of the archangel Ga-
> briel shared with all created things the imperfection aris-
> ing from their association with matter.[38]

Here we have a vigorously consistent way of handling the
problem if one wishes to retain revelation along with the Platonic
dualism! The parallel with the early Christian heresy of docetism
is not hard to see: to preserve Christ from the rigors of the human condition, He was declared to be a man only in appearance,
not in reality. The liberal evangelicals employ this same operation, though less thoroughly, when they elevate the "spiritual"

content of Scripture—or its entirety viewed "revelationally"—to a realm of untestable infallibility.

Would it not be better simply to recognize that there is no compelling reason whatever to accept Zen becomingness or Platonic dualism? To be human is not necessarily to err, as Jesus surely demonstrated by His incarnate life. And if this is admitted, one can hardly gainsay His promise to lead other men by His Spirit into all truth. Such truthfulness is claimed by the biblical writers for themselves and by Jesus for them. Let us not spoil this all-important doctrine "through philosophy and vain deceit, after the tradition of men, after the rudiments of the world, and not after Christ."

2. *The missing autographs.* If the Bible is inerrant, where is that inerrancy to be located? Not in translations of the text, since these are but approximations of the original; not in printed texts, for these are but representations of manuscript copies, subject to correction by comparison with them; not in the manuscript copies themselves, since they likewise endeavor, with greater or less fidelity, to reproduce the manuscripts on which they are dependent. Unless, therefore, one wishes to maintain that a given stream of transmission or translation was kept inviolable by God (and Scripture itself nowhere gives ground for such an affirmation), inerrancy must be said to reside in the original manuscripts written by the biblical authors, i.e., in the autographs of Scripture.

But precisely here the critic of inerrancy sees hopeless absurdity. When conservative evangelicals (e.g., the scholarly membership of the Evangelical Theological Society) declare that "the Bible alone, and the Bible in its entirety, is the Word of God written, and therefore inerrant in the autographs," they appeal to a chimerical standard, for not a single biblical autograph has apparently survived! All existent copies of the text are admittedly erroneous, but a non-existent original is supposedly error-free!

Stated in this way, the inerrancy position appears as epistemologically nonsensical as the infallible-where-untestable viewpoint of some liberal evangelicals. But a little reflection will show that this is by no means the case. Consider the situation for books in general prior to the invention of printing with movable type in the West. Virtually no autographs have survived, and we are therefore dependent upon copies. Does this mean that we can say nothing meaningful concerning the originals? Certainly not, for the entire body of sophisticated technique comprising the field of Textual Criticism has been developed precisely to make possible the effective reconstruction of the original on the basis of copies. Textual Criticism is a standard tool employed in dealing with all ancient authors, and the result is that no one feels troubled by such phraseology as "Plato said x" or "Cicero said y." These propositions are, to be sure, a shorthand for prolix assertions of the form: "On the basis of accepted principles of textual analysis, we conclude that the best copies of Plato/Cicero do in fact represent the lost autographs when they say x/y." Very seldom is this lengthy propositional form employed, for the judgments of Textual Criticism are highly objective (based on vigorously testable principles) and so universally accepted that the establishment of a reliable text comes to *mean* the representation—in the sense of re-representation—of the autograph. The same is true of many works written since the invention of printing, where only the printed texts and not the autographs exist today (e.g., the writings of Shakespeare). Is it absurd to assert "Shakespeare says, 'To be or not to be,' " in the absence of Shakespeare's own manuscript? Hardly, for Textual Criticism allows us to establish a firm printed text which re-presents the no longer existent autograph.

But what about the case of an allegedly *inerrant* writing? How can Textual Criticism ever re-present that? If errors exist even in the best and earliest copies, is it not an asylum of ignorance to claim that if we did have the originals, these mistakes would not exist in them? The answer to this latter question would certainly be yes *if* (a) the number of errors increased or even remained constant as one moved back through the textual tradition toward the time of original composition, and (b) the conservative evangelical, to solve alleged biblical errors and contradictions, hypothesized that the autographs differed materially and unjustifiably from the best copies in existence. However, (a) the number of textual errors steadily diminishes as one moves back in the direction of the lost autographs, reasonably encouraging the supposition that could we entirely fill in the interval between the originals and our earliest texts and fragments (some New Testament papyri going back to the 1st century itself), all apparent errors would disappear; and (b) the conservative evangelical only appeals to the missing autographs over against existent best texts in those limited and specific instances (such as the recording of numerals) where independent evidence shows a very high probability of transcriptional errors from the very outset. Whereas the believer in scriptural inerrancy will appeal (with good reason, since the phenomenon is common) to the likelihood that a very early transcriptional error produced a numerical contradiction in the extant texts, he will hardly attempt to explain alleged disharmony in the Gospel accounts of the first Easter morning by claiming that the autographs of three of the four Gospels contained no mention of the subject!

In short, the conservative evangelical handles the autograph issue relative to the Bible just as a secular literary scholar handles the identical problem in reference to other ancient and many modern texts; both give the benefit of doubt to their materials, and neither should be accused of naïveté for doing so. The conservative biblical scholar goes farther, to be sure, in that he gives *maximal* benefit of doubt to his Book, but that also is justified if he has maximal reason for doing so: the clear testimony of the divine Christ that Scripture is to be trusted in all it teaches or touches.

3. Fallible sense experience and infallible Scripture. Recent critics of biblical inerrancy have developed what they consider to be an unassailable argument against the traditional position. Let us hear philosopher George Mavrodes' formulation of the critique, since he takes as his *point de depart* the issue of the missing autographs just discussed:

> It is a mistake to suppose that A[utograph]-infallibility closes any question in the sense of making available an answer which is impervious to scientific attack. For A[utograph]-infallibility provides us with no answers at all until it is combined with the results of textual science. . . . If we accept the doctrine of A[utograph]-infallibility, then, we must expose ourselves, in theology as well as in other matters, to whatever fallibility and uncertainty such a reliance upon science involves.[39]

The thrust of this argument is that one has no right to make an absolute claim for the Bible (its inerrancy) when the scriptural text can only be arrived at by a non-absolute procedure (textual science). Putting the argument more generally, as Daniel Fuller does in his reply to the criticisms of Clark Pinnock: "Induction . . . means letting criticism control all aspects of the knowing process from beginning to end"; thus one's view of Scripture, derived from an inductive investigation of the Bible, cannot possibly involve "absolute certainty." [40]

There is an important truth resident in this argument, and it was well expressed by B. B. Warfield in a passage which Fuller himself cites approvingly:

> We do not adopt the doctrine of the plenary inspiration of Scripture on sentimental grounds, nor even, as

we have already had occasion to remark on *a priori* or general grounds of whatever kind. We adopt it specifically because it is taught us as truth by Christ and His apostles, in the Scriptural record of their teaching, and the evidence for its truth is, therefore, as we have also already pointed out, precisely that evidence, in weight and amount, which vindicates for us the trustworthiness of Christ and His apostles as teachers of doctrine. Of course, this evidence is not in the strict logical sense "demonstrative"; it is "probable" evidence. It therefore leaves open the metaphysical possibility of its being mistaken. But it may be contended that it is about as great in amount and weight as "probable" evidence can be made, and that the strength of conviction which it is adapted to produce may be and should be practically equal to that produced by demonstration itself.[41]

Evidence for biblical inerrancy (whether viewed from the angle of Textual Criticism or from the more general perspective of Apologetics) is never *itself* inerrant, but this by no means makes the inerrancy claim irrational. Warfield (like Fuller) is perfectly willing to admit that his case is a probability case, yet (unlike Fuller) he affirms the inerrancy of the Bible in *all* matters to which it refers—not just to those "germane to salvation" (whatever they may be!). Why? because, as he correctly observes, the evidence that Christ (God Himself incarnate) held to exactly this inerrancy view of Scripture "is about as great in amount and weight as 'probably' evidence can be made" and thus warrants conviction on our part.

The weight of Christ's testimony to Scripture is so much more powerful than any alleged contradiction or error in the text or any combination of them, that the latter must be adjusted to the former, not the reverse. Warfield did not fall into Lessing's ditch ("The accidental truths of history can never become the proof of necessary truths of reason"), for this would have been to capitulate to the old Platonic dualism in a new guise. Nor did he tumble into the logical trap that swallows Mavrodes and Fuller: confusing the value of a result with the means of obtaining it (the genetic fallacy). In 1669 the German alchemist Hennig Brand discovered phosphorous by boiling toads in urine: the method left a good deal to be desired, but the result was phosphorous nonetheless. Textual science and other inductive procedures may not be perfect, but when applied to data of earth-shaking consequence they can yield a divine Savior and His clear testimony to a perfect Book.[42]

CONCLUSION: THE STAKES COULD
NOT BE HIGHER

At the beginning of this essay we encountered the ghostly
silence of a contemporary church that has lost its trumpet of
proclamation and finds even an uncertain sound often beyond
its feeble capacities. Along the way we met liberal Protestants,
modern Catholics, and mediating evangelicals whose views of
biblical authority make it impossible for them unqualifiedly
to declare of Holy Writ: "Thus saith the Lord." Yet the tenets
of a non-inerrancy approach to the Bible have been found wanting in logic and theological adequacy, and the key objections
to total scriptural infallibility have collapsed when subjected
to detailed analysis.

What, then, prevents us from embracing the church's historic
position on Scripture? Is it that we are unaware of what really
is at stake? The case presented above forces us to acknowledge
that only an entirely trustworthy Scripture allows for the possibility of clear theological thinking (since a tainted revelation
means a hopeless confusion of divine truth with human error).
But this observation seems "theoretical"—unrelated to our
personal ministries and service.

Perhaps we are slow to recognize what is at stake in the
conflict over the extent of biblical authority because we do not
feel, as some have felt in our time, the breath of Antichrist
and the pressure of demonic forces that would twist the world
into his unholy image. A theologian particularly well acquainted
with the German scene—and certainly no "fundamentalist"—
makes the following highly significant observation:

> In the years of Nazi persecution, the Confessional Church
> minister's Biblical interpretation was a near-fundamental-
> ism. "Es steht geschrieben"—"it is written" was his
> answer to every question. A few short years later Bult-
> mann's radical Biblical criticism was a burning issue in
> Germany. But only after General Eisenhower's armies
> had liberated Western Germany. Probably any church
> in a situation of crisis reverts to something as near
> fundamentalism as makes no odds.[43]

Does this not say something terribly important as to what
is at stake in the inerrancy issue? In crisis, there is no alternative to proclamation that "makes no odds." Under such
conditions, anything less than total assurance in Christian proclamation is betrayal of Christ and sure defeat. But how can

one possibly say, "it is written," without a Scripture that is entirely trustworthy? We need to become aware that *all* of life is really crisis in a sinful world where the battle between Christ and the powers of evil never ceases for a moment. What is at stake? Your effectiveness in that battle, and mine. Let us not tarnish and corrode our only effectual weapon—"the sword of the Spirit, which is the word of God."

NOTES

[1] Geoffrey Gorer and Ronald Searle, *Modern Types* (London: Cresset Press, 1955), pp. 66-69.

[2] Malcolm Muggeridge, *Jesus Rediscovered* (Garden City, N.Y.: Doubleday, 1969), p. 142. Admittedly, Muggeridge's conversion did not wipe out all his theological confusions or philosophical blindspots; but where he stands on the side of the angels (and he does so remarkably often) we quote him with approbation.

[3] Ian Henderson, *Power without Glory: A Study in Ecumenical Politics* (London: Hutchinson, 1967), *passim*.

[4] Cf. *COCU: The Official Reports of the Four Meetings of the Consultation* (Cincinnati: Foward Movement Publications [1966]), especially p. 52.

[5] Charles Merrill Smith, *The Pearly Gates Syndicate, or How to Sell Real Estate in Heaven* (Garden City, N.Y.: Doubleday, 1971), pp. 193-96. Smith, it should perhaps be noted, is by no means a theological conservative.

[6] Smith alludes to the French *cocu*, "cuckolded."

[7] "The Death of 'Relevance,'" *Time*, October 11, 1971, p. 64. See, as examples of Berger's penetrating studies of the contemporary church scene, his *The Noise of Solemn Assemblies* and *A Rumor of Angels*. For clarification, the reader should again be reminded that we are not tendentiously trying to prove a point by quoting those whose theology is our own; Berger could certainly not be regarded as theologically conservative.

[8] *Spectrum of Catholic Attitudes*, ed. Robert Campbell, O.P. (Milwaukee: Bruce, 1969), pp. 56-57.

[9] *Ibid.*, p. 32. Cf. Campbell's parallel volume, *Spectrum of Protestant Beliefs* (Milwaukee: Bruce, 1968), to which the present writer was one of the five contributors.

[10] Hans Küng, *Infallible? An Inquiry*, trans. Edward Quinn (Garden City, N.Y.: Doubleday, 1971), pp. 218-21. Cf. Montgomery, *Ecumenicity, Evangelicals, and Rome* (Grand Rapids, Mich.: Zondervan, 1969), pp. 103-104 ("Hans Küng on Justification").

[11] *Lexicon de l'Eglise Nouvelle*, ed. Maurice Lelong, O. P. (Forcalquier, France: Robert Morel, 1971), *in loco*.

[12] Donald C. Masters, F.R.S.C., *The Rise of Evangelicalism* ([Toronto: Evangelical Publishers, 1961]), p. 15. The lectures comprising this publication appeared originally in the *Evangelical Christian*.

[13] For an interesting example of a contemporaneous "liberal evangelical" attack on Louis Gaussen's inerrancy position, see Ulysse Gaussen, *Etude sur la Théopneustie des Saintes Ecritures de Louis Gaussen. Thèse présentée à la Faculté de Théologie protestante de Strasbourg ... pour obtenir le grade de Bachelier en théologie* (Strasbourg: G. Silbermann, 1867).

[14] James T. Burtchaell, C.S.C., *Catholic Theories of Biblical Inspiration since 1810: A Review and Critique* (Cambridge, Eng.: Cambridge University Press, 1969), pp. 1-2.

[15] For a very recent editorial reaffirmation of this position on the part of *Christianity Today*, see "The Infallible Word" (June 20, 1973), pp. 26-27.

[16] Cf. Montgomery, *Crisis in Lutheran Theology* (2 vols., 2d ed.; Minneapolis: Bethany Fellowship, 1973); *Time*, July 23, 1973 (Religion: "Battle of New Orleans"), and August 20, 1973 (Letters); *Affirm*, III/4 (September, 1973).

[17] Jeffrey K. Hadden, *The Gathering Storm in the Churches* (Garden City, N.Y.: Doubleday, 1969), pp. 41, 251. Our table is a composite of Hadden's Table 8 and Appendix Table I.

[18] *Ibid.*, p. 53 (Table 18). The decline in belief in specific substantive doctrines,

though subject to age correlations in such areas as the Virgin Birth, is not as pronounced quantitatively as the decline in belief in a literally reliable, totally veracious Bible. Otherwise stated, "the *proportional* differences representing the extreme age groups is considerably less than was the case on the items dealing with how scripture should be interpreted." Hadden accounts for this by noting that "denominationalism," rather than acceptance of the Bible's teachings because they are taught by the Bible, "appears to be significant in determining what a minister actually believes about traditional theology" (p. 54). If this interpretation is correct (and it certainly seems to fit the facts), one may well contemplate the sad future of christological teachings as the influence of the institutional church (denominationalism) steadily weakens. Indeed, such weakening of denominational religiosity is one of the main characteristics of the present church scene. If the Bible can no longer sustain Christ, what makes us think denominationalism will be capable of doing so?

¹⁹ Daniel P. Fuller, "The Nature of Biblical Inerrancy," *American Scientific Affiliation Journal*, XXIV/2 (June, 1972), p. 50. Cf. Clark H. Pinnock, "In Response to Dr. Daniel Fuller," *Evangelical Theological Society Journal*, XVI/2 (Spring, 1973), pp. 70-72.

²⁰ Terence, *Heauton timoroumenos* (163 B.C.), Act I, Sc. 1.

²¹ John Henry Cardinal Newman, *The Idea of a University*, ed. Charles Frederick Harrold (new ed.; New York: Longmans, Green, 1947), pp. 45-46.

²² Cf. David K. Cornelius and Edwin St. Vincent, *Cultures in Conflict: Perspectives on the Snow-Leavis Controversy* (Chicago: Scott, Foresman, 1964).

²³ Jacques Barzun, *The House of Intellect* (New York: Harper Torchbooks, 1961), p. 11.

²⁴ Henry Evelyn Bliss, *The Organization of Knowledge and the System of the Sciences*, with an Introduction by John Dewey (New York: Henry Holt, 1929), p. 409. H. E. Bliss was creator of the Bliss Bibliographic Classification.

²⁵ Ernest Cushing Richardson, *Classification: Theoretical and Practical* (3d ed.; New York: H. W. Wilson Company, 1930), p. 9.

²⁶ Burtchael, *op. cit.* (in note 14), p. 224.

²⁷ Alfred Loisy, *Mémoires pour servir à l'histoire religieuse de notre temps* (3 vols.; Paris: Nourry, 1930-1931), I, 237.

²⁸ *Ibid.*, III, 246; and cf. Albert Houtin & Félix Sartiaux, *Alfred Loisy: sa vie, son oeuvre*, ed. Emile Poulat (Paris: C.N.R.S., 1960), p. 157.

²⁹ Robert Pease, *The Associate Professor: A Novel* (New York: Simon and Schuster, 1967), pp. 113-14.

³⁰ See, for example, Pierre Marcel, "Our Lord's Use of Scripture," in *Revelation and the Bible*, ed. Carl F. H. Henry (Grand Rapids, Mich.; Baker Book House, 1958), pp. 121-34.

³¹ For a fuller development of this point, see Montgomery, "Inspiration and Infallibility: A New Departure," in *The Suicide of Christian Theology* (Minneapolis: Bethany Fellowship, Inc., 1970), pp. 314-55.

³² Fuller, *loc. cit.* (in note 19 above).

³³ Virgil C. Aldrich, *Philosophy of Art* ("Foundations of Philosophy"; Englewood Cliffs, N.J.: Prentice-Hall, 1963), p. 92.

³⁴ Clarification of the precise scope of the intentional fallacy may be in order, particularly in light of the (laudatory) emphasis placed on macro-intention and micro-intention in Professor Pinnock's essay, "Limited Inerrancy: A Critical Appraisal and Constructive Alternative" appearing in this same volume. The intentional fallacy, it should be carefully noted, does *not* apply to the inductive determination of an author's purpose by the examination of the work he has written; such efforts to derive the larger or lesser purposes of composition are part and parcel of all responsible interpretation of literature, written creative or didactic. One commits the intentional fallacy, rather, when one performs either or both of the following operations: (1) the author's alleged intent is derived *extrinsically*—from outside the work to be interpreted—and is then forced on the work regardless of the natural meaning of the work taken by itself; and (2) the author's alleged intent, obtained either from outside his composition or even within the composition, is employed as a *reductionistic principle* for discounting what he has in fact said in his work or the truth-value of it. In short, one can and should try to learn an author's purpose in writing, but this must be learned through analysis of his composition itself, and must not be used as a critical principle to evacuate his work of its substantive content. Analysis of intent ought to function ministerially—as a servant —not magisterially—as lord and master—in interpreting a text; it is properly a *hermeneutic*, not a *critical* tool.

35 Fuller himself hesitates to do so, for he states that "if some aspect of these biblicaι events which is an essential of revelation did not happen, then it would destroy the truth of Scripture." But can we not conclude (using his intentional fallacy) that he really did not "intend" to make this damaging qualification after all?! Less facetiously, his qualification is without practical value, for he nowhere defines what makes an event or aspect of an event "essential to revelation" (as compared with biblical events or aspects that are not). He calls them "redemptive," but what in Scripture is unrelated to redemption? Luther rightly perceived that "the whole Scripture is about Christ alone everywhere" (*Vorlesung über den Römerbrief*, 1515-16, ed. J. Ficker [4th ed.; Leipzig, 1930], p. 240). One is left with the impression that when the chips are down for the liberal evangelical, the infallibly "revelational" or "redemptive" in Scripture can easily become synonymous with the not-yet-criticized.

36 E.g., Roman Catholic theologian Bruce Vawter: "A human literature containing no error would indeed be a contradiction in terms, since nothing is more human than to err" (*Biblical Inspiration* [Philadelphia: Westminster, 1972]).

37 Julia V. Nakamura, *The Japanese Tea Ceremony: An Interpretation for Occidentals* (Mount Vernon, N.Y.: Peter Pauper Press, 1965), pp. 29-37. In Japanese legend, tea originated with Daruma, who founded Zen Buddhism; the tea ceremony is thus on the deepest level an Eastern religio-philosophical liturgy.

38 A. J. Arberry, *Revelation and Reason in Islam* (London: Allen & Unwin, 1971), p. 24.

39 George I. Mavrodes, "Science and the Infallibility of the Bible," *American Scientific Affiliation Journal*, XIX/3 (September, 1967), 92. Cf. also his papers, "The Language of Revelation," *American Scientific Affiliation Journal*, XVIII (December, 1966), pp. 103-107, and "Revelation and Epistemology," in *The Philosophy of Gordon H. Clark*, ed. Ronald H. Nash (Philadelphia Presbyterian and Reformed Publishing Co., 1968), pp. 227-56.

40 Daniel Fuller, "On Revelation and Biblical Authority," *Evangelical Theological Society Journal*, XVI/2 (Spring, 1973), pp. 67-69.

41 B. B. Warfield, *The Inspiration and Authority of the Bible*, ed. Samuel G. Craig (Philadelphia: Presbyterian and Reformed Publishing Co., 1948), pp. 218-19.

42 "Mavrodes fails to see that the epistemological route by which one arrives at Biblical truth does not determine the value of what one arrives at—any more than the use of a less than perfect map requires one to reach a city having corresponding inadequacies" (Montgomery, "Gordon Clark's Philosophy of History," in *The Philosophy of Gordon H. Clark* [*op. cit.*], p. 390, and in *Where Is History Going?* [Minneapolis: Bethany Fellowship, Inc., 1972], p. 180). See also Montgomery, "Inductive Inerrancy," in *The Suicide of Christian Theology* (*op. cit.*, in note 31 above), pp. 356-58.

43 Henderson, *op. cit.* (in note 3 above), p. 180.

2

"SOLA SCRIPTURA" IN HISTORY AND TODAY

J. I. Packer

"*Sola* Scriptura"—by Scripture *only*—is a Reformation slogan which stands for the Reformer's total view of how the Bible should function as an authority in the conscience of the individual and in the church's corporate life. This view is more complex than the slogan might suggest, and a major part of this survey will be spent elucidating it. Then we shall attempt a bird's-eye view of how the Reformers' principle has fared since their day, and we shall end by reflecting on some of the factors involved in maintaining it in ours. Our own belief that the Reformers' view was and is essentially right will not be disguised, and our hope is that the evidence to be passed in review will go some small way towards justifying it.

THE MEANING OF "SOLA SCRIPTURA"

To the Reformers, the principle of bowing to the authority of Scripture was basic in all that they did and taught. Melanchthon called *sola Scriptura* the formal principle of the Reformation, *sola fide* being its material principle. In articulating the principle of *sola Scriptura*, as in so much else, Luther was the pioneer. Many have traced how, from the positive declaration that to hear or read the Scripture is nothing else than to hear God [1]—a conviction common to the whole Christian church from the earliest times—Luther was led to set the authority of "the infallible Word of God" (*verbum Dei infallibile*) [2] over that of popes, councils, church fathers, and tradition in all its forms, until on April 18, 1521, at Worms, when called on by

Johann von Eck, Official General of the Archbishop of Trier, to renounce his alleged errors, he spoke these tremendous words: "Unless I am convinced by testimonies of Scripture or evident reason (*ratione evidente*)—for I believe neither the Pope nor Councils alone, since it is established that they have often erred and contradicted themselves—I am the prisoner of the Scriptures cited by me, and my conscience has been taken captive by the Word of God; I neither can nor will recant anything, since it is neither safe nor right to act against conscience. God help me. Amen." [3] What Luther thus voiced at Worms shows the essential motivation and concern, theological and religious, of the entire Reformation movement: namely, that the Word of God alone must rule, and no Christian man dare do other than allow it to enthrone itself in his conscience and heart.

Luther's reference to "evident reason" as a source of conviction does not cut across the principle of Scripture *only*, for "reason" here means precisely "logical inference from biblical principles." Luther rejected the idea that fallen man's rational reflection could be a source of religious truth apart from the Bible, and when he envisaged reason trying to pronounce on divine things independently of Scripture he called it "the devil's whore." This is his distinction between the *magisterial* use of reason, which he condemns as a damnable expression of human pride, and the *ministerial* use of it, which he treats as right and necessary. [4] None of the Reformers were irrationalists! But all of them, with Luther, insisted that it is by Scripture only that God and His grace may be known and our souls fed. For Luther, "*Sola Scriptura* was not only the battle-cry of the crusade," writes Arthur Skevington Wood; "it was the polestar of his own heart and mind." [5] All that Luther was and did he owed to the Bible. The same could be said of all the Reformers, who in this as in other matters were a remarkably homogeneous body of men.

What was new here? Not the idea that the Bible, being God-given, speaks with God's authority—that was common ground to both the Reformers and their opponents, and was indeed at that time an unquestioned Christian commonplace, like the doctrine of the Trinity. Nor was there anything new in the Reformer's insistence that Bible reading is a sweet and nourishing activity for Christan people. What was new was the belief, borne in upon the Reformers by their own experience of Bible study, that Scripture can and does interpret itself to the faithful from within—Scripture is its own interpreter, *Scrip-*

tura sui ipsius interpres, as Luther put it [7]—so that not only does it not need Popes or Councils to tell us, as from God, what it means; it can actually challenge Papal and conciliar pronouncements, convince them of being ungodly and untrue, and require the faithful to part company with them. From the second century on, Christians had assumed that the traditions and teachers of the church, guided by the Holy Spirit, were faithful to the biblical message, and that it was safe to equate Church doctrine with Bible truth. The Reformers tested this assumption by the self-interpreting Scripture which they found they had and discovered that the assumption was mostly justified in the case of the fathers (save that apart from Augustine none of them seemed to be quite clear enough on the principle of salvation by grace and not even Augustine had fully grasped imputed righteousness).[8] In relation, however, to the pronouncements of Mediaeval popes and councils and the teaching of the "sophists" (scholastic theologians), the assumption was beyond all hope and rescue. It was no part of the Reformer's case to affirm that there was no value at all in the church's tradition of witness and theology; their point was simply that church tradition, which offered itself as exposition and application of Bible teaching,[9] should be tested by the Scriptures which it sought to subserve in order to check that it had not run off the track. This was part of the meaning of "only" in the slogan "by Scripture *only*"; as Scripture was the only *source* from which sinners might gain true knowledge of God and godliness, so Scripture was the only *judge* of what the church had in each age ventured to say in her Lord's name.[10]

It would be wrong to view Reformation theology as the projection into words of an experience, but equally it would be wrong to forget that it was born out of a tremendous renewal of Christian experience. The Reformation was a spiritual revival, if any movement in Christendom ever was; and at its heart was a renewed awareness both of what Scripture says about God and also that what Scripture says, God says. Luther's own *Türmerlebnis* ("discovery in the tower") in 1514 illustrates this: God there taught him the meaning of the divine righteousness in Romans 1:17 and how the just, i.e. justified man lives by faith, so that, in Luther's own words, "I felt just as though I had been born again, and believed I had entered Paradise through wide-opened doors." [13] It was with this experience, as Dr. Skevington Wood says with perfect justice, that "the Protestant Reformation really started." [14] But the presupposition of the experience was that what Scripture says has divine authority, and had Luther not vividly felt that, his insight into Paul's meaning in Romans 1:17 would have had for him no more than historical interest—as indeed is the case with many moderns who agree that Luther's exegesis of Paul is right but have no sense of its being God's message to them. In truth, the root and matrix of the Reformation experience of God was the conviction that what Scripture declares is God's authentic message to us who hear and read it.

In affirming Holy Scripture to be the only source of true knowledge of God, and the only judge of the truth or otherwise of Christians' beliefs, the Reformers set their faces against any trust in natural theology. They based their distrust of it on a denial, not of God's general revelation, in the manner of Karl Barth, but of fallen man's ability to apprehend general revelation correctly. Quite apart from the fact that general revelation, as described by Paul in Romans 1:18-23, 32, 2:12-16 (the passages on which the Reformers based their view), tells of God only as Creator, Lawgiver, and Judge, and not as Redeemer of sinners, fallen man's proud intellect (so the Reformers held) always distorts what comes through to him from general revelation by his own self-willed speculation or self-induced obtuseness. In face of the nonbiblical scholastic theology of the Roman church and the fantastic idolatries of the pagan world, the Reformers argued constantly that those who do not in humility and self-distrust allow the Bible to teach men its message about God and grace will never have their false notions of God corrected, nor see the light of saving truth, but will walk in darkness forever; only those who become pupils of Scripture will find the true God, and eternal life.

Theologically, and religiously too, this point is bound up with another: namely, the clear understanding of the ministry of the Holy Spirit which blossomed at the Reformation in a way that was quite without precedent since the Apostles Paul and John laid down their pens. Warfield held that the most appropriate of all possible titles for Calvin was "the theologian of the Holy Spirit," and it is certainly true that in the pages of the Institutes we find, briefly but powerfully expressed, a fully worked-out account of the dispensation of the Spirit in bringing us through the Scriptures the knowledge and life of God in Christ —an account which historically proved epoch-making.[11] Yet the fact is that all Calvin's points about the Spirit's work with the Word were made by Luther before him,[12] and can be amply paralleled from other Reformation divines. As we said before, these theologians were an uncommonly homogeneous body of men, and the extent to which they are at one on central issues is most striking. Theologically, the Reformers' grasp of the nature and power of the Spirit's ministry sprang straight from the Scriptures, which as scholarly Renaissance men they read, not to allegorize in terms of inherited ideas as Mediaeval preachers had done, but to enter into the thinking of the authors; and, reading them thus, they learned from God's penmen of the Spirit's covenanted work in Christians and in the church. Subjectively, however, what determined the emphasis which they gave to the Spirit's ministry was the fact that, reading the Scriptures not just as scholars but as Christians, conscious of the darkness of their own minds and praying for light, they had enjoyed in answer to their prayers a deep personal experience of the Spirit's inner witness to the authenticity of Scripture as God's Word, and of the Spirit's power to use what was written as a source of instruction, hope and strength.

Calvin makes this clearer than anyone in some magnificent sentences declaring that this conviction is the universal outcome of the Spirit's inner witness to Scripture—that is, His bestowal of spiritual sight so that we perceive in Scripture the Divine light that shines forth from it. Calvin writes:[15]

> Let it therefore remain a fixed point, that those whom the Holy Spirit has inwardly taught rest firmly upon Scripture, and that Scripture is indeed self-authenticated, not is it right that it be subjected to proof and arguments; but that it attains the certainty in our eyes that it merits by the witness of the Spirit. Even if it wins reverence for itself by its own majestic quality (*majestate*), it only affects us seriously when sealed on our hearts by the Spirit. Enlightened by his power, we do not believe that Scripture is from God on our own judgment or that of others; but, rising above human judgment, we declare it utterly certain (just as if we saw God's own divinity there) that by men's ministry it has flowed to us from God's own mouth . . . we are fully conscious that we hold the unconquerable truth . . . we feel the unmistakable power of the divine majesty living and breathing there. . . . Such, then, is the conviction that does not require reasons; such the knowledge with which the best reason agrees—that is, in which the mind knows surer and steadier repose than in any reasons; such the awareness (*sensus*) which cannot be born save by heavenly revelation. *I speak only of what each believer experiences in himself*, save that my words fall far short of a just account of it.

Again:[16]

> The power which is peculiar to Scripture appears from
> the fact that no human writings, however skilfully pol-
> ished, are able so to affect us at all. Read Demosthenes
> or Cicero; read Plato, Aristotle, or any of that crowd;
> they will wonderfully allure, delight, move and thrill you;
> but betake yourself from them to read the sacred book,
> and willy-nilly it will so affect you, move your heart and
> fix itself in your very marrow that compared with the
> force of that realisation (*sensus*) the impression made by
> the orators and philosophers will just about vanish away.
> So it is easy to see that the Holy Scriptures, which so far
> surpass in their effect all the gifts and graces of human
> endeavour, *breathe out something divine.*

Therefore Calvin can confidently oppose the claim of the
Anabaptist "enthusiasts" that their private revelations were
Spirit-given, the common awareness of Christians that it is
through the Word, and as confirmer of the Word, that the Spirit
of God is truly known.[17]

> The Lord has so bound together our certainty concern-
> ing his word and his Spirit that firm reverence for the
> Word possesses our minds when the Spirit shines to make
> us behold God's face there, and we in turn embrace the
> Spirit with no fear of being deceived when we recognise
> him in his own image, that is, in the word. . . . God . . .
> sent down the Spirit by whose power he has delivered the
> word to complete his work by effective confirmation of
> the word . . . as the children of God . . . see themselves
> bereft of all the light of truth without the Spirit of God,
> so they are aware that the word is the instrument by
> which the Lord bestows on believers the illumination of
> His Spirit. They know no other Spirit than Him who
> dwelt and spoke in the apostles, *him by whose oracles
> they are repeatedly recalled to the hearing of the Word.*

It is apparent that an overwhelmingly vivid awareness of
Scripture as God's Word to us was central to the Reformation
experience, or none of these paragraphs could ever have been
written; and it is apparent also that to the extent that this awareness is absent the Reformers' understanding of what *sola Scriptura* means cannot be sustained.

The Reformers' whole understanding of Christianity, then, depended on the principle of *sola Scriptura*: that is, the view that
Scripture, as the *only* Word of God in this world, is the *only*
guide for conscience and the church, the *only* source of true
knowledge of God and grace, and the *only* qualified judge of the

church's testimony and teaching, past and present. This view rests upon a further series of principles, several of which have been hinted at already, but which may now conveniently be presented in order, thus:

(1) God's people need instruction from God, as a teacher informing and educating his pupils, because their minds are blind and ignorant through sin, and it is beyond their power to work out any true knowledge of God for themselves.

(2) God intends to enlighten and teach us, and so bring us to faith and knowledge of Himself in Christ, by the Spirit through the Scriptures. That is why the Scriptures exist, that is what they are for, and that is how their character as a *canon* should be understood. "Canon" means a rule or a measuring-rod: the Reformers' concept was that the function of a measuring-rod for faith and life is through God's appointment fulfilled by this unique composite *textbook*, of which He himself is both author and interpreter.

(3) The Scriptures were so directly produced ("spoken" or "dictated") by the Holy Spirit that there is no room for doubt that whatever they teach God himself teaches.

(4) As would be expected of documents that were written, not to mystify, but to be understood, the Scriptures are essentially clear in their meaning and do not need an authoritative human voice to speak for them as if they were intrinsically obscure. In any case, no such authoritative voice is available: the infallibility which the Mediaevals claimed for the church does not exist.

(5) Scripture teaching is sufficient for our guidance in all matters of faith and life, and there is no need, just as there is no possibility, of supplementing the Bible from any other source of revelation.[18]

(6) Through the inner witness of the Spirit, Christians recognize that the Scriptures "breathe out something divine" and come with God's own authority to all who hear or read them. The church is "a witness and a keeper of Holy Writ,"[19] but it is not in the last analysis the church's testimony, as such which gives certainty concerning either the nature of Scripture or the extent of the canon. The church's certainty about the canon rests finally, after all has been said that can be said about the history and pedigree of the separate books, on the Spirit-given awareness that they bear divine witness to Christ, and God himself speaks to us what they say.

(7) As the Spirit who inspired these books attests them to us as the Word from God, so He enables us to understand them

in their true theological sense, as a complex unity of witness to our Lord and Saviour Jesus Christ, who in one way or another is the *scopus* (end in view, goal, object or aim) of them all.

(8) The biblical message which is God's teaching stands over the church and over individual Christians, God's pupils, at all times, to judge correct and amplify their understanding of, and witness to, God's works and ways. To differ from the Bible is to differ from God, and so to be wretchedly wrong.

(9) The people of God must wait on the ministry of his Word by those whom he has qualified for this task. This is the way the church must feed its faith and nourish its life. Where the Word is not faithfully preached and taught, spiritual darkness and death always and necessarily supervene.

On three issues involved in the above account something further needs to be said, to make the Reformers' view quite clear in face of modern discussions.

(1) *The Authority of Scripture.* Authority is a relational and hierarchical concept with a wide range of applications. It needs to be said explicitly that when the Reformers ascribe authority to Scripture they are not just thinking of a relative human authority which the biblical writers might be held to have by virtue of their religious experience or expertise, or of the fact that their witness to God's acts of revelation and redemption in history is near to being first-hand and is in any case of better quality than any other available to us. Many today construe biblical authority in these terms, but such a view falls far short of the Reformers' meaning. They were concerned to ascribe to the Scriptures an absolute divine authority, springing from the fact that God gave them and now says to us what they say. The inspiration of the prophets, whose human utterances were also and equally oracles of God, were to the Reformers the model of all biblical inspiration, while the universal and permanent application of statute law (a principle exhibited in Scripture in the abiding authority of the God-given Mosaic law over Israel) was the model for their belief that Scripture as a whole is God's instruction and guide for all his people in every age. Because God is God, his authority is ultimate and final; and because all Scripture is divinely inspired, final divine authority, in the sense of an absolute claim on our credence and our obedience, attaches to all that it has to say. James Barr draws a useful distinction between "hard" and "soft" concepts of authority, as follows: "A 'hard' idea would mean that the authority of the Bible was (i) antecedent to its interpretation and (ii) general in its application. The

reader or user of the Bible would be expected to *expect* that biblical passages would be authoritative and therefore illuminating; . . . and this expectation would be firm *before* the interpretation was carried out, and not therefore be a decision based afterwards upon the results of the interpretation. A 'soft' idea of authority would suggest that authority was (i) posterior to interpretation and (ii) limited accordingly to the passages where an authoritative effect had in fact been found." [20] While most modern Protestants espouse a "soft" view of biblical authority, that of the Reformers was as "hard" as could be.

(2) *The Clarity of Scripture.* The Reformers have sometimes been suspected of holding that Spirit-taught Bible students would find no difficulties in Scripture, nor would they need to bring to Scripture technical knowledge of a linguistic, cultural and historical sort in order to find out its meaning. Whatever currency these ideas may have had in later pietistic circles, they were no part of the Reformers' view. This appears from their own exegetical practice, which made the fullest use possible in their day of all these technical resources; it appears too from their demand for a learned ministry, which was based on their conviction that preaching and teaching require a high degree of disciplined scholarship; and their own statements show that they fully recognized that the Bible contains passages whose meanings are elusive. But when Erasmus spoke largely and loosely about the obscurity of Scripture, Luther replied as follows: [21]

> I certainly grant that many *passages* in the Scriptures are obscure and hard to elucidate, but that is due, not to the exalted nature of their subject, but to our own linguistic and grammatical ignorance; and it does not in any way prevent us knowing all the *contents* of Scripture. For what solemn truth can the Scriptures still be concealing, now that the seals are broken, the stone rolled away from the door of the tomb, and that greatest of all mysteries brought to light—that Christ, God's Son, became man, that God in Three in One, that Christ suffered for us, and will reign for ever? And are not these things known, and sung in our streets? Take Christ from the Scriptures—and what more will you find in them? You see then, that the entire content of the Scriptures has now been brought to light, even though some passages which contain unknown words remain obscure.

And he went on to say that if anyone finds the Bible wholly

obscure the fault is not in the Bible, but in him—he is spiritually blind, and cannot discern Christ, needs the help of the Holy Spirit to make him see.

Calvin, too, believed that the substance of the biblical message was clear, and the fact that he never saw cause to change his mind on any point of doctrine throughout almost thirty years of theological writing of itself lends confirmation to his belief; yet, As T. H. L. Parker notes, he was not "authoritarian in exegesis. Very frequently he will leave the precise meaning of a word, clause, or even sentence undecided ... he will sometimes change his mind on the exegesis of a passage ..." [22] Like Luther, Calvin insisted that the essential message was plain, but allowed that the meanings of some passages were uncertain. (And he said he did not understand the book of the Revelation at all!)

There are circles today in which it is fashionable to highlight the remoteness of the biblical world from ours and the problematical nature of the composition and background of the biblical books, and on this basis to ask whether it can be wise or fruitful to expect ordinary Christians to be benefited, as distinct from perplexed, by personal Bible reading. Thus, for instance, D. E. Nineham writes: "It is perhaps a pity that the proposed new Anglican catechism appears to regard the private reading of the Bible as mandatory for every literate member of the Church. Is that realistic ... ?" [23] This is a return to Erasmus, and the Reformers' comment on it would certainly be the same as Luther's to Erasmus: namely, that if you have eyes for Christ as the *scopus* of Scripture, according to its own testimony to itself, you will find that, just as the grace of the biblical Christ is relevant to you, so the essence of the biblical witness to Him is clear to you. Millions of Bible-readers in the world today will testify that this indeed is so.

(3) *The Unity of Scripture.* A further contemporary fashion is to dwell on the contrasts of style and vocabulary found within the Bible, and on this basis to deny that there is any such thing as "*the* biblical theology" at all. The suggestion is that what we have, rather, in the Bible as a whole, and in the New Testament particularly, is a series of distinct theologies balancing each other, to which we do violence if we try to integrate them into one. Gospel harmonies, for instance, are misguided endeavours; we best grasp the witness of the gospels to Jesus Christ not by combining them, as the church has been doing since Tatian, but by noting the differences between them.

Similarly, the theologies of Luke-Acts, Paul, Hebrews and the Johannine writings should be separated out and kept distinct, so that each can be appreciated in its divergence from the others. James Barr acts as sounding-board for this approach when, describing the current flow of opinion about the Bible, he writes: "There is less confidence in the idea that the Bible must be read 'as a whole.' There are those who feel, on the contrary, that the diversity and disagreement found within the Bible is a more sure characteristic of its nature and a more promising clue to its meaning . . . If the emphasis on the Bible 'as a whole' grew up in reaction against the purely analytic interests of scholars, so in turn the strivings after synthesis in post-war exegesis ended up by seeming like old-fashioned harmonization and made people turn again with relief to analysis as a fresher approach. Once again, therefore, we find that people are giving different values to different parts of the Bible." [24]

The Reformers would have seen this approach as abusing a half-truth, a monumental case of getting hold of the wrong end of the stick. Calvin, who came to the Bible as a gifted linguist and literary man, shows himself every whit as sensitive as modern scholars are to the verbal and stylistic differences between one author and another, and he was not alone in this. But what the Reformers found was that when the Bible is allowed to interpret itself from within, on the basis that "the mind of the Spirit is understood when the text of the document is understood," [25] then as the various parts of each individual book join up together by internal thematic links, so do the various books with each other to form a single coherent body of teaching. The verbal and conceptual resources of the different writers vary, but the theology which they teach is one. The Reformers took Scripture "literally" in the sense that they abandoned the arbitrariness of allegorizing, treated the historical character of the documents seriously, and concentrated on discovering what the human writer had in mind and why he was concerned to say it. Handling the Bible so, they found in it unity of doctrine, in a way that Mediaeval exegesis never had. Their expository method as theologians both reflected and confirmed their discovery: they built up their accounts of each matter inductively, by adducing successive Scriptures bearing on each theme. This was what Warfield meant when he said that Calvin's theological method "was persistently, rigorously, some may even say exaggeratedly, *a posteriori.* All *a priori* reasoning here he not only eschewed but vigorously repelled. His instrument of research was not logical amplification but exegetical investigation." [26] What was true of Calvin was true of Luther before him, and of all the Reformation masters. To Calvin, the grace of Christ the Mediator, and the history of the covenant of grace which Christ mediated through successive dispensations, are the two over-arching and complementary themes which run through all the Bible and hold it together.[27] Luther also has this insight, though the key to the unity of Scripture of which he makes most is the apparent antithesis of law and gospel: God, says Luther, first drives us out of ourselves through the law (His "strange work") so that He may draw us as needy sinners to the Christ of the gospel promise, of whom the Old Testament said much and the New Testament is full to overflowing.[28] Both Luther and Calvin labored to present Bible teaching as a coherent corpus of instruction from God the Holy Spirit about God and ourselves—the redeeming work in history of the God who made us, and the godliness to which knowledge of this should give rise in all human lives.[29]

It is surely clear that the Reformation tradition of exegesis, with its unitive, evangelical, Christocentric thrust and its unqualified acceptance as from God of all that Scripture is found to teach, prompts uncomfortable questions about its modern counterpart which stresses differences within the Bible, real or alleged, as the clue to understanding it. Did the Reformers succeed in showing that beneath the surface diversity of the documents lies a deep unity of evangelical teaching? If so, how can we regard a type of exegesis which does not show this as other than a failure? If unity is inescapable when exegesis is adequate, failure to find unity shows only that exegesis has been inadequate. But in that case the movement of thought described by Professor Barr must be judged, not an advance, but a regression. We may and must allow that if a unitive exegesis cannot be made convincing the Bible falls apart and the principle of *sola Scriptura* is exploded. But with that we must also insist that if a unitive exegesis can be vindicated, then the viability of the principle is established and its challenge becomes inescapable.

"SOLA SCRIPTURA" IN CHRISTIAN HISTORY

In the older Lutheran and Reformed churches of Western Europe and the British Isles, in conservative Presbyterian, Congregational, Baptist and Methodist circles, and now in the fast-growing Pentecostal churches, *sola Scriptura* has been enthroned as the architectural and critical principle of all sound theology. On the history of this principle over more than four centuries we make the following comments.

(1) *The extent of unanimity among its adherents has been remarkable.* If one reviews the historic Lutheran, Reformed, Anglican, Congregational and Baptist confessions, or compares, for example, Calvin's *Institutes* with the systematic theologies of F. Pieper the Lutheran, Charles Hodge and Louis Berkhof the Presbyterians, E. A. Litton and W. H. Griffith Thomas the Anglicans, W. B. Pope the Methodist and A. H. Strong the Baptist, or if one examines the preaching and spirituality of churches which actively upheld *sola Scriptura* as a principle for determining faith and action, what impresses is the oneness of overall outlook and the width of the area over which substantially identical positions were taught. Whether those involved felt close to each other as they sparred over points of specific agreement, or defended their denominations against criticism, is perhaps doubtful; but what is not doubtful is that those who historically have held to *sola Scriptura*, recognizing no *magisterium* save that of the Bible itself, have been at one on all essentials and on most details too, in a very striking way. If evidence tending to confirm the clarity of Scripture is called for, this fact will surely qualify.

(2) *The matters on which adherents of this principle have differed have been secondary.* To the traditional Roman Catholic complaint that Protestant biblicism produces endless divisions in the church, the appropriate reply is twofold: firstly, the really deep divisions have been caused not by those who maintained *sola Scriptura*, but by those, Roman Catholic and Protestant alike, who rejected it; second, when adherents of *sola Scriptura* have split from each other the cause has been sin rather than Protestant biblicism, for in convictional terms the issues in debate have not been of the first magnitude. Leaving aside the deep unorthodoxies of sects like Mormons and Jehovah's Witnesses—and their hostility to the Christian tradition and distrust of ordinary canons of biblical scholarship obliges one to put them in a class by themselves—one finds that the main theological issues that have divided Protestants who hold to *sola Scriptura* have been these: (1) how to understand God's sovereignty in salvation—the issue between Calvinists on the one hand and Arminians and Lutherans on the other: (2) how to understand the presence of Christ in the

Lord's Supper—the issue between Lutherans and other Protestants: (3) how far, if at all, Scripture legislates in the realm of church order—the issue between Flacians and "adiaphorists" in Lutheranism, and between the Puritans Cartwright and Travers on the one hand and Whitgift and Hooker on the other in Elizabethan England: (4) how the churches should be related to the state—the issue in debates about establishment throughout the world since the seventeenth century: (5) whether churchmen's children may properly be baptized in infancy or not—the issue between Baptist and all other Protestant churches: (6) what circumstances will surround the Lord's return—the issue between postmillennialists, premillennialists, and amillennialists. Other issues debated within Protestantism—anthropological, Christological, soteriological—have involved abandoning the Reformers' view of biblical inspiration, and thus defecting from *sola Scriptura* in its original sense, so we leave these questions out of account. (That lowered views of Scripture produce endless division within the churches is a fact too well known to need comment here, and we forbear to dwell on it.)

What are we to say to these six matters of debate? First, that whatever divisions they may have occasioned in the past it is very arguable that, being in reality secondary questions, they need not, and ideally would not have this effect. Second, that it is also very arguable that in each of these cases unexamined assumptions brought to the task of exegesis, rather than any obscurities arising from it, were really at the root of the cleavage. The trouble was that presuppositions were read into Scripture rather than read out of it, as follows:

(1) The first debate seems to have sprung from the assumption made by some that if man's free agency and responsibility were to be affirmed as Scripture affirms them, then God's absolute control of human action which Scripture also affirms must be denied.

(2) The second debate seems to have arisen because there were exegetical questions about our Lord's words of institution at the Last Supper which the Swiss Reformers raised and Luther would not face.

(3) The third debate reflected a taking for granted by some that apostolic acts in ordering church life have normative force for later generations, whether or not anything to this effect is said in the text, and equally that practices in the church which lack direct biblical sanction by precept or precedent are prohibited.

(4, 5) The fourth and fifth debates reflected the presupposition that Scripture must legislate on the issues in question, even though no biblical author addresses himself to either.

(6) The sixth debate reflects an unexamined difference of assumptions as to what constitutes "literal" exegesis of prophetic Scriptures.

It is a confusion to blame the principle of *sola Scriptura* for conflicts which sprang from insufficient circumspection in exegesis.

(3) *To limit God's sovereignty is to undermine "sola Scriptura."* This is not simply because the Bible views God's sovereignty as unlimited, though it does; it is because any such limitation strikes at the truth of inspiration. If God is not in absolute control of free human acts generally, then he was not in absolute control of the writings done by the biblical authors, and it cannot in that case be fully true that "the mind of the Spirit is understood when the text of the document is understood." It was inevitable that Arminian and Deist theology, which both take God's governing hand away from man's self-determined actions, should have produced lowered views of inspiration and a style of exegesis which convicted the inspired authors of making mistakes. Kant was being no more than a good Deist, with his own epistemological trimmings, when he denied that God can send us verbal messages. The unwillingness of the neo-orthodox, Barth, Bultmann and their followers to equate the normative Word of God with what the Bible says, and their preference for identifying the Word with what the biblical writers are thought to have meant despite what they said, or with Christ beyond the Bible rather than the Bible itself, or with a subjective psychic event rather than the objective truth that causes it, shows that they too do not wish to be lumbered with the historic doctrine of inspiration, and that in turn points to the fact that they too have an inadequate grasp of God's sovereignty over all His world. (This is an inadequacy which Barth's view of history and Bultmann's view of nature have in fact long made plain: [30] it has undoubtedly been the fundamental weakness in the theologies of both men.) The *sola Scriptura* which Protestants of this kind may profess in refusing to turn for knowledge of God to any extra-biblical source (e.g., the Roman Catholic *magisterium*) has to be differentiated from the *sola Scriptura* of the Reformers, whose essential point was that the teaching of the Bible is to be received as instruction from God without any qualification at all. The Reformation principle of *sola Scriptura* presup-

poses the Reformation view of God, and cannot be maintained apart from it.

MAINTAINING "SOLA SCRIPTURA" TODAY

What has been said suggests three concluding points.

(1) *The necessary of upholding "sola Scriptura."* It is inescapable that, as this principle determines one's whole account of Christianity, so one cannot abandon it without one's whole view of Christianity changing, more or less, at fundamental level. This is so whether the abandonment takes the form of giving up belief in absolute divine sovereignty and plenary biblical inspiration, or of accepting the Roman claim that a charisma of interpretive infallibility attaches to popes, councils, and their dogmas. For this reason the latest stage in the general ecumenical discussion of Holy Scripture (in which, of course, Roman Catholic scholars take their share) must be judged intensely depressing. Accomplished biblical scholars like D. E. Nineham, Christopher Evans and James Barr[31] reject all concepts of a revealed Word of God or a *Heilsgeschichte* that is normative for faith. The era when ecumenical Bible study was shaped by the concerns of Barth and Cullmann has ended. Barr notes in contemporary theological thought "a shift in the locus of authority, or indeed an abandonment of the concept of authority altogether." "The older theology," he continues, "seems to us today to have suffered from an authority neurosis; in all diversities there was an attempt to proceed from an agreed authority centre, defined and known in advance, which would serve as criterion in doubtful questions... Today we are content to have criteria which are less clear, to leave the nature of authority to emerge at the end of the theological process rather than to be there in defined form at the beginning."[32] This is as sad as it is clear. Barr is opting for a theological programme which sees Christianity as an historical phenomenon of which biblical and theological study is one continuing aspect, and he views the theological task humanistically as a venture in analytical description and free construction. On his programme, what authority the end-product has will presumably be decided by estimating its coherence as an historical analysis on the one hand and its vitality as a stimulus to discussion on the other; and the question of its *truth*, in the sense of whether it squares with God's view of things or not, will never be raised. Thus the "authority neurosis" of older Protestant theology, and the

"really pathological" concern of fundamentalists and others to learn from Scripture how to discriminate between orthodoxy and heresy, i.e. true and false belief,[33] will be transcended and left behind. It is not unknown for intelligent persons of neurotic and pathological opinions to diagnose the views of others of being neurotic and pathological, and the question arises whether that is not happening here; but, intriguing as that question is, we cannot pursue it now. Our only present point is that current theological developments, as illustrated by the views of Barr, confirm beyond all doubt what our earlier analysis indicated—namely, that those who wish to affirm any concept of *Heilsgeschichte* (particularly a divinely interpreted *Heilsgeschichte*), or any concept of a revealed Word of God (particularly one that is identical with the Bible) must do so on the basis of the Reformation principle of *sola Scriptura*, or they will not be able to do it at all.

(2) *The importance of vindicating a unitive theological exegesis of Scripture.* In the passage quoted above, Barr continues by predicating his approach on the existence in the Bible of "a multiplicity of theologies." "The older theological principle, if I do not misjudge it," he continues, "did not think in this way: rather, it set forth a criterion or authority which would, it was implied, generate the 'right' theology . . . There was a strict line between the one authority and the one true theology." [34] Again we may be grateful to Professor Barr for his clarity; this is exactly correct, and the Reformers' principle of *sola Scriptura* will only appear viable or credible if it can be shown that a unitive biblical exegesis which plots the "strict line" to true theology is actually plausible. Is this, in the present state of studies, an impossible task? Certainly current exegesis, which has theological pluralism in its presuppositions and method, has such pluralism in abundance in its conclusions; but we do well to remember this has not always been the way of scientific biblical study. On the dust-jacket of the most recent volumes of the new Scottish translation of Calvin's New Testament commentaries to come into my hands, the three which contain his Harmony of the Synoptic Gospels, it says: "These are the classic commentaries of the Reformation which laid the basis for all later scholarly exegesis of the Bible and which are proving as 'modern' as ever in their honest careful handling of the text, and in the relevance of their exposition to our deep religious and human needs. The interpretation . . . makes the Bible live and speak not only to the preacher and

the scholar but to the common man concerned to understand the Word of God." Yet the exegesis of Calvin, who over a quarter of a century expounded almost all the Bible in his own distinctive and distinguished way, was unitive through and through, as indeed that of Protestant commentaries generally was till fairly recent times. Could it be that the dust-jacket is right, and that Calvin's theological exegesis points a way which is still open to us today, if we will take it? But if so, we must face the fact that many of our contemporaries are sure that Calvin's road is not open, and the contrary can only be established in face of their skepticism when theological exegesis of Scripture which is both contemporary and unitive is actually produced. Here, perhaps, is the major task for evangelical scholarship in the next generation. General apologetics for biblical theism and the formal principle of *sola Scriptura* may keep the invading waters at bay, but only theological work which makes credible to modern doubters the inner unity of the message of the two Testaments and the sixty-six canonical books will turn the tide. In this twentieth century, the most sustained quest for exegesis of the kind described has been that of Karl Barth: and if we think that his venture was not wholly a success, it behooves us not to dismiss his objective, but to take the task in hand ourselves and try to do better. No general return to *sola Scriptura* can be expected today or tomorrow till the inner unity, consistency and coherence of the Bible message has been demonstrated to the Christian world afresh.

(3) *The cruciality of divine sovereignty in the case for "sola Scriptura."* The customary apologetic for biblical authority operates on too narrow a front. As we have seen, faith in the God of Reformation theology is the necessary presupposition of faith in Scripture as "God's Word written,"[35] and without this faith *sola Scriptura* as the God-taught principle of authority more or less loses its meaning. We may wish to defend against criticism our inherited evangelical habit, learned from the Westminster Confession, of dealing with the Bible, as the *principle* of true theological knowledge, prior to any other subject in the body of divinity; but we must never lose sight of the fact that our doctrine of God is decisive for our concept of Scripture, and that in our controversy with a great deal of modern theology it is here, rather than in relation to the phenomena of Scripture, that the decisive battle must be joined.[36]

NOTES

[1] Luther, *Weimarer Ausgabe (WA)*, ed. J. C. F. Knaske & others, (Weimar, 1883-), pp. 3, 14; 4, 318 (Commentary on the Psalms, 1513-15).

[2] *WA* 2. 279 (disputation with Eck, 1519).

[3] *WA*, 7, 838. On the question whether the words "Here I stand, I cannot do otherwise," which were added in the first printed version, were really spoken by Luther on that occasion, see R. Bainton, *Here I Stand: A Life of Martin Luther* (New York: New American Library Mentor Books, 1955). In any case, Luther put these words into print in the following year in a striking passage from his reply to "King Heinz" (Henry VIII, of England!): "For me it is enough that King Heinz cannot quote a single Scripture.... I place against the sayings of all Fathers, and every artifice and word of angels, men and devils, the Scripture and the gospel. *Here I stand, here I bid defiance, here I strut about and say, God's Word for me is above everything.* I will not give a hair though a thousand Augustines, a thousand Heinz-churches" (a reference to Henry's position as "supreme head" of the Church of England) "were all against me, and I am certain that the true church with me holds fast to the Word of God" (*WA*, 10 II, 256).

[4] B. A. Gerrish writes: "We must carefully distinguish: (1) natural reason, ruling within its proper domain (the Earthly Kingdom); (2) arrogant reason, trespassing upon the domain of faith (the Heavenly Kingdom); (3) regenerate reason, serving humbly in the household of faith, but always subject to the Word of God. Within the first context reason is an excellent gift of God; within the second, it is Frau Hulda, the Devil's Whore; within the third, it is the handmaiden of faith." (*Grace and Reason: a Study in the Theology of Luther* [Oxford: Oxford University Press, 1962], p. 26). Gerrish notes that Calvin's *Institutes* II.ii "amounts to a summing-up" of Luther's view of reason in fallen man (p. ix).

[5] Arthur Skevington Wood, *Luther's Principles of Biblical Interpretation* (London: Tyndale Press, 1900), p. 7.

[6] Cf. the following remark of Luther's: "I will not waste a word in arguing with one who does not consider that the Scriptures are the Word of God; we ought not to dispute with a man who thus rejects first principles" (cited without reference by A. M. Renwick in *Evangelical Quarterly*, XIX/2 [April, 1947], 114).

[7] *WA*, 7, 97.

[8] Augustine was by far the most admired and influential of the Fathers among the Reformers, particularly for his doctrine of grace formulated against Pelagianism. Misled by the meaning of *"justificare"* in Latin, he understood justification as God's work of making sinners subjectively righteous by pardoning their sins and infusing into them the grace of love (*caritas*).

[9] This was the Patristic view of tradition, which Mediaeval divines did not wholly abandon: see R. P. C. Hanson, *Tradition in the Early Church* (London: SCM, 1962), and G. Tavard, *Holy Writ or Holy Church* (London: Burns & Oates, 1959). The later theory that Scripture and tradition are two distinct and complementary sources of doctrine was not explicitly taught by the Council of Trent, though following Melchior Cano, Canisius and Bellarmine most Roman Catholics from the sixteenth century to the present day have assumed the contrary. See J. R. Geiselmann in *Christianity Divided*, ed. D. J. Callahan, H. A. Obermann, D. J. O'Hanlan (London and New York: Sheed and Ward, 1962), pp. 39ff.

[10] Cf. Westminster Confession I.x: "The supreme Judge, by which all controversies of religion are to be determined, and all decrees of councils, opinions of ancient writers, doctrines of men, and private spirits, are to be examined, and in whose sentence we are to rest, can be no other but the Holy Spirit speaking in the Scriptures."

[11] B. B. Warfield, *Calvin and Augustine* (Philadelphia: Presbyterian and Reformed, 1956), p. 484. Warfield continues: "It was [Calvin] who first related the whole experience of salvation specifically to the working of the Holy Spirit, worked it out in its details, and contemplated its several steps and stages in orderly progress as the product of the Holy Spirit's specific work in applying salvation to the soul.... What Calvin did was, specifically, to replace the doctrine of the Church as the sole source of assured knowledge of God and sole institute of salvation, by the Holy Spirit.... The *Institutes* is, accordingly, just a treatise on the work of God the Holy Spirit in making God savingly known to sinful man, and bringing sinful man into holy communion with God...." (pp. 485 ff).

[12] The reader can begin to verify this by consulting R. Prenter, *Spiritus Creator* (Philadelphia: Muhlenberg Press, 1953).

[13] *WA*, 54, 187.

[14] Wood. *op. cit.*, p. 7.

[15] *Inst.* I. vii. 3.

[16] *Inst.* I. viii. 1.

[17] *Inst.* I. ix. 3.

[18] Cf. Article VI of the Anglican Thirty-Nine Articles: "Holy Scripture containeth all things necessary to salvation: so that whatsoever is not read therein, nor may be proved thereby, is not to be required of any man, that it should be believed as an article of the Faith, or be thought requisite or necessary to salvation."

[19] Article XX.

[20] James Barr, *The Bible in the Modern World* (London: SCM, 1973), p. 27.

[21] *The Bondage of the Will*, tr. and ed. J. I. Packer and O. R. Johnston (London: James Clarke, 1937), p. 71 (*W.A.*, 18, 607).

[22] T. H. L. Parker, *op. cit.*, pp. 79f.

[23] *The Church's Use of the Bible Past and Present*, ed. D. E. Nineham (London: SPCK, 1963), p. 162.

[24] Barr, *op. cit.*, p. 6. It seems that this view is now imminent in the World Council of Churches, at any rate at the secretariat level. Pekr Beyerhaus blames "the breakdown of the exegetical preparation for Bangkok" as "the depth of the hermeneutical crisis in the WCC. There is as common conviction that the Bible is the authoritative and reliable basis for Christian faith and ministry. Scripture is seen by many as a collection of different historical documents, justifying to the experiences of salvation and understandings of the divine will at the time they were written. But these witnesses, it is felt, do not necessarily agree among themselves" (*The Evangelical Response to Bangkok*, ed. Ralph Winter [South Pasadena: William Cary Library], pp. 110f.). See also p. 58.

[25] The phrase comes from T. H. L. Parker's account of Calvin's exegetical method in *Calvin's New Testament Commentaries* (London: SCM, 1971), p. 68).

[26] Warfield, *op. cit.*, p. 481.

[27] Cf. *Inst.* II.ix-xi.

[28] Luther's sense of the unity of the New Testament comes out vividly when he writes in the preface to his German translation of it: "we must get rid of the delusion that there are four gospels . . . the New Testament is one book . . . there is only one gospel, only one book in the New Testament, only one faith, and only one God . . ." (*WA*, 6, 2).

[29] This is where both differ from many modern exponents of the unity of the Bible who unite in terms of "biblical theology" or "*Heilsgeschichtich*" standpoint. The latter commonly treat the biblical witness to God's saving acts in history as spotty and unreliable, more or less; Luther and Calvin, however, put implicit trust in it, as the teaching of the Holy Spirit.

[30] Barth will not attempt a Christian view of history, and is equivocal on the continuity of God's saving act in Christ with the rest of world history. Bultmann's rejection of the physical miracles ascribed in the gospels to Christ, and of His virgin birth and bodily resurrection, reveal a mechanistic, uniformitarian view of nature as rigid as that of any Deist. For both, wherever else God's control may be a reality, it does not seem to be so in the material order.

[31] Cf. Nineham, *op. cit.*, and "*The use of the Bible in Modern Theology*," *Bulletin of the John Ryland's Library* lii (1969), pp. 178-99; Evans, *Is "Holy Scripture" Christian?* (London: SCM, 1971); Barr, *op. cit.*

[32] Barr, *op. cit.*, p. 113.

[33] *Ibid.*, p. 147.

[34] *Ibid.*, p. 114.

[35] The phrase is from Anglican Article XX.

[36] For an excellent and conclusive example of such a battle, see the critique of Dewey M. Beegle's view of Scripture by Cornelius Van Til in his mimeographed class syllabus *In Defence of the Faith, I: The [Protestant] Doctrine of Scripture* (Ripon, Calif.: Den Dulk Christian Foundation, (1967), pp. 72-87.

3

LESSONS FROM LUTHER ON THE INERRANCY OF HOLY WRIT

John Warwick Montgomery

A most dangerous method of resolving arguments is the appeal to human authority. A disagrees with B; A cites great man C in his behalf; B claims that great man D supports his view; and the discussion degenerates into an attempt on the part of A to show that his authority is superior to B's, while B endeavors to demonstrate the superiority of *his* authority. In the course of such discussions the protagonists generally forget the real point at issue, namely, the relative value of the evidence marshalled by the authorities appealed to. In the final analysis, it is not the judgment of the alleged authority that determines the question, but the value of his evidence. Why? because, God excepted, authorities are like the rest of us: they can make mistakes.[1]

On the vital question of the extent of biblical reliability, therefore, we must be particularly careful not to engage in a "can-you-top-this" appeal to theologians and church leaders through the centuries, as if their judgments would ipso facto arbitrate the question. Ultimately, the issue of scriptural inerrancy can be settled only by the evidence to which all authorities on the subject must themselves necessarily appeal: the claims made by the God of Scripture, through prophets, apostles, and His incarnate Son, concerning the Bible's entire truthfulness.

But, having accepted this important caveat, we must not go to the opposite extreme and neglect the judgments of history's greats as to the reliability of Scripture. It is surely of more than routine significance that belief in the unqualified accuracy of Holy Writ conditioned the thinking of nearly all influential western minds from the beginning of the Christian era to the rise of modern secularism in the 18th century. Conceivably— though the notion hardly accords with the arrogance of modernity—Augustine, Aquinas, Michelangelo, Luther, Calvin, Pascal, Bach, Kepler, Wesley, and a host of others too numerous to mention may have had better reason to hold to scriptural authority than 20th century man has to reject it.

Were we allowed to pose the question as to the Bible's inerrancy to but a single figure in western history outside of the scriptural writers themselves, the choice of Luther would be entirely natural. Robert Southey, poet laureate of England, did not hesitate to formulate a new beatitude: "Blessed be the day of Martin Luther's birth! It should be a festival only second to that of the nativity of Jesus Christ." [2] Perhaps this strikes us as excessive, but we can hardly gainsay Carlyle's parallel historical judgment:

> The Diet of Worms, Luther's appearance there on the 17th of April, 1521, may be considered as the greatest scene in modern European history; the point, indeed, from which the whole subsequent history of civilization takes its rise. The world's pomp and power sit there, on this hand; on that, stands up for God's truth one man, the poor miner Hans Luther's son. Our petition—the petition of the whole world to him was: "Free us; it rests with thee; desert us not." Luther did not desert us. It is, as we say, the greatest moment in the modern history of men—English Puritanism, England and its Parliaments, America's vast work these two centuries; French Revolution; Europe and its work everywhere at present—the germ of it all lay there. Had Luther in that moment done other, it had all been otherwise. [3]

No individual in the entire history of the church has had the revolutionary impact upon its development that Luther exercised; and all branches of Protestantism—the third great division of the Church Militant—stand equally and directly in his debt. Ought not such a man's attitude to biblical authority have more than passing interest to Christians today who are concerned with the same problem?

It is the thesis of this essay that we have much to learn, not only positively but also negatively, from Luther's attitude to the Bible. Even his misconceptions were those of a great man, and therefore instructive. Though he did not possess the systematic spirit of a philosopher, he had the scholar's mind and the teacher's heart.[4] His vast literary legacy thus provides us with a very full picture as to how he regarded the Holy Scriptures and expected his students and readers to view them. Let us take our place, then, in Luther's classroom, and—retaining our critical faculties to be sure—go to the corpus of his writings[5] and to the existential heart of his career to learn his way of approaching Holy Writ. Our specific interest is to determine whether the great Reformer considered the Bible entirely, or only partially, revelatory: did he, or did he not, view it as inerrantly the Word of God?[6]

LUTHER ON THE TRUSTWORTHINESS OF SCRIPTURE

To say that the Bible was important to Luther is as informative as to say that mathematics was important to Einstein. Anyone who has the slightest acquaintance with the Reformer's work knows that for him the Scriptures and the Scriptures alone were the only true source of true theology and the place where he rediscovered the central teaching of the Christian religion: that a man is saved, not by what he does, but by what God as already done for him in Jesus Christ. A passage such as the following—from one of Luther's sermons on John 3:16—is entirely typical:

> If a different way to heaven existed, no doubt God would have recorded it, but there is no other way. Therefore let us cling to these words, firmly place and rest our hearts upon them, close our eyes and say: Although I had the merit of all saints, the holiness and purity of all virgins, and the piety of St. Peter himself, I would still consider my attainment nothing. Rather I must have a different foundation to build on, namely, these words: God has given His Son so that whosoever believes in Him whom the Father's love has sent shall be saved. And you must confidently insist that you will be preserved; and you must boldly take your stand on His words, which no devil, hell, or death can suppress. ... Therefore no matter what happens, you should say: There is God's Word. This is my rock and anchor. On it I rely, and it remains. Where it remains, I, too, remain; where it goes, I, too, go. The Word must stand, for God cannot lie; and heaven and earth must go to

ruins before the most insignificant letter or tittle of His Word remains unfulfilled.[7]

The great momumental statues of Luther are indicative of his lifelong attitude toward Scripture. They invariably show the Reformer holding an open Bible. This is true of the statue by Siemering in Eisleben, the East German town where the Reformer was born and died[8]; Schadow's statue of Luther in the Wittenberg town square; and—greatest of all, with six replicas in the United States alone—the statue by Rietschel at Worms, commemorating Luther's stand before the Emperor. Those who wished to give the Reformer permanent artistic representation could not think of him apart from the Bible.

But the centrality of Scripture in Luther's experience is conceded even by those who claim that he did not hold to the inerrancy of the Bible. Their argument goes that Luther's strong affirmations of scriptural authority apply to its *Christic* content, which he experienced so deeply; as for the biblical "details," Luther was impatient with them and ought not to be regarded as a modern plenary inspirationist. This is the position espoused by Köstlin in his standard older treatment of Luther's theology,[9] and more recently by the Dutch Luther-scholar Kooiman in his influential book, *Luther and the Bible* (warranting the extended review given to it in my Addendum to the present essay). Philip Watson, in his otherwise masterly study, *Let God Be God!* writes: "For Luther, all authority belongs ultimately to Christ, the Word of God, alone, and even the authority of the Scriptures is secondary and derivative, pertaining to them only inasmuch as they bear witness to Christ and are the vehicle of the Word." [10] Neo-orthodox theologian J. K. S. Reid echoes this theme, concluding: "For Luther, Scripture is not the Word, but only witness to the Word, and it is from Him whom it conveys that it derives the authority it enjoys." [11]

What can be said in critique of this interpretation of Luther's bibliology? Much, but one point is all that is needed: the view is simply not Luther's. (The story comes to mind of the barrister who was ready to give twelve reasons why his client was not in court; but after hearing the first—the client had died the night before—the judge did not bother to hear the other eleven.) Listen to some of Luther's representative—and often pungent—affirmations on the extent of inerrant biblical authority: "It is impossible that Scripture should contradict itself; it only appears so to senseless and obstinate hypocrites." [12] "Everyone knows that at times they [the fathers] have erred as men will; therefore, I am ready to trust them only when they prove their opinions from Scripture, which has never erred." [13] "Mr. Wiseacre is a shameful, disgusting fellow. He plays the master if he can discover that [in our Bible translation] we have perchance missed a word. But who would be so presumptuous as to maintain that he has not erred in any word, as though he were Christ and the Holy Spirit?" [14]

To argue that Luther located the trustworthiness of Scripture only in its theological or Christic aspect, not in its "details," is to misunderstand the very heart of the Reformer's conception of the Bible. It was his belief, from the days of his earliest theologizing, that "the whole Scripture is about Christ alone everywhere." [15] Heinrich Bornkamm confirms this by numerous illustrations in his comprehensive study, *Luther and the Old Testament*, and, faithful as he wants to be to the Reformer, is troubled by it: "Any research which thinks historically will have to give up, without hesitation or reservation, Luther's scheme of Christological prediction in the Old Testament." [16] But surely if Luther saw Christ everywhere in Scripture, to say that he considered only the Christological material inerrant is to talk nonsense. For Luther, all genuine Scripture was Christic, and all of it was inerrant. Thus comments such as the following abound in his expositions of the Bible:

> He who carefully reads and studies the Scriptures will consider nothing so trifling that it does not at least contribute to the improvement of his life and morals, since the Holy Spirit wanted to have it committed to writing.[17]

> We see with what great diligence Moses, or rather the Holy Spirit, describes even the most insignificant acts and sufferings of the patriarchs.[18]

> Who can think this through to his satisfaction? A man [Jonah] lives three days and three nights in solitude, without light, without food, in the midst of the sea, in a fish, and then comes back. I dare say that is what you would call a strange voyage. Indeed, who would believe it and not consider it a lie and a fable if it did not stand recorded in Scripture? [19]

> The two incidents—that not a bone of the Lord Christ was broken and that His side was opened with a spear— do not appear to be of any particular significance. And yet, since the evangelist John adduces clear testimonies of Scripture, proving that Moses (Ex. 12:46) and Zechariah (12:10) predicted these things centuries before, we

must confess that they are of great importance, no matter how insignificant the incidents seem to be; for the
Holy Spirit does not speak anything to no purpose and in
vain.[20]

Just as Christ is everywhere present in Scripture, so the
Holy Spirit is everywhere its Author. Declares Luther: "In
the article of the [Nicene] Creed which treats of the Holy
Spirit we say, 'Who spake by the prophets.' Thus we ascribe
the entire Holy Scripture to the Holy Spirit." [21] "Not only
the words which the Holy Spirit and Scripture use are divine,
but also the phrasing." [22] "The Holy Spirit is not a fool
or a drunkard to express one point, not to say one word, in
vain." [23]

Luther's straightforward belief in Scripture's inerrancy cannot be downplayed as representing only his "callow youth"
or—*mutatis mutandis*—his "senile old age." From his commentaries on the Psalms of 1513-1516, written before the posting
of the Ninety-Five Theses ("All the words of God are weighed,
counted, and measured") [24] to his final major attack on the
papacy in 1545, the year before his death ("Let the man
who would hear *God* speak read Holy Scripture"),[25] the Reformer's attitude to Scripture remains categorical. He embraces
the bibliology of the historic church: "St. Augustine, in a letter
to St. Jerome, has put down a fine axiom—that only Holy
Scripture is to be considered inerrant." [26]

How else can we explain Luther's unshakeable appeal to
Scripture in his debates with Romanists such as Eck, or his
reliance on Scripture when, at Worms, the Emperor himself
thundered against him and his very life hung in the balance?
How else can we make sense of his concentration on the single
scriptural phrase, "This is My body," when in dialogue with
Zwingli at the Marburg colloquy, and in numerous treatises
he wrote on the Real Presence against the sectarians? [27]
When we stand awestruck in that little cell at the Wartburg
castle where Luther strove to translate Scripture so "every
ploughboy could hear God's Word" and see there a printed
edition of Luther's translation with his painstaking marginal
corrections—to bring his rendering into the closest verbal accord
with the original—and remember that he kept up this "sweat
and toil" all his life to produce editions of his German Bible
always better than the earlier ones; can we doubt that he
was serious in claiming that only belief in Scripture as entirely
Christ's Word sustained him? "No one would have persuaded
me by favors or gold to translate a book," he said more than

once; "I have done it for the sake of my Lord Christ." [28]

Thus the classic treatments of Luther's scriptural position—the foremost in English being Reu's *Luther and the Scriptures*—conclude that he did indeed hold to the inerrancy of the Bible.[29] Of considerable significance is the criticism leveled against Luther by the great rationalist historian of dogma Adolf von Harnack: he "confounded the word of God and the Sacred Scriptures" and consequently did not "break the bondage of the letter. Thus it happened that his church arrived at the most stringent doctrine of inspiration."[30] On examining the efforts of theologians of less historical objectivity (such as Seeberg and Emil Brunner) to argue that Luther held a limited inspiration view, Theodore Engelder commented in his indispensable work, *Scripture Cannot Be Broken:* "It is one of the mysteries of the ages how theologians who claim to be conversant with Luther's writings can give credence to the myth that Luther did not teach Verbal, Plenary Inspiration. . . . [But] the moderns are going to believe the myth till doomsday." [31]

A MYSTERIOUS MYTH MEDITATED

Why the persistence of this myth in spite of Luther's Scripture-controlled life and biblical affirmations by the thousands? [32] In large part, certainly, because of the common human failing we all have to want great men to agree with us. It is most interesting to observe that a Neo-orthodox such as Brunner discovers a Luther who refuses to identify "the letters and words of the Scriptures with the Word of God," [33] while a post-Bultmannian advocate of the New Hermeneutic such as Ebeling finds a Luther who devotes himself "to the service of the word-event in such a way that the word becomes truly word." [34] How easy it is to meet a Luther who is one's own mirror image! This tendency is especially strong among those whose theological position allows such transformations in principle, that is to say, among liberal theologians who will not accept an objective, determinative standard for their beliefs, but who allow their own experience a constitutive role in the creation of theology. Such theologians are used to bending Scripture to fit their own ideas or the dictates of the Zeitgeist, so performing the same operation on Luther comes easily. To be sure, confessional Christians are also subject to this temptation, but their willingness in principle to subject themselves to biblical teaching whether they like it or not makes them less likely to twist the subsequent history of the church to fit their interests; if they do it, they act against their own principles, which cannot be said for liberals embracing the famous "hermeneutical circle" of Bultmannianism.[35] The remedy, however, is the same for all reworkings of history in the interest of the present, whoever performs them: let the primary documents correct modern misinterpretations. Let Luther speak for himself.

But precisely here the knowledgeable opponent of Luther-as-plenary-inspirationist steps forward to plead his case on far better, and apparently primary source, grounds. The argument is that Luther's practice belied his profession where scriptural authority was concerned, for (1) Did the Reformer not handle Scripture with utmost freedom when he translated it? (2) Was he not indifferent to contradictions and errors, showing that his real concern lay only with the central theological teachings of the Bible? and (3) Does not his wholesale rejection of books from the very Canon of Scripture prove beyond question that he could not have taken every word of the Bible as God's Word?

A worthwhile *point de départ* for our response is the caution expressed by Paul Althaus—a caution made even more valuable when we recall that Althaus is embarrassed by Luther's belief in the infallibility of Scripture: "It is not a question of how far Luther may have gone in one-sided or forced interpretations of the Scripture. Neither would we speak about his criticism of the canon. These matters do not alter the fact that Luther—even when he criticized Scripture—never wanted to be anything else than an obedient hearer and student of the Scripture." [36] Precisely. Even if the worst could be shown concerning Luther's treatment of the Bible in practice (which is hardly the case, as we shall immediately see), it would be manifestly unfair to use this to negate his repeated asseverations that he believed in an inerrant Scripture. Where would any of us be, inconsistent sinners that we are, if our practice were allowed to erase our profession? Just as the problem-passages in Scripture must not be allowed to swallow up the Bible's clear testimonies to its entire reliability, but must be handled in light of these testimonies, so Luther's treatment of Scripture must always be viewed from the standpoint of the unequivocal words we have heard him express again and again: "The Scriptures have never erred." With this perspective clearly in mind, let us examine in turn each of the apparent deviations of Luther's scriptural practice from his biblical profession.

(1) *Luther As Free Translator.* Even in his own time the Reformer was criticized by his theological opponents for render-

ing Scripture into German too freely. In particular, he was castigated for inserting the word "alone" into his translation of Romans 3:28 ("a man is justified by faith *alone* without the deeds of the law"). Since the word "alone" does not appear in the original text, his Roman Catholic opposition saw clear evidence of Luther's willingness to modify Scripture to fit his own doctrinal peculiarities and experience, rather than to subject these to God's objective revelation. Modern critics of biblical inerrancy who want Luther on their side find his action in this regard ground for holding that he did not really consider the Bible *verbally* inspired—else how could he have altered its verbal content?

The answer to this charge is, of course, that it seriously misunderstands the translator's work. No sensible translation can match the original text word for word. Some years ago a nincompoop who had studied biblical languages for a short time at the Bible Institute of Los Angeles embarked upon a project which would finally provide a definitively faithful rendering of the Scriptures into English. The fundamental translating principle was that "each word of the Original is given only one exclusive English rendering." The result—the so-called "Concordant Version"—contains such gems as: "And saying is God, 'Roaming is the water with the roaming, living soul, and the flyer is flying over the earth on the face of the atmosphere of the heavens' " (Gen. 1:20).[37] The result is exactly the opposite of what the translator desired: God's Word is hopelessly obscured. Indeed, the more faithful one wants to be to an original text, the more careful he ought to be to render it so idiomatically that it really will convey the full impact and exact signification of the original text in the second language.

As one of the greatest translators the world has ever known— he did singlehandedly for German-speaking peoples what required an entire corps of King James translators to do for the Anglophonic world—Luther knew full well what was required to produce a great translation. Listen to his own defense of his rendition of Romans 3:28:

> I knew very well that the word *solum* [solely] does not stand in the Latin and Greek texts, and the papists had no need to teach me that. True it is that these four letters s-o-l-a do not stand there. At these letters the asinine dunces stare as a cow stares at a new gate. Yet they do not see that this is the meaning of the text and that the word belongs there if a clear and forceful

German translation is desired. I wanted to speak German, not Latin or Greek, since I had undertaken to speak German in the translation. It is the nature of our German language that when speaking of two things, one of which is granted while the other is denied, we use the word "solely" along with the word "not" or "no." Thus we say: The farmer brings only grain and no money; no, I have no money, but only grain; I have only eaten, not drunk; did you only write, and not read it? There are innumerable cases of this kind in daily use. . . .

We must not, as these jackasses do, ask the Latin letters how to speak German; but we must ask the mother in the home, the children on the street, the common man in the market place, how this is done. Their lips we must watch to see how they speak, and then we must translate accordingly. Then they will understand us and notice that we are talking German with them.[38]

So conscientious was Luther to convey the exact force of each word of the Hebrew and Greek texts that he even visited the butcher to find out the German terms for the parts of animals mentioned in the accounts of Levitical sacrifice. In all this incredible labor it was the Reformer's confidence in the text as God's very Word that impelled him to give it the best German rendering possible. Hear his testimony:

This I can say with a good conscience: I have used the utmost faithfulness and care in this work, and I never had any intention to falsify anything. I have not taken nor sought nor won a single penny for it. Neither do I intend to win honor by it (that God, my Lord, knows); but I did it as a service to the dear Christians and to the honor of One who sits above, who does so much good to me every hour that if I had translated a thousand times as much or as diligently, I still should not deserve to live a single hour or to have a sound eye. All that I am and have is due to His grace and mercy, aye, to His precious blood and bitter sweat. Therefore, God willing, all of it is to be done to His honor, joyfully and sincerely. If scribblers and papal jackasses abuse me, very well, let them do so. But pious Christians and their Lord Christ praise me; and I am too richly repaid if only a single Christian recognizes me as a faithful worker.[39]

Paradoxically, therefore, Luther's fidelity to the original text of Scripture was the very cause of his seemingly free translations, since only thus could he convey God's Word with precise accuracy in his native tongue. By the same token, the ease with which he sometimes treats the received text indicates not a cavalier attitude toward the Bible, but just the opposite. If the existing texts posed problems, it might be in the interests of God's inerrant Word as originally given to emend the faulty transmitted version to vindicate His trust-worthiness. In reviewing a number of typical examples of Luther's textual modifications, Skevington Wood properly observes:

> Luther's recognition of biblical inerrancy was confined to the original autographs, and was not tied to the transmitted text. This gave him the freedom to query the accuracy of the existing readings and on occasion to offer emendations of his own. . . .
>
> But it must be emphasized that Luther allowed himself this freedom only within the limits already prescribed—namely, that infallibility attaches solely to the original autographs of Scripture. He had no thought of doubting the reliability of the underlying text. His aim was to reach it.[40]

(2) *Luther As Bible Critic.* But—our anti-inerrancy Luther interpreters hasten to remind us—the problem does not lie merely with Luther's translations or his textual conjectures; this is the mere surface of the iceberg. What about his indifference to contradictions and errors in the text when he cannot resolve them? and what about his judgments—one must call them Higher Critical judgments—on the scriptural writings themselves?

Köstlin argues that whereas with reference to "saving truth . . . it is to Luther inconceivable that there should be any contradiction whatsoever, or any error, in the canonical Scriptures whose origin is to be traced to the Holy Spirit," the Reformer attaches "no great importance" to such problems in the biblical "narratives of external historical events."[41] Köstlin's evidence is that in several instances Luther does not provide a resolution of the historical problems he observes in the biblical materials. "Nor did he hesitate, finally, to acknowledge even *patent errors*."[42] The single passage cited: Stephen's speech in Acts 7, where Luther considers Moses rather than Stephen correct in regard to Abraham's call (v. 2) and notes that Stephen, in relying on the Alexandrian version of the Old Testament, cites an inaccurate statistic (v. 14). To be sure, it is rather odd that Luther, "who here expresses his mind so freely as to the reliability of books and their contents, should, under other circumstances, as especially in the sacramental controversy, cling so stubbornly to the very letter of the Scriptures." [43]

As even Köstlin must admit, where historical problems exist in the text Luther "labors with conscientious assiduity and acumen to remove the difficulties." [44] It is precisely where he does not succeed in resolving the problem that what Köstlin and others have called his posture of "no great concern" appears. This is not an indifference to the problems (otherwise Luther would hardly have "labored assiduously" to solve them) nor an indifference to alleged errors in Scripture; it is just the opposite: because the Reformer is so convinced that God's Word cannot err or contradict itself, he refuses to be shaken by an unresolved difficulty. His confidence in the entire trustworthiness of the Bible allows him to do what he said he always did in regard to the mystery of the Holy Trinity: like a peasant, he doffed his cap and he went his way.

Klug, in his recent Free University of Amsterdam doctoral dissertation, goes in detail into Luther's style of handling alleged factual errors and contradictions in Scripture. His discussion is worth quoting in extenso—particularly since he refers in passing to Luther's supposed acknowledgement of "patent error" in Acts 7.

> He [Luther] endorses every honest effort to reconcile problems to the extent possible: "Therefore answers that are given in support of the trustworthiness of Scripture serve a purpose, even though they may not be altogether reliable." His position is the same in connection with Haran's age, if Abraham was the elder brother and married Haran's daughter, Sarah. Luther allows for the possibility that Haran married a widow, and "that the daughter was brought along with the mother." Thus he seeks to squelch what he calls "the foolhardy geniuses who immediately shout that an obvious error has been committed" by averring that finally "it is the Holy Spirit alone who knows and understands all things." With truly wry touch Luther adds: "I wanted to call attention to these facts, . . . in order that no one might get the impression that we either have no knowledge of such matters or have not read about them." Luther likewise dealt with the problem of reconciling Genesis 12:4 with Acts 7:2, the accounts of Moses and Stephen concerning Abraham's age at the time of his departure from Haran. He grants that while "each of the two is a trustworthy witness, . . . they do not agree with each other." His suggested solution is to rely on Moses' historical accuracy and to suggest that Stephen is emphasizing not details as

much as the fact that God discloses Himself and His mercy through the promised Seed, Christ.

Undoubtedly, this sort of dutiful and childlike surrender when the problem went over his head, appears naive and evasive to much of modern scholarship, which boldly enters in where Luther—and the angels—feared to tread. But Luther resolutely refused to budge one inch from the Holy awe he felt before the Holy Spirit's handiwork in Scripture. This is all the more remarkable in view of the fact that as translator over a period of years Luther had to take that Scripture literally apart to get its meaning into his native German. To imply that it contained error was to him not only contrary to what the Scripture itself testified concerning its truthfulness and inerrancy, but, above all, an insolent affront to God who gave it.[45]

Retorts the liberal Luther-interpreter: And yet the Reformer's Prefaces to the Bible books he translated display an attitude which today would be termed Higher Critical! Here Luther was introducing the common man to the Scripture, and he obviously wanted him to be concerned, not with traditional questions of the consistency of the text or its authorship, but solely with the gospel message.[46] Of the Book of Isaiah, Luther writes: Isaiah "does not treat them [the three subjects of the book: preaching against sin and proclaiming the coming of Christ's Kingdom; prophesying about Assyria; and prophesying concerning Babylon] in order and give each of these subjects its own place and put it into its own chapters and pages; but they are so mixed up together that much of the first matter is brought in along with the second and third, and the third subject is discussed somewhat earlier than the second. But whether this was done by those who collected and wrote down the prophecies (as is thought to have happened with the Psalter), or whether he himself arranged it this way according as time, occasion, and persons suggested, and these times and occasions were not always alike, and had no order—this I do not know." Similarly of Jeremiah: The prophetic subjects he treats "do not follow one another and are not reported in the book in the way that they actually came along. . . . There is often something in a later chapter which happened before that which is spoken of in an earlier chapter, and so it seems as though Jeremiah had not composed these books himself, but that parts of his utterances were taken and written into the book. Therefore one must not care about the order, or be hindered by the lack of it." Luther says in his Preface to Hosea: "It appears as though this prophecy of Hosea was not fully and entirely written, but that pieces and sayings out of his preaching were arranged and brought together into a book." Are not these remarks of Luther the sentiments of a scholar who, though he had the misfortune to live before the era of modern biblical criticism, nonetheless thought in Higher Critical terms?

In a word: no. Luther admittedly points up non-chronological arrangement within biblical books, and, as a possible explanation for this, suggests later compilation by one or more persons other than the author to whom the book is traditionally attributed. This may seem like Higher Critical concession, but it is nothing of the kind. The modern biblical critic combines with such judgments as to inner arrangement and authorship of biblical materials one or more of the following assumptions: (i) Miracles and genuine prophecies do not occur (thus, for example, portions of Isaiah are attributed to a "Second-" or "Third-Isaiah" who wrote them after the events supposedly prophesied). (ii) The non-chronological arrangement of the biblical material involves factual errors and internal contradictions; indeed, the discovery of such faults in the text is a prime means of determining organizational lapses in the scriptural writings and therefore instances of multiple authorship. (iii) The ultimate editors or compilers did their work in a far from perfect manner: coming after—sometimes long after—the materials they deal with, they can and often do misunderstand them and render the resultant text confusing and misleading. The task of Higher Criticism thus comes into being: to strike back behind the present text to its (supposed) sources so as to discover their original signification.

Luther would have been horrified at all three of these Higher Critical assumptions. (i) As we have already seen, his approach to the entire Bible was so thoroughly Christocentric that he found genuine prophecies of Christ everywhere in the Old Testament—to such an extent that even a scholar as sympathetic to Luther's mind-set as Heinrich Bornkamm asserts that contemporary man must "give up, without hesitation or reservation, Luther's scheme of Christological prediction in the Old Testament." [47] For Luther, miraculous prophecy was the heart of the Old Testament, and his questions as to the authorship or internal arrangement of biblical books never impugned their supernatural character. (ii) The same thing can be said—and has been said many times in our essay to this point—with regard to alleged biblical contradictions and errors. Luther categorically, and in principle, rejected the idea of an errant Scripture, and his observation of non-chronological order in some biblical books was in no sense negative criticism of these books. Luther recognized the obvious fact that an author or editor has every right to organize his material on a non-chrono-logical basis. Just as the gifts of the Spirit are diverse, so are the possible schemes for putting a book together. (iii) Most important of all, Luther's suggestion that a biblical book might have been written down by someone other than the tradi-tional author had nothing whatever to do with the modern conception that scriptural books are unreliable compilations reflecting inaccurate later editorializing. If an ultimate redactor was involved, Luther believed him to be no less than the Holy Spirit, who, in such activity as in His inspiration of biblical writers in general, guaranteed the truth of scriptural utterances. Typical of Luther's approach to this matter are his prefatory remarks on the Psalms, which (as we have seen) he agreed might well be a compilation:

> The Psalter ought to be a dear and beloved book, if only because it promises Christ's death and resurrection so clearly, and so typifies His Kingdom and the condition and nature of all Christendom that it might well be called a little Bible. It puts everything that is in all the Bible most beautifully and briefly, and constitutes an "Enchiri-dion," or handbook, so that I have a notion that the Holy Spirit wanted to take the trouble to compile a short Bi-ble and example-book of all Christendom, or of all the saints.

Where compilation is involved, the Holy Spirit is the compiler, and "we must stand by the words of the Holy Spirit." [48] So far distant is Luther's "biblical criticism" from the rational-istic Higher Criticism that becomes articulate in the deistic 18th century, grows to maturity in the anthropocentric 19th century, and dominates the world of contemporary biblical schol-arship.[49] While Higher Criticism poses its questions in a pos-ture of rationalistic dominance over the text, Luther asks his questions of God's Word on his knees. The contrast could hardly be sharper.

(3) *Luther As Independent Canonist.* Those who would draw the Reformer into the orbit of limited biblical infallibility have saved their most powerful salvo until last. If—they argue with smug satisfaction—you continue to read Luther's Prefaces to his Bible translations, and come to those for the New Testament, you find that Luther actually went *beyond* most radical higher critics of our own time: he removed entire books from their

place in the Canon of Scripture! Using his newly rediscovered doctrine of salvation-by-grace-alone-through-faith as a personal criterion of canonicity, he judged certain New Testament books as canonically inferior, hardly worthy of canonical status at all. Surely this is biblical criticism writ large: the "internal criticism" of the Canon of Scripture. Post-Bultmannian Luther scholar Gerhard Ebeling commends Luther for it: "The manner in which Luther used this internal criticism of the canon is well known, though perhaps not as well known as it should be; he placed the Epistle to the Hebrews and the Epistle of James after the Johannine epistles, and the unnumbered series of what now become the last four New Testament writings, namely, the Epistle to the Hebrews, the Epistle of James, the Epistle of Jude, and the Revelation of St. John outside the numbered sequence of the other twenty-three books of the New Testament; he also made value judgements, 'which are the authentic and noblest books of the New Testament,' and correspondingly negative utterances about other New Testament writings." [50]

In his general Preface to the New Testament of 1522, Luther says of James that it is "really an Epistle of straw," for "it has nothing of the nature of the gospel about it." The Reformer goes into more detail in his Preface to the Epistle itself: "James does nothing more than drive to the law and to its works. Besides, he throws things together in such disorderly fashion that it seems to me he must have been some good, pious man, who took some sayings of the Apostles' disciples and threw them thus on paper; or perhaps they were written down by someone else from his preaching." Luther employs the "straw" motif again, though much less harshly, in his Preface to Hebrews: it is "a marvellously fine Epistle," yet "my opinion is that it is an Epistle put together of many pieces, and it does not deal systematically with any one subject." Although, as the author "himself testifies (Heb. 6:1), he does not lay the foundation of faith, which is the work of the Apostles, nevertheless he does build finely thereon with gold, silver, precious stones, as St. Paul says in I Cor. 3:12. Therefore we should not be hindered, even though wood, straw, or hay are perhaps mixed in with them, but accept this fine teaching with all honor; though, to be sure, we cannot put it on the same level with the apostolic epistles." Concerning Jude, Luther states that "the ancient fathers excluded this Epistle from the main body of the Scriptures," and "therefore, although I value this book, it is an Epistle that need not be counted among the chief books which are to lay the foundations of faith." Finally, in his 1522 Preface to the Revelation of St. John, Luther is supposed to sum up his philosophy of individualistic, internal theological criticism of the Bible: "Let everyone think of it as his own spirit leads him. My spirit cannot accommodate itself to this book. For me this is reason enough not to think highly of it: Christ is not taught or known in it. But to teach Christ is the thing which an Apostle is bound above all else to do, as Christ says in Acts 1:8, 'Ye shall be my witnesses,' Therefore I stick to the books which give me Christ, clearly and purely."

What can be said in answer to such apparently powerful primary-source evidence? Much in every way! Let us begin with some textual considerations. Even in his strongest remarks on the four antilegomena (Hebrews, James, Jude, Revelation), Luther intersperses positive comments and makes quite plain that the question of how to treat these books must be answered by his readers for themselves. If he can speak of James as an "Epistle of straw," lacking the gospel, he can also say of it—simultaneously: "I praise it and hold it a good book, because it sets up no doctrine of men but vigorously promulgates God's law." Since Luther is not exactly the model of the mediating personality—since he is well known for consistently taking a stand where others (perhaps even angels) would equivocate—we can legitimately conclude that the Reformer only left matters as open questions when he really was not certain as to where the truth lay. Luther's ambivalent approach to the antilegomena is not at all the confident critical posture of today's rationalistic student of the Bible.

Especially indicative of this fact is the considerable reduction in negative tone in the revised Prefaces to the biblical books later in the Reformer's career. Few people realize—and liberal Luther interpreters do not particularly advertise the fact [51]—that in all the editions of Luther's Bible translation after 1522 the Reformer dropped the paragraphs at the end of his general Preface to the New Testament which made value judgments among the various biblical books and which included the famous reference to James as an "Epistle of straw." [52] In all the editions after 1522 Luther also softened the critical tone of his Preface to the Epistle itself; in 1522 he had written: James "wants to guard against those who relied on faith without works, and is unequal to the task *in spirit, thought, and words, and rends the Scriptures and thereby resists Paul and all Scripture*," but he subsequently dropped all the words after "unequal to the task." He also omitted the following related comment: "One man is no man in worldly things; how then should this single man alone [James] avail against Paul and all the other Scriptures?" Moreover, Luther's short and extremely negative Preface to the Revelation of St. John was completely dropped after 1522, and the Reformer replaced it with a long and entirely commendatory Preface (1530).[53] Because "some of the ancient fathers held the opinion that it was not the work of St. John the apostle," Luther leaves the authorship question open, but asserts that he can no longer "let the book alone," for "we see, in this book, that through and above all plagues and beasts and evil angels Christ is with His saints, and wins the victory at last." In his original, 1532 Preface to Ezekiel, Luther made a cross-reference to the Revelation of St. John with no hint of criticism; in his later, much fuller Preface to Ezekiel, he concludes on the note that if one wishes to go into prophetic study more deeply, "the Revelation of John can also help."

True enough, all the editions of Luther's German Bible—right to the last one he himself supervised (1545)—retain the classification by which the four antilegomena are grouped together, in a kind of bibliographical ghetto, after the other books.[54] Comments remain in the Prefaces (e.g., Romans) indicating that Luther always held to a hierarchy of biblical books, with the Gospel of John and Romans constituting the empyrean. A careful study of Luther's remarks on and treatment of James throughout his career has shown that, wholly apart from the Prefaces, the Reformer consistently held a low view of the book's utility.[55] Yet in fairness to Luther, is not this frank attitude just the recognition of what we all must admit, however high our view of scriptural inerrancy, namely that the biblical books do not all present the gospel with equal impact? Even the fundamentalist of fundamentalists distributes portions of the Gospel of John and not II Chronicles. Wesley was saved at Aldersgate listening to the reading of Luther's Preface to Romans; it would not have surprised Luther—nor should it surprise us—that the effect was not produced by the reading of the Preface to Obadiah. To paraphrase George Orwell, all the Bible books are equal, but some are more equal than others. Moreover, the successive editions of Luther's German Bible show the Reformer concerned that the general public not be led away from any portion of Scripture by his own personal opinions or prejudices.

But does our response really meet the issue? Is not the

key issue that Luther did not personally regard the antilegomena *as* Scripture in the full sense? His manner of cataloging them apart as an unnumbered unit exactly parallels his way of dealing with the Old Testament Apocrypha; does not this make plain that Luther was personally revising the Canon? And was he not doing it purely on the subjective ground that certain books did not accord well with his personal religious experience?

We must admit that in one sense Luther does reevaluate the Canon, though haltingly, tentatively, sensitively—not at all like a modern radical critic—and certainly not as a spokesman for the church (we have already noted his hesitancy to influence others at this point). As for his reasons for reopening the canonical question, they were not at all as subjective, arbitrary, and cavalier as they are often made to seem. In his Preface to Jude we heard Luther say: "Although I value this book, it is an Epistle that need not be counted among the chief books which are to lay the foundations of faith"; why? "The ancient fathers excluded this Epistle from the main body of the Scriptures." Again and again in his Prefaces we find Luther arguing in this vein: "Up to this point we have had to do with the true and certain chief books of the New Testament. The four which follow have from ancient times had a different reputation." "This Epistle of St. James was rejected by the ancients." "Many of the fathers also rejected this book [Revelation: Luther's Preface of 1522] a long time ago." Here Luther appeals not to subjective considerations but objectively to the judgments of the early church, specifically to what Jerome says in his *De viris illustribus*, chap. 2, and to what Eusebius reports in his *Ecclesiastical History*, Bk. II, chap. 23 and Bk. III, chap. 25. The negative evaluations of antilegomena by certain church fathers were certainly unjustified, as history proved, but Luther had every right to raise the question in terms of the fathers. Unless one is going to make the fatal error of accepting the content of Scripture because the institutional church has declared it such (which necessarily subordinates Scripture to Church and brings the Protestant back to his Romanist vomit), there is no choice but to refer canonicity questions to the earliest judgments available historically concerning the apostolic authority of New Testament books. Christ promised to the apostolic company a unique and entirely reliable knowledge of His teachings through the special guidance of His Holy Spirit (John 14:26), so the issue of the apostolicity of New Testament writings has always been vital for the church. As a theologian, Luther had the right, even the responsibility, to raise this issue, and did not become a subjectivist by doing so.

However, it would be impossible to claim that Luther's questioning of the antilegomena was motivated purely by historical concerns. (What, indeed, in the Reformer's life, was ever so motivated? One of his favorite sayings was that he did his best theological work when angry!) Is it not indicative that the Revelation of St. John gains in stature for him as he sees its apologetic possibilities vis-à-vis the papacy ("the whore that sitteth on the seven hills," etc.)? Is it pure coincidence that James, the New Testament book which Luther cares for the least, is the one that stresses works the most—that seems most in tension with the Pauline doctrine at the heart of Luther's entire "Copernican revolution in theology": salvation by grace alone through faith, apart from the deeds of the law?

Here, if anywhere, those arguing against Luther's biblical orthodoxy have a point. Though it is unfair to call him a subjectivist on the canonical question, there is no doubt that he developed a personal criterion of canonicity that took its place alongside of apostolicity and perhaps even swallowed it up. He unabashedly states this new criterion in his Preface to James: "All the genuine sacred books agree in this, that all of them preach and inculcate Christ. And that is the true test by which to judge all books, when we see whether or not they inculcate Christ.[56] For all the Scriptures show us Christ (Rom. 3:21), and St. Paul will know nothing but Christ (I Cor. 2:2). Whatever does not teach Christ is not apostolic, even though St. Peter or St. Paul does the teaching. Again, whatever preaches Christ would be apostolic, even if Judas, Annas, Pilate, and Herod were doing it."

The dangers in such an approach to canonicity are legion, and they were fully recognized by Luther's own contemporaries—not only by his theological opponents but also by his colleagues and supporters. Thus, as early as 1520, Luther's Wittenberg University co-reformer Bodenstein von Carlstadt—hardly a traditionalist (his radically negative attitude to ecclesiastical adiaphora eventually caused his rupture with Luther)—condemned Luther's rejection of James and argued that one must appeal either to known apostolic authorship or to universal historical acceptance (*omnium consensus*) as the test of a book's canonicity, not to internal doctrinal considerations. [57] In spite of certain deficiencies in Carlstadt's treatment, a 19th century student of the subject was certainly right in noting that unlike Luther on the Canon, "Dr. Bodenstein's reforming approach was based on history and not on feelings, on critical evaluation and not on piety." [58] As is well known, the church that carries Luther's name has never adopted his canonical judgments.

Though it is understandable that, passionate reforming spirit that he was, Luther would reintroduce the doctrine of salvation by grace through faith everywhere, it is unfortunate that he misused it as a canonical criterion. One must first establish the Canon and then set forth all that the canonical books teach: canonicity before doctrine. If one reverses the procedure, personal doctrinal emphasis, however commendatory, may turn into weapons by which genuine Scripture is rejected or downplayed unnecessarily. Had Luther begun with a purely historical view of the Canon, he would have been forced to discover the entire compatibility between James and Paul; his misleading criterion of canonicity opened the floodgates to subjectivity—in spite of his best intentions—and shortcircuited the kind of exegesis of James that would have revealed its harmony with Pauline teaching and its vital complementary place in the corpus of New Testament doctrine.[59]

Having delivered these blasts against our hero,[60] we must nonetheless take away from the anti-inerrancy critic with one hand what we have apparently bestowed upon him with the other. Luther's canonical deficiencies in no sense impugn his belief in the entire infallibility of Holy Writ! How can this be? Simply because, as Adolf Hoenecke well put it:

> One must distinguish well between the extent of the Canon and the inspiration of the books which are canonical without question. Here Wilhelm Walther says correctly that for Luther the extent of the Canon was an open question, but the books that were canonical were absolutely authoritative for him as the inspired Word of God. But this distinction is always being overlooked. Modern theologians always want to draw conclusions from Luther's remarks concerning individual books as to his attitude towards the Word in general and its inspiration and thus make Luther share their liberal views regarding inspiration.[61]

Perhaps the point can be made most clearly and effectively by two analogies. Imagine that your essayist (who has made himself objectionable for many years by his hard-nosed defense of the inerrancy of Scripture) is one day confronted on the street by a guru-like figure carrying a huge pulpit Bible. Jumping suddenly at me with a religious whoop, the guru opens this Bible, points to a section and says in a booming voice:

"Is this or is this not verily the Word of God?" I look at the open Bible and find that the Pittsburg telephone directory for 1973 has been carefully bound in. "No," I reply, "this is not the Word of God." "Aha," shrieks the guru. "Just as I suspected. Your professions of the inerrancy of Scripture are but sounding brass and tinkling cymbal. You outrightly reject the Word of God. It would be bad enough if you denied individual verses; but your impiety knows no bounds: you reject whole portions of the Word." The point does not require belaboring: to deny the inerrancy of what I consider non-canonical (non-biblical) hardly means that I do not believe in the infallibility of what I *do* regard as Scripture.

Or if the first analogy is too bizarre or personal (or too personally bizarre), take the widely recognized difference between Roman Catholics and Protestants cn the canonical acceptance of the Old Testament Apocrypha. If a Roman Catholic were to tell you as a Protestant that all your claims to hold to the plenary authority of Scripture are worthless because you downgrade Tobit and II Maccabees, would the argument impress you as logical? Hardly, for you cannot properly be judged as to your doctrine of inspiration except with reference to books you accept as genuinely revelatory, i.e., canonical. Reu asks the inevitable rhetorical question: "How can Luther's opinion about a non-canonical book change our findings concerning his attitude toward the canonical books?" [62]

And here Luther makes himself (as usual) unambiguously plain:

> I have learned to ascribe the honor of infallibility only to those books that are accepted as canonical. I am profoundly convinced that none of these writers has erred. All other writers, however they may have distinguished themselves in holiness or in doctrine, I read in this way: I evaluate what they say, not on the basis that they themselves believe that a thing is true, but only insofar as they are able to convince me by the authority of the canonical books or by clear reason. [63]

WHAT TO LEARN FROM LUTHER

In present-day evangelical circles, the battle over the inerrancy of Scripture is in full swing. Can anything be learned from the 450-year old example of Luther? Our instinctive response is a negative, for as evangelicals—representatives of a tradition that attains self-awareness only in the 18th century, after the modern secular era has begun—we look not to the past for help, but to future possibilities or to present experience.[64]

But here precisely we lose the battle before it starts. For we do not recognize that it is our very heritage of present-directed, experiential-orientated religion that has betrayed us. How can evangelicals so easily give up the full authority of Scripture? we ask helplessly. The answer is simply that evangelicals have seldom placed the stress on Scripture that they place on the personal experience of salvation, so it has never been too difficult for them to accept the specious argument that the inerrancy of the Bible need not be maintained as long as the saving gospel is witnessed to. Is it really so strange that the Reformation principle of *Sola Scriptura* should lose its imperative in circles (and they are not limited to the South!) where the following typical description applies?

> The Southerner's God tends to be immediately accessible to his emotions; only with the greatest difficulty can he grasp a description of an objective concept of assurance. The note of mystery in the knowledge of God is obscured, inasmuch as the divine presence is reckoned to be near at hand. The Kingdom of God is brought into the present through the miracle of conversion. In some quarters of popular regional piety, relations with deity become "chummy"—God is essentially one's partner, guardian, and benefactor, a sentimental picture which omits the dimension suggested by classical Christianity's "terrible presence of God." In any case, God is deemed knowable under stated conditions. For example, church revivals and mass evangelistic crusades are predicated on the assumption that souls will be saved, on the spot; if congregations pray and witness, and if the preacher is "Christ-centered," men will be born again.
>
> Since the knowledge of God is primarily connected to a man's emotions, southern evangelicals are apt to correlate uncritically the upsurges of a person's emotions with the divine presence. This truth was vividly illustrated by the reaction of an evangelical leader to his visit to a football rally at a church-related college, during which a student led the well-wishers in singing several "gospel choruses": "I have never felt the presence of God more real in any church than I did on that football field tonight." [65]

In point of fact, not only do evangelicals tend to let their present spiritual experience dominate over biblical teaching; their new theologians expressly pick up this theme to justify a non-inerrancy approach to Scripture. Donald Bloesch, for example, first lays down as axiomatic (and it is: but only to the Neo-orthodox and to evangelicals!) that "revelation is essentially an encounter between the living Christ and the believer," and then finds it painless to convince his readers that the Bible is but a "relative or dependent norm" which, taken by itself, has to be considered "fallible and deficient"; thus "the indefeasible criterion is not simply the Word but the Word and the Spirit." [66] "What we advocate," he writes, "is that evangelicalism rediscover the mystical elements in its own piety and tradition" [67]—and he appeals to Luther as one who "illustrates the position of evangelical fideism." [68]

But this is exactly what Luther was *not*, and if we could once catch the vision of the difference, it might be just the factor needed to pull us out of our present bibliological bog. Declared Luther: "You are just and holy from outside yourself. It is through mercy and compassion that you are just. It is not my disposition or a quality of my heart, but something outside myself—the Divine Mercy—which assures us that our sins are forgiven." [69] After considering a host of such passages illustrating Luther's fundamental theme that salvation is entirely *extra nos*, a conscientious Roman Catholic scholar concluded:

> Luther was able to discover the certainty of salvation solely because he broke free of his entanglement with the subjective, inner world and turned to the objectively valid message of salvation. . . . If we were to use the ideas of contemporary psychology—naturally, *mutatis mutandis*—we might say: Luther found peace and the certainty of salvation by releasing himself from his introverted attitude and adopted that of an extrovert, the "world outside" being understood of course as God's world of salvation. What he was as a religious man and as a theologian, he became precisely by turning away from his subjective states and towards the objective. [70]

Adolf Köberle, author of the classic, *The Quest for Holiness*, makes the same point concerning Luther's perspective on experience, and contrasts it sharply with another religious lifestyle (does it not uncomfortably remind one of evangelicalism—at least of the Bloesch variety?):

> Mystical-spiritualist enthusiasm also knows the certainty of salvation. . . . But when inner experience, an exalted mood, the strength of visions, are made the measure of belief, the person is involved in a dubious dependence on

the ups and downs of his psyche, of his subjectivity.
... The reason for salvation lies solely in the loving and
redeeming will of God. Of course such a certainty demands personal faith. It is also possible, according to
Luther, for this grasp of faith to be accompanied by experience and feeling. But what goes on in the soul in this
respect can never be the reason for certainty of salvation. We live solely on the gift that is offered to us.[71]

To "turn to the objectively valid message of salvation" and
to "live solely on the gift offered to him" Luther had to have
a Scripture whose message was itself indefeasible. Its reliability
could not be dependent upon any personal experience, or the
very saving relation with Christ would be put in jeopardy.
At Worms, when his life was on the line, there could be no
mixing of God's Word with man's word or God's inerrant Truth
with man's experiential vagaries:

> Unless I am convinced by the testimonies of the Holy
> Scriptures or evident reason (for I believe in neither the
> Pope nor councils alone, since it has been established that
> they have often erred and contradicted themselves), I
> am bound by the Scriptures that I have adduced, and my
> conscience has been taken captive by the Word of God;
> and I am neither able nor willing to recant, since it is
> neither safe nor right to act against conscience. God help
> me. Amen.[72]

"Conscience captive to God's inerrant Word": that is the
strength of Luther's reform. So convinced was he that to put
the Spirit's leading or spiritual experience in tandem with Scripture would bring all theology to ruin that he expended tremendous energy fighting the *Schwärmer* of his day—the religious
enthusiast or spiritualist who set his own feelings above Holy
Writ.[73] Radical reformer Thomas Müntzer considered himself sufficiently led by the Spirit to cry, "Bible, Babel, bubble!"
Luther's reply was that apart from the inscripturated Word
he would not listen to Müntzer even if "he had swallowed
the Holy Ghost, feathers and all." [74]

Let us learn from Luther both positively and negatively.
His experiential criterion of canonicity shows how even a great
theologian committed to the objective, theocentric authority
of God's Word can slip into subjective, anthropocentric thinking.
If this was possible for Luther, is it any wonder that the lesser
theological lights of our own day easily fall victim to the parallel
temptations of using their spiritual experience to create a "canon
within the canon" and a Bible that is not indefeasible in its

own right? We should remember how readily the experiential pietism of the late 17th century became the rationalism of the 18th century, and see the dangers in our own revivalistic heritage. The weaknesses in our heritage should impel us to strike back into Christian history beyond the evangelical revivals to the Reformation for guidance in the present crisis of scriptural authority. No one can offer us better resources in this life-or-death struggle than Luther, for he knew what it was to stand alone before a hostile world with nothing but Scripture to speak for him. With Luther as our model, the words of the great 19th century French Protestant leader Théodore Monod can become our confession too: "We will not appeal to experience—only to the Word of God." [75] And if the forces minimalizing scriptural commitment seem at times to drive us to sadness and bewilderment, Luther's example will permit us to join the saints of three and a half centuries ago when they sang,[76]

> As true as God's own Word is true,
> Not earth or hell with all their crew
> Against us shall prevail.

Addendum
OVER AGAINST WORDS
OF ANGELS AND DEVILS

A review of
Luther and the Bible, by Willem Jan Kooiman, translated by John Schmidt (Muhlenberg Press, 1961, 243 pp.)*

The Luther research movement of the last half century, stemming largely from the work of Karl Holl and the editors of the great *Weimarer Ausgabe* of the Reformer's writings, has virtually revolutionized our understanding of Luther's theology and world view. As with most such movements of European

---

* First published in *Christianity Today*, February 16, 1962, and now reprinted with slight omissions

origin, considerable time elapsed before American scholars and, more especially, pastors and laymen, became aware of the new emphasis; and it is safe to say that even now many non-Lutherans are unacquainted with the results of the new Luther research. Roland Bainton's *Here I Stand* has provided an excellent biographical introduction to the Reformer on the basis of recent scholarship, and now, with the translation from the Dutch of Kooiman's *Luther and the Bible*, we have perhaps the best theological starting point for those who would understand the essence of Luther's thought in regard to Scripture and Gospel.

The most striking characteristic of Luther's biblical approach, as revealed in this excellent study by a professor of church history at the University of Amsterdam, is undoubtedly its diametric opposition to the presuppositions of large segments of present-day Protestant biblical scholarship. "Luther sees the whole truth of the Gospel already revealed, even though veiled, in the Old Testament. Just like the New, it is 'full of Christ'" (p. 209). "How completely he means this is made clear by the fact that he placed a '*Praefatio Jhesu Christi*' (a prefatory word from Christ himself) in the edition of the Psalter to be used by the students. This introduction consists of Bible passages directly or indirectly spoken by Jesus, intended to show that he is the true Author of the Psalms" (p. 32). In his treatment of the Bible, Luther was "not concerned with a mere collection of individual texts, but with the Author who stands behind them and wishes to reveal himself through them" (p. 84).

Not only in regard to the unity of the Bible, but also in the matter of its power and authority, Luther holds a position unacceptable to many moderns. "We see the essential elements of Luther's theology appearing early. Christ is the content of the scripture and he desires to come to us through them, both in his judgment and grace. *Sola Scriptura* (scripture alone) is the same as *solus Christus* (Christ alone)" (p. 42). "For Luther the Bible itself is a weapon with which God fights in his great and comprehensive battle against Satan. With it he defeats his enemy and gives victory to those who believe in him. And it is because of this fact that 'every word of the scriptures is to be weighed, counted, and measured'" (p. 54). The following assertions by Luther are as typical of him as they are disturbing in the present theological milieu: "Over against all the statements of the fathers and of all men, yes, over against words of angels and devils, I place the scriptures"

(p. 80); "I have learned to ascribe the honor of infallibility only to those books that are accepted as canonical. I am profoundly convinced that none of these writers have erred" (p. 78).

Two negative criticisms of Kooiman's volume are in order, though one of these will be leveled at publisher and not author, and neither is to be considered sufficient to detract from the general value of the book. First, Professor Kooiman's very accurate depictions of Luther's views suffer on occasion from the conclusions that he draws from them. Thus, in spite of the wealth of material indicating that Luther held as "strong" a view of biblical inspiration as possible apart from Romanist mechanical inspirationism, the author insists on claiming that Luther was no "verbal inspirationist" (p. 236). This is true, of course, if we equate verbal inspiration with dictational inspiration, but such an equation muddies the theological water. Granted, the verbal inspiration controversy postdates Luther, but it is difficult to feel after reading Kooiman, that Luther, if he lived today, would not in fact consider "verbal inspiration" the biblical view most congenial to his own. In line with Kooiman's negative attitude toward verbalism, one finds in chapter 17 that the author attributes an anti-bookishness to Luther; that this is inconsistent with a proper understanding of the Reformer's life and thought will be seen in this reviewer's article on "Luther and Libraries" in his *In Defense of Martin Luther* (Milwaukee: Northwestern Publishing House, 1970).

A second criticism has to do with the treatment of Kooiman's book at the hands of its publisher. Copy editing is substandard (bibliographical citations are inconsistent and frequently at variance with accepted practice—e.g., on p. 93 Bornkamm's *Luther's World of Thought* is cited in English translation, but on p. 239 it is cited in the German original with no indication of English translation); the index is abominable (e.g., "Ein Deutsch Theologian" is entered under E: and the strange entry "Random comments by Luther" appears under R!); misprints are evident (e.g., on p. 25, "Erdmans" for "Eerdmans"; on p. 50, "profeticus" for "propheticus"—cf. p. 31); no indication is given as to the date of the original edition from which the translation was made; there is poor registration and typographical smearing throughout the book; and even the spinecloth on my copy is unaligned. Surely a book of the quality and importance of Kooiman's volume deserves better bibliographical dress than this.

John Warwick Montgomery

NOTES

[1] Not *"must* make mistakes" but *"can* and often *do* make mistakes." For our discussion of the misleading axiom, *Errare est humanum*, see Chapter One of the present work.

[2] Quoted in P. C. Croll (ed.), *Tributes to the Memory of Martin Luther* (Philadelphia: G. W. Frederick, 1884), p. 39.

[3] *Ibid.*, pp. 49-50. Cf. Junius B. Remensnyder, *What the World Owes Luther* (New York: Revell, 1917), *passim.*

[4] See E. Harris Harbison, *The Christian Scholar in the Age of the Reformation* (New York: Scribner, 1956), pp. 103-35; and F. V. N. Painter, *Luther on Education* (St. Louis, Mo.: Concordia [1889]), *passim.*

[5] Citations will be made to the standard, critical *Weimarer Ausgabe (WA).*

[6] I have dealt elsewhere with the related hermeneutic question (did Luther regard Scripture as objectively perspicuous?) and shall not therefore treat that subject here; see "Luther's Hermeneutic vs. the New Hermeneutic," in my *In Defense of Martin Luther* (Milwaukee: Northwestern Publishing House, 1970), pp. 40-85; also in my *Crisis in Lutheran Theology* (2d ed.; 2 vols.; Minneapolis: Bethany Fellowship, 1973), I, pp. 45-77.

[7] *WA*, 10 III, 162 (*Kirchenpostille*—a sermon collection which Luther considered his "very best book").

[8] A photograph of this statue appears in my *Suicide of Christian Theology* (Minneapolis: Bethany Fellowship, 1970), p. 22.

[9] Julius Köstlin, *The Theology of Luther in Its Historical Development and Inner Harmony*, trans. from the 2d German ed. by Charles E. Hay (2 vols.; Philadelphia: Lutheran Publication Society, 1897), II, pp. 252-57.

[10] Philip S. Watson, *Let God Be God! An Interpretation of the Theology of Martin Luther* (London: Epworth Press, 1947), p. 175.

[11] J. K. S. Reid, *The Authority of Scripture: A Study of the Reformation and Post-Reformation Understanding of the Bible* (London: Methuen, 1957), p. 72.

[12] *WA*, 9, 356.

[13] *WA*, 7, 315; cf. *WA*, 15, 1481: "The Scriptures have never erred."

[14] *WA*, 38, 16.

[18] *Vorlesung über den Römerbrief*, 1515-16, ed. J. Ficker (4th ed.; Leipzig, 1930), p. 240.

[16] Heinrich Bornkamm, *Luther and the Old Testament*, trans. E. W. and R. C. Gritsch; ed. Victor I. Gruhn (Philadelphia: Fortress Press, 1969), p. 262.

[17] *WA*, 42, 474 (on Gen. 12:11-13).

[18] *WA*, 44, 91-92 (on Gen. 32:21-24).

[19] *WA*, 19, 219 (exposition of Jonah [1536]).

[20] *WA*, 52, 811 (on John 19:25-37).

[21] *WA*, 54, 35.

[22] *WA*, 40 III, 254 (on Ps. 127:3).

[23] *WA*, 54, 39 (discussion of Gen. 19:24 and I Chron. 17:10).

[24] *WA*, 3, 486 (*Dictata super Psalterium*, at Ps. 73:19-20).

[25] *WA*, 54, 263 (*Wider das Papsttum zu Rom, vom Teufel gestiftet*).

[26] *WA*, 34 I, 347 (sermon on John 16:16-23 [1531]); for evidence of the genuineness of the sermon, see *WA* 34 II, 572. Luther was quite correct in attributing belief in the inerrancy of Scripture to Augustine; see Charles Joseph Costello, *St. Augustine's Doctrine on the Inspiration and Canonicity of Scripture* (Washington, D. C.: Catholic University of America, 1930), especially pp. 30-31. The letter from Augustine to Jerome to which Luther refers is doubtless the one containing the following passage (Luther expressly quotes it in *WA*, 7, 308): "I confess to your charity that I have learned to defer this respect and honor to those Scriptural books only which are now called canonical, that I believe most firmly that no one of those authors has erred in any respect in writing" (Augustine, *Epistolae*, 82. i.3).

[27] In particular: "That These Words of Christ, 'This Is My Body,' etc., Still Stand Firm Against the Fanatics," in *Word and Sacrament III*, ed. Robert H. Fischer, Vol. XXXVII of *Luther's Works*, American Edition, ed. Jaroslav Pelikan and Helmut T. Lehmann (Philadelphia: Fortress Press, 1961).

[28] *WA-T* (*Tischreden*), II, No. 2623b [recorded by Cordatus, 21-31 August 1532]. Cf. M. Reu, *Luther's German Bible: An Historical Presentation Together with a Collection of Sources* (Columbus, Ohio: Lutheran Book Concern, 1934), *passim.*

[29] M. Reu, *Luther and the Scriptures* (Columbus, Ohio: Wartburg Press, 1944); this exceedingly important publication was reissued, with corrections to the notes, as the August,

1960, issue of *The Springfielder* (Concordia Theological Seminary, Springfield, Illinois). Cf. also the essays, "Luther's *Sola Scriptura*" by Lewis W. Spitz, Sr., and "Luther As Exegete" by Douglas Carter, both included in my *Crisis in Lutheran Theology (op. cit.* [in note 6 above]), II, pp. 123-38; and "Luther and the Bible" by J. Theodore Mueller, in *Inspiration and Interpretation,* ed. John F. Walvoord (Grand Rapids, Mich.: Eerdmans, 1957), pp. 87-114. A. Skevington Wood, in his valuable book, *Captive to the Word. Martin Luther: Doctor of Sacred Scripture* (Exeter, Eng.: Paternoster Press, 1969), marshals considerable primary source evidence to support his contention that "Luther's doctrine of inspiration is inseparably linked with that of inerrancy" (p. 144; see the full discussion, pp. 135-47). Eugene F. A. Klug comes to the same conclusion in his Free University of Amsterdam doctoral dissertation, *From Luther to Chemnitz. On Scripture and the Word* (Kampen: J. H. Kok, 1971), pp. 105-114.

[30] Adolf von Harnack, *Outlines of the History of Dogma,* trans. Edwin Knox Mitchell; intro. Philip Rieff (Boston: Beacon Press, 1957), pp. 561-62. (Cf. Jaroslav Pelikan, "Adolf von Harnack on Luther," in Pelikan's *Interpreters of Luther: Essays in Honor of Wilhelm Pauck* [Philadelphia: Fortress Press, 1968], pp. 253-74.) Harnack's recognition-cum-critique of Luther's belief in scriptural inerrancy is echoed by Paul Althaus: Luther "basically accepted it [the Bible] as an essentially infallible book, inspired in its entire content by the Holy Spirit. It is therefore 'the word of God,' not only when it speaks to us in law and gospel and thereby convicts our heart and conscience but also—and this is a matter of principle—in everything else that it says.... Here is the point at which the clarity of Luther's own Reformation insight reached its limit. For it was at this point that Luther himself, in spite of everything, prepared the way for seventeenth century orthodoxy.... Theology has had plenty of trouble in the past—and in many places still has—trying to repair this damage by distinguishing between the 'Word of God' in the true sense and a false biblicism" (*The Theology of Martin Luther,* trans. Robert C. Schultz [Philadelphia: Fortress Press, 1966], pp. 50-52).

[31] Theodore Engelder, *Scripture Cannot Be Broken: Six Objections to Verbal Inspiration Examined in the Light of Scripture,* pref. W. Arndt (St. Louis, Mo.: Concordia, 1944), pp. 290-91 n.

[32] W. Bodamer observes that over a thousand unequivocal assertions identifying Scripture with the Word of God can be found in only ten volumes of Luther's collected works; in his article he quotes a hundred of them ("Luthers Stellung zur Lehre von der Verbalinspiration," *Theologische Quartalschrift,* 1936, pp. 240 ff.).

[33] Emil Brunner, *The Theology of Crisis* (New York: Scribner, 1929), p. 19; see also his *Revelation and Reason,* trans. Olive Wyon (Philadelphia: Westminster Press, 1946), pp. 273-76. Cf. Paul King Jewett, *Emil Brunner's Concept of Revelation* (London: J. Clarke, 1954), and the same author's essay, "Emil Brunner's Doctrine of Scripture," in *Inspiration and Interpretation (op. cit.* [in note 29 above]), pp. 210-38.

[34] Gerhard Ebeling, "The New Hermeneutics and the Early Luther," *Theology Today,* XXI (April, 1964), pp. 45-46. Cf. my essay, "Luther's Hermeneutic vs. the New Hermeneutic," *op. cit.* (in note 6 above), *passim.*

[35] See Montgomery, "Toward a Christian Philosophy of History," *Where Is History Going?* (reprint ed.; Minneapolis: Bethany Fellowship, 1972), pp. 182-97.

[36] Althaus, *op. cit.* (in note 30 above), p. 5.

[37] Cf. *The Concordant Version: A Contribution to the Battle for the Bible,* and a host of other pamphlets illustrating and defending this remarkable exegetical operation (all published by Concordant Publishing Concern, Los Angeles and Saugus, California).

[38] *WA,* 30 II, 636-37 (*Sendbrief vom Dolmetschen* [1530]).

[39] *Ibid.,* p. 640.

[40] Skevington Wood, *op. cit.* (in note 29 above), pp. 145-46.

[41] Köstlin, *op. cit.* (in note 9 above), II, pp. 255-56.

[42] *Ibid.* (Köstlin's italics).

[43] *Ibid.,* p. 257.

[44] *Ibid.,* p. 255.

[45] Klug, *op, cit.* (in note 29 above), pp. 109-110. Klug's primary source citations of Luther are to be found in *WA,* 42, 425-26, 431, and 460.

[46] Thus implies Concordia Seminary (St. Louis) professor and "moderate" Lutheran Edgar Krentz in his editorial introduction to the reprint in pamphlet form of Luther's *Prefaces to the New Testament,* trans. Charles M. Jacobs, rev. E. Theodore Bachmann (St. Louis, Mo.: Concordia [1967]). This reprint has been made from Vol. XXXV of the American Edition of *Luther's Works,* which contains all the Prefaces—both for the Old and for the

New Testament. The complete set of Prefaces is also conveniently available in Vol. VI of the Philadelphia Edition of *Luther's Works* (Charles M. Jacobs' unrevised translation).

[47] See above, our text at note 16.

[48] *WA*, 42, 23 (on Gen. 1:6).

[49] Cf. Part Two of Thomas Paine's *Age of Reason, Being an Investigation of True and Fabulous Theology* (1795); *Religion, érudition et critique à la fin du XVIIe siècle et au début du XVIIIe* by Baudouin de Gaiffier *et. al.* (Paris: Presses Universitaires de France, 1968); Jerry Wayne Brown, *The Rise of Biblical Criticism in America, 1800-1870* (Middletown, Conn.: Wesleyan University Press, 1969).

[50] Gerhard Ebeling, *The Word of God and Tradition*, trans. S. H. Hooke (Philadelphia: Fortress Press, 1968), p. 120.

[51] Krentz, in his reprint of the New Testament Prefaces (*op. cit.* in note 46 above), gives no indication whatever that the depreciatory remarks on James were omitted from the general Preface to the New Testament in the editions from 1534 on.

[52] *WA-DB* (*Deutsche Bibel*), VI, 10.

[53] *WA-DB*, VII, 404 and 406 ff.

[54] *WA-DB*, VI, 12-13.

[55] Wilhelm Walther, *Luthers spätere Ansicht über den Jacobusbrief. Zur Wertung der deutschen Reformation* (Leipzig, 1909), especially pp. 170 ff. The evidence is summarized in Reu, *Luther and the Scriptures* (*op. cit.* [in note 29 above]), chap. iii. Here belongs Luther's widely quoted—though but a table-talk—remark: "Some day I will use James to fire my stove" (*WA-T*, V. 5854 [unknown date, perhaps 1540]).

[56] Or "deal with Christ/lay emphasis on Christ" (*Christum treiben*).

[57] Carlstadt, *De canonicis Scripturis libellus* (Wittenberg, 1520), para. 50.

[58] Samuel Berger, *La Bible au XVIe siècle* (Geneva, Switz.: Slatkine Reprints, 1969), p. 96; cf. the whole of chap. vi ("Luther et Carlstadt"), pp. 86-96. Berger is quite wrong, however, to locate the "origins of biblical criticism" in the 16th century and to argue that the Reformation in general operated only with the "material principle" (justification by grace through faith), subordinating the "formal principle" (Holy Scripture) to it. On Carlstadt's radicalism—well characterized as moderate illuminism—cf. Fritz Blanke, "Anabaptism and the Reformation," in Guy F. Hershberger (ed.), *The Recovery of the Anabaptist Vision* (Scottdale, Pa.: Herald Press, 1957), p. 57.

[59] Cf. my essay, "Some Comments on Paul's Use of Genesis in his Epistle to the Romans," *Evangelical Theological Society Bulletin* [now: *Journal*], IV (April, 1961), 4-11.

[60] However, we have to agree (for once!) with Lessing when he declares: "In such reverence do I hold Luther, that I rejoice in having been able to find some defects in him, for I have been in imminent danger of making him an object of idolatrous veneration. The proofs that in some things he was like other men are to me as precious as the most dazzling of his virtues" (quoted in Croll, *op. cit.* [in note 2 above], p. 29).

[61] Adolf Hoenecke, *Ev.-Luth. Dogmatik*, ed. W. and O. Hoenecke (4 vols.; Milwaukee: Northwestern Publishing House, 1909), I, 362. Cf. Francis Pieper's excellent discussion of the whole question of "Luther and the Inspiration of Holy Scripture," in his *Christian Dogmatics* (4 vols.; St. Louis, Mo.: Concordia, 1950-1957), I, 276-98.

[62] Reu, *Luther and the Scriptures*, *loc. cit.* (in note 55 above).

[63] *WA*, 2, 618 (*Contra malignum Iohannis Eccii iudicium ... Martini Lutheri defensio* [1519]). The early date of this affirmation is noteworthy: two years after the posting of the Ninety-Five Theses.

[64] Cf. Bruce Shelley, "Sources of Pietistic Fundamentalism," *Fides et Historia*, V/1-2 (Fall, 1972 and Spring, 1973), 68-78.

[65] Samuel S. Hill, Jr., *Southern Churches in Crisis* (New York: Holt, Rinehart, and Winston, 1967), p. 87.

[66] Donald G. Bloesch, *The Ground of Certainty: Toward an Evangelical Theology of Revelation* (Grand Rapids, Mich.; Eerdmans, 1971), pp. 71-74.

[67] *Ibid.*, p. 155.

[68] *Ibid.*, p. 178. That Bloesch sees himself as a spokesman for contemporary evangelicalism is evident from his more recent book, *The Evangelical Renaissance* (Grand Rapids, Mich.: Eerdmans, 1973).

[69] *WA*, 40 II, 353.

[70] Stephanus Pfürtner, O.P., *Luther and Aquinas—a Conversation*, trans. Edward Quinn (London: Darton, Longman & Todd, 1964), pp. 107-108.

[71] Adolf Köberle, "Heilsgewissheit," *Evangelisches Kirchenlexikon*, ed. H. Brunotte and

O. Weber (Göttingen, 1956 to date), II, 90-91. Cf. Wilhelm Pauck: Luther's "own position was that of a theonomous Biblicism, i.e., in the Bible he found the Word of God, by faith in which God could became *his* God. Thus he overcame a heteronomous objectivism which excludes personal commitment, as well as an autonomous subjectivism which disregards super-personal authority" (*The Heritage of the Reformation* [Boston: Beacon Press, 1950] p. 4).

[72] *WA*, 7, 836-38.

[73] See Regin Prenter, *Spiritus Creator*, trans. John M. Jensen (Philadelphia: Muhlenberg Press, 1953), especially Pt. II ("In the controversy with the Enthusiasts").

[74] *WA*, 17 I, 361-62. On Müntzer, see the balanced essay by Hans Hillerbrand in his *A Fellowship of Discontent* (New York: Harper, 1967), pp. 1-30, 167-70.

[75] Théodore Monod, *The Gift of God* (London: Morgan and Scott, 1876), p. 13. These addresses were originally delivered in English; the following year a French edition was published in Paris with the title, *Le don de Dieu*.

[76] "Fear not, O little flock, the foe" (Altenburg), Stanza 3, lines 1-3, in *Lyra Germanica*, trans. Catherine Winkworth (New York: Standford & Delisser, 1858), p. 17. Altenburg published this hymn in 1631, during the Thirty Years War; it was soon called Gustavus Adolphus' battle song, for he sang it often with his army, the last time just before the battle of Lützen.

4

CALVIN'S VIEW
OF SCRIPTURE

J. I. Packer

The biggest problem facing anyone who attempts a paper on Calvin's view of Scripture is simply *embarras de richesse.* Far more material presents itself than can be properly treated in the space available. Calvin held that a particular understanding of the relations between Church, Bible and Holy Spirit was essential to the maintaining of undistorted Christianity, and he laboured to focus and flesh out that understanding all through his working life. To systematize, expound and apply the teaching of Scripture was, as he saw it, his supreme task, the fruits of which now fill 59 large volumes of the *Corpus Reformatorum.*[1] Having first written his *Institutes of the Christian Religion* as a layman's pocket-book of six chapters,[2] he laboured from the second (1539) to the sixth (1559) edition to perfect it as a student's introduction to Bible study and in particular to his own commentaries[3]; and the index pages of the latest translation list almost 7,000 biblical references scattered through the 1,500 pages and 80 chapters of the full-grown work.[4] Through his commentaries, which covered most of the Bible,[5] he became the father of modern critical and theological exegesis—a field in which, four centuries after, he is still, right up with the leaders.[6] On his death-bed in 1564 he told his fellow-pastors what he had sought to do, and, as he believed, had done: [7]

> As for my doctrine, I have taught faithfully, and God has given me grace to write, which I have done faithfully as I could; and I have not corrupted one single passage of Scripture nor twisted it so far as I know;

and when I studied subtlety, I have put all that under my feet, and have always aimed at being simple. I have written nothing out of hatred against anyone, but have always set before me what I thought was for the glory of God.

As Kenneth S. Kantzer rightly says, had Calvin been allowed to choose an honorific title of the Mediaeval type he would have wished to be called Doctor, not of Predestination, but of Sacred Scripture.[8] Was he not, after all, a pastor, and was not the pastor's first task, according to the *Ordinances* which he himself drew up to be the Geneva church's constitution after his return from exile in 1541, "to proclaim the Word of God so as to teach, admonish, exhort and reprove?" [9] Thus Calvin saw his calling; and in the course of his thirty year quest for faithful simplicity in handling the Word of God, he produced more material expressing or reflecting his view of Scripture than has ever been brought together in print.[10]

PROBLEMS AND PITFALLS

With all this material to draw on, and bearing in mind the lucid consistency of all Calvin's work, one might have expected the study of his view of Scripture to be problem-free. But this is not so, for three reasons.

First, what Calvin says of the nature of Scripture has that oddly elliptical and paradoxical quality which led Bauke in 1922 to diagnose Calvin's way of thought as *complexio oppositorum*, the weaving together of things apparently exclusive of each other.[11] This quality, which is certainly a mark of Calvin's theology, would be widely held today to reflect not intellectual arbitrariness but theological acumen, in that Calvin sees the *complexio oppositorum* in biblical Christology-divinity *and* humanity, majesty *and* lowliness, the disclosing *and* concealing of glory—as a paradigm for thought about both the Church and the Scriptures. Whether or not Calvin's mind really worked this way—and it is hard to prove either that it did or that it did not, or whether it was simply that, as with many quick thinkers, his mind habitually made jumps—there is certainly a problem of opposites in his view of Scripture. For T. H. L. Parker, this is "probably the most difficult problem in all his theology." [12] Parker analyses it as "a question of relating the numerous passages where he speaks of the Holy Spirit 'dictating' the Scriptures to the prophets and apostles, his 'amanuenses,' and the no less frequent places where he treats the text as a human production and, as such, sometimes incorrect on matters of fact. Some scholars emphasize the one side, some the other. Doumergue will distinguish between the form and content of Scripture and say with Gallican [*sic*] fervour: 'it is not the words that are important, it is the *doctrine*, the *spiritual doctrine*, the *substance*.' But Professor Dowey considers that Calvin 'believes the revelation to have been given word for word by the Spirit.' Both views are quite right and can be supported easily by quotations from Calvin's writings." [13] What are we to make of this state of affairs?

Second, scholars have inevitably brought their own preoccupations to Calvin, asking him to answer questions which are more theirs than his and seeking to show either, if they are Reformed men, that they can quote him in substantial support of the views they already espouse or, if they stand in non-Calvinist traditions, that he really is guilty of holding positions which they themselves have already rejected. Thus, for instance, C. A. Briggs and Doumergue's clan[13] find in Calvin a willingness to go along with them in denying that all the Bible tells us is true,[14] while Lutheran scholars like Seeberg and Methodists like R. E. Davies, who themselves accept the fallibility of Scripture, convict Calvin of teaching a "mechanical" view of divine dictation (though how can they justify the application to him of so anachronistic an adjective does not appear).[15] Again, French Reformed writers like Lobstein and Pannier who with Schleiermacher saw the religious consciousness as the true source of theological convictions have interpreted Calvin's doctrine of the Spirit's inner witness as foreshadowing this view,[16] while the great B. B. Warfield, heir as he was to the Butlerian type of anti-Deist apologetic which had been standard in American Presbyterian theology since there was such a thing,[17] understood *Institutes* I. viii as a list of arguments from which the witnessing Spirit leads us to conclude that the Bible is divine, and which thus become the direct grounds of our faith in it.[18] But neither of these views is correct, as we shall see. These examples show sufficiently how preconceptions can deflect judgment in the study of Calvin's view of Scripture.

Third, Calvin did not have to face all the problems about the Bible that we face. He was not under pressure from epistemological problems about how God can be known and teach truths, nor from historical problems about the contents of biblical narratives, nor from problems raised by the account of this world which the natural sciences give, nor from theological problems about whether inspiration could extend to the very words used; nor was he up against the post-Kantian dualism which affirms God's presence in man's psyche but effectively denies his Lordship over the cosmos as such—the dualism which is the basic presupposition, more or less explicit, of all the different classes of problems noted in our list. A. D. R. Polman is right when he says: "With the Apostolic Christian Church of all ages Calvin confesses the divine inspiration of the Sacred Scriptures. He considers it a catholic truth which is completely beyond dispute. Never does Calvin present a thetical exposition of this doctrine; not in the *Institutes*, not in his *Commentaries*, nor in any other work of his. . . . He does not discuss the subject, but presupposes it." [19] Calvin's problem had to do with the message and authority of Scripture—how the Bible sets forth Christ and grace; how the Spirit authenticates and interprets the Word to us, making it both self-evidencing and clear to us; how Christ teaches and rules his people through the ministry of the Word. These were matters which Calvin had to debate, on the one hand with the Church of Rome, which set itself in the place belonging to the Spirit, as authenticator and interpreter of the Word, and on the other hand with the Anabaptists, who put the "internal word" of supposed private revelation in the place belonging to the Scriptures, as the instrument of God's rule over his people's lives. But he did not have to vindicate biblical inspiration and inerrancy against either Rome or the Anabaptists, for neither denied that the Bible came from God. Thus Calvin could skate lightly over areas where evangelicals today have to stand and fight, and this has sometimes prompted the false inference that he did not attach as much importance to maintaining the total truth of Scripture as modern evangelicals do. But this is wrong. The reason why Calvin never argued this point is not that it was not important to him, but that it was not denied. Why should he spend his strength breaking down open doors? The occasionally unguarded way in which he phrases his thoughts about slips in the biblical text, so making possible in our time ascription to him of the belief that in its detail Scripture can err, is actually a witness to the reality of Christian consensus on inerrancy in his time. Calvin did not bother to guard his flanks, because there was in his situation nothing to guard them against. (In fact, close examination shows that inerrancy is presupposed as axiomatic even in his comments on these slips, as we shall shortly see.)

THE KNOWLEDGE OF GOD

The best way to approach Calvin's account of Scripture, as

indeed of everything in the *Institutes*, is via reflection on the famous sentence with which the work opens: "Almost all the wisdom we possess, that is to say, true and sound wisdom, consists of two parts: the knowledge of God and of our-selves." [20] As Dr. Battles observes, these are "decisive words" which "set the limits of Calvin's theology and condition every subsequent statement." [21] We should note the following points.

(1) Calvin speaks of "our wisdom." Who are the "we"? Not mankind as such, but the people of God, believers whose faith seeks understanding. Calvin's stance throughout the book is that of a Christian helping his fellow-Christians to add to their faith knowledge, and in understanding to be men.

(2) Calvin connects knowledge of God and of ourselves. Knowledge of God's gifts to us in our present state of weakness, dependence and misery brings knowledge of his goodness and resourcefulness; knowledge of God's moral perfection brings knowledge of our sinfulness, need of grace, and unfitness to approach him.[22] Thus, knowledge of God and self grow to-gether, in the form of an increasing and deepening awareness of unlimited grace meeting unlimited need.

(3) Calvin means by knowledge of God more than knowledge about him or a bare acknowledgment of his existence. "The knowledge of God, as I understand it, is that by which we not only conceive that there is a God, but also grasp what benefits us and makes for his glory, what in short brings profit. Nor shall we say that God, strictly speaking, is known where there is no religion or godliness." [23] "We are called to a knowledge of God which does not just flit about in the brain, content with empty speculation, but which, if we rightly grasp it and it takes root in our heart, will be solid and fruitful." [24] "Knowledge of God is not identified with cold speculation, but brings with it worship of him." [25] The total concept of knowing God which emerges as the *Institutes* proceeds is of acknowledging him as he reveals himself in Scripture; giving him honour and thanks for all things; abasing oneself before him as a sinner, and learning of him as he speaks of salvation; believing on the Christ whom he sets forth as our Saviour; loving Father and Son with a love that answers the love shown by them to us; living by faith in the promises of mercy given us in Jesus Christ; cherishing the hope of a joyful resurrection; obeying his law, and seeking his glory in all relationships and commerce with created things. Knowledge of God thus comprehends both true theology and true religion. But true theology means acknowledg-ing, just as true religion means worshipping, God in his dual relationship to us as both Creator and Redeemer.[26] From

what source do we learn of God in this dual relationship? Only from the Scriptures. This, in Calvin's view, is where the Bible comes in.

SCRIPTURE NEEDED AND PROVIDED

Calvin's first and basic point about the Bible, in the *Institutes* as elsewhere, is that we *need* it. Though self-revealing action by God the Creator goes on all the time, creating in the human heart an inescapable awareness of "one above," men's sinful perversity and blindness of mind is such that, instead of "tuning in" correctly, they distort the Creator's self-revelation into some kind of lie. So "general" or "natural" revelation (to use the terms of later formalized theology) never produce either true natural theology or true worship. The Creator's self-disclosure in his works, which would have sufficed for a life-giving relationship between him and men "if Adam had remained upright," [27] now leads only to falsehood and idolatry, calling forth condemnation, and that is the present state of the non-Christian world. So (to quote the title of *Institutes* I.vi), "Scripture is needed as guide and teacher for anyone who would come to God the Creator." As for knowledge of God as Redeemer, this was first given in biblical history, from the patriarchs to Christ, and is the main burden of the biblical record: it is no part of general revelation, so once again Scripture is needed as guide and teacher if we are to come to a knowledge of God's saving grace.

Calvin brings this thought into focus by the use of three favourite figures: the maze, the spectacles and the schoolmaster. Man, by nature, says Calvin, is stuck in a labyrinth of which he does not know the plan, and from which he cannot find his way out unaided. His sinful wrong-mindness always takes him up blind alleys of idolatry, where he wanders lost. "Scarcely a single person has ever been found who did not fashion for himself an idol or phantom in God's place." [28] But God in love reaches down to us in our lostness and gives us the guidance of the Scriptures, which are like a thread leading us out of the maze of ignorance and misconception into knowledge of the one true God. "Thread" is Calvin's own metaphor[29]; and his image of the spectacles makes the same point. "Just as, when you put before old or bleary-eyed and weak-sighted men even the most beautiful book, though they may recognize that there is something written they can hardly make out two words, yet with the aid of spectacles will begin to read distinctly; so Scripture, gathering into one the otherwise muddled-up knowledge of God in our minds, dispels the darkness and shows us the true God clearly." [30] Thus through the Scriptures God himself becomes our instructor, and we must humbly consent to have it so, saying good-bye to the world of theological fantasy and speculation in order to enroll in the school of the Word. "We should hold that, for true religion to shine on us, we must begin by being taught from heaven; and that no man can have the least knowledge of true and sound doctrine without having been a pupil of the Scriptures. Hence it is that when we reverently embrace what God has been pleased to testify there concerning himself, the beginning of true understanding emerges. And not only perfect faith, complete in every way, but all right knowledge of God, is borne of [this] obedience." [31] Thus the Scriptures should be seen first and foremost as a gift of grace to benighted sinners, who without them could never have known God at all; and we need to have it firmly fixed in our minds that disregard of the Scriptures is as perverse and ungrateful as it is disastrous.

THE NATURE OF SCRIPTURE

God gave the whole Bible, and thereby constituted it all his Word for all time. Calvin's classic statement on this deserves extended quotation.[32]

When it pleased God to raise up a more visible form of the church, he willed to have his Word set down and sealed in writing. . . . He commanded also that the prophecies be committed to writing and be accounted part of his Word. To these at the same time histories were added, also the labour of the prophets, but composed under the Holy Spirit's dictation. I include the psalms with the prophecies. . . . That whole body [*corpus*], therefore, made up of law, prophecies, psalms and histories was the Lord's Word for the ancient people. . . .

Let this be a firm principle: No other word is to be held as the Word of God, and given place as such in the church, than what is contained first in the Law and the Prophets, then in the writings of the apostles. . . . [The apostles] were to expound the ancient Scripture and to show that what is taught there has been fulfilled in Christ. Yet they were not to do this except from the Lord, that is, with Christ's Spirit going before them and in a sense dictating their words. . . . [They] were sure and genuine penmen [*certi et authentici amanuenses*] of

the Holy Spirit, and their writings are therefore to be considered oracles of God: and the sole office of others is
to teach what is provided and sealed in the Holy Scriptures.

Calvin's view of inspiration is, as we have seen, nowhere
spelt out in formal analysis. Nonetheless, we can focus it clearly
enough by attention to four key notions which recur when he
deals with the Scriptures. The first notion is *os Dei*, "the mouth
of God," a biblical phrase pointing to the Creator's use of
human language to address us. The second notion is *doctrina*,
"doctrine" or "teaching," which is the instruction that these
verbal utterances convey. "Teaching from God's mouth," or
putting it more simply and dynamically, "God *speaking - teaching - preaching*," is the heart of Calvin's concept of Holy Scripture. The third notion is "dictation" as a term for the work
of the Holy Spirit in relation to the part played by the human
authors in producing the biblical documents. The fourth notion
is "condescension" as a characterization of God's method and
style of verbal instruction.

(1, 2) Calvin's view of Scripture as doctrine coming from
God's mouth is made explicit by remarks in his *Commentary
on the Pastoral Epistles*. Says he concerning II Timothy 3:16
("All Scripture is given by inspiration of God, and is profitable
for doctrine, for reproof, for correction, for instruction in righteousness"):

He [Paul] commends the Scripture, first, on account
of its authority, and, second, on account of the utility
that springs from it. In order to uphold the authority of
Scripture, he declares it to be divinely inspired [*divinitus
inspiratam*]: for if it be so, it is beyond all controversy
that men should receive it with reverence. . . . Whoever
then wishes to profit in the Scriptures, let him first of
all lay down as a settled point this—that the law and the
prophecies are not teaching [*doctrinam*] delivered by the
will of men, but dictated [*dictatam*] by the Holy Ghost. . . .
Moses and the prophets did not utter at random what
we have from their hand, but, since they spoke by divine
impulse, they confidently and fearlessly testified, as was
actually the case, that it was the mouth of the Lord
that spoke [*os Domini loquutum esse*]. . . . We owe to
the Scripture the same reverence which we owe to God,
because it has proceeded from Him alone, and has nothing
of man mixed with it [*nec quicquam humani habet admix-
tum*].

The full authority which they [the scriptures] obtain with the faithful proceeds from no other consideration than that they are persuaded that they proceeded from heaven, as if God had been heard giving utterance to them.[33]

Clear signs that God is its speaker [*manifesta signa loquentis Dei*] are seen in Scripture, from which it is plain that its teaching [*doctrinam*] is heavenly.[34]

Being enlightened by him [the Holy Spirit] . . . we are made absolutely certain . . . that it [Scripture] has come to us by the ministry of men from God's very mouth [*ab ipsissimo Dei ore ad nos fluxisse*]. [35]

These statements are very emphatic, and their meaning admits of no doubt.

(3) Calvin's frequent references to the Holy Spirit "dictating" Scripture and using the biblical writers as his amanuenses may well sound startling and even uncouth in modern ears. However, his use of the notion turns out on inspection to be both clear and sober. Positively, as Warfield, Kantzer and others have shown,[36] this is a theological metaphor conveying the thought that what is written in Scripture bears the same relation to the mind of God which was its source as a letter written by a good secretary bears to the mind of the man from whom she took it—a relation, that is, of complete correspondence and thus of absolute authenticity. Psychologically, there are no implications whatever of any supression or diminution of the free cooperative functioning of the penmen's minds as the Spirit led them. Peter and Paul express their own thoughts as well as the judgment of the Spirit; tradition, observation and memory entered into the writings of the prophets; David wrote out of his own experience and expressed what was in his heart; each writer wrote in his own style, according to his own personality.[37] Calvin will, indeed, go so far as to say of the expressions of total hopelessness voiced by the author of Psalm 88:

I think he . . . gave utterance to those confused conceptions which arise in the mind of a man under affliction. . . . Nor is it wonderful that a man endued with the Spirit of God was, as it were, so stunned and stupefied when sorrow overmastered him, as to allow unadvised words to escape from his lips.[38]

Calvin's view is that it was this that God wanted to happen, that it was because the psalmist was Spirit filled that it did happen, and that precisely this constituted the dictating process:

for Calvin defines the Spirit's purpose of instruction in this psalm as, not to communicate truth about the after-life (prayers are not revelatory or didactic or definitive of doctrine in the way that sermons and oracles are!), but rather to give universal expression to the desperate feelings which spiritual men actually have in times of distress, and so to furnish "a form of prayer for encouraging all the afflicted who are, as it were, on the brink of despair, to come to [God] himself." [39] Hence, the Spirit included in the inspired product "apparently harsh and improper" expressions which sprang spontaneously from the psalmist's depressed state of mind. [40] But if the process which Calvin calls dictation can include this, then clearly we are wholly in the realm of theological metaphor and not at all in that of mechanistic psychology. [41] About the descriptive psychology of inspiration Calvin has nothing to say, and would doubtless have said, if asked, that this was a mystery beyond our fathoming.

What Calvin is saying about the nature of Scripture by his use of the first three notions—*os Dei, doctrina, and dictation*—can be stated thus: All Scripture has the character of the prophetic oracles, in the sense that all Scripture has a dual authorship. The prophets began their sermons by announcing: "Thus saith the Lord" (literally, "oracle of Jehovah"). This was to say, in effect, that the words which they spoke were to be heard and received as words from God: what came from their mouth was actually coming from God's mouth. So it is, says Calvin, with all Scripture; not only the prophets, and the law, and those other passages where the claim to divine authorship is explicit, but also the psalms and the wisdom writings and the history books of both Testaments and the New Testament epistles, and indeed all sixty-six books of the Bible. All Scripture has the same double aspect: it consists of words of men which are also words of God and so is to be received, every particle of it, as having proceeded from God's very mouth.

(4) And in this we see God's "condescension." God in his great love deigns to talk our language so that we may understand Him. More than that, he stoops to talk our language in an earthy and homespun way, sometimes "with a contemptible meanness of words" (*sub contemptibili verborum humilitate*). [42] His purpose in this is not simply to keep us humble, though that is part of it; his first aim is to help us to understand, and his simple method of speech is thus a gesture of love first and foremost. On the "earthly things" (i.e. Jesus's parable

of a fresh birth) referred to in John 3:12, Calvin comments: "God ... condescends to our immaturity [*se ille ad nostram ruditatem demittit*]. ... When God prattles to us [*balbutit*] in Scripture in a clumsy, homely style [*crasse et plebeio stylo*], let us know that this is done on account of the love he bears us." [43] One sign of love to a child is that one accommodates to the child's language when talking to him, and this, says Calvin, is how God in his love accommodates to our childishness in spiritual things. T. H. L. Parker puts this thought strikingly as follows: "Calvin frequently expresses this [accommodation] under the simile of an adult (usually he means a mother) communicating with a child and confining herself to concepts, syntax, and vocabulary that he can understand. With a very small child this becomes baby-talk hardly recognisable as the same language that the mother normally speaks. Now Calvin obviously assumes that by means of this to an adult barely comprehensible language the mother genuinely expresses her meaning to the child, and the child genuinely comprehends that meaning. So God 'prattles' or 'babbles' with man in the Scriptures." [44] Thus genuine human weaknesses and limitations exhibited sometimes almost paraded—in the biblical text should be seen as also, and equally, signs of how "undignified" God is ready to become in order to teach us and bring his love home to us effectively. The earthly life and death of the Son of God is, of course, a further and supreme sign of the same thing.

INERRANCY?

At this point a closer look may be taken at the places where Calvin seems at first sight to be detecting biblical errors. The issue that arises, both in interpreting Calvin and in modern Protestant debate about the Bible, is: Does the Bible's divine origin entail its total truth? or does God's "babbling," his self-humbling in revelation, extend to the point where the words which he uses, or sanctions, put forward as true at least some statements of detail which are not true? Many moderns affirm that it does and have fathered their view on to Calvin, as we saw; but the evidence shows that Calvin's real view was the opposite. The attribution to him of a willingness to admit error in Scripture rests on a superficial mis-reading of what he actually says. The handful of passages in his commentaries which have on occasion been taken as affirming or implying that he thought particular biblical writers had gone astray prove on inspection to fall into the following categories.[45]

(1) Some are reminders of points where God has accommodated Himself to rough-and-ready forms of human speech, and tell us only that in such cases God is evidently not concerned to speak with a kind or degree of accuracy which goes beyond what these forms of speech would naturally convey. Thus, for instance, Calvin warns us that we must not expect to learn natural science (he specifies astronomy) from Genesis I, which is written in popular phenomenal language.

(2) Others say only that particular texts show signs of having been altered in the course of transmission. Thus, for instance, Calvin tells us that "by mistake" Jeremiah's name has somehow "crept in" (*obrepserit*, his regular word for unauthentic textual intrusions) in Matthew 27:9. There is a similar comment on "Abraham" and the seventy-five souls in Acts 7:14-16.

(3) Others deal with cases where apostolic writers quote Old Testament texts loosely; Calvin's point in this group of comments is invariable that the apostles quote paraphrastically precisely in order to bring out the true sense and application—a contention strikingly supported by the modern discovery that this was standard practice among the rabbis at that time.

(4) Others deal with a few points of what we might call formal inaccuracy by suggesting that in these cases no assertion was intended, and therefore no error can fairly be said to have been made. The inference is clearly unexceptionable if the premise can be established for where no assertion is intended the question of falsehood and error cannot arise. An example of this class of statements is Calvin's denial that the evangelists meant at every point to write narratives which were chronologically ordered, leading to the claim that since they did not intend to connect everything chronologically, but on occasion preferred to follow a topical or theological principle of arrangement, therefore they cannot be held to contradict each other when they narrate the same events in a different sequence. Another example (which Professor John Murray, perhaps rightly, thinks unhappy and "ill-advised," but which clearly comes in this category) is Calvin's suggestion that in Acts 7:14 (the seventy-five souls) and Hebrews 11:21 (Jacob's staff) the writer may have chosen to echo the Septuagint's mistranslation of the Hebrew of Genesis rather than correct it, lest he disconcert his readers or distract them from the point he was making, which was not affected by the mistranslation one way or the other. In these cases, Calvin implies, alluding to the incidents in the familiar words of the Greek Bible would not involve asserting either that the Septuagint translation was correct

or that it expressed the true facts at the point where it parted company from the Hebrew. On neither of these issues would the New Testament writer be himself asserting anything, and consequently his formal inaccuracy in echoing the substantial inaccuracy of the Septuagint would not amount to error (false assertion) on his part. Whether this line of explanation be accepted or not, it is clear that, so far from admitting that biblical authors fell into error, Calvin's concern in his treatment of all these passages is to show that they did no such thing: and this is what matters for us at present.

Rupert Davies concludes his survey of the passages in question by saying that the most they can possibly prove is that Homer may have nodded—in other words, that in the course of thirty years of theological writing so prolific as to fill fifty-nine large volumes of the *Corpus Reformatorum* Calvin may on three or four occasions have broached a suggestion about a text which did not fit his doctrine of Scripture quite as well as he thought it did. "The instances quoted by Doumergue," writes Davies, "are but drops in a bucket of unquestioning reverence for the words of Holy Scripture, and indicate at most that he was very occasionally in a long career untrue to one of his most dearly-cherished ideas." [46] This in itself should be enough to dispose of the assumption, made too readily by Doumergue and others, that these few passages are significant for Calvin's view of inspiration; at most, they merely show even Calvin could on occasion fail to be quite consistent with himself. And even this may be thought to concede too much. It might be rash to affirm that Calvin's handling of all four groups of texts which we mentioned was right in every particular, but it is not at all hard to maintain that it does involve not the least inconsistency with his doctrine of inspiration.

THE AUTHORITY OF SCRIPTURE

We turn now from the question of the nature of Scripture to that of its authority, which to Calvin was, as we saw, the central point needing to be argued against both Roman Catholics and Anabaptists. The key chapters on this topic in the *Institutes* are I.vii, I.ix and IV.viii. Their headings indicate at once the thrust of Calvin's argument, for they read as follows: "By what witness Scripture must be confirmed, namely, that of the Spirit, so that its authority may be established as certain: and that it is a wicked falsehood, that its credibility depends on the judgment of the Church" (I.vii); "Fanatics, abandoning Scripture and flying over to revelation, cast down all the principles of godliness" (I.ix); "The power of the Church with respect to articles of faith; and how in the Papacy, by unbridled license, the Church has been led to corrupt all purity of doctrine" (IV.viii). The position Calvin takes may be summarized under five heads.

(1) The claim of Scripture to be believed and obeyed does not derive from the say-so of the church. When Augustine declares that had he not been moved by the authority of the church, he would not have believed, what he means is that the spectacle of the church's faith prepared his mind to receive Christian truth on its own terms. Rome's claim that the proper object of faith is her teaching, as such, and that canonical Scripture is to be received on her authority, is no less presumptuous than the parallel claim that canonical Scripture must be interpreted according to Roman tradition. There is no basis whatever on which such claims can be made.

(2) The authority of Scripture does not rest on any judgment passed by the inquiring intellect. Rational arguments drawn from the remarkable qualities of Scripture—its majesty, consistency, antiquity, preservation, and so forth—can perform a real service in preparing us to acknowledge its inspiration and authority, and by showing such acknowledgement, which is an act of faith, to be eminently reasonable. But the true ground on which the authority of the Bible rests, Calvin maintains, is its divine authorship, the fact that it came from the mouth of the Lord. Its claim to rule our minds and lives is absolute, just because it is the Word of God. This is the precise point argued in *Institutes* I.viii: "So far as human reason goes, sufficiently firm proofs are at hand to establish the credibility of Scripture." Calvin spends this chapter exhibiting in relation to Scripture, a truth which, for the honour of God and the furtherance of faith in man, he illustrates in many contexts: namely, that faith accords with reason, while unbelief is utterly unreasonable and absurd, for it flies in the face of facts and evidence. This is what his display of "firm proofs" is meant to show. He does not, however, suppose either that he can produce faith in Scripture by reasoning, or that the Christian's Spirit-given sense of the Bible's divine authority will necessarily rest on or be given through these or any other "firm proofs" previously known and weighed.[47] Insofar as the believer's sense of God's authority in Scripture (which, as we shall see, is a divine judgment formed by the Spirit in our mind) is linked with any

prior human judgment it grows out of pondering the Church's corporate judgment of the Bible rather than any "rational" arguments about its intrinsic qualities. At best, these may clear away rubbish in the mind and so make way for faith, but faith itself, by its very nature, is grounded on something higher than either the "proofs" or the church's corporate witness. The last paragraph of the chapter brings this out clearly:

> There are other reasons, neither few nor weak, for which the dignity and majesty of Scripture may not only be affirmed in godly hearts, but excellently maintained against the wiles of its disparagers; yet these of themselves are not strong enough to provide a firm faith, until our heavenly Father, by revealing his own majesty there [i.e., in Scripture], lifts reverence for Scripture beyond the realm of controversy. Therefore, Scripture will ultimately suffice for a saving knowledge of God only when certainty about it is founded on the inward persuasion of the Holy Spirit. Indeed, these human testimonies which are there to confirm it will not be without value [*inania*] if, as secondary aids to our feebleness, they follow along with that chief and highest testimony; but those who wish to prove to unbelievers that the Bible is the Word of God are acting foolishly: for only by faith can this be known.[48]

(3) Scripture is, in the last analysis, self-evidencing and self-authenticating, says Calvin, as divine realities always are: those who have faith recognise its divine character in the immediate, unanalysable way in which one recognises a colour or a taste, by physical sense. About this perception of the divinity of Holy Scripture no more can be said than that it happens, and that inner certainty on the point is the sure sign that it has happened. If we ask: what brings it about? Calvin's answer is: the inner witness of the Holy Spirit. Calvin's conception of the inner witness is not of a particular kind of experience or feeling, as such, but of a work of inward enlightenment whereby, through the medium of external verbal testimony, divine realities come to be recognised and embraced for what they are. Thus, it is through this inward enlightenment that we perceive the truth of the deity and mediation of Jesus, as set forth in the biblical gospel, and receive Him as the Saviour of our souls. And it is through this same inward enlightenment that we recognise the divinity of the Scriptures, as witnessed to by Christ, prophets, psalmists and apostles, and receive them, according to their own self-attestation, as the Word of God to rule our lives. In a well-known sentence from the *Institutes,*

which we quoted in part before, Calvin writes: "Enlightened by Him [the Spirit], we no longer believe that Scripture is from God either on our own judgment or on that of others; but, in a way that surpasses human judgment, we are made absolutely certain, just as if we beheld there the majesty [*numen*] of God Himself, that it has come to us by the ministry of men from God's very mouth." [49] The inner witness of the Spirit opens blind eyes of the heart and gives us spiritual sight, and in consequence we discern and bow to the divine authority—the right to rule, the claim to dominate—which is inherent in and shines out from the Scriptures, as the Word of the speaking God.[50]

Calvin never formally discusses the principle of canonicity, and all that is explicit about it in the *Institutes* is his dismissal of the Roman claim that the historic church must determine our view of the limits of the canon as offering mockery and insult to the Holy Spirit.[51] It is natural to suppose that to his mind the witness of the Spirit was decisive: since the impact on us which through this witness the inspired books make is unique,[52] the very fact that impact will show the church the difference between Spirit-dictated books and all others. But his position is not entirely clear. Calvin treats authorship by an inspired man (prophet or apostle) is a *sine qua non* of canonicity, yet he is able to accept the whole traditional canon while allowing that the authorship of some books is to some extent an open question; so it would seem that the basis of his acceptance is more than a scholar's probability—judgment about literary pedigree.[53] What Calvin does in cases of doubtful authorship is to appeal, not to the church's historic attestation as such (which could not in any case be decisive for him, since the church can be wrong), but to the "marks of divinity" in the subject matter of the attested yet doubtful books, marks discernible through comparison with the contents of undoubted biblical books. Kantzer writes: "In Calvin's understanding of the matter, if a book bears the majesty or marks of divinity, it must then have been produced by inspiration and, therefore, must be accepted as the authoritative Word of God. The two lines of thought are interchangeable. If a book was produced by a chosen prophet of God, it must be reckoned as inspired. On the other hand, if a book bears upon its pages the marks of divinity, it must have been given by God through a prophet. By this latter means Calvin makes his final decision with respect to the canonicity of the Epistle of Second Peter (*sic*)." [54] Yet it is only, on Calvin's view, through the inner witness of the Holy Spirit that "marks of divinity" can be recognised in any book, and so certainly on this matter be reached. The fact that Calvin clearly thinks he has an answer ready should any Roman Catholic say that without the church's guidance neither Calvin nor any other Protestant can know the limits of the canon, must surely mean that he thought the canonical books were self-evidencing in the way described, as is summarily stated in Article IV of the Gallican and Article V of the Belgic Confessions.[55] Yet, when all is said and done, it is odd that, in view of the importance of the question, Calvin should have left us to infer his view from a few incidental remarks, and not anywhere discussed it fully.

(5) The authority of Scripture depends, not only on what it is in itself, but also on God's purpose for it. Calvin's thesis is not only, nor even primarily, that Scripture, being inspired, is fit to be our guide; his main point, overarching all detailed discussions, is that God intends it to be our guide, and so obliges us to use it as a rule of faith and life. God wills that the Scriptures should be the only source and guide for the church's teaching and the Christian's faith because he wants to be his own witness to himself, revealing Christ to his people from the Word and bringing them through him to the life of grace and the grace of life. This is why the Word must be preached faithfully in the church: such preaching is the will of God, the climactic act of worship and obedience, and the supreme means of grace.[56] This, says Calvin, is the true way for God's people, which the Reformed churches have found, and the Roman and Anabaptists fraternities have tragically missed. Neglecting the use which God has authoritatively charged us to make of his authoritative Scripture, they both dishonour him and miss the path of life.

Space does not allow any proper discussion here of Calvin's theological exegesis of Scripture. Suffice it to say that, as he thought of the whole process of revelation in Trinitarian terms—the Son revealing the Father and the Spirit being sent by Father and Son to inspire and authenticate and interpret the written record in order that we might come to the Father through the Son—so he found the whole Bible's end-in-view (*scopus*) in Jesus Christ, the eternal Word of the Father and Mediator of all the revelation that has ever been given;[57] and he broke new ground in expounding both Testaments as a unity of historical testimony to the one Christ. But that takes us beyond Calvin's view of Scripture to his handling of it, and is thus matter for another essay at another time.

The task of this paper was to report rather than assess, and it is no part of our task to assert the inerrancy of Calvin. Yet the power and insight of the Geneva divine, here as in other matters, command the deepest admiration, and we cannot forbear to voice our conviction that no approach to Scripture can be richer or more right-minded than that which Calvin worked out.

NOTES

[1] *Ioannis Calvini opera quae supersunt omnia*, ed. N. W. Baum, E. Cunitz, E. Reuss, P. Lobstein and A. Erichson (Brunswick and Berlin: C. A. Schweiske, 1863-1900). This standard edition of Calvin's writings comprises Vols. 29-87 of the *Corpus Reformatorum* (cited as *CR*). Even these volumes do not exhaust the material available, and twelve further volumes under the title *Supplementa Calviniana*, ed. E. Mulhaupt and others, are currently in process of publication (Neukirchen: Neukirchener Verlag).

[2] Published in 1536; its length—520 pp.—is about the length of the New Testament from the beginning of Matthew to the end of Ephesians (*Calvin: Institutes of the Christian Religion*, ed. J. T. McNeill, trans. F. L. Battles (2 Vols., London and Philadelphia, 1960), p. xxxiv).

[3] In the Preface to the edition of 1539 and all later editions, Calvin wrote: "My intention in this work was so to prepare and train aspirants after sacred theology in reading the Divine Word that they might have an easy access to it and then go on in it without stumbling. For I think I have so embraced the sum of religion in all its parts and arranged it systematically [*ordine*] that if anyone grasps it aright, he will have no difficulty in determining both what he ought especially to seek in Scripture, and to what end [*scopum*] he should refer everything contained in it.... And if I shall hereafter publish any commentaries on Scripture, I shall always condense them and keep them short, for I shall have no need to undertake lengthy discussions on doctrines, and digress into *loci communes*. By this method the godly reader will be spared great trouble and boredom provided he approaches the commentaries forearmed with a knowledge of the present work as a necessary weapon." (Translation based chiefly on T. H. L. Parker, *Calvin's New Testament Commentaries* [London: SCM, 1971], p. 53, a more accurate rendering than is found elsewhere.) Parker, *op. cit.*, chaps. 2 and 3, points up Calvin's importance as the first commentator of the modern type: whereas Bucer and Melanchthon had written commentaries revolving partly or wholly round doctrinal themes (*loci communes*) Calvin put all the doctrinal material into the *Institutes* and then wrote *running* commentaries on the flow of thought in the text.

[4] *Institutes* (ed. J. T. McNeill), II, 1553-92.

[5] Calvin wrote commentaries on every New Testament book except II and III John and Revelation (which he once professed not to understand), and on the Pentateuch, Joshua, Psalms and Isaiah. Translations of these, plus his printed lecture-sermons on the other prophets, fill forty-five volumes of the Calvin Translation Society edition (reprinted by Eerdmans, Grand Rapids, Michigan, in 1948). The stylistic level of the commentaries is very similar to that of the lecture-sermons.

[6] Calvin's New Testament commentaries are currently being retranslated, under the editorship of D. W. and T. F. Torrance (Edinburgh: Oliver and Boyd and St. Andrew's Press, 1959 to date).

[7] *CR* 9, 893b.

[8] Kantzer, "Calvin and the Holy Scriptures," in *Inspiration and Interpretation*, ed. J. F. Walvoord (Grand Rapids, Mich.: Eerdmans, 1957), p. 115. Kantzer's essay, plus A. D. R. Polman, "Calvin on the Interpretation of Scripture," *John Calvin: Contemporary Prophet*, ed. J. T. Hoogstra (Grand Rapids, Mich.: Baker Book House, 1959), pp. 97 ff., and B. B. Warfield, "Calvin's Doctrine of the Knowledge of God," in his *Calvin and Calvinism* (Philadelphia: Presbyterian & Reformed Publishing Co., 1956), pp. 29 ff., have been of special help in preparing the present study.

[9] Text in *Documents of the Continental Reformation*, ed. B. J. Kidd (Oxford: Oxford University Press, pp. 589 ff.

[10] "No exhaustive work which sets forth Calvin's doctrine of Scripture and especially of inspiration has appeared yet either in English speaking lands or on the continent" (Kantzer, *op. cit.*, p. 116, n. 6).

[11] H. Bauke, *Die Probleme der Theologie Calvins* (Leipzig: J. C. Hinrichs, 1922).

[12] Parker, *op. cit.*, p. 56.

[13] Ibid., p. 57. J. K. S. Reid, *The Authority of Scripture* (London: Methuen, 1957), pp. 54ff., lists authorities on both sides. Parker, *loc. cit.*, has a delightful footnote: "An American writer would make me, along with Professors Niesel, Reid, and Wallace, a child of Doumergue. . . . But, awed as I am by Doumergue's historical and antiquarian industry, I cannot think so highly of him as an interpreter of Calvin's theology."

[14] The passages in Calvin to which Briggs appeals in *The Bible, the Church and Reason* (New York: Scribners, n.d.), pp. 24, 219 ff., are faithfully dealt with by John Murray in his work, *Calvin on Scripture and Divine Sovereignty* (Philadelphia: Presbyterian & Reformed Publishing Co., 1960), pp. 12ff.

[15] R. Seeberg, *Lehrbuch der Dogmengeschichte* (Leipzig: J. C. Hinrichs, 1920-1933), IV/2, 613; R. E. Davies, *The Problem of Authority in the Continental Reformers* (London: Epworth, 1946), p. 114.

[16] P. Lobstein, *La connaissance religieuse d'après Calvin* (Paris and Lausanne, 1909), pp. 76ff.; J. Pannier, *Recherches sur la formation intellectuelle de Calvin* (Paris: Librairie Alcon, 1931), p. 85.

[17] This apologetic was designed to build up Christian belief step by step on the assumption of a neutral and uncommitted starting point—an approach going back through Butler and Aquinas to Origen and the Apologists. It does not seem to fit in with Calvin's view of the natural man.

[18] Warfield, *op. cit.*, pp. 74-80. Kantzer *op. cit.*, pp. 126, n. 47, and 132, n. 62, claims that Warfield misses Calvin's point. Calvin is saying that the arguments can do no more than prepare for and confirm faith in Scripture, while the ground of faith is not the argument at all, but Scripture's own divine quality, immediately perceived through the Spirit's witness.

[19] Polman, *op. cit.*, pp. 97, 102. Polman notes (pp. 100f.) how completely Calvin's view of inspiration coincides with Augustine's: "A limited concept of inspiration is foreign to their thought and they both express in most emphatic language the absolute dependence of Bible writers upon the Spirit."

[20] *Inst.* I. i.l.

[21] *Inst.* (Trans. Battles [*op. cit.* in note 2 above]), I, 36, n. 3.

[22] This is a summary of *Inst.* I. i.

[23] *Inst.* I. ii.1. "Godliness" translates *pietas*.

[24] *Inst.* I. v. 9. Kantzer (*op. cit.*, p. 117, n. 7) lists sample adjectives which Calvin applies to true knowledge of God. The list includes "certain," "deeply rooted," "permanent," "pure," and "undistorted."

[25] *Inst.* I. xii. 1.

[26] For the purpose of expository analysis, Calvin devotes Book I of the *Institutes* exclusively to knowledge of God as Creator, and Book II entirely to knowledge of God as Redeemer. He is not however suggesting—and would indeed deny—that it was possible to have either without the other.

[27] *Inst.* I. ii. 1.

[28] *Inst.* I. v. 12. Battles (*op. cit.* [in note 2 above], I, 64f., n. 36) observes that Calvin often uses the labyrinth image "as a symbol of human frustration and confusion."

[29] *Inst.* I. vi. 3.

[30] *Inst.* I. vi. 1.

[31] *Inst.* I. vi. 2.

[32] *Inst.* IV.viii. 8f.; cf. I. vi, 2.

[33] *Inst.* vii. 1.

[34] *Inst.* I. vii. 4.

[35] *Inst.* I. vii. 5

[36] Warfield, *op. cit.*, pp. 62ff; Kantzer, *op. cit.*, pp. 138 ff.

[37] See *ibid.*, p. 139, and references there cited.

[38] *Commentary on the Psalms* (Calvin Translation Society ed.), III, 410.

[39] *Ibid.*, p. 407.

[40] *Ibid.*, p. 410.

[41] Kantzer (*op. cit.*, p. 140, n. 97) observes that the word "dictate" has in Calvin a broad,

metaphorical use. Nature, common sense, experience and one's feelings all "dictate" courses of action. Equally, the Holy Spirit "dictates" by confirming in the heart that the teaching one has heard is from God (*Inst.* IV. vii. 5). Any strong urging or pressure to accept, do or produce something could, it seems, be described as "dictation." Perhaps when the Spirit is said to have dictated the Scriptures, the metaphor carries the thought not only of actual correspondence between the divine intention and what was actually written, but also of the Spirit's sovereignty in bringing this about.

[42] *Inst.* I. viii, 1, referring to the New Testament preaching of the Kingdom. As a literary man, Calvin was conscious of poor style, in the Scriptures as elsewhere, and he accepted the view of his time—and of the Corinthians before him (cf. I Cor. 1, 2)—that unadorned, unrhetorical expression was always poor style.

[43] *Commentary on John, ad loc.*

[44] Parker, *op. cit.*, p. 58. Parker understands God's condescension as the mere fact that he uses human language at all, rather than the homeliness with which he uses it; thus he does not quite do justice to Calvin's point.

[45] For an excellent discussion of these passages, see John Murray *op. cit.*, pp. 11-31.

[46] Davies, *op. cit.*, p. 116.

[47] This is where Warfield's interpretation of the chapter goes astray.

[48] *Inst.* I.viii. 13.

[49] *Inst.* I.vii. 5.

[50] Kantzer correctly analyses the nature of the Spirit's inner witness as "the Spirit's working immediately upon the mind and heart of the elect to form within the human soul and to seal upon it His own Divine judgment as to the truth and authority of Scripture" (*op. cit.*, p. 133). His whole discussion of the Spirit's witness (pp. 127-37), though scholastic in expression, is excellent in substance.

[51] *Inst.* I. vii. 1.

[52] Cf. *Inst.* I. viii, 1 quoted on p. 47.

[53] See Calvin's prefaces to his Commentaries on, e.g., 2 Peter and Hebrews. He classes Hebrews among "apostolic writings," although he is sure Paul did not write it and does not know who did. Calvin's view of the relation between the human authorship and the divine authority of biblical books appears from his comment as to the identity of Mark: who he was "is of little importance to us, provided only we believe that he is a properly qualified and divinely appointed witness who committed nothing to writing but as the Holy Spirit directed him, and guided his pen" (*Harmony of the Gospels* [Calvin Translation Society ed.], I, xxxviii). It is hard to see how the source of such a persuasion can, in the last analysis, be other than the sense of divinity called forth by the contents of the book through the witness of the Holy Spirit.

[54] Kantzer, *op. cit.*, p. 151.

[55] The Gallican Confession, having listed the 66-book canon says: "We recognize these books to be canonical and the very sure rule of our faith, not so much by the common accord and consent of the Church, as by the inward witness and persuasion of the Holy Spirit, who makes us distinguish them from all other ecclesiastical books." Warfield (*op. cit.*, pp. 93ff.) queries whether this was really Calvin's view, pointing out that he never himself affirmed it like this, but these doubts seem implausible. Had Calvin thought the Gallican Confession in error, when it achieved its statement on this point by changing Calvin's own draft, is it credible that he would not have said so? Whether he could have regarded as good drafting the Confession's "not so much," and its omission of all reference to the contents of the books, which gives its statement a very fideistic cast, is of course another question.

[56] *Inst.* IV.viii, and I. ix; cf. Polman *op. cit.*, pp. 103ff.

[57] *Inst.* IV. viii. 5.

5

WARFIELD'S CASE FOR BIBLICAL INERRANCY

John H. Gerstner

A 1970 Brown University dissertation has shown the unity of Princeton Seminary's theology from its founding father, Archibald Alexander, continued in its most famous systematic theologian, Charles Hodge, and climaxed in its most distinguished Reformed scholar, Benjamin Breckenridge Warfield. W. A. Hoffecker in his thesis, "The Relation between the Objective and the Subjective Elements in Christian Religious Experience: a Study in the Systematic and Devotional Writings of Archibald Alexander, Charles Hodge and Benjamin Breckenridge Warfield," [1] discusses both the thought and piety of these men in their backgrounds, their formal writings and their devotional literature. Carefully, fairly and critically considering these three faces of the three men Dr. Hoffecker comes to this general conclusion that although the historical context had changed greatly over the century "yet the Princeton theology remained virtually unchanged." [2]

Among the contributions of these Princetonians, Warfield's major one was clearly the doctrine of the inspiration of the Bible. His was not only the major contributions of the whole "Old Princeton" to that major theme, but it may well be the greatest contribution to the theme ever made by any Christian scholar before or since. As John R. Mackay wrote in a bibliographical article shortly after the death of Warfield in 1921:

Looking over this series of articles, one makes bold to say that not in the whole range of Christian literature will one find the exegetical facts, upon which the doctrine of the plenary Inspiration of the Scriptures rest, brought out so fully and established after so severely scientific a manner as they are brought to light in the foregoing articles on Inspiration by Professor Warfield. I submit that his work on Inspiration on this account marks in this department of theology an epoch.[3]

Notwithstanding, some of his contemporaries and many modern scholars think that Warfield's magnificent effort failed and may even have damaged the cause of true biblical inspiration. In his own life time, C. A. Briggs formidably opposed the Warfield-Princeton doctrine on all points. James Orr, who edited the *International Standard Bible Encyclopedia*, invited Warfield, because of his undoubted ability and knowledge, to write the article on inspiration although the editor himself did not find the position completely satisfying. Warfield's former president, close associate and eulogist Francis Lindey Patton maintained that a certain probability element in the Warfield position precluded the absoluteness of his conclusions.[4] Tom Torrance, writing in 1954 on the occasion of the publication of *The Inspiration and Authority of the Bible*, faults the writer, whose greatness he acknowledges, for a certain scholastic rationalism which Torrance does not really prove.[5] Emil Brunner, as a guest lecturer at Princeton Seminary in 1937, defended his own view of inspiration by appealing to Charles Hodge against Warfield who, Brunner maintained, had driven the historic Princeton doctrine to an extreme in verbal inerrancy.[6] Dr. Cornelius Van Til regards the entire Princeton School's case for inspiration harmed by an underlying doctrine of the autonomy of man derived from Bishop Butler—justifying his own Introduction to Presbyterian and Reformed Publishing Company's new 1948 edition of Warfield's *Works* by his agreement with Warfield's position on the absolute necessity of biblical revelation.[7] The author of the ablest recent doctoral dissertation on Warfield's theory of revelation, J. J. Markarian, after very carefully stating and weighing the Princetonian's case, concludes that it fails of its purpose because "in his zeal to deal with historical criticism he was driven into the extreme position of suspending the truth of the Christian faith upon the ability of the scholar to beat back the attacks against Jesus's historicity."[8] An earlier Yale Ph.D. dissertation on the apologetics of Warfield had come to a similar conclusion.[9]

Dr. Jack Rogers' *Scripture in the Westminster Confession*, while not a major study on Warfield, does take deliberate aim at his interpretation of the Westminster Confession's doctrine of inspiration because Warfield's errant view on inerrancy (as Rogers thinks) has led even modern Princeton (which is normally allergic to Warfield) to sin. In Roger's opinion, Warfield's error is in projecting his own view of biblical inerrancy to the Westminster divines who (with the possible exception of George Gillespie) did not share it.[10]

Probably the most severe modern critic of the Old Princeton doctrine of Scripture is Ernest R. Sandeen, who sees this doctrine as reaching its peak in Warfield. In 1970 he published *The Roots of Fundamentalism: British and American Millenarianism 1800-1930*.[11] Of particular interest to us is chapter five: "Biblical Literalism: Millennialism and The Princeton Theology." Here Sandeen represents nineteenth century Fundamentalism as centering its case for biblical authority on Christian religious experience. When criticisms against inerrancy increased, however, the movement turned to Princeton Seminary for help and especially to Warfield—"probably the most intellectually gifted professor ever to teach on that faculty." [12] Because of the influence and typicality of this critique we will set it forth more fully and critically.

First, Sandeen attempts to drive a wedge between the Westminster Confession of Faith and the Princeton theology, saying that the Confession "insists that only the witness of the Holy Spirit can convince any man that this [the inspiration of the Bible] is so, whereas Hodge prefers to argue that the Scriptures are the Word of God because they are inspired." [13] This reveals, on Sandeen's part, an inability to understand the positions involved. The Confession's statement about the Bible, "Our full persuasion and assurance of the infallible truth, and divine authority thereof, is from the inward work of the Holy Spirit, bearing witness by and with the Word in our hearts," follows a recital of proofs whereby the Bible "doth abundantly evidence itself to be the Word of God." [14] In other words, the proof or evidence that the Bible is the Word of God is one thing; the persuasion of acceptance of this evidence is another. The Confession recognizes the nécessity of evidence prior to persuasion and so states; Hodge recognizes the necessity of evidence prior to persuasion and so states. Sandeen fixes on the persuasion element in the Confession and the evidence element in Hodge and, of course, notes a difference. But let him compare the evidence element in both

and let him compare the persuasion element in both and he
will note an essential agreement. This is the author who
a few pages later accuses Warfield of an "inability to understand
history"!

Having manufactured (unintentionally, we assume) a non-
existent difference between the Confession and Princeton
(Hodge), Sandeen next proceeds to manufacture (unintentionally, we again assume) a non-existent difference between Hodge
and Warfield. On page 119 Sandeen quotes these words from
Hodge: "If the sacred writers assert that they are the organs
of God . . . then, *if we believe their divine mission*, we must
believe what they teach as to the nature of the influence under
which they spoke and wrote" (italics ours). On page 120, Sandeen
writes: "For Charles Hodge's depending upon previously acquired biblical reverence, Benjamin Breckenridge Warfield sub-
stituted the externally verified credibility of the apostles as
teachers of doctrine. . . . Thus he shifted the ground on which
Charles Hodge had established the proof of the doctrine of
inspiration and made Princeton's dependence upon external
authority complete." One does not have to read anything in
Hodge but what Sandeen has quoted to recognize that Sandeen's
"shift of ground" is pure fiction. We underlined the words
in Hodge "if we believe their [the apostles'] divine mission"
because they are quite equivalent to Warfield's "externally
verified credibility of the apostles as teachers of doctrine."
One can see throughout Hodge's many writings that he, no
less than Warfield, accepted the Bible with the noted "reverence" for the same reason that Warfield did, namely, that
they were sanctioned by verified messengers of God.

Sandeen is not yet finished: he must manufacture (unintentionally, we still assume) a difference between Princeton's
founder Archibald Alexander and both Hodge and Warfield.
How? He quotes Alexander: "In the narration of well-known
facts, the writer [of Scripture] did not need a continual
suggestion of every idea but only to be so superintended as
to be preserved from error." [5] This is taken to mean that
Alexander did not hold verbal inspiration (while, in fact, Sandeen's interpretation shows that Sandeen does not understand
verbal inspiration). Practically equivalent statements can be
found in all verbal inspirationists, as, for example, in Warfield
himself:

> This mode of revelation differs from prophecy, properly
> so called, precisely by the employment in it, as is not
> done in prophecy, of the total personality of the organ

of revelation, as a factor. It has been common to speak of the mode of the Spirit's action in this form of revelation, therefore, as an assistance, a superintending, a direction, a control, the meaning being that the affect aimed at—the discovery and enunciation of Divine truth—is attained through the action of the human powers—historical research, logical reasoning, ethical thought, religious aspiration—acting not by themselves, however, but under the prevailing assistance, superintendency, direction, control of the Divine Spirit.[16]

The second Princetonian position identified by Sandeen is inerrancy, which he claims to have been an innovation—though he offers no proof of it. In this context our author charges that Princeton, by championing inerrancy, "in a sense seemed to risk the *whole Christian faith* upon one proved error." [17] This is so dreadful a misrepresentation that while one is wondering how anyone who knows anything about the Princeton theologians could write it, Sandeen immediately goes on to mention that Warfield most certainly did distinguish between the Christian religion and the inerrancy of the Bible; but then Sandeen has the audacity to call that a "compromise" by which Warfield was able to have his cake and eat it too. That Sandeen really meant this slanderous and utterly unsubstantiated remark is seen in the still more slanderous statement about the whole school several pages later (p. 130): they manifested a "continuing tendency to treat every opponent of the Princeton theology as an atheist or non-Christian."

The third alleged distinctive of the Princeton theology—and the especial responsibility, according to Sandeen, of A. A. Hodge and Warfield—was appeal to the autographa. To this point we will return later.

So we see that though it is generally recognized by all that Warfield is one of the greatest champions of biblical inspiration; at the same time many (if not most) modern scholars seem to think that his effort in this regard was one of the greatest of failures. To put it in other words, the absolute errancy in Warfield is seen in his doctrine of the inerrancy of Scripture. Warfield would like that juxtaposition and would readily admit that if the Bible is not totally inerrant his greatest work is virtually totally errant. And to those who, like Kuyper and Van Til, agree that his doctrine of inerrancy is true but his method of proving it is not, he would say the reverse: Kuyper and Van Til's doctrine is true but their method of proving it is not.

So as we now consider Warfield's case for inerrancy the reader is invited to judge whether the doctrine of inerrancy is or is not true and whether Warfield's case for it is or is not true. This paper is not entitled "Warfield's Doctrine of Inerrancy" but "Warfield's Case for Inerrancy." It will include the doctrine, of course, but will deal with more than the doctrine itself. Were we handling only the doctrine itself we would begin and end with Warfield's exposition of the relevant passages of the Bible from which alone he derives his doctrine of inerrancy. But because we are attempting to state Warfield's case for inerrancy we must begin back of the Bible itself. In fact, we must start at the starting point of Warfield's own thought about thought. Here we will briefly consider four points: (1) sense experience, (2) understanding, (3) will, and (4) reason. Having considered Warfield's epistemology, we then proceed to the object of knowledge, which for Warfield is revelation. So we shall take up natural revelation in three topics: (1) the natural sense of God, (2) the theistic proofs, and (3) tradition. Finally, we shall turn to our third and major topic—a supernatural revelation. Under this head we deal with (1) supernatural revelation *to* men (revelation proper); (2) supernatural revelation *through* men (inspiration); and (3) supernatural revelation *from* men (transmission and interpretation).

I. THE STARTING-POINT

1. Sense Experience

Although a theologian and not a philosopher, Warfield did not write much about sense experience—and yet it seems to be his epistemological starting point. Kraus notes that Warfield begins with first principles (including reliance on sense perception *à la* Reid) and criticizes him accordingly. Warfield, according to Kraus, having made this presupposition "proceeded to pile up evidence which was calculated to force mental assent apart from voluntary response as though first principles could, after all, be proven." But Warfield did think they could be proven because one could not think without them. His approach may or may not be correct but it cannot truly said to be internally inconsistent.

2. The Understanding

While sense experience may be the starting point, that does not imply for Warfield that there is nothing in the mind before sense data stamp their story. He would probably have answered John Locke as Wilhelm Leibniz did: "There is nothing in the mind before sense experience except the mind itself"—though with a somewhat different implication. Warfield seems to have been in the orthodox Old Princeton philosophic tradition of Scottish Realism, according to which there are the "intuitions" of the mind which are not, as Norman Kraus supposed, "innate ideas."

In Warfield's study of Augustine's theory of knowledge he appears to be setting forth his own. For example, he interprets Augustine as a rationalist in the sense that "the reason acting under laws of its own supplies the forms of thought without which no knowledge can be obtained; whether by sensation or experience." [18] Even in relation to faith, reason takes a priority of order. "It was fully recognized by Augustine—as by Sir William Hamilton—that an activity of reason underlies all 'faith.' " [19]

It is clear that Warfield belongs to the Scottish Realistic philosophical approach of Old Princeton and not to the Dutch presuppositionalism of his great and much-admired contemporary, Abraham Kuyper. When Warfield in 1898 wrote the introduction to the English translation of Kuyper's most noted work, *The Encyclopedia of Theology*, he seemed only vaguely aware of the ominous apologetical difference. He expressed his great appreciation of Kuyper without criticism, though noting that the *Encyclopedia*

> is marked above all, however, by the frankness with which it is based on the principles of the Reformed The-ology—with which it takes its starting point 'from what Calvin called the *Semen Religionis*, or the *Sensus Divini-tatis in ipsis medullis et visceribus hominis infixus*,' so as to grant at once that it must seem as foolishness to him who chooses a different point of departure; and with which also it builds up its structure on the assump-tion of the truth of its Reformed presuppositions, and allows at once that it separates itself so much from the point of view of all other systems.[20]

Although the volume contains a detailed and devastating critique of Hodge's Old Princeton approach, Warfield did not see fit to comment, unless the above statement expresses a muffled, implicit misgiving.

By 1903 when Warfield wrote the "Introductory Note" to F. R. Beattie's *Apologetics*[21] he expressed far greater concern. Still regarding Kuyper as "one of the really great theologians of our time," Warfield now greatly laments his depreciation of apologetics. Kuyper taught that there is a sense of deity in every man which impels him to seek God, and that the new birth opens man to the reception of God's revelation of Himself in Scripture and to its exposition. But before that, says Warfield, we must assure ourselves that there is knowledge of God in Scripture; and before *that* that there is knowledge of God in the world; and before *that* that this knowledge is open to men; and before *that* that there is a God to know. Apologetics is, therefore, the first and not the last theological discipline. To be sure, a Christian must stand *in* Scripture but first he must *have* Scripture. God gives faith, indeed; but that faith is a conviction grounded in reason. The "prepared heart" alone will respond to the reasons but there must be reasons to which it can respond. Warfield cites the Reformed formula *argumentum propter quod credo* (reason because of which I believe). Christianity, he insists, is uniquely "the apologetic religion." "Sin has not destroyed or altered in its essential nature any one of man's faculties although . . . it has affected the operation of them all."

3. The Will

Warfield on the will seems to have been strongly influenced by Jonathan Edwards, as was his own mentor, Charles Hodge. Writing a most penetrating article on "Edwards: The New England Theology" for Hastings' *Encyclopedia of Religion and Ethics*, he remarks that "Edwards stands out as the one figure of real greatness in the intellectual life of colonial America." [22] "His analytical subtlety has probably never been surpassed." [23] So far from supposing that Edwards' theology led to the breakdown of New England theology, Warfield believed that it delayed that collapse more than a hundred years.[23]

The will follows the understanding. This is especially clear in the matter of faith. The religious pattern of choice follows the same natural pattern. In "rational religion" conviction passes into confidence. Faith is the will acting on religious evidence; true faith is the renewed will acting on true, or Biblical, evidence. Faith is not arbitrary but is determined by reason.[25] Faith and fact normally coincide. "Christianity," Warfield writes, "has thus from the beginning ever come to men as the rational religion making its appeal primarily to the intellect." [26] In his essay entitled "Apologetics," he spells out the primacy of intellect: "It seems to be forgotten that though faith be a moral act and the gift of God, it is yet formally conviction passing into confidence; and that all forms of conviction must rest on evidence as their ground; and it is not faith but reason which investigates the nature and validity of this ground." [27] In like manner he had defended Augustine from the charge of fideism by citing this statement—obviously with his own imprimature—from the Bishop of Hippo: "If . . . it is rational that, with respect to some great concerns which we find ourselves unable to comprehend, faith should precede reason, there can be no question but that the amount of reason which leads us to accord faith, whatever that amount may be, is itself anterior to faith." [28]

Precisely because of this primacy of reason to faith, Scripture must first be authenticated to provide a rational basis for its acceptance. This sentiment is expressed throughout Warfield's works, but it is the special point of his "Introductory Note" to Beattie's *Apologetics* to argue that a person "must first have the Scriptures authenticated to him as such, before he can take his starting point in them."

It is interesting that by 1919 Warfield had seen presuppositionalism, even in the Calvinists he so greatly admired, as a great threat to a reasonable approach to Christian faith. It is also interesting that the seminary (Westminster) which was founded to perpetuate the Calvinism Warfield held so dear has generally advocated the presuppositionalism he so much feared. We shall later note this in Dr. Van Til but here it is well to remember that not only Westminster, but most of those who lean heavily on him for their inerrancy doctrine, have deviated from Warfield's "case for inerrancy." For example, Klaas Runia, in his *Karl Barth's Doctrine of Holy Scripture*,[29] manifestly prefers Warfield's doctrine of Scripture to Barth's but equally favors Barth's epistemological approach to Scripture to Warfield's. He acknowledges the circular reasoning involved but seems to glory in it. Markarian, too, thinks that Warfield saw the fideistic point in soteriology but missed it in apologetics.[30] This same root error is supposed to have blinded Warfield to what Doumergue and Dowey saw, namely, that John Calvin did not wait to prove the Bible before he trusted it.[31]

Before we leave this Warfieldean starting point we must inquire about his view of the "noetic influence of sin," i.e., the question of reason apart from regeneration. Clearly he held to the Calvinistic doctrine of total depravity.[32] He does not extensively articulate its effect on the understanding because, apparently, he had to stress in his day (as Calvin did not in his) what the mind *could* see rather than what it could *not* see. But he notes that the will responds to what "the mind takes for evidence," [33] not to the evidence per se. If we look again at the citation above that analyzed faith rests on "conviction" and conviction "on evidence" (the "nature and validity" of which reason investigated), we note that "nature and validity" do not necessarily include power or what Edwards called "strength of the motive." For Warfield, this factor *may* have been beyond mere cognition, as it was in Edwards. Here sin's discoloration may have been at work. Certainly in his indictment of Pelagianism Warfield insists that the disease of sin has penetrated the will itself and men "cannot" love and do good. Therefore, the question the Pelagians cannot answer is: Who will make the "dry bones" live? [39] Still, corrupted or not, the reason must and can investigate the "nature and validity" of the "ground."

It should be noted here, though it will be more adequately discussed later, that Warfield of course recognized and emphasized the truth that the Holy Spirit must make the evidence appealing: "The supernatural redemption itself would remain a mere name outside of us and beyond our reach were it not realized in the subjective life by an equally supernatural application." [35] But it was "evidence" that the Holy Spirit made appealing. Köstlin, the great Luther scholar of last century, took the rather modern view that Calvin rested his case on the internal testimony of the Holy Spirit and not on the "indicia." Warfield's answer was to quote Calvin, stressing what he thought to be the answer to Köstlin: "These *indicia* will produce no fruit until they can be 'confirmed' by the internal testimony of the Spirit." [36] One can see Warfield's intention here: to show that for Calvin the Holy Spirit only "confirmed" the *indicia* as proofs. He is no doubt right and relevant. Nevertheless, it would be even more to Warfield's purpose to prove from Calvin's chapters that the word "fruit" in this quotation refers to spiritual and not mere rational fruit.

II. NATURAL REVELATION

Having surveyed Warfield's theory of the instruments of knowledge, we turn now to the content of that knowledge. First we consider what is revealed to us from the world within and around us.

1. Natural Sense of Deity ("Sensus divinitatis")

In referring to Kuyper's approach we saw that Warfield made a special point of the Dutch Calvinist's reliance on the natural sense of deity. He clearly approved of it. We see from his other writings that he found the same position strongly advocated by John Calvin,[37] and by Augustine as well.

2. The Theistic Proofs

Warfield, who admires Kuyper's belief in the sense of deity in every man, goes beyond him. With Calvin, Warfield embraces the theistic arguments also. After surveying the Reformer's handling of the proofs, Warfield notes in an approving summary that "the proofs for the existence of God on which we perceive Calvin thus to rely has been traditional in the Church from the first age."[38] Nevertheless, Warfield admits, "in richness as well as fulness of presentation he [Calvin] is surpassed here by Zwingli, and it is to Melanchthon that we shall have to go to find among the Reformers a formal enumeration of the proofs for the divine existence."[39]

So, too, in our twentieth century of apologetic Reformers we find the traditional arguments for God. The causal argument seems to underlie every apologetic position Warfield takes, yet he seems never to address himself to the subject directly. So we must present his thinking on this crucial matter obliquely.

Speaking of the origin of all things, Warfield writes: "In creation, therefore, the Christian man is bound to confess a frankly supernatural act—an act above nature, independent of nature, by which nature itself and all its laws were brought into existence."[40] Here he states this as confessional fact, but, judging from his thought in general, he accepts this fact of God as the only adequate explanation of what has come into being. This parallels his approach to special revelation. The entire development of the argument in his "Divine Origin of the Bible" is that human means could not account for—be the adequate cause of—the Bible.[41] This is also the principal motif in *Counterfeit Miracles*: miracles can only come from God for purposes of revelation; therefore, all outside the biblical sphere are necessarily "counterfeit" (he then attempts to confirm that theory by a critique of alleged post-biblical miracles). In the article "Kikuyu, Clerical Veracity and Miracles," Warfield maintained that miracles are not merely above nature or our understanding of it (*supra naturam*) but against nature (*contra naturam*), requiring an adequate cause, the Creator of nature himself.[42] In the well-known statement that supernaturalism is the essence of Christianity, evangelicalism the essence of Protestantism, and particularism the essence of Calvinism,[43] the most basic of these is the first. Supernaturalism is the essence of Christianity because, for Warfield, it is the only possible causal explanation of it.

Again, purpose in the universe can only be explained by divine choice—not by chance. "Type," says Warfield, "will never form the thought of Pure Reason if stirred to eternity." [44] Why so? Because "what chance cannot begin the production of in a moment, chance cannot complete the production of in an eternity." [4] Dice, however often rolled, will never turn up double sevens. He cites even his contemporary biologists as tacitly recognizing this when they begin to talk of "leaps" in nature.

Warfield also uses what is sometimes called the anthropological argument. The image of God, he argues, characterizes man and cannot be erased (Gen. 5:5, 9:6; I Cor. 11:7; Heb. 2:5f.). He further cites evolutionary thinking in favor of man's derivation from one ancestor. The idea of race is outside the Bible's teaching; it stems from human pride, exhibited first at Babel and then in the polygenism of classical Greece, revived at the Renaissance and now well-nigh universal. [46]

So we see Warfield continuing the Old Princeton tradition. And precisely here Dutch Calvinism was parting from the Scottish-American-Princeton Calvinism. Kuyper had attempted thoroughly to refute and repudiate Charles Hodge on this very matter which Warfield had avoided mentioning in his Preface to Kuyper's *Encyclopedia*. Nor did Warfield ever really answer Kuyper. Some, such as Bernard Ramm, appear to think that Warfield was in certain respects crypto-Kuyperian. However, there is no indication that Warfield ever did move in Kuyper's apologetic direction, though their friendship continued and Warfield was responsible for the invitation to Kuyper to deliver the Stone Lectures at Princeton. Incidentally, these famous addresses on *Calvinism* [47] avoid discussion of the apologetic divergence between Princeton and Amsterdam. We recall no important point in the lectures with which Warfield would not have concurred. Significantly, J. Gresham Machen, the "scholarly fundamentalist" considered by C. A. Russell the last in the great line of Hodge and Warfield [48] and the founder of Westminster Theological Seminary, remained—in spite of the Kuyperian Van Til—in the Old Princeton tradition. [49]

3. Tradition

A third source of natural revelation is tradition. Although this has played a significant role in earlier orthodox thinkers such as Richard Baxter, Theophilus Gale and Jonathan Edwards, and in some contemporary scholars, such as the Lutheran Paul Althaus, it received little attention from Warfield. He seems to accept the fact that tradition continued to illumine heathenism: "Edenic revelation must have lingered among the nations but we do not know how long." [50] Gentile nations were affected merely as individuals, with Abimilech and Pharaoh receiving revelation only as it affected Israel, while Melchizedek, Jethro and Balaam are puzzles for Warfield.[51] Acts 14:16 shows that, in general, God did not impart special revelation to the nations at this time. But there is little further development of the point and we have not found a single article by Warfield devoted to this theme exclusively. We are inclined to think that his confidence in the theistic proofs as more universal, more apparent, and more conclusive relegated tradition to a place of "benign neglect."

III. SUPERNATURAL REVELATION

The epoch-making second edition of Karl Barth's *Römerbrief* appeared about the time B. B. Warfield died. With that commentary the way of the "new orthodoxy" swept over the world. Natural theology and natural revelation were buried unceremoniously, and supernatural revelation—"Senkrecht von Oben"—became the new kerygma. Gone were labored arguments and theistic proofs, and before many pages of the *Kirchliche Dogmatik*, Barth had, instead of using apologetics, declared its utter folly. In fact, he insisted that what was philosophical was not Christian and what was Christian was not philosophical. Meanwhile, Warfield slept peacefully in his grave and these words from "The Biblical Idea of Revelation" could well have been inscribed as his apologetic epitaph: "Without general revelation, special revelation would lack that basis in the fundamental knowledge of God as the mighty and wise, righteous and good, maker and ruler, of all things, apart from which the further revelation of the great God's intervention in the world for the salvation of sinners could not be either intelligible, credible or operative." [52] Nowhere was the antithesis between the old and new orthodoxy sharper than in these two positions regarding proof and in these two persons, B. B. Warfield and Karl Barth.

For Warfield, natural revelation was the indispensable foundation for supernatural revelation; for Barth, supernatural revelation was the only foundation (if one can even speak of a foundation) for natural revelation. For Warfield, natural revelation would lead logically to supernatural revelation; for Barth, supernatural revelation would paradoxically posit natural revelation. For Warfield, natural revelation, properly understood and accepted, was a bridge to supernatural revelation; for Barth, supernatural revelation was known only as a leap of faith and natural revelation as a correlation of gratuitous assumption.

1. *Supernatural Revelation to Men (Revelation Proper)*

(1) Supernatural cause (miracle) as evidence of supernatural revelation. Warfield believed, as Francis Bacon did, that miracles were not necessary to prove God; nature did that. Nature, as we have seen, yielded her theistic proof. God revealed himself through the creation and preservation of the universe:

> The heavens are telling the glory of God;
> and the firmament proclaims his handiwork.
> Day to day pours forth speech,
> and night to night declares knowledge. (Ps. 19:1-2)

This was revelation from God-as-God to man-as-man.[53]

But *supernatural* revelation was from God as Judge and Savior to man as sinner.[54] Each of these revelations "is incomplete without the other." [55] For Warfield, God could not address himself to man as a sinner unless he had first identified himself by addressing man as man. Man, knowing his Creator to exist, could well understand God speaking to man the sinner in the role of Judge and Savior.

So miracle, or supernatural causality, is the crux of Warfield's case for special, supernatural, divine revelation. This was not only the Old Princeton position but the Old Christian tradition from the second century apologists to the present.

However, since the eighteenth-century Enlightenment, many theologians—such as Friedrich Schleiermacher—have apologized *for* rather than *with* miracles. Instead of believing that God was especially revealing himself as indicated by the presence of miracles, they have argued for revelation in spite of the alleged miracles. For example, instead of miracles proving the revelation of Chirst, the revelation of Christ was used as the proof of miracles. Revelation was taken on faith and miracles were deduced from that revelation, rather than the miracles serving as facts from which the revelation was inferred.

Consequently, although miracles were no more foundational to Warfield's case for divine revelation than for Alexander's and Hodge's, they received greater emphasis in Warfield. By Warfield's time, miracles were no longer so universally accepted by Christian scholars as they had been in Alexander's and even Hodge's days. As Hoffecker has well said: "Because Warfield could not assume an historical faith he concentrated his effort on arousing it." [56]

Dr. Rogers, in his previously cited work, *Scripture in the Westminster Confession*, maintains that the Westminster divines believed the Bible to point to the person of Christ rather than to proofs. Warfield (and he interpreted the Westminster divines as of the same mind as himself) argued that the Bible offered *proofs of a person*, the divine Christ. Rogers sees Scripture in the Westminster theologians merely as a direct witness to Christ who needs no proof, while Warfield viewed their Scripture citations as proof that the confessional witness to Christ as divine was actually true. Faith rested on this evidence, according to Warfield, while it contained its own evidence, or, rather, needed none, according to Dr. Rogers.

(2) "Counterfeit Miracles." If Warfield was concerned with anything more than miracles it was "counterfeit miracles." These were closer home! In his defense of true miracles and their significance Warfield was opposing the rationalistic ideology of the Enlightenment which had spread everywhere by the turn of the century; his attack on counterfeit miracles was in opposition to the charismatic tendency which was only beginning to take shape then and has reached massive proportions in our time. Although Pentecostalism began in earnest at the turn of the century and has only poured over the banks of Warfield's as well as the other "main-line" denominations in the form of Neo-pentecostalism since 1960, producing a flood of literature in its train, Warfield's *Counterfeit Miracles* remains the ablest critique yet of the fundamental principles at stake.

In Warfield's thinking, counterfeit miracles were of two basic kinds: internal and external.

(2a) Counterfeit internal "miracles." For Warfield, it was a perversion of the internal witness of the Holy Spirit to the Christian heart (precious as it was to him) when that experience was used as proof of the supernatural revelation of Scripture. This it was never intended to be. One must not employ the *testimonium internum Spiritus sancti* as a demonstration when, in fact, it is a confirmation. The internal testimony seals to the heart what external miracles provide for the mind. To make the internal experience a substitute for external miracle at once eliminates the role of the true miracle and changes the nature of the internal experience.

(2b) Counterfeit external "miracles." W. B. Eerdmans Pub-

lishing Co. did a service to mankind by republishing Warfield's
Counterfeit Miracles—but they undid it by the change in title
to *Miracles Yesterday and Today*. People who get their cue
to books by titles alone would be totally misled by the new
title if they did not know Warfield. His original title, admittedly
rather flamboyant for a classical scholar, tells the story. In
Warfield's judgment, the "yesterday" miracles of the biblical
period, and only those of the biblical period, are genuine. All
post-apostolic, "today" miracles are spurious. All non-biblical
"miracles" are "counterfeit miracles." The contents of the
volume make this plain: "The Cessation of the Charismatia;"
Patristic and Mediaeval Marvels"; "Roman Catholic Miracles"; "Irvingite Gifts"; "Faith-Healing"; "Mind-Cure."

Warfield has an interesting comment on miracles in his
previously mentioned article, "Kikuyu, Clerical Veracity and
Miracles." [57] His running critique of Professor Sanday's position shows that Sanday's emphatic statement, *"Miracles did actually happen"* really meant that miracles never did happen!
Why? The Anglican scholar distinguished between miracles
supra naturam (which he accepted) and *contra naturam* (which
he did not), but for Warfield miracles were such precisely because they were contrary to or different from God's usual or
natural way of working. Sanday refused just this definition of
miracles. In his critique Warfield notes that since Sanday had
been a competent critic all his life and his own Gospel criticism
had pertained to the *contra naturam* miraculous working of
Christ, Sanday's rejection of this definition of miracle showed
that his initial assumption against miracles had dominated all
his researches.

2. Supernatural Revelation Through Men (Inspiration)

(1) Reason for inspiration. Warfield now has a supernatural
revelation of God to men. It has been clearly revealed to its
recipients, to whom it has also been miraculously demonstrated
to be from God. But if this revelation is to come not only to
individuals but to mankind in general, it must be *communicated*
through these individuals. Here an obvious danger arises. How
is mankind to know that those who have indeed encountered
God have accurately relayed and interpreted the revelation?
I learned once of a gift some people gave me which was never
relayed to me. Even though it was given, it has never yet reached
me. But even if it reached me by the person who was to deliver
it, how would I know it was the gift which was originally sent?
Only those who sent it could ultimately assure me. Warfield

teaches that the God who gave his revelation to individuals saw to it that they delivered it to mankind by his actually speaking through these individuals himself. This is what Warfield called inspiration, and it is this doctrine to which he has given definitive statement and defense.

(2) The definition of inspiration. Early in his career Warfield defined the doctrine which he devoted much of his life to developing and defending and from which he never departed. Although known as a Princetonian and identified in the distinguished succession of Alexander, Hodge, Vos, Green, Wilson and Machen, Warfield began his career at Western Theological Seminary in 1880. His inaugural address there defined inspiration as the "extraordinary influence (or, passively, the result of it) exerted by the Holy Ghost on the writers of our Sacred Books, by which their words were rendered also the words of God, and therefore, perfectly infallible." Anyone familiar with Warfield knows that reflected in all his work is this classical Christian position that "what Scripture says, God says."

(3) The proof of inspiration. How does Warfield prove the Bible to be inspired as defined? Because (he will attempt to show) the Bible says so. When it is further asked, Do we not have to assume the Bible is inspired if we would believe it when it says it is inspired? Warfield answers: No, we need not and we do not. Rather, we believe the writers of the Bible, because they have been shown, independently of an assumed inspired Bible, to be the accredited messengers of the God who cannot lie or err. The miracles which attested them established their "credit as proposers" (Locke), as has been shown above. God, who cannot lie, would not accredit messengers who, in his name, could and might lie. His accrediting of them is not quite tantamount to his inspiring them because it is conceivable that he could have revealed himself to them and then left them to communicate or not communicate that experience in their own fallible terms. But if he did that, he would never, after accrediting them, have permitted them to say otherwise. And if he did inspire their inscripturation of the message, he would never have allowed them to deny this. So, in brief, Warfield's proof of inspiration is in two *non-circular* stages: first, the Bible teaches its own inspiration, and second, God, having accredited its writers as his messengers independently of an inspired Bible, would never have permitted them to err or lie in so teaching.

This line of reasoning, incidentally, shows us how essential Warfield's whole apologetic case is to his case for inspiration.

Natural revelation and special revelation are woven together in a seamless garment. Or, to change the metaphor to one which Warfield himself used in another connection, a perfect vase would have to be totally free of defect, for one infinitesimal blemish would destroy it as a *perfect* vase.

To show that the Bible does, in fact, teach its own inspiration, Warfield enlists his best exegetical efforts. His texts range all over the Bible, Old Testament and New. He deals with minutiae and general principles. He enters into criticism, to exegesis ant to sermonizing. Without doubt, in the total corpus of Warfieldean literature the majority of it concerns the "inspiration and authority of Scripture."

It may help merely to list the articles in the most recent collection of some of Warfield's writings on his favorite theme[58] to give a clue to the scope of his labors:

> "The Biblical Idea of Revelation"
> "The Church Doctrine of Inspiration"
> "The Biblical Idea of Inspiration"
> "The Real Problem of Inspiration"
> "The Terms 'Scripture' and 'Scriptures'
>   as Employed in the New Testament"
> " 'God-inspired Scripture' "
> " 'It Says': 'Scripture Says': 'God Says' "
> "The Oracles of God"
> "Inspiration and Criticism"

For two reasons (besides space) we need not enter here into a full exposition of Warfield on inspiration. First, many have already written on this subject. To mention a few: There is the important older article by T. M. Lindsay, "The Doctrine of Scripture in the Reformers and the Princeton School." [59] F. L. Patton's oration following the death of Warfield is significant.[60] W. M. Counts produced an important Master's Thesis in 1959 at the Dallas Theological Seminary on Warfield's doctrine of inspiration. In 1961, C. N. Kraus did a formidable doctoral dissertation at Duke on "The Principle of Authority in the Theology of B. B. Warfield, W. A. Brown, and G. B. Smith." Trites wrote a useful Th.M. thesis at Princeton on "B. B. Warfield's View of the Authority of Scripture" (1962). W. Behannon's Th.D. dissertation dealt with "Benjamin B. Warfield's Concept of Religious Authority." [61] Livingston's Yale thesis, to which we have referred, bears on Warfield's view of inspiration, though its concentration is on his apologetic. Daniel Fuller's article, "Benjamin Breckenridge Warfield's View of Faith and History," [62] is important, and his recent joint article with Clark Pinnock ("On Revelation and Biblical Authority") [63] debates the issues. We have already mentioned Rogers' fine critical comments on the Warfield doctrine. Probably the best extensive—though essentially critical—study is the work of J. J. Markarian, "The Calvinistic Concept of the Biblical Revelation in the Theology of Benjamin Breckenridge Warfield." [64]

Secondly, and more to the point, it is not essential to our purpose to present a full exposition of Warfield's doctrine of inspiration. We are trying to set forth his *case* for inspiration and this is much more comprehensive than his *doctrine* of inspiration. Hence we need consider his doctrine of inspiration only sufficiently to explain it clearly and see its place in his "case."

There were, in Warfield's opinion, three major biblical texts on inspiration and to these he gave special attention. [65] They are: John 10:35, II Tim. 3:16, and II Peter 1:20-21, the greatest being II Tim. 3:16. His treatment of that single *locus classicus* gives us his perspective. He insists that the crucial word "theopneustia" in II Tim. 3:16 does not mean "*in*spired of God." The Greek term, he says, refers not to in-spiring, but only to "spiring" or spiration. God breathed out the Scriptures and they are the outflowing of his power. "Scriptures are," Warfield concludes, "a divine product, without any indication of how God has operated in producing them." [66]

(4) The method of inspiration. Warfield had relatively little to say about the method of inspiration as he believed the Bible itself had very little to say on the subject. The great theopneustic passage, as he interpreted it, revealed only the THAT of inspiration, not the HOW. According to our exegete, the same is true of most other biblical passages relevant to this theme.

However, Warfield found some intimations in the Bible of its method of inspiration. There is the great Petrine statement (II Peter 1:20, 21): "No prophecy ever came by impulse of man, but men moved by the Holy Spirit spoke from God." The crucial verb here is $\varphi\epsilon\rho\acute{\epsilon}\omega$, "move or bear along." Admittedly, the writers are described as passive in one sense, but at the same time Warfield insists that "reception itself is a kind of activity." The point, he reminds us, is that there is "no ground for imagining that God is unable to frame his own message in the language of the organs of his revelation without its thereby ceasing to be, because expressed in a fashion natural to these organs, therefore purely His message." [67] *Concursus* is Warfield's view: he sees Scripture in a true sense human but still divine.[68] The main idea which seems most to have impressed Warfield was, whatever the method of inspiration, it assured as end product the pure and unalloyed, infallible and authoritative Word of God.

In his zeal for the divine purity of the sacred text, Warfield at times overstated himself—and even overstated John Calvin. He rightly maintained that Calvin never meant to teach "dictation" but only "that the result of inspiration is as if it were by dictation"; but then Warfield adds, "free from all human admixture." [69] Both Calvin and Warfield denied any *sinful* or *errant* admixture but neither really went so far as to deny "all *human* admixture." The whole "concursus" concept is against such a notion. One can only remark that while talking about inerrancy, Warfield on this occasion spoke errantly! By this slip he seems to give some substance to the oft-heard charge that the orthodox doctrine of inspiration is docetic. This is most unfortunate, for Warfield did not mean that; and, as we have seen above, he labors the point that docetism and mechanical inspiration are not taught by the church either explicitly or implicitly.

(5) The extent of inspiration. For Warfield, the extent of inspiration was the canon, the whole canon and nothing but the canon. We have noted that in his view the end result of inspiration is that "what the Bible says, God says." The crucial question then becomes, What is the Bible? or—more specifically—What is the extent of the Bible? i.e., What is the canon?

Among his many writings on the canon and aspects of it are:

> "Lectures and Abstracts on the New Testament Text, Language and Canon" (unpublished MS, 1878)
> *Syllabus on the Canon of the New Testament in the Second Century* (Pittsburgh, 1881)
> "The Canonicity of Second Peter," *Southern Presbyterian Review* (1882)
> "The Christian Canon," *The Philadelphian* (June, 1887)
> *The Formation of the Canon of the New Testament* (Philadelphia: American Sunday School Union, 1892)

In all these studies, Warfield assumes the individual scholar's ability and responsibility to ascertain the canon. Always the practitioner of the Protestant principle of the right of private judgment, he consciously rejects the viewpoint of the traditionalists. The canon, he insisted, is a collection of inspired books. The statement of a Roman Catholic scholar that he believed the Bible to be the inspired Word of God because his Church told him so and had the Church said that Aesop's *Fables* were inspired he would have believed that, would be no more blasphemous than non-sensical to Warfield.

Warfield faces the traditionalist question in his study of Augustine's famous remark: "I would not have had God as father if I had not had the Church as mother." Warfield first gives an extensive survey of the saying in its original context and the history of its interpretation. He seems to agree, not with Luther (who regarded the statement merely as one of Augustine's errors) but with Calvin (Augustine meant that the Church was the instrument by which he learned of God and not that she was the source of spiritual knowledge, which, rather, came from the Bible).[70]

But if Warfield opposed ecclesiastical authority as the criterion of canon, he was even more opposed to subjectivism. He was understandably cool to the sentiment Coleridge expressed in his well-known adage, "That is inspired which inspires me," and he would equally have rejected Karl Barth's later characterization of inspired Scripture as "das mich findet." In his "Introductory Note" to Beattie's *Apologetics*, Warfield designates rationalism and mysticism as the two great enemies of apologetics. In 1917 he takes up the question of "Mysticism and Christianity."[71] In this essay he shows that mysticism tends to degenerate into rationalism, and even more commonly into pantheism. Mysticism is based on feeling and is necessarily inarticulate. It must use the language that is at hand. We hear of "Christian mysticism," but all true Christianity rests on external authority while all mysticism is purely internal[72] and is therefore the antithesis of Christianity. "The history of mysticism only too clearly shows that he who begins by seeking God within himself may end up by confusing himself with God." As G. K. Chesterton says bluntly: "Jones worships Jones." "Christ" in this view "enters the heart not to produce something new but to arouse what was dormant."[73]

Between the authoritarian Roman claim on the one hand and the mystical or subjectivistic claim on the other, Warfield saw *apostolicity* as the genuine criterion of canon. To be, sure, Christ himself authenticated the Old Testament, but the authentication of the Gospel records about Christ and the rest of the New Testament literature depended squarely on apostolic authorship or sanction. In "The Formation of the Canon of the New Testament,"[74] Warfield carefully distinguishes the gradual recognition of the New Testament canon from the immediately

recognized principle of canonicity. The apostles from the beginning imposed the Old Testament and their own and others'
writings as the law of the church. This was recognized in the
New Testament itself and in the post-apostolic age. "The principle of canonicity was not apostolic authorship," insists Warfield,
"*but imposition by the apostles as 'law.'*" For example, Paul
in 1 Tim. 5:18 imposed a text from the non-apostle Luke. Of
course, there was considerable confusion in the early churches
about the application of this criterion, but Warfield warns that
"we must not mistake the historical evidences of the slow cir-
culation and authentication of these books over the widely-
extended church, for evidence of slownesss of 'canonization'
of the books." [75]

3. Supernatural Revelation from Men
(Transmission and Interpretation)

(1) The transmission of the inspired revelation. Though in
reality we have finished our study of Warfield's case for biblical inerrancy, a rather prevalent contemporary confusion
necessitates two further steps. Even if we grant Warfield's
inerrant Scriptures, some charge, the Scriptures as transmitted
are not the same Scriptures as were inspired. So all is lost
anyway. Even if God has revealed himself and inerrantly inspired his accredited messengers, unless we can say that he
has infallibly transmitted the inerrant Bible down to this moment, Warfield's case for inerrancy is lost because his inerrant
Scriptures are lost.

This criticism of Warfield has often been raised. In his own
time, Charles A. Briggs made the point which was answered
by a joint work of Warfield and A. A. Hodge.[76] In our day,
appeal to autographs is widely censured as a desperate innovation. We heard one scholar recently refer to such an appeal
as "weasel words." Probably the most serious criticism has
come from Ernest R. Sandeen, to whom we referred earlier.

Sandeen has been very critical of the apologetic use of the
autographa, especially Warfield's use of them. Sandeen maintains that appeal to the autographa was surreptitiously slipped
into the apologetic arsenal, having never been explicitly "mentioned by Warfield and [A.A.] Hodge." [77] He interprets this
as a tactical "retreat" or "hedging" "as more errors appeared
and could not be dismissed as flecks in the Parthenon." [78]
But, as a matter of fact, appeal to the autographa is the generally assumed teaching of Reformed orthodoxy. H. Heppe notes

this in his *Reformed Dogmatics* and cites the seventeenth century German Calvinist, Cocceius, as an example: " 'Whence it follows that they [the biblical writers] never deviated from the thing to be written about by infirmity of memory or of λογισμός nor by lack of skill or care in the use of *words*. So that every *word*, as being contained in *letters* which were sacred as signs, should be accepted and held as the word of the H. Spirit, useful and most wisely compounded to meet every exigency of edification *without the slightest danger*.' " [79] Since Reformed theologians in Europe, as well as at Princeton, never contended for the precise infallibility of the transmitted test, they almost always, logically and inevitably—not because of some craven fear of textual critics—defended the inspiration and inerrancy of the autographa only. So Sandeen's censuring of Warfield as a clever innovator gives him too much credit. Appeal to autographa was standard in Reformed orthodoxy. The only reason that it is not conspicuous in Charles Hodge and the earlier Princetonians is that no general attack on inspiration, as in Warfield's day, necessitated their laboring the matter.

True, some Reformed theologians believed that God perfectly preserved the text which he perfectly inspired. According to this theory, the autographa and the transmitted text were identical. Needless to say, this extreme position was a minority report which Warfield never accepted. Rather, he stood with the Reformed consensus and the scholarly world in general in not identifying our present text with the autographa but researching to ascertain how closely it approximated the inspired original. With most textual specialists, he found this approximation so great as to approach identity. "The autographic text of the New Testament is distinctly within reach of criticism in so immensely the greater part of the volume, that we cannot despair of restoring to ourselves and the Church of God, His book, word for word, as He gave it by inspiration to men." [80]

(2) The interpretation of the inspired revelation. Here we offer virtually a postscript to a postscript. How persons interpret the inerrantly inspired Scriptures has no necessary doctrinal relation either to the Scriptures' inspiration or to their inerrancy. But interpretation is the most important matter of all where the individual's own relation or Christian growth is concerned. The Scriptures will do him no good—and will indeed bring judgment upon him—if he unsoundly interprets them ("which the ignorant and unstable twist to their own destruction" [II

Pet. 3:16]. "This is the man to whom I will look," says the Lord: "he that is humble and contrite in spirit, and *trembles at my word*" (Is. 66:2). What one does with Scripture affects him, not Scripture. So, strictly speaking, interpretation is irrelevant to Warfield's case for inerrancy. Nevertheless, some indication of the way one of the greatest defenders of the inerrant Scripture used it must interest anyone concerned either with Scripture or with Warfield. So we proceed to comment briefly, first, on Warfield's hermeneutical method, and, second, on the vital issue of the relation between hermeneutics and regeneration.

(2a) The hermeneutical method. There was nothing unique about the hermeneutics of B. B. Warfield. He simply stood, as scholarship in general must, for the gramatico-historical approach. Those who would follow his steps in interpreting Scripture should go to his *Manuscript Materials of the New Testament.*

These steps Warfield illustrated profusely throughout the corpus of his writings. In his wide assortment of biblical and technical discussions, essays, sermons, and in almost all of his doctrinal discourses ranging from "Predestination" to the "Millennium" and from "Jesus' Alleged Confession of Sin" to "Whether Few are Saved?", Warfield practices what he preaches.

(2b) The relation of hermeneutics to the regenerate heart. In spite of all the charges that Warfield is coldly scientific, utterly objective, completely abstract in his theorizing, and aristocratic and aloof in his personal manner, he emerges as a theologian of the heart. Hoffecker, who has pondered this theme most thoroughly, comes to this studied conclusion: "In Warfield's devotional writings we have found the same themes which we find in Alexander and Hodge." [81] Warfield emphasized heart above head and insisted that ministers' problems did not arise from too much in the head, but too little in the heart.

Warfield believed that unregenerate men could study and even understand the Word of God, for it was open and available to rational human nature. The Dutch Calvinists, Warfield felt, saw too great a difference between the unregenerate and the regenerate. After all, "Christianity has from the beginning ever come to men as the rational religion making its appeal primarily to the intelligence." [82] But though the unregenerate could rationally grasp the doctrines of the Bible, they would not be grasped *by* them unless enlivened by the Holy Spirit. This

truth climaxes Warfield's lecture on "Christian Supernaturalism": "The redemption of Christ is . . . no more central to
the Christian hope than the creative operations of the Holy
Spirit upon the heart: and the supernatural redemption itself
would remain a *mere name outside of us and beyond our reach*,
were it not realized in the subjective life by an equally supernatural application." [83] With fervor Warfield endorses Calvin's
famous insistence on the inseparability of the Word and the
Spirit. The Word could not be *savingly* understood apart from
the Spirit and the Spirit could not be *savingly* experienced
apart from the Word.[84]

Nothing shows Warfield's personal religion more affectingly
than his concern for the spiritual welfare of his students. Stickler
that he was for the highest academic standards, he was also
the author of "Spiritual Culture in the Theological Seminary." [85] If, as some say, the theological seminary is the
place a man is most likely to lose his religion, this would
not have been true of Warfield's Princeton. After all, what
could be a greater testimony to a professor's piety than insisting
that a theological seminary should be a means of grace? [86]

CONCLUSION

Warfield's case for biblical inerrancy has been stated and
tried—and we, unlike Markarian, have not found it wanting.
Not Warfield's case was wanting, but, we fear, Markarian's
understanding of it. Like other uninspired humans, Warfield
erred on occasion, but not at the point of maintaining the inerrancy of Holy Scripture. His parting words to all who would
demonstrate errors in the Bible remain a permanent challenge:

> Let (1) it be proved that each alleged statement occurred
> certainly in the original autographa of the sacred book
> in which it is said to be found. (2) Let it be proved that
> the interpretation which occasions the apparent discrep-
> ancy is the one which the passage was evidently intend-
> ed to bear. It is not sufficient to show a difficulty, which
> may spring out of our defective knowledge of the circum-
> stances. The true meaning must be definitely and certainly
> ascertained, and then shown to be irreconcilable with other
> known truth. (3) Let it be proved that the true sense of
> some part of the original autographa is directly and nec-
> essarily inconsistent with some certainly known fact of his-
> tory, or truth of science, or some other statement of
> Scripture certainly ascertained and interpreted. We be-
> lieve that it can be shown that this has never yet been

successfully done in the case of one single alleged instance of error in the Word of God.[87]

NOTES

[1] Unpublished Ph.D. dissertation, Brown University, 1970.

[2] Page 356.

[3] John R. Mackay, "B. B. Warfield—A Bibliography," *The Expositor*, Eighth Series, XXIV (July, 1922), 37.

[4] Francis Lindey Patton, "Benjamin Breckenridge Warfield," *The Princeton Theological Review* XIX (1921), 369-91. Cf. also C. Norman Kraus, "The Principle of Authority in the Theology of Benjamin Breckenridge Warfield, Wm. Adams Brown, and Gerald Birney Smith" (unpublished Ph.D. dissertation, Duke University, 1961), p. 270.

[5] *Scottish Journal of Theology* VII, No. 1 (March, 1954), 104ff. Torrance writes: "Here we are given an account of inspiration that is eminently sober and scholarly, and which is grounded upon an exposition of the Biblical teaching itself. Thus presented, it is a view which must be reckoned with, and not one to be set aside under an opprobrious label like 'American fundamentalism'—which is only too often done by Liberal reactionaries." After the criticism we mentioned, Torrance concludes that Warfield's work is one "of great scholarship and power which has much that is essential to offer us today."

[6] Cf. below our discussion of Sandeen (who mistakenly made the same point).

[7] Warfield, *The Inspiration and Authority of the Bible*, ed. Samuel G. Craig (Philadelphia: Presbyterian and Reformed Publishing Co., 1948), pp. 3-68.

[8] J. J. Markarian, "The Calvinistic Concept of the Biblical Revelation in the Theology of Benjamin Breckenridge Warfield" (unpublished Ph.D. dissertation, Drew University, 1963), p. 75.

[9] Wm. Livingston, "The Princeton Apologetic as Exemplified by the Work of Benjamin Breckenridge Warfield and J. Gresham Machen: A Study in American Theology, 1880-1930" (unpublished Ph.D. dissertation, Yale University, 1948).

[10] Jack Rogers, *Scripture in the Westminster Confession* (Grand Rapids, Mich.: Eerdmans, 1967), *passim*. Cf. also Rogers' essay, "Van Til and Warfield on Scripture in the Westminster Confession of Faith," in E. R. Gechan (ed.), *Jerusalem and Athens* (Nutley, N. J.: Presbyterian and Reformed Publishing Co. 1971), where Rogers finds Van Til as well as Warfield wrong and the Westminster Confession of Faith correct in teaching that "The Bible offers not proofs, but a person to persuade us" (p. 165).

[11] Ernest R. Sandeen, *The Roots of Fundamentalism* (Chicago: University of Chicago Press, 1970).

[12] *Ibid.*, p. 115.

[13] *Ibid.*, p. 119.

[14] Westminster Confession of Faith, chap. i, line 5.

[15] Quoted in Sandeen, *op. cit.*, pp. 123-24.

[16] Warfield, "The Biblical Ideal of Revelation," in *The Inspiration and Authority of the Bible*, p. 95.

[17] Sandeen, *op. cit.*, p. 126 (italics ours).

[18] Warfield, "Augustine's Doctrine of Knowledge and Authority," in his *Studies in Tertullian and Augustine* (New York: Oxford University Press, 1930), p. 140.

[19] Warfield, "On Faith in its Psychological Aspects," in his *Studies in Theology* (New York: Oxford University Press 1932), p. 325. This sentence ends with the words: "and an act of 'faith,' underlies all knowledge." We omitted it in the text because we think it not germane to that context but include it here for fulness' sake.

[20] Warfield, "Dr. Abraham Kuyper": Introductory note to the English translation of Kuyper's *Encyclopaedie*, 1898 (reprinted by Eerdmans in 1954); also accessible in Meeter's *Selected Shorter Writings of Benjamin Breckenridge Warfield* (Nutley, N. J.: Presbyterian and Reformed Publishing Co., 1972), pp. 453-54.

[21] F. R. Beattie, *Apologetics, or The Rational Vindication of Christianity* (Richmond, Va.: The Presbyterian Committee of Publication, 1903), "Introductory Note" by B. B. Warfield, pp. 19-32.

[22] *Studies in Theology*, p. 515.

[23] *Ibid.*, p. 528.

[24] *Ibid.*, p. 532.

[25] Warfield, "Psychological Aspects of Faith," in *Studies in Theology*, p. 317.

[26] Warfield, "The Right of Systematic Theology," *Presbyterian & Reformed Review*, VII (July, 1896) 456.

[27] Warfield, "Apologetics," in *Studies in Theology*, p. 15.

[28] Augustine, *Epist.* 120, chap. 3, cited by Warfield in *Studies in Tertullian and Augustine*, p. 171.

[29] Grand Rapids, Mich.: Eerdmans, 1962.

[30] Markarian, *op. cit.*, p. 88.

[31] *Ibid.*, pp. 99ff.

[32] Cf. Warfield, "Repentance and Original Sin," *Union Seminary Magazine*, X (February, 1899), 169-74. In "On Faith in its Psychological Aspects," Warfield writes: "Even as sinner man cannot but believe in God. . . . But his consciousness of dependence on God no longer takes the form of glad and loving trust" (*Studies in Theology*, p. 339).

[33] Warfield, "Psychological Aspects of Faith," in his *Studies in Theology*, p. 318.

[34] Warfield, *The Plan of Salvation* (rev. ed.; Grand Rapids, Mich.: Eerdmans, 1942), chap. 2.

[35] Warfield, "Christian Supernaturalism," in his *Studies in Theology*, p. 44.

[36] *Institutes*, I, vii, 4-5, quoted by Warfield in his *Calvin and Calvinism* (New York: Oxford University Press, 1931), pp. 88-89 (cited by Markarian, *op. cit.*, p. 96).

[37] Warfield, *Calvin and Calvinism*, chap. 2.

[38] *Ibid.*, p. 147.

[39] *Ibid.*, pp. 148-49.

[40] Warfield, *Studies in Theology* (New York: Oxford University Press, 1932) p. 35.

[41] Warfield, *Revelation and Inspiration* (New York: Oxford University Press. 1927) pp. 429ff.

[42] *Princeton Theological Review*, XII, No. 4 (October, 1914), 572 f.

[43] Warfield, *Plan of Salvation*, p. 115.

[44] Warfield, "On the Antiquity and Unity of the Human Race," in his *Studies in Theology*, p. 245.

[45] *Ibid.*, p. 247.

[46] *Ibid.*, pp. 250 f. Seely's attack on this essay is, according to Buswell in his essay, "Warfield and Creationist Anthropology," based on attributing positions to Warfield that he did not in fact hold (*Journal of the American Scientific Affiliation*, XVIII, No. 4 [1966], 117-20).

[47] Published by Revell in 1899.

[48] *Journal of Presbyterian History*, Spring 1973, pp. 41ff.

[49] W. D. Livingston, "The Princeton Apologetic as Exemplified by the Work of B. B. Warfield and J. G. Machen: A Study in American Theology, 1880-1930" (unpublished Ph.D. dissertation, Yale University, 1948).

[50] Warfield, "The Biblical Idea of Revelation," in his *Inspiration and Authority of the Bible*, p. 78.

[51] *Ibid.*, pp. 78f.

[52] Warfield, "The Biblical Idea of Revelation," in his *Inspiration and Authority of the Bible*, p. 75.

[53] *Ibid.*, p. 74.

[54] *Ibid.*

[55] *Ibid.*, p. 75.

[56] Hoffecker, *op. cit.*, p. 312.

[57] *Princeton Theological Review* (*op. cit.* in note 42 above), XII, 529ff.

[58] Warfield, *The Inspiration and Authority of the Bible* (*op. cit.* in note 7 above). Note that this collection includes only a small number of the articles he wrote on biblical authority, and some of his essays remain even today in manuscript.

[59] *The Expositor*, 1895.

[60] F. L. Patton, "Benjamin Breckenridge Warfield," *The Princeton Theological Review*, XIX (1921), 369-91.

[61] Unpublished Th.D. dissertation, Southwestern Baptist Theological Seminary, 1963.

[62] *Bulletin of the Evangelical Theological Society*, XI, No. 2 (Spring, 1968), 75-83.

[63] *Journal of the Evangelical Theological Society*, XVI, No. 2 (Spring, 1973), 67ff.

[64] Markarian, *op. cit.* (in note 8 above).

[65] Of course, Warfield surveyed all relevant passages. In this connection, his "Biblical Idea of Revelation" (in *The Inspiration and Authority of the Bible*) is characteristic.

[66] "The Biblical Idea of Inspiration," in *The Inspiration and Authority of the Bible*, p. 133.

[67] Warfield, "The Biblical Idea of Revelation," in *The Inspiration and Authority of the Bible*, p. 93.

[68] *Ibid.*, p. 95. Warfield developed this theme in his essay, "The Divine and Human in the Bible," *The Presbyterian Journal*, May 3, 1894.

[69] *Calvin and Calvinism*, p. 64.

[70] *Studies in Tertullian and Augustine*, pp. 199ff. Warfield paraphrases Augustine's argument thus: "The upshot of it is that if no clear proof of Manichaeus' apostleship is to be found in the Gospel, I shall credit the Catholics rather than you; while if there is such to be found in the Gospel I shall believe neither them nor you. Where then is your demonstration of the apostleship of Manichaeus—that I should believe it? Of course I do not mean that I do not believe the Gospel. I do believe it, and believing it I find no way of believing you. You can point out neither in it nor in any other book faith in which I confess, anything about this absurd apostleship of Manichaeus. But it is certainly evident that your promise to demonstrate to me your tenets signally fails in this case on any supposition" (p. 201). Augustine's teaching everywhere is that the Church is "the vehicle rather than the seat of authority."

[71] *The Biblical Review*, II (1917), 169-91 (reprinted in *Studies in Theology*, pp. 649-66).

[72] *Ibid.*, p. 659.

[73] *Ibid.*, p. 664.

[74] Originally published by the American Sunday School Union in 1892, and reprinted in Warfield's *Inspiration and Authority of the Bible*, pp. 411ff.

[75] *Ibid.*, p. 416.

[76] Cf. L. A. Loetscher, *The Broadening Church* (Philadelphia: University of Pennsylvania Press, 1954), pp. 30-32, 50-56, 61, 68, and *Theology Today*, XII, No. 1 (April 1955), pp. 27f. Cf. my "American Calvinism Until the Twentieth Century," in J. T. Hoogstra (ed.), *American Calvinism* (Grand Rapids, Mich.: Baker Book House, 1957), pp. 38-39.

[77] Sandeen, *op. cit.* (in note 11 above), p. 128.

[78] *Ibid.*, p. 130.

[79] Cocceius, quoted in H. Heppe, *Reformed Dogmatics*, rev. and ed. E. Bizer; trans. G. T. Thomson (London: George Allen and Unwin, 1950), pp. 17-18. (Italics ours, except the last phrase.) Reformed theology generally accepted the inspiration even of the Hebrew vowel points, (incorrectly) believing them to have been part of the original text.

[80] Warfield, *An Introduction to the Textual Criticism of the New Testament* (Toronto: S. R. Briggs, 1887), p. 15.

[81] Hoffecker, *op. cit.*, p. 344.

[82] Warfield, "The Right of Systematic Theology," *Presbyterian and Reformed Review*, VII (July, 1896), p. 456.

[83] Warfield, "Christian Supernaturalism, "in *Studies in Theology*, p. 44 (italics ours).

[84] In his essay on "Apologetics," Warfield puts the matter this way: "Of course mere reasoning cannot make a Christian; but that is because a dead soul cannot respond to evidence. The action of the Holy Spirit in giving faith is not apart from evidence; and in the first instance consists in preparing the soul for the reception of the evidence" (*Studies in Theology*, p. 15).

[85] Address to Princeton Seminary's incoming students on September 20, 1903.

[86] Cf. Warfield, *The Religious Life of Theological Students* (an address delivered at the Autumn Conference at Princeton Theological Seminary, October 4, 1911, and published as a pamphlet at Princeton in 1911).

[87] A. A. Hodge and B. B. Warfield, "Inspiration," p. 242 (cited by Sandeen, *op. cit.*, p. 129).

6

LIMITED INERRANCY: A CRITICAL APPRAISAL AND CONSTRUCTIVE ALTERNATIVE

Clark H. Pinnock

INTRODUCTION

According to the testimony of Jesus, God in an act of gracious condescension has communicated with mankind in human language and given us his written Word which is wholly reliable and true. It is hardly surprising that the church, following her Master, has until recently with only rare exceptions concurred with this Christian doctrine. Although some scholars like Piepkorn have sought to discredit the notion of inerrancy by showing it to be of recent vintage, the crucial fact to notice is that biblical inerrancy has been the common persuasion from the beginning of the church.[1] Even if it could be shown that inerrancy as a technical term were recent, the point would be of only *formal* and *not material* significance, since, whatever term was used, the idea of ascribing error to the Scriptures has always been unthinkable. To take a famous example, Augustine's attitude towards the complete veracity of Scripture is both clear and typical of the Christian viewpoint. When he encountered difficulties in the text of the Bible, he always sought to harmonise and adjust them in accordance with his view of biblical inerrancy. He wrote,

> The evangelists could be guilty of no kind of falsehood, whether it was of the type designed intentionally to deceive or was simply the result of forgetfulness.[2]

143

The complete trustworthiness of the Bible is the historic Christian position.

Despite this fact the term inerrancy has become less and less popular. Some of the reasons given to explain this are not convincing. For example, it is objected that inerrancy is a term which applies better to material in Scripture of a strictly factual nature, and not to such forms as lyric poetry, ethical exhortation, or parable. Even granting the point, there are two things to be said. First, factual matters are crucially important to the Christian faith so that a term which upholds their solidity is needed. Second, the term can be applied analogously to all the literary forms in Scripture to indicate their integrity. Another objection to inerrancy has to do with the dynamism of the Word of God. It is felt that if the Word were fixed once and for all in a document, it would be a lifeless archive, without power to address new situations that arise. Without wandering too far afield we may observe that an archival document, if it be the constitution, for example, has real meaning and significance for the community which it, in a real sense, brought into being. This canon of inerrant Scripture is the definitive expression of God's will for his people, and is for those who believe far from lifeless or irrelevant. Clearly, the current hesitancy over inerrancy does not rest on objections such as these.

It is important that the *real* cause for the defection from belief in the inerrancy of the Bible be recognised. Up until the end of the eighteenth century, it was taken for granted that the biblical statements on whatever subject were reliable and true. We have only to think of the care with which Luther, for example, in his commentary on Genesis considered which rivers they were which flowed out of Eden. Even what appear to be minor details were regarded as true. What accounts for the change of attitude? The new factor we have to recognise is the massive assault on the Christian faith of secular science and negative criticism. The entire biblical framework of history and doctrine has been repudiated by a substantial segment of modern culture, including the theological sector. Theology since then has been a continual attempt to come to terms with this fundamentally new situation. The result in biblical studies is that the Scriptures are now looked at from a completely different perspective. Instead of regarding the Bible as the written Word of God, negative biblical critics begin with the assumption that it is an ordinary human book, and find within it numerous difficulties of every kind, which they are pleased to call errors. The inerrancy of the Bible can not, they feel, survive the scrutiny of critical study. The modern view of the Bible finds it to be "teeming with contradictions, errors and imperfections." [3]

There are *three* basic ways to respond to the allegation that there are errors in the Bible. One could follow Augustine's lead and seek to solve the problems uncovered by critical study, no doubt a painstaking and difficult task. Conservative evangelicals have always felt that this option was the only consistent one a Christian could adopt. It is the position of this paper and will be discussed further in the last section.

At the opposite extreme, theology could simply recognise the loss of biblical inerrancy and hunt around for a way to do theology without relying on the foundation of a reliable Bible. Unfortunately, once biblical inerrancy is surrendered, it is far from clear on what ground Christian truth can be predicated. Very few modern theologians appeal to the Bible as warrant or authorisation for their opinions. At most they tend to appeal to biblical patterns or themes that illuminate the views they are putting forward. The result has been rather plainly a crisis in theological method. [4] Somewhere in between these two options there lies a *via media*, a third possibility.

I. LIMITED INERRANCY

The third way of coping with difficulties in the Bible is to limit inerrancy to a certain stratum or dimension of biblical teaching, or to redefine inerrancy so that it is unaffected by certain types of errors. We should note at the outset that this is quite a conservative position, requiring a modification and not rejection of inerrancy. Only a person of very traditional loyalites would even try to retain the concept of inerrancy at all. This explains why our examples of limited inerrancy occur in Roman Catholic and evangelical Protestant theology from whose strong historic position people are trying to emancipate themselves without appearing to do so.

The tradition of inerrancy in Catholic theology of recent times makes a fascinating study. [5] It is the dramatic story of a shift from the absolute to the limited inerrancy of the Bible. At the Reformation period, Rome declared her confidence in Scripture "as having been dictated either orally by Christ or by the Holy Ghost, and preserved in the Catholic Church in unbroken succession" (Trent, Fourth Session). Later on at the First Vatican Council she reaffirmed this position, insisting that biblical revelation contained no errors and had God for its author (Chapter 2, "Of Revelation"). And in various encyclical letters since then popes have made it unmistakably clear that the inerrancy of the Bible is the position of the Roman Church.[6]

Prior to the twentieth century then there had been only occasional and unofficial divergencies from this strong stand. Erasmus, for example, while commenting on Matthew's gospel, noticed the less than literal way that citations from the Old Testament were given, and suggested that in these unimportant matters the Holy Spirit left the inspired writers to their own devices, including their faulty memories. His liberal approach was followed by some other authors like William Holden who, in a work published in 1652, limited inspiration and inerrancy to the doctrinal matters of Scripture. Anywhere else, he reasoned, no inspiration would be required, and the sacred writers could only rely there on that kind of divine assistance that ordinary Christians can expect. His view was quickly condemned by the Sorbonne, but it did not disappear. It set in motion the effort to limit the extent of inspiration and the scope of inerrancy which would continue to be appealing to certain minds. Even John Henry Newman, in a tract defending biblical inspiration written in 1884, limited inerrancy to what should be considered material to the Bible's purpose. Newman did not think that a sacred writer would be safeguarded from all error when he merely mentioned something in passing or said something quite incidental to his primary purpose. In actual practice, however, Newman did not want to restrict errors only to the *obiter dicta*, because he used his principle to absolve us from believing certain things the biblical writers certainly did want to teach. But these men were not typical of their age or church. They were like voices crying in the wilderness, for during the whole period leading up to Vatican Two the official stand of the Catholic Church was clear and decisive. The only way open to Catholic biblical scholars to deal with biblical problems was *within* the framework of inerrancy. This was done by making full use of the literary forms of the Bible. By recognising the truth of each literary form, it was possible to avoid imputing error even where by modern standards error was involved. By adjusting the freedom from error to the degree of affirmation intended by a biblical text, it was possible to handle many biblical difficulties without seeming to contravene the official tradition of inerrancy.[7]

Vatican Two represents a turning point in the history of

Catholic dogma on this matter. What it said about the nature of Scripture should make us very hesitant in repeating the cliche, "Rome never changes." The original draft scheme on revelation which was offered to the first session of the Council by the theological commission expressed the old view. It stated that Scripture is "absolutely immune from error" and was phrased in the language of the old curial Catholic theology. The Council rejected it outright, not even accepting it as the basis for further discussion. The commission was enlarged and went to work on a fresh statement. After much debate, the fifth draft was finally approved and promulgated by the Council. The crucial sentence reads:

> Therefore, since everything asserted by the inspired authors or sacred writers must be held to be asserted by the Holy Spirit, it follows that the books of Scripture must be acknowledged as teaching firmly, faithfully, and without error that truth which God wanted to put into the sacred writings for the sake of our salvation. (Divine Revelation, 11)

The statement, like so many others at the Council, is a compromise. It is deliberately ambiguous so that the old and the new views of the Bible can alike appeal to it. But Rome had not been ambiguous on this point before; therefore, it should be considered as a victory for the progressives. Now for the first time inerrancy can be predicated of and limited specifically to the truth God willed for the sake of our *salvation*. The Bible is no longer held to be inerrant in all its assertions. It is certain only when it serves as the vehicle of divine salvific intention. In this way the Council effectively repealed the earlier Catholic view of complete inerrancy.[8]

In a seemingly parallel development, evangelical Protestant scholar Daniel P. Fuller has also sought to limit inerrancy to the saving or revelatory content of the Bible. Finding a statement of the Bible's purpose in 2 Timothy 3:15 he maintains that we should proportion inerrancy to this saving intention "to make men wise unto salvation." Inerrancy should only be expected in the case of those biblical assertions 'which teach or rightly imply knowledge that makes men wise unto salvation'. This soteric truth he also refers to as "revelational knowledge."[9] On other matters, not considered soteric, Scripture may and does in fact err. Fuller gives such examples as the chronology of Abraham's life in Stephen's speech, the mustard seed, the time span of Genesis 5, etc. To be fair we must say that Fuller concedes very little, and always upholds Scripture where it counts. We must also admit that Fuller's two brief articles are not much to base a firm opinion on as to his real meaning. In a response to my criticism of his theology at this point he protested that he had been misunderstood. But even the text of his protest contains the same ambiguity. He wants to define the macro-purpose of the Bible in soteric terms, and proportion inerrancy to it.[10]

II. CRITICAL APPRAISAL

In order to be candid and fair, we must admit to limiting inerrancy ourselves, not to a macro-purpose elevated above the text, as in the view just described, but to the intended teaching of each passage of Scripture.[11] For example, we would distinguish between formal and material errors. Figures of speech are good examples of material error. We say the glutton's eyes are bigger than his stomach, the fog was as thick as pea soup, and it was raining cats and dogs. Materially, the falsity of such statements is obvious, and yet we would hardly accuse a person of error who chooses to talk in this way. Obviously his intention has not been to speak literally or precisely, but rather figuratively to convey a vivid impression. Such "errors" do not concern us. It is formal error that disturbs us, the error which really represents a false judgment, and a lack of conformity with reality. It is the intention of the individual author which is the crucial thing.

In another vein, Packer suggests that we distinguish between the *subjects* about which the Bible speaks and the *terms* in which it speaks of them. When the biblical writers wished to speak of their experiences in the natural world, they did so "using such modes of speech about the natural order and human experience as were current in their days, and in a language that was common to themselves and their contemporaries." [12] Had Bultmann kept such a distinction in mind he would not have tried to rest his demythologising proposal so heavily on such expressions as that found in Philippians 2:10. Paul's purpose there is not to teach us the structure of the world, but the relation of all its creatures to their Lord. The question of authorial intentionality is critical, and can be applied to many longstanding biblical problems. It is entirely proper to ask with Carnell what the prupose of the Chronicler was in recording the public genealogies, with Kantzer as to Luke's purpose in recording the historical allusions in Stephen's speech, and with Harrison what kind of speech the term "rib" is in Genesis 3.[13]

Restricting inerrancy to the sense intended by the inspired

writer is not, in our judgment, any basis for speaking of limited inerrancy. It simply respects the meaning which the writer wished to convey rather than some other. The message of the writer is the message of the Bible, and to that, and that alone, inerrancy refers. The position which we are criticising, however, does not correlate inerrancy to the intention of Scripture as each several passage requires. Instead it relates it to a macro-purpose, salvation truth, with which it feels free to limit inerrancy. This we consider to be a precipitous doctrinal move for these reasons.[14]

1. It is certainly true that Scripture has a macro-purpose, designed to lead men to Jesus Christ and to salvation. (2 Tim. 3:15) It is a handbook of salvation. Its overarching purpose is not to teach science or general history, which men can discover on their own, but the facts of salvation which God has revealed for our benefit. As Jesus told the unbelieving Jews of his day, Scripture is not an end in itself, it is a means to the end of finding life in himself (John 5:39-40). He made it plain that his own person and work was the hermeneutical clue to the whole Bible (Luke 24:27, 44). This purpose is carried out by all the Scriptures.

But to convert this valid theological principle into a critical scalpel is to *misuse* it. It was not meant to give us license to limit inerrancy as we please. Jesus and his apostles received *all* Scripture as God's written Word in an attitude of total trust. They accepted not only what we might be pleased to call the primary intent of a passage, but the secondary details as well. They took all the declarative statements of Scripture as reliable and true. It is difficult to avoid the impression when reading Roman Catholic discussions of this matter that the question as to whether the Magisterium teaches inerrancy looms even larger than the more important question whether Jesus taught it. If we take him as our guide, the only proper way to discover divine truth would be, not to sift the biblical teaching according to a somewhat general principle we call the intention to convey saving truth, but to enquire of *each passage* what its inerrant teaching is.

2. We freely grant that it is possible to distinguish soteric from non-soteric truth in the Bible. We all do this whenever we make a judgment as to what constitutes heresy. The denial of Christ, for example, surely cuts one off from salvation in a way that denial of Anti-christ does not. Orthodox theologians have often made the distinction between fundamental and non-fundamental doctrines in this way (e.g., Quenstedt). However,

they did not regard this as giving them a dispensation from accepting the non-fundamental doctrines of the Bible.[15] After all, although some biblical truths are more heavily soteric than others, all of them are still biblical *truths*. This differentiation does not give us the right to consider them errant or irrelevant. In fact, if we do that, we surrender the only sound method of building theology. Since our knowledge of things divine derives from Scripture, the whole structure of theology is ready to collapse as soon as the trustworthiness is given up. If we say, as Vatican II does, that inspiration guarantees only those truths necessary to salvation, the question arises, how much we need to know to be saved. The way is open for someone to come along with the opinion that he need know very little. Very little, then, is inerrantly taught in Scripture.[16]

Surely it is wiser and truer to recognise that the Bible is a seamless garment. We are not to pluck out a thread and discard the cloth. "*All* Scripture is God-breathed." Like Paul, we believe everything laid down by the law or written in the prophets (Acts 24:14). Its truth is all intertwined in a most complex unity. He discredits its authority who limits its reliability. This proposal of limited inerrancy is a misdevelopment in theology which could have serious and tragic consequences. Limited inerrancy is a halfway house on the way to unlimited errancy. It is a position, a slope not a platform. Like the term marriage, inerrancy is absolute and cannot easily be limited without ceasing to be a useful term. We expect those who at present seek to limit inerrancy in the near future to disavow the term altogether, which is precisely what less conservative Christians have done.

III. CONSTRUCTIVE ALTERNATIVE

The Bible is the Word of God in the words of men. It did not drop down out of heaven. It was mediated through authors whose humanity was real and tangible. We should not be offended at that. As C. S. Lewis wrote:

> The same divine humility which decreed that God should become a baby at a peasant woman's breast, and later an arrested field preacher in the hands of the Roman police, decreed also that he should be preached in a vulgar, prosaic, and unliterary language. If you can stomach the one, you can stomach the other.[17]

Scripture comes to us in a form that invites critical questions as to date, text, authorship, meaning, composition, etc. The high view of biblical inerrancy does not obstruct honest criticism or seek to deny that real difficulties exist. It only directs us to handle them in a more Christian, and less perilous manner than the view we have been reviewing.

Undoubtedly the most important single fact to keep in mind when approaching difficulties in Scripture is the attitude of Jesus Christ toward it. No Christian can afford to disregard that fact. The real issue in inspiration is to be kept steadily before us. We do not abandon our Lord's doctrine of Scripture without abandoning *him* as a reliable teacher of doctrine. This is the issue to be courageously faced. There is an enormous weight of evidence on behalf of the high biblical doctrine of inspiration. We cannot go ahead and negatively criticise the Bible as if it did not exist. It is not as if this fact should create in us an indifference or complacency regarding the seriness of the biblical problems, as if we had the right to rid ourselves of them through strained exegesis or artificial harmonising. If a difficulty cannot be solved in a convincing way, let it remain unsolved. The simple point is that the attitude of Jesus and his apostles toward Scripture creates within us a powerful presumption in favour of the reliability of the Bible, a presumption that leads us to regard the difficulties as inconsistent with inerrancy in appearance only. We are driven to believe on the strength of the testimony of our Lord that the inspiration of the Bible is finally consistent with its phenomena.

Not that this presumption has been adopted arbitrarily or for sentimental reasons. For we believe the presumption to be an eminently rational one. As Warfield put it:

> We adopt it specifically because it is taught us as truth by Christ and His apostles, in the scriptural record of their teaching, and the evidence for its truth is, therefore, as we have also already pointed out, precisely that evidence, in weight and amount, which vindicates for us the trustworthiness of Christ and His apostles as teachers of doctrine.[18]

In our approach to biblical difficulties then we do *not* give equal weight to the phenomena and to the doctrine of inspiration, as Beegle does.[19] How could a yet-to-be-solved and usually trivial detail in the narrative possibly count against or rank with our Lord's express teaching? The only possible approach for the Christian must be to begin with the doctrine of his Lord and test it out in relation to the phenomena of Scripture. As Montgomery puts it, Christ's doctrine of inspiration is the *Gestalt* or pattern which gives us the clue how to go about treating the difficulties. He writes:

> To know how to treat biblical passages containing apparent errors or contradictions, we must determine what kind of book the Bible is. . . . And how does one correctly determine the nature and extent of scriptural authority? Not by staring at genealogical difficulties or ancient king-lists as [to use Luther's figure] a cow stares at a new gate, but by going to the Bible's central character, Jesus Christ, who declared himself to be God incarnate by manifold proofs, and observing his approach to Scripture.[20]

Put in this way, it is obvious that the stakes are very high. Nothing less than the authority of Jesus is on the line. We must be very careful indeed, and very sober, when we test out his doctrine in relation of biblical difficulties. Should the facts prove to be inconsistent with the testimony of our Lord, it is well that we know it, and know its clarity, with the full realisation of the consequences.

There is a good deal of wisdom, theological and otherwise, when we consider difficulties secondary to firmly established principles. After all, there are difficulties in the way of believing anything. Philosophers have denied causality and the existence of other selves because neither are visible entities. If we waited until all the difficulties were removed before we believed anything, we would believe nothing. Bavinck put it this way:

> Who wants to wait with his faith in Scripture until all objections are removed and all contradictions reconciled, never comes to faith.[21]

Warfield wrote along the same lines:

> Who doubts that the doctrines of the Trinity and of the Incarnation present difficulties to rational construction? Who doubts that the doctrines of native demerit and total depravity, inability and eternal punishment raise objections in the natural heart? We accept these doctrines and others which ought to be much harder to credit, such as the biblical teaching that God so loved sinful man as to give his only-begotten Son to die for him, not because their acceptance is not attended with difficulties, but because our confidence in the New Testament as a doctrinal guide is so grounded in unassailable and compelling evidence, that we believe its teachings despite the difficulties which they raise. We do not and we cannot wait until all these difficulties are fully explained until we yield to the teaching of the New Testament the fullest confidence of our minds and hearts. How then can it be true that we are to wait until all difficulties are removed before we can accept with confidence the biblical doctrine of inspiration? [22]

Because of our confidence in Jesus Christ, and in light of the doctrine of inspiration which he taught, we accept the high doctrine of the inerrancy of Scripture *before* we are able to adjust all the phenomena of Scripture to it. We walk by faith and not by sight. It would be a strange thing if the doctrine of inerrancy had no difficulties to face. But this fact will no more induce us to disbelieve the doctrine than do the difficulties we face in other areas of Christian truth. Who, for example, declines to believe in the Trinity because he has difficulty explaining it?

A good deal of the problem is cleared up once we learn to distinguish between *difficulties* and *proven errors.* Only the latter are incompatible with biblical inerrancy, and not the former. And when it comes to establishing errors in Scripture we would be wise, not only theologically, but also critically to exercise some caution. A few theses on the subject of biblical difficulties are in order.

1. These difficulties which people place in opposition to the biblical doctrine of inspiration are few of them newly discovered, and many of them enjoy highly probable solutions already. Indeed, one of the difficulties the conservative critic faces in this area is the conspiracy of silence which surrounds these solutions. It is rare indeed to discover the non-evangelical critic taking any cognizance of well-argued alternatives to his own negative conclusions (for example, M. H. Segal on the composition of the Pentateuch). When we take into account the full range of evangelical biblical studies, recently completed, or now in progress, we get the distinct impression that biblical difficulties are a steadily vanishing number.[23] If anything, the climate is becoming more and not less hospitable for biblical inerrancy.

2. All the evidence is not yet in. It is extremely important that the data which it is claimed will overthrow a given conviction be present and available for careful investigation. According to Yamauchi, this is far from being the case. Of the evidence which has survived bearing on the biblical account only a fraction has been surveyed, a fraction of that excavated, a fraction of that examined and published. The significance of this is that it is unfair to dismiss the written records of Scripture on the basis of evidence as yet so fragmentary.[24]

3. There is a class of difficulties so spurious that they can be swept under our feet. They do not lead us to the new view of the Bible, but arise from it. They are concocted by clever but hypercritical minds and hardly merit a painstaking reply.

C. S. Lewis refers to such difficulties in a delightful essay on "Modern Theology and Biblical Criticism." In it Lewis, the literary critic, expressed doubt in the critical judgment of many who consider themselves biblical scholars. Although they spend a good deal of time in the biblical text, he felt they spent too little in literature at large, and thus developed no truly literary taste and no standards of comparison for testing their results. He gives several examples of what he means. In one of them he reviews one of Bultmann's critical exercises in which he carefully carves up the text of Mark 8, finding in it several strata pasted together. Lewis comments:

> Logically, emotionally, imaginatively, the sequence [of Mark 8] is perfect. Only a Bultmann could think otherwise.[25]

As one who has watched reviewers reconstructing the genesis of his own books, Lewis had reason for being skeptical. Not one of the attempts ever was right. We really must insist that biblical criticism be removed from the realm of idle speculation, and conducted only where there is objective evidence for testing the conclusions. There is a way to read the Bible that is fault-finding because it is negative in orientation. There is also a faithful way of reading this book which believes the promises of God and sweeps difficulties such as these under its feet.

4. Finally, we must remember that critics are seriously divided amongst themselves on many of the alleged errors in the Bible. How often a lecturer in religion will state dogmatically that "modern scholarship" has concluded that such and such a position is no longer tenable. In fact there is no such unanimity in biblical studies. Of course there have been scholars to cast doubt on each and and every tenet of the Christian faith. But there have always been, and there are now, other scholars no less competent and learned who support these very positions. How many classes studying the Pentateuch in our ostensibly unaligned departments of religion or liberal theological seminaries are ever told of the complete repudiation of the dominant literary theory by C. H. Gordon, renowned archeologist and Near Eastern scholar? The evangelical student needs to acquaint himself with the full breadth of the debate on such issues so that he will not be pressured into a defeatist posture.[26]

The importance of these various principles is to show that the distinction between difficulties and proven errors is critically, as well as theologically, wise. On both counts it makes sense to follow Augustine's example when he wrote:

If we cannot reconcile such a contradiction [as between a teaching of the Bible and a piece of secular evidence] we are to suspend judgment, not doubting either the Holy Scripture or the results of human observation and reasoning, but believing that it is possible, given sufficient knowledge and understanding, to reconcile the apparent contradiction.[27]

Only such an attitude upholds the integrity of our Lord's teaching authority, and at the same time keeps close to the actual evidence.

Is such a line of defense unfalsifiable in principle? Has it protected itself with such a wall of presumption that no conceivable amount of evidence could ever dislodge it? Certainly not! Many evangelicals are quite prepared to admit the possibility that evidence might turn up which would seriously undermine their confidence in the inerrancy of Scripture. It is the only approach consistent with an attitude open to the evidence. There is nothing shocking about such an admission. If it could be shown that Christ was not raised or that God did not exist, our religion and theology would certainly be in ruins. But admitting a possibility is quite a different thing from expressing an expectation or making a prediction. We would have to say immediately that inerrancy has not yet been falsified, and we do not expect that it ever will. Whatever we may theoretically allow, our knowledge of Jesus Christ and his Word is sufficiently sure as to make this possibility a practical impossibliity. We can go even further and state that the issues being what they are, we would require evidence of a most compelling variety. Nothing less than clear demonstration would be sufficient to demolish a presumption about inerrancy, firmly established as it is on the clear testimony of Jesus Christ. Warfield comments:

If it would be a crime to refuse to consider most carefully and candidly any phenomena of Scripture asserted to be inconsistent with its inerrancy, it would be equally a crime to accept the asserted reality of phenomena of Scripture, which, if real, strike at the trustworthiness of the apostolic witness to doctrine, on any evidence of less than demonstrative weight.[28]

Summing up, it is hard to resist citing Warfield once again:

The question is not, whether the doctrine of plenary inspiration has difficulties to face. The question is, whether these difficulties are greater than the difficulty of believing that the whole church of God from the beginning has been deceived in her estimate of the Scriptures committed to her charge—are greater than the difficulty of believing that the whole college of the apostles, yes and Christ himself at their head, were themselves deceived as to the nature of those Scriptures which they gave the church as its precious possession, and have deceived with them twenty Christian centuries, and are likely to deceive twenty more before our boasted advancing light has corrected their error,—are greater than the difficulty of believing that we have no sure foundation for our faith and no certain warrant for our trust in Christ for salvation. We believe this doctrine of the plenary inspiration of the Scriptures primarily because it is the doctrine which Christ and his apostles believed, and which they have taught us. It may sometimes seem difficult to take our stand frankly by the side of Christ and his apostles. It will always be found safe.[29]

CONCLUSION

We should remind ourselves in closing of the practical importance of the position we have been defending. We are contending that God is true and truthful, that Jesus Christ should be believed in his teaching about Scripture, and that the reader of God's Word will not be deceived or led astray by anything he reads there. These are large issues, far from merely academic. As soon as we limit or modify, as the limited inerrancy position does, the complete trustworthiness of the Bible, we cast doubt on its competence as our supreme norm set theology adrift, and undermine the grounds of the believer's confidence in God's Word.

The doctrine of biblical inerrancy does not belong to that list of soteric Christian teachings we referred to earlier. A person can certainly be saved without believing it. Yet it is by no means irrelevant to the list, since what is proclaimed and believed does ultimately depend upon one's attitude to this Book. Limiting or abandoning inerrancy lands us in theological quicksand and leads in the long run to placing in jeopardy the Christian proclamation. We do not want to exaggerate. The discussion on biblical inerrancy is a family discussion amongst Christians. We freely acknowledged that an enormous amount of valuable biblical study and preaching is being done by those who do not agree with us on this point. Nevertheless we think it right to issue the warning where the denial of inerrancy can easily lead.

When one is under attack, Nicole has observed, it is always

a temptation to shorten the lines of defense and to surrender what may appear to be costly outposts. Such strategies of withdrawal, as the theory of limited inerrancy is, are often advocated with the best of intentions.[30] Obviously some well-meaning Christians have decided to surrender an element of biblical truth, namely, complete inerrancy, in the mistaken belief that it is peripheral and has no vital bearing on essential Christian truth. Whatever the intentions, the effects of this concession are disastrous. The almost inevitable result is further concessions and a weakening of the foundations. We need to voice our concern before the full implications of this theory work themselves out in theology and life.

NOTES

[1] Arthur Carl Piepkorn, "What Does 'Inerrancy' Mean?" *Concordia Theological Monthly* XXXVI (1965), 577-93. Contrast Robert D. Preus, "Notes on the Inerrancy of Scripture," in John Warwick Montgomery (ed.), *Crisis in Lutheran Theology* (2 vols.; 2d ed.; Minneapolis: Bethany Fellowship, 1973), II, 34-47.

[2] *De Consensu Evangelistarum*, II. xii. 29. See also Charles J. Costello, *St. Augustine's Doctrine on the Inspiration and Canonicity of Scripture* (Washington: Catholic University of America, 1930).

[3] *The Pelican Guide to Modern Theology*, III: *Biblical Criticism*, ed. Robert Davidson and A. R. C. Leaney (Harmondsworth, Middlesex: Penguin, 1970), 20.

[4] D. H. Kelsey, "Appeals to Scripture in Theology," *Journal of Religion*, XLVIII (1968), 1-21; G. D. Kaufman, "What Shall We Do With the Bible?" *Interpretation* XXV (1971), 95-112. The rejection of biblical inerrancy has led, in our judgment, to what J. D. Smart calls *The Strange Silence of the Bible in the Church* (Philadelphia: Westminster, 1970).

[5] C. M. Martini, "Inspirazione e verita nella Sacra Scrittura," *Civilta Cattolica* CXX (1969), 241-251; N. H. Cassern, "Inerrancy after Seventy Years: the Transition to Saving Truth," *Science et Esprit* XXII (1970), 189-202; R. E. Murphy and C. J. Peter, "The Role of the Bible in Roman Catholic Theology," *Interpretation* XXV (1971), 78-94.

[6] For the documentation, see David F. Wells, *Revolution in Rome* (Downers Grove, Ill.: Inter-Varsity Press, 1972), pp. 29f.; Bruce Vawter, *Biblical Inspiration* (Philadelphia: Westminster, 1972), pp. 70-75, 132.

[7] J. Forestell, "The Limitation of Inerrancy," *Catholic Biblical Quarterly* XX (1958), 9-18; P. Zerafa, "The Limits of Biblical Inerrancy," *Angelicum* XXXIX (1962), 92-119; Vawter, *op. cit.*, pp. 132-43.

[8] For the full story of the debates surrounding the development and eventual adoption of the constitution on revelation, see H. Vorgrimmler (ed.), *Commentary on the Documents of Vatican II* (New York: Herder, 1969), III, 155-172. Hans Küng has expressed his displeasure that the phrase 'without error' (undoubtedly present due to papal pressure) should have been retained at all. In the future the Vatican Two statement will probably seem conservative indeed if Catholic progressives pursue their present direction. Küng, *Infallible? An Inquiry* (New York: Doubleday, 1971), p. 214.

[9] D. P. Fuller, "The Nature of Biblical Inerrancy," *Journal of the American Scientific Affiliation* XXIV (1972), 47, 50, and "Benjamin B. Warfield's View of Faith and History," *Bulletin of the Evangelical Theological Society* XI (1968), 80-82.

[10] In a letter printed in *Christian Scholars Review*, III (1973), 330-33.

[11] "It [inspiration] extends to everything which any sacred writer asserts to be true," C. Hodge, *Systematic Theology* (London: James Clarke, 1960), I, 163.

[12] J. I. Packer, *'Fundamentalism' and the Word of God* (London: Inter-Varsity Fellowship, 1958), pp. 96f.

[13] E. J. Carnell, *The Case for Orthodox Theology* (Philadelphia: Westminster, 1959),

pp. 102-110; K. S. Kantzer, "Christ and Scripture," *HIS Magazine* [Inter-Varsity Christian Fellowship], XXVI (January, 1966), 17; R. K. Harrison, *Introduction to the Old Testament* (Grand Rapids, Mich.: Eerdmans, 1969), pp. 555f.

[14] Warfield's critique of the limited inerrancy position continues to be relevant. See his *Inspiration and Authority of the Bible* (Philadelphia: Presbyterian and Reformed Publishing Co., 1948), pp. 169-226.

[15] See, for example, F. Pieper, *Christian Dogmatics* (4 vols; St. Louis, Mo.: Concordia, 1950), I, 80-93.

[16] Cf. David F. Wells, *op. cit.*, p. 218.

[17] C. S. Lewis, Introduction to J. B. Phillips' *Letters to Young Churches* (London: Bles, 1947).

[18] Warfield, *op. cit.*, p. 218.

[19] D. Beegle, *The Inspiration of Scripture* (Philadelphia: Westminster, 1963), p. 14.

[20] John Warwick Montgomery, *The Suicide of Christian Theology* (Minneapolis: Bethany, Fellowship, 1970), p. 358.

[21] Bavinck is cited by Klaas Runia, *Karl Barth's Doctrine of Holy Scripture* (Grand Rapids, Mich.: Eerdmans, 1962), p. 110.

[22] Warfield, *op. cit.*, pp. 215f.

[23] An older work is J. W. Haley, *An Examination of the Alleged Discrepencies of the Bible* (reprinted.; Grand Rapids: Baker, 1958). Some newer titles are: Raymond F. Surburg, *How Dependable is the Bible?* (New York: Lippincott, 1972); K. A. Kitchen, *Ancient Orient and the Old Testament* (Chicago: Inter-Varsity, 1966).

[24] Edwin Yamauchi, *The Stones and the Scriptures* (New York: Lippincott, 1972).

[25] C. S. Lewis, *Christian Reflections*, ed. Walter Hooper (Grand Rapids: Eerdmans, 1967), pp. 152-66.

[26] For a discussion of Gordon's views, see R. K. Harrison, *op. cit.*, pp. 78-81, 515f.

[27] Cited in J. I. Packer, *God Speaks to Man: Revelation and the Bible* (Philadelphia: Westminster, 1965), p. 20, n. 1.

[28] Warfield, *op. cit.*, p. 218.

[29] *Ibid.*, p. 128.

[30] Roger Nicole, "The Inspiration of Scripture: B. B. Warfield and Dr. Dewey M. Beegle," *Gordon Review*, VII (1963), 108.

7

GOD AND BIBLICAL LANGUAGE: TRANSCENDENCE AND IMMANENCE

John M. Frame

One of the most persuasive and frequent contemporary objections to the orthodox view of biblical authority goes like this: the Bible cannot be the word of God because *no* human language can be the word of God. On this view, not only the Bible, but human language *in general*, is an unfit vehicle—unfit to convey infallibly a message from God to man.

This objection takes various forms, three of which I shall discuss:

1. Some linguists and philosophers of language have suggested that language is never completely true—that the undeniable discrepancy which always exists between symbol and reality (the word "desk" is not a desk, for instance) injects falsehood into every utterance. This contention is sometimes buttressed by the further assertion that all language is metaphorical, figurative—and thus can never convey the "literal" truth. There is, however, something odd about any view which attributes falsehood to all language. For one thing, the assertion that "all sentences are false" is self-refuting if taken literally; and if we don't take it literally, what does it mean? Perhaps

the real point is that language never conveys the *"whole* truth"—
that it never conveys the truth with absolute precision or
absolute comprehensiveness. But consider: (a) Some sentences
are, in one sense, perfectly precise and comprehensive. Take
"Washington is the capitol of the United States": could that
fact be stated more precisely? more comprehensively? (b)
Of course, even the aforementioned sentence is not comprehensive in the sense of "saying everything there is to say"
about Washington and the U.S. But no human being ever
tries to say all that, at least if he has any sense at all! Nor
does the Bible claim to say "everything" about God. The claim
to infallibility does not entail a claim to comprehensiveness
in this sense. And where no claim to comprehensiveness is
made, lack of comprehensiveness does not refute infallibility.
(c) Nor is imprecision necessarily a fault. "Pittsburgh is about
300 miles from Philadelphia" is imprecise in a sense, but it
is a perfectly good sentence and is in no usual sense untrue.
An "infallible" book might contain many imprecise-but-true
statements of this sort. Granting, then, that there is a sense
in which language never conveys the "whole truth," we need
not renounce on that account any element of the orthodox view
of biblical authority.

More might be said about this first form of the objection
we are discussing—its reliance upon the discredited referential
theory of meaning, its strangely generalized concept of "metaphor," its dubious presuppositions about the origin and development of language, its ultimate theological roots. These topics,
however, have been adequately discussed elsewhere,[1] and my
own interests and aptitudes demand that I press on immediately
to other aspects of the problem. The following discussion will
raise some basic issues which I trust will shed further light
on this first area of concern.

2. If the first form of our objection was raised primarily
by linguists, philosophers of language and their entourage, the
second form (though similarly focussed on language) arises
out of broader epistemological and metaphysical concerns. In
the 1920s and 30s, the philosophy of logical positivism attempted
to divide all philosophically important language into three categories: (a) tautologies ("A book is a book," "Either it is raining
or it is not raining"), (b) contradictions ("It is raining and
it is not raining," "The table is square and it is not square"),
and (c) assertions of empirical fact ("There is a bird on the
roof," "The President has put price controls on beef"). Tautologies, on this view, were said to be true purely by virtue

of the meanings of the terms, and contradictions false on the same account. Empirical assertions could be either true or false, and their truth or falsity was said to be ascertainable by something like the methods of natural science. When someone claims to state a fact, but upon examination it turns out that this "fact" cannot be verified or falsified by such methods, then, said the positivists, this utterance is not a statement of fact at all; it is not an "empirical assertion"; it is neither true nor false. Such an unverifiable utterance may have a use as poetry, expression of feeling or the like, but it does not state any fact about the world; it is (to use the positivists' technical term) "cognitively meaningless," it does not measure up to the "verification criterion of meaning." On such grounds, the positivists dismissed metaphysical statements ("Mind is the absolute coming to self-consciousness") and theological statements ("God is love") as cognitively meaningless. Ethical statements ("Stealing is wrong") also were seen, not as statements of fact, but as expressions of attitude, commands, or some other non-informative type of language.[2]

As a general theory of meaningfulness, logical positivism was too crude to last very long. Disputes quickly arose over what methods of verification were to be tolerated, how conclusive the verification or falsification must be and other matters too technical to discuss here. Many felt that the whole project was to some extent a rationalization of prejudice—not an objective analysis of what constitutes "meaningfulness," but an attempt to get rid of language distasteful to various philosophers by constructing a "principle" arbitrarily designed for that purpose.[3]

No thinker of any consequence today subscribes to the "verification principle" as a general criterion of meaningfulness. One aspect of the positivists' concern, however, is very much with us. Although we do not buy the whole logical positivist theory, many of us are quite impressed with the basic notion that *a fact ought to make a difference*. This concern is vividly presented in the oft-quoted parable of Antony Flew:

> Once upon a time two explorers came upon a clearing in the jungle. In the clearing were growing many flowers and many weeds. One explorer says, 'Some gardener must tend this plot.' So they pitch their tents and set a watch. No gardener is ever seen. 'But perhaps he is an invisible gardener.' So they set up a barbed-wire fence. They electrify it. They patrol with bloodhounds. (For they remember how H. G. Wells's *The Invisible Man* could be both

smelt and touched though he could not be seen.) But no shrieks ever suggest that some intruder has received a shock. No movements of the wire ever betray an invisible climber. The bloodhounds never give cry. Yet still the Believer is not convinced. 'But there is a gardener, invisible, intangible, insensible to electric shocks, a gardener who has no scent and makes no sound, a gardener who comes secretly to look after the garden which he loves.' At last the Sceptic despairs, 'But what remains of your original assertion? Just how does what you call an invisible, intangible, eternally elusive gardener differ from an imaginary gardener or even from no gardener at all?' [4]

If there is *no difference* between "invisible gardener" and "no gardener," then surely the dispute between Believer and Sceptic is not about facts. If there is no difference, then talk of an "invisible gardener" may be a useful way of expressing an attitude toward the world, but it cannot make any empirical assertion about the world. Flew is not asking the Believer to verify his view in some quasi-scientific way (although one suspects that is what would make him most happy); he is simply asking him to state what *difference* his belief makes.

As we might suspect, Flew thinks that much language about God makes "no difference." Believers say that "God is love" even though the world is full of cruelty and hatred. How does such a God differ from a devil, or from no God at all? And if "God is love" makes no difference, how can it be a fact? how can it be, as the positivists liked to say, "cognitively meaningful"?

Flew does not suggest that *all* religious language succumbs to this difficulty, or even that all language about God is in jeopardy. He seems to be thinking mainly of what "often" happens in the thought of "sophisticated religous people." [5] Still, his knife cuts deep. Can any Christian believer offer a straightforward answer to Flew's concluding question, "What would have to occur or to have occurred to constitute for you a disproof of the love of, or of the existence of, God?" [6] Our first impulse is to say with the apostle Paul, "If Christ hath not been raised, then is our preaching vain, and your faith is also vain." [7] The Resurrection shows that God does make a difference! Disprove the Resurrection, and you disprove God. The Resurrection (but of course not only the Resurrection!) demonstrates the great difference between God and no-God. But push the argument back another step: What would have to occur or to have occurred to constitute for you a disproof of the *Resurrection*? Do we have a clear idea of how the Resurrection may be falsified? Paul appeals to witnesses,[8] but the witnesses are dead. What if a collection of manuscripts were unearthed containing refutations of the Christian message by first century Palestinian Jews? And what if these manuscripts contained elaborate critiques of the Pauline claim in I Cor. 15, critiques backed up with massive documentation, interviews with alleged witnesses, etc. And then: what if the twenty-five most important New Testament scholars claimed on the basis of this discovery that belief in the physical Resurrection of Christ was untenable!? Would that be sufficient to destroy our faith in the Resurrection? It would be hard to imagine any stronger sort of "falsification" for any event of past history. And I don't doubt that many would be swayed by it. But many would not be. I for one would entertain all sorts of questions about the biases of these documents and those of the scholars who interpreted them. I would want to check out the whole question myself before conceding the point of doctrine. And what if I did check it out and found no way of refuting the anti-Resurrection position? Would that constitute a disproof? Not for me, and I think not for very many professing Christians. We all know how abstruse scholarly argument can be; there are so many things that can go wrong! In such a situation, it is not difficult to say "Well, I can't prove the scholars wrong, but they may be wrong nonetheless." And if the love of Christ has become precious to me, and if I have been strongly convinced that the Bible is his word, I am more likely to believe what he says in I Cor. 15 than to believe what a lot of scholars say on the basis of extra-biblical evidence. Could we *ever* be persuaded that the Resurrection was a hoax? Perhaps; but such a change would be more than a change in opinion; it would be a loss of faith. In terms of Scripture, such a change would be a yielding to temptation. For our God calls us to believe his Word even when the evidence appears against it! Sarah shall bear a son, even though she is ninety and her husband is a hundred![9] God is just, even though righteous Job must suffer! The heroes of the faith believed the Word of God *without* the corroboration of other evidence: they walked by faith, not by sight.[10] As long as we remain faithful, God's Word takes precedence over other evidence.

Flew's objection, therefore, is not to be lightly dismissed. There is a sense in which, not only the language of "sophisticated religious people" but even the language of simple Christian believers, fails to measure up to his challenge. God-language *resists* falsification. It is difficult to say what would refute a faith-assertion; for faith requires us to resist all temptation to doubt within the faith-language, no terms can be specified for renouncing the faith-assertions; for faith *excludes, prohibits,* such renouncement.

Does this, then, mean that the Resurrection "makes no difference"? We hope not! We certainly want to say that it *does* make a difference. Yet we find it difficult to say what would refute our belief in the Resurrection. We find it difficult to conceive of any state of affairs in which we would abandon our belief. We find it difficult to say what the Resurrection rules out. And thus we find it difficult to state *what difference it makes!* Perhaps, then, talk of the Resurrection does not really concern any empirical fact. Perhaps all God-talk is cognitively meaningless. And perhaps, then, God cannot be spoken of at all in human language. And if that is true, all talk of Scripture as the Word of God is clearly nonsense.

This, then, is the second form of the objection which I stated at the beginning of the paper, the second way in which human language is said to be disqualified as a medium of divine speech. Let us briefly examine the third form of the objection before presenting our response:

3. The third form of our objection is more distinctively theological. Karl Barth, for example, suggests on theological grounds that human language is unfit to convey truth about God:

> The pictures in which we view God, the thoughts in which we think Him, the words with which we can define Him, are in themselves unfitted to this object and thus inappropriate to express and affirm the knowledge of Him.[11]
>
> The Bible, further is not itself and in itself God's past revelation, but by becoming God's Word it attests God's past revelation and is God's past revelation in the form of attestation.... Attestation is, therefore, the service of this something else, in which the witness answers for the truth of this something else.[12]

This sort of point, which is very common in twentieth-century theology, is essentially a religious appeal to the divine transcendence. God is the Lord, the creator, the redeemer. To him belong all praise and glory. How can any human language ever be "fitted" to the conveyance of his word? Surely human language, like everything human and finite, can only be a servant, confessing its own *un*fitness, its own *in*adequacy. The Bible cannot *be* revelation; it can only *serve* revelation. To claim anything more for human language, for the Bible, is to dishonor God, to elevate something finite and human to divine status. To claim anything more is to think of revelation "in abstraction from" God himself and from Jesus Christ.[13] It is not just a mistake; it is an impiety.

At the same time, Barth does insist that the words of revelation have an importance:

> Thus God reveals Himself in propositions by means of language, and human language at that, to the effect that from time to time such and such a word, spoken by the prophets and apostles and proclaimed in the Church, becomes His Word. Thus the personality of the Word of God is not to be played off against its verbal character and spirituality. . . .
>
> The personification of the concept of the Word of God . . . does not signify any lessening of its verbal character.[14]

The words are still unfit; they are not themselves revelation; they are not necessarily true themselves, but they witness to the truth of "something else." Nevertheless the words are important, because from time to time God may use them to communicate with man. Even when they are false, they are God's instruments. God uses them, however, not as true propositional representations of his message, but as the instruments for an encounter that no human language is fit to describe.

Barth, therefore, like Flew, argues that God cannot be truly spoken of in human language. Here, it would seem, the resemblance between Barth and Flew ceases; for Barth argues "from above," Flew "from below." Barth argues that God is too great for language; Flew argues that language cannot speak meaningfully of God. But are the two positions really that far apart? Thomas McPherson suggests that an alliance is possible between the logical positivist philosophers and theologians like Rudolph Otto (McPherson might also have cited Karl Barth in this connection) who stress the transcendence of God over language:

> Perhaps positivistic philosophy has done a service to religion. By showing, in their own way, the absurdity of what theologians try to utter, positivists have helped to suggest that religion belongs to the sphere of the unutterable. And this may be true. And it is what Otto, too, in his way, wanted to point out. Positivists may be the enemies of theology, but the friends of religion.[15]

Enemies of *some* theology!—not of Otto's theology, nor of Barth's, nor of Buber's (to which McPherson refers in a footnote), nor (I would judge) of the broad tradition of dialectical and existential theologies of the twentieth century. In positivism and in these modern theologies, God belongs to the sphere of the unutterable, and human language (when "cognitively meaningful") belongs to the sphere of the humanly verifiable. Let us then consider the Flew problem and the Barth problem as one.

RESPONSE

Religious language is "odd" in a great number of ways. Not only does it tend to resist falsification, as Flew has pointed out; it also tends to claim certainty for itself, as opposed to mere possibility or probability.[16] It also tends to be connected with *moral* predicates—as if disbelief in it were a *sin*, rather than a mere mistake.[17] It is frequently spoken with great passion; with Kierkegaard we tend to be suspicious of allegedly religious language which seems detached or uncommitted.

On the other hand, religious language is in some respects very "ordinary," very similar to other language. It is not a techinical, academic language like that of physics or philosophy; it is the language of ordinary people. It is not restricted to some limited and distinctive compartment of human life; rather it enters into all human activities and concerns. We pray for the healing of a loved one, for help in a business crisis; we seek to "eat and drink to the glory of God." [18] We believe that our faith "makes a difference" in the real world, that God can enter into all the affairs of our life and make his presence felt. In this respect, the "action of God in history" is like the action of *anyone* in history. God can change things, can make them different. And what he does does not occur unless he chooses to do it. God makes a difference, and in that sense he is *verifiable*—much as the existence of any person is verifiable (or so, at least, it appears to the simple believer!). Few religious people would claim that their faith is a blind leap in the dark. They have "reasons for faith." These reasons may be the technical theistic arguments of the philosophers, or simply the childlike appeal to experience, "He lives within my heart." One who really believes (as opposed to one who merely drifts along in a religious tradition) believes for a *reason*, because he thinks God has somehow made his presence felt, because God now *makes a difference*—to him!

Religious language, then, is "odd" and it is "ordinary." If an analysis of religious language is to be adequate, it must take *both* features into account, not just one of them. Flew and Barth do not reflect very much upon the "ordinariness" of religious language. They seem to imply that it is a sort of delusion, for it makes a claim to verifiability which cannot on analysis be sustained, or because it betrays a spirit of human pride, because it brings God down to man's level. For Barth at least, we gather that the "ordinariness" of religious language is a mark of its *humanity*, a mark of its *unfitness* to convey the word of God. There is, however, another interpretation of the data—one which does not write off the "ordinariness" of religious language as a delusion, one which accounts both for the verifiability of religious statements and for their tendency to resist verification, one which illumines the ways in which Scripture itself speaks of God.

Religious language is language of *basic conviction*. It is the language by which we state, invoke, honor, advocate (and otherwise "bring to bear") those things of which we are most certain, those things which are most important to us, those things which we will cling to even though we must lose all else. Not all language of "basic conviction" is religious in the usual sense. Many people who consider themselves irreligious have "basic convictions" of some sort. If fact, it may well be disputed whether anyone can avoid having *some* basic conviction—whether it be a faith in reason, in material success, in a philosophical absolute, or in a god. But all language which *is* religious in the usual sense is language of basic conviction.

Someone may object that for many people their religion is *not* their most basic commitment. A man may mumble through the church liturgy every Sunday while devoting his existence almost exclusively to acquiring political power. For him, surely, the liturgy does *not* express his "basic commitment." True; but that is because there is something wrong! A man like this we call a hypocrite; for the liturgy is *intended* to express basic conviction and our fanatical politician utters the words deceitfully. He does not *really* "believe in God, the father almighty" in the sense of biblical faith, though he says he does. His real faith is in something else. The man is a liar. But his lying use of the language does not change the meaning of it, which is to confess true faith in God.

All of us have basic convictions, unless possibly we are just confused. Positivists do too—and Barthians! And insofar as we try to be consistent, we try to bring all of life and thought into accord with that basic conviction.[19] Nothing inconsistent with that conviction is to be tolerated. An inconsistency of that sort amounts to a divided loyalty, a confusion of life-direction. Most of us, at least, try to avoid such confusion. The conviction becomes the paradigm of reality, of truth and of right, to which all other examples of reality, truth and right must measure up. As such, it is the cornerstone of our metaphysics, epistemology and ethics. It is not, be it noted, the *only* factor in the development of a system of thought. Two people may have virtually identical "basic commitments" while differing greatly in their systems of thought. The two will both try to develop systems according with their common presupposition, but because of differences in experience, ability, secondary commitments and the like, they may seek such consistency in opposite directions. But though the "basic commitment" is not the *only* factor in the development of thought (and life), it is (by definition) the most important factor.

We have suggested that religious language is a subdivision of "basic-commitment language." The next point is that basic-commitment language in general displays the same kinds of "oddness" and "ordinariness" that we have noted in religious language. We state our basic commitments as certainties, not merely as possibilities or probabilities, because our basic commitments are the things of which we are most sure, the paradigms of certainty against which all other certainties are measured. Basic commitments are paradigms, too, of *righteousness*; challenges to those commitments invariably seem to us unjust because such challenges if successful will deny our whole reason for living. And basic-commitment language is (almost tautologically) the language of *commitment*, not of detached objectivity. And to these "oddnesses" we must add the oddness of resistance to falsification.

Take a man whose basic commitment in life is the earning of money. To him, the legitimacy of that goal is a *certainty*, beyond all question. When that goal conflicts with other goals, the basic goal must prevail. Questions and doubts, indeed, may enter his mind; but these questions and doubts are much like religious temptations. Insofar as he takes them seriously, he compromises his commitment; he becomes to that extent double-minded, unstable. He faces then a crisis wherein he is challenged to change his basic commitment. Under such pressure he may do so. But then the new commitment will demand the same kind of loyalty as the old one. Challenges *must* be resisted. Evidence against the legitimacy of the commitment must be somehow either ignored, suppressed, or accounted for in a way that leaves the commitment intact. "Are people starving in India? We must be compassionate, of course; but the best means of helping the poor is by teaching them the virtues of free enterprise and self-help: if everyone were truly dedicated to earning money there would be no poverty. We do them no favor by compromising our commitment"! A rationalization? It might not seem so to one so committed, especially if no other answer to the poverty question lies close at hand.

Let us rephrase Flew's question as it might be addressed to the mammon-worshipper: What would have to occur or to have occurred to constitute for you a disproof of the primacy of money-making? What would have to happen to cause him to abandon his faith? Well, one simply cannot say in advance! Committed as he is, he devoutly hopes that *nothing* will bring about such a change. He not only hopes, he *knows* (or so he thinks)—because he interprets all reality so as to accord with that commitment. Some event, indeed (we can't say what), may cause him to change—if he yields to the temptation of regarding that event from a non-mammon perspective. He changes them because he has already compromised; it is like a change in religious faith.

The basic-commitment language is "odd" indeed; but it is also "ordinary." It is not something strange or esoteric; we use it all the time. It enters into every area of life, simply because it is so basic, so important. It is important because it "makes a difference"—more difference than anything else. Without it nothing would make sense. All of experience, then, "verifies" the validity of the commitment. We can "prove" our commitment true in any number of ways. The evidence is there.

But how can a commitment be verifiable and nonverifiable at the same time? How can it present proof, and at the same time resist falsification by contrary evidence? The resolution of this paradox gets us to the heart of the matter. Think of a philosopher who is committed to establishing all truth by the evidence of his senses. Sense-experience is his criterion of truth. What evidence would disprove that criterion? In one sense none; for if sense-experience is truly his criterion, then all objections to the criterion will have to be verified through sense-experience. They will have to be tested by the criterion they oppose. "Disproof," as with other basic commitments, will come only when there is something like a crisis of faith. At the same time, all evidence *proves* the criterion. The philosopher will argue very learnedly to establish his conviction. He will refute contrary claims, he will produce carefully constructed arguments.

The arguments, of course, will be "circular." Arguments for the sense-criterion must be verified by the sense-criterion itself. The philosopher must argue for sense-experience by appealing to sense-experience. What choice does he have? If he appeals to something else as his final authority, he is simply being inconsistent. But this is the case with any "basic commitment." When we are arguing on behalf of an absolute authority, then our final appeal must be to that authority and no other. A proof of the primacy of reason must appeal to reason; a proof of the necessity of logic must appeal to logic; a proof of the primacy of mammon must itself be part of an attempt to earn more money; and a proof of the existence of God must appeal in the final analysis to God.

Such arguments are circular; but they are also arguments! A "proof" of, say, the primacy of reason, can be highly persuasive and logically sound even though, at one level, circular. The circularity is rarely blatant; it lurks in the background. One never says "Reason is true because reason says it is." One says instead, "Reason is true because one must presuppose it even to deny it." The second argument is just as circular as the first. Both presuppose the validity of reason. But in the second argument the presupposition is implicit rather than explicit. And the second one is highly persuasive! The irrationalist cannot help but note that he is (in many cases) presenting his irrationalism in a highly rational way. He is trying to be more rational than the rationalists—a contradictory way to be! He must decide either to be a more consistent irrationalist (but note the paradox of that!) or to abandon his irrationalism. Of course he might renounce consistency altogether, thus renouncing the presupposition of the argument. But the argument shows him vividly how *hard* it is to live without rationality. The argument is circular, but it draws some important facts to his attention. The argument is persuasive though circular because down deep in our hearts we *know* that we cannot live without reason.[20]

Some circular arguments are persuasive to us, others not. Those circular arguments which verify the most basic commitments of our lives are by definition the *most* persuasive to us. And because we believe those commitments true, we believe that those arguments ought to be persuasive to others too. A Christian theist, while conceding that the argument for God's existence is circular, nevertheless will claim that the argument is sound and persuasive. For he devoutly believes that his position is true, and he believes that it can be recognized clearly as such. He believes that God made men to think in terms of *this* circularity, rather than in terms of some competing circularity.[21]

Basic-commitment language, therefore, is both "odd" and "ordinary"; it resists falsification, it refuses to be judged by some antithetical commitment; yet it accepts the responsibility to verify itself. It accepts the responsibility of displaying whatever rationality and consistency it may claim.

What is Antony Flew's "basic commitment"? To reason? To "academic integrity" of some sort? To a secular ethic? To religious agnosticism? I don't know, but I would assume that he has one, since he does not seem like the sort of person who accepts values unreflectively. And more can be said: If with the Bible we divide the human race into Christian and non-Christian, those who know God and those who don't, those who love God and those who oppose him, clearly Flew by his writings has identified himself with the God-opposing group. If this self-identification truly represents his heart commitment, then according to Scripture Flew is committed to "hindering the truth" of God, "exchanging the truth of God for a lie." [22] According to Scripture, he is committed at a basic level to opposing, contradicting, resisting the truth of God which in some sense he nevertheless "knows." [23] This commitment too will be unfalsifiable and yet self-verifying, for it is a basic commitment; and for all its irreligiosity it is logically like a religious commitment. Let us illustrate by a parody on Flew's parable:

Once upon a time two explorers came upon a clearing in the jungle. A man was there, pulling weeds, applying fertilizer, trimming branches. The man turned to the explorers and introduced himself as the royal gardener. One explorer shook his hand and exchanged pleasantries. The other ignored the gardener and turned away: "There can be no gardener in this part of the jungle," he said; "this must be some trick. Someone is trying to discredit our previous findings." They pitch camp. Every day the gardener arrives, tends the plot. Soon the plot is bursting with perfectly arranged blooms. "He's only doing it because we're here—to fool us into thinking this is a royal garden." The gardener takes them to a royal palace, introduces the explorers to a score of officials who verify the gardener's status. Then the sceptic tries a last resort: "Our senses are deceiving us. There is no gardener, no blooms, no palace, no officials. It's still a hoax!" Finally the believer despairs: "But what remains of your original assertion? Just how does this mirage, as you call it, differ from a real gardener?"

A garden indeed! How convenient that we should be talking about gardens—for that is where the Bible's own story begins. Adam and Eve lived in a garden, and they knew the divine

Gardener. He talked to them, worked with them, lived with them; until one day Eve—and Adam!—denied that he was there. Irrational it was, for sin is at its root irrational. And Scripture tells us that ever since that day sinners have been guilty of the same irrationality. God is verifiable, knowable, "clearly seen" in his works;[24] but men still—"irrationally" because sinfully—deny him. To the Christian, the denials lapse into cognitive meaninglessness—an attempt to evade God by using atheistic language to describe a patently theistic world.

From a "neutral" point of view, both Flew and the Christian are in the same boat. Both have beliefs which are "odd" and "ordinary"; resistant to falsification, yet verifiable on their own terms. But of course there is no "neutral" point of view. You are either for God or against Him. You must place yourself in one circle or the other. Logically, both systems face the difficulties of circularity. But one is true and the other is false. And if man is made to know such things, then you can tell the difference.[20] You *know* you can! [20]

Our response to Flew, in short, is that (1) He has only told half the story: religious language does resist falsification, as he says; but it also often claims to be verifiable in terms of its own presuppositions. (2) These epistemological peculiarities attach to all "basic-commitment language," not just to religious or Christian language—and thus they attach to unbelieving language as well. Therefore, these considerations may not be urged as a criticism of Christianity. They are simply descriptive of the human epistemological condition. (3) Scripture pictures the *unbeliever* as the truly ridiculous figure, who ignores patent evidence and makes mockery of reason, on whose basis *no* knowledge is possible. To the Christian, the unbelieving circle is, or ought to be, absurd: something like "Truth is a giant onion; therefore truth is a giant onion."

Flew, therefore, does not succeed in showing religious language to be "cognitively meaningless"; and therefore he fails to show that human language cannot speak of God. But what of the third form of our objection? What of Karl Barth? Should we simply leave him behind?

Let us go back to the "oddness" and "ordinariness" of religious language, and Christian language in particular. The oddness of Christian language derives from the transcendence of God, and the ordinariness of it derives from God's immanence. Christian language is odd because it is the language of basic commitment; and the transcendence of God's Lordship demands that our commitment be basic. This language is odd because it expresses our most ultimate presuppositions; and these presuppositions are the demands which God makes upon us—nothing less. It is odd because it attempts to convey God's demands—his demands for all of life. It will not be "falsified" by some secular philosophical criterion, because God will not be judged by such a criterion. "Let God be true, though every man a liar." [25] God's own word, the paradigm of all Christian language, is therefore *supremely* odd.

Christian language is "ordinary," verifiable, because God is not only the transcendent Lord; he is also "with us," close to us. These two attributes do not conflict with one another. God is close to us *because* he is Lord. He is Lord, and thus free to make his power felt everywhere we go. He is Lord, and thus able to reveal himself clearly to us, distinguishing himself from all mere creatures. He is Lord, and therefore the most central fact of our experience, the least avoidable, the most verifiable.

And because God's own word is supremely odd, it is supremely ordinary. Because it is supremely authoritative, it is supremely verifiable. Because it furnishes the ultimate presuppositions of thought, it furnishes the ultimate *truths* of thought.

Barth's argument essentially reverses this picture (derived from Scripture) of God's transcendence and immanence. To Barth, God's transcendence implies that he *cannot* be clearly revealed to men, clearly represented by human words and concepts. This view of God's transcendence contradicts the view of God's immanence which we presented. Similarly, Barth has a view of God's immanence which contradicts the view of transcendence which we presented. To Barth, the immanence of God implies that words of merely human authority, words which are fallible, may from time to time "become" the word of God. Thus the only authority we have, in the final analysis, is a fallible one. The only "word of God" we have is a fallible human word. God does not make authoritative demands which require unconditional belief; he does not determine the presuppositions of our thought; he does not resist all falsification—rather he endorses falsehood and sanctifies it.

Well, who is right? Does God's transcendence include or exclude an authoritative verbal revelation of himself to men? Note that this question must be faced squarely. It is not enough to say that revelation must be seen in the context of God's transcendence; for that transcendence has been understood in different ways, and one must therefore defend his particular view of it. One does not get into the heart of the matter by saying that one view sees revelation "in abstraction from" God's lordship; for the two sides do not agree on the nature of this lordship or the relation that revelation is supposed to sustain to that lordship.

Both views claim Scriptural support. Barth can appeal to the basic creator-creature relationship as presented in Scripture: man is a creature; his ultimate trust must rest solely in God. To put ultimate confidence in something finite is idolatry. Human words are finite. Therefore to put ultimate confidence in Scripture is idolatry. And in a fallen world, such confidence is all the more foolish; for human words are sinful as well as finite. Sinful speech can never perfectly honor God. The Gospel precisely requires us to *disown* any claim to perfection, to confess the *inadequacy* of all human works, to cast all our hope on the mercy of God. How can we put ultimate trust in human words and in God's mercy at the same time?

Barth's view can be stated very persuasively as long as it focuses on the general facts of creation and redemption. Scripture *does* condemn idolatry; it *does* condemn reliance on merely human means of salvation. But when this view turns specifically to the concept of revelation, its unbiblical character becomes obvious. For Scripture itself never deduces from God's transcendence the inadequacy and fallibility of all verbal revelation. Quite to the contrary: in Scripture, verbal revelation is to be obeyed without question, *because* of the divine transcendence:

> Hear, O Israel: The Lord our God is one Lord: and thou shalt love the Lord thy God with all thy heart, and with all thy soul, and with all thy might. And these words, which I command thee this day, shall be in thy heart; and thou shalt teach them diligently unto thy children, and shalt talk of them when thou sittest in thy house, and when thou walkest by the way, and when thou liest down, and when thou risest up. . . . Ye shall diligently keep the commandments of the Lord your God, and his testimonies, and his statutes, which he hath commanded thee.[26]

One who serves God as lord will obey his verbal revelation without question. One who loves Christ as Lord will keep his commandments.[27] God's lordship, transcendence, demands unconditional belief in and obedience to the words of revelation; it *never* relativizes or softens the authority of these words. But how can that be? Is Scripture itself guilty of idolizing human words? The answer is simply that Scripture does not regard verbal revelation as merely human words. Verbal revelation, according to Scripture, is the Word of *God*, as well as the word of man. As with the incarnate Christ, verbal revelation has divine qualities as well as human qualities. Most particularly, it is divine as to its *authority*. To obey God's word is to obey *Him*; to disobey God's word is to disobey *Him*. Unconditional obedience to verbal revelation is not idolatry of human words; it is simply a recognition of the divinity of God's own words. It is the deference which we owe to God as our creator and redeemer.

Dishonoring the divine is just as sinful as idolizing the creature. The two are inseparable. To disobey God is to obey something less than God. When we turn from God's words, we idolize human words. If Scripture is right, if verbal revelation does have divine authority, then it is Barth's view which encourages idolatry. For Barth's view would turn us away from proper deference to God's words, and would have us instead make a "basic commitment" to the truth of some other words— our own, perhaps, or those of scientists, or those of theologians.

These considerations do not prove that Scripture is the word of God. They do show, however, that the biblical doctrine of divine transcendence does not compromise the authority of verbal revelation. One may, indeed, prefer Barth's concept of transcendence to the biblical one; but such a view may not be paraded and displayed as the authentic Christian position.

We conclude, then, that the "objection" before us is unsound in all of its three forms. Human language *may* convey the infallible word of God, because God is *lord*—even of human language!

NOTES

[1] One helpful discussion of these matters from an orthodox Christian perspective can be found in Gordon H. Clark, *Religion, Reason and Revelation* (Phila.: Presbyterian and Reformed, 1961), pp. 111-50.

[2] The classical exposition of logical positivism in the English language is A. J. Ayer, *Language, Truth and Logic* (New York: Dover, 1946).

[3] One of the sharpest debates was over the status of the verification principle itself. Surely it was not to be regarded as a tautology; but it did not seem to be "verifiable" either in any quasi-scientific sense. Was it then to be dismissed as "cognitively meaningless"? Ayer himself (see above note) came to the view that the verification principle was a "convention" (see his introduction to the anthology *Logical Positivism* [Glencoe, Ill.: Free Press, 1959] p. 15). He maintained that this "convention" had some basis in ordinary usage, but admitted that it went beyond ordinary usage in crucial respects.

[4] Antony Flew, *et al.*, "Theology and Falsification," *New Essays in Philosophical Theology*, ed. Antony Flew and Alasdair MacIntyre (London: SCM Press, 1955), p. 96.

[5] *Ibid.*, p. 98.

[6] *Ibid.*, p. 99.

[7] I Cor. 15:14.

8 I Cor. 15:5-8.

9 Gen. 17:16-17.

10 Heb. 11. The contrast between faith and sight alludes to II Cor. 5:7.

11 Karl Barth, *Church Dogmatics*, Vol. II: *The Doctrine of God*, ed. G. W. Bromiley and T. F. Torrance; trans. T. H. L. Parker, W. B. Johnston, H. Knight, and J. L. M. Haire (New York: Scribner, 1957), Pt. 1, p. 188.

12 *Ibid.*, Vol. I: *The Doctrine of the Word of God*, trans. G. T. Thomson (New York: Scribner, 1936), Pt. 1, p. 125.

13 *Ibid.*, pp. 155ff.

14 *Ibid.*, pp. 156f.

15 Thomas McPherson, "Religion as the Inexpressible," *New Essays in Philosophical Theology*, ed. Antony Flew and Alasdair MacIntyre (London: SCM Press, 1955), pp. 140f. In a footnote, McPherson notes a similar view in Martin Buber's *I and Thou*.

16 Note Ludwig Wittgenstein's interesting discussion of this point in *Lectures and Conversations on Aesthetics, Psychology and Religious Belief, Compiled from Notes taken by Yorick Smythies, Rush Rhees and James Taylor*, ed. Cyril Barrett (Oxford: Blackwell, 1966), pp. 53-59. Wittgenstein seems to make the extreme suggestion that religious belief *never* is "probable" in character. Wittgenstein obviously never spent much time around seminary students and academic theologians!

17 Cf. *ibid.*, p. 59.

18 I Cor. 10:31.

19 Some readers may be helped here by the observation that there are many different degrees of "basicness" among our convictions. All of our convictions govern life to some degree. When someone disagrees with one of our opinions, we naturally tend to try to defend it—either to refute our opponent's argument or to show that his position is compatible with ours. The learning process is such that we always try to interpret new knowledge in such a way as to minimize disturbance to past opinions. Some opinions we hold more tenaciously than others. It is fairly easy to convince me that I am wrong about, say, the team batting average of the Pittsburgh Pirates. It is much more difficult to persuade me that the earth is flat! In the first instance, citation of one presumable competent authority is enough. In the second instance, the intrinsic unlikelihood of a flat earth would bring into question the competence of any "presumably competent authority" who held such a position. Nevertheless, if there were a full-scale revolution among scientists over systems of measurement, and cogent reasons could be given for reverting to a flat earth view, I might be persuaded to reconsider. Some convictions, then, we relinquish less easily than others; and the "most basic convictions" (which we focus upon in the text of the article) are relinquished least easily of all. In fact, we *never* relinquish those unless at the same time we change in our basic concept of rationality.

20 *How* do we know? That's hard to say; but we do. Some circular arguments simply are more plausible than others. "Truth is a giant onion, for all true statements are onion shoots in disguise." That argument is best interpreted as a circular one, the conclusion being presupposed in the reason offered. But there is something *absurd* about it. "Reason is necessary, for one must use reason even in order to deny it." That too, is circular, but it seems much more plausible. A sceptic might say that the second argument seems plausible because it is *our* argument, while the first is not.

"Knowledge" itself is dreadfully hard to define. Logicians, epistemologists and scientists have devoted countless hours to the task of finding criteria for genuine knowledge. Yet knowledge may not be defined as the observance of any such criteria. Knowledge occurred in human life long before there was any science of logic or epistemology or biology, and people still gain knowledge without referring to such disciplines. These disciplines try to conceptualize, define, understand a phenomenon which exists independently of those disciplines. They do not make knowledge possible. And their concepts of knowledge change rather frequently. It would be presumptuous indeed to suppose that these disciplines have succeeded at last in defining everything which constitutes "knowledge." Thus, if the recognition of plausibility in a circular argument does not fit any existing technical criteria of "knowledge," then so much the worse for those criteria.

The fact is that recognition of such plausibility is a type of knowledge which epistemologists are obligated to note and account for. "Basic convictions" cannot be avoided; and such convictions may be proved only through circular argument. Therefore circular argument is unavoidable, at the level of basic conviction. This sort of circularity is not a defect in one system as opposed to others. It is an element of all systems. It is part of the human condition.

It is altogether natural, then, that the term "knowledge" be applied to basic convictions, and if no technical account has yet been given of this sort of knowledge, then such an account is overdue.

Within a particular system, the basic convictions are not only truths; they are the most certain of truths, the criteria of other truths. If we deny the term "knowledge" to these greatest of all certainties, then no lesser certainty can be called "knowledge" either. And no epistemologist may adopt a view which, by doing away with all knowledge, does away with his job! Knowledge is not an ideal; it is not something which we strive for and never attain. It is a commonplace of everyday life. It is the job of epistemologists to account for that commonplace, not to define it out of existence. One may not define "knowledge" in such a way as to require us to transcend our humanity in order to know. One must defer to the commonplace. And "knowledge of basic principles" is part of that commonplace.

[21] These are the terms in which the matter must be phrased. The controversy is between competing circularities, not between circularity and non-circularity.

[22] Rom. 1:18, 25.

[23] Rom. 1:19-21a; note the phrase *gnontes ton theon*, "knowing God."

[24] Rom. 1:20.

[25] Rom. 3:4.

[26] Deut. 6:4-7, 17.

[27] John 14:15, 21, 23; 15:10. On these matters, cf. my other essay in this collection.

8

SCRIPTURE SPEAKS
FOR ITSELF

John M. Frame

What does Scripture say about itself? The question is both momentous and commonplace.

It is momentous: the self-witness of Scripture has been for centuries the cornerstone of the orthodox Christian argument for biblical authority. For one thing, there would never be any such argument unless there were reason to believe that Scripture *claimed* authority. If Scripture renounced all claim to authority, or even remained neutral on the subject, there would not be much reason for Christians today to claim authority *for* Scripture. But if Scripture *does* claim authority over us, then we are faced with a momentous challenge indeed! Acceptance or rejection of that claim will influence every aspect of Christian doctrine and life.

Furthermore, the authority of Scripture is a doctrine of the Christian faith—a doctrine like other doctrines—like the deity of Christ, justification by faith, sacrificial atonement. To prove such doctrines, Christians go to Scripture. Where else can we find information on God's redemptive purposes? But what of the doctrine of the authority of Scripture? Must we not, to be consistent, also prove *that* doctrine by Scripture? If so, then the self-witness of Scripture must not only be the *first* consideration in the argument; it must be the final and decisive consideration also.

Now of course someone may object that that claim is not competent to establish itself. If the Bible *claims* to be God's word, that does not prove that it *is* God's word. That is true in a sense. Many documents claim to be the word of some god or other. The Koran, the Book of Mormon and countless other books have made such claims. In no case does the claim in itself establish the authority of the book. The claim must be compared with the evidence. But the evidence through the presuppositions furnished by, among other things, our religious convictions. A Christian must look at the evidence with Christian assumptions; a rationalist must look at the evidence with rationalistic assumptions. And the Christian finds his most basic assumptions in the Bible!

As I have argued elsewhere,[1] it is impossible to avoid circularity of a sort when one is arguing on behalf of an *ultimate criterion*. One may not argue for one ultimate criterion by appealing to another. And the argument over Scriptural authority is precisely an argument over ultimate criterion!

We must not, of course, simply urge non-Christians to accept the Bible because the Bible says so. Although there is much truth in that simplicity, it can be misleading if stated in that form without further explanation. A non-Christian must start where he is. Perhaps he believes that Scripture is a fairly reliable source, though not infallible. He should then be urged to study Scripture as a historical source for Christian doctrine, as the *original* "source." He will be confronted with the claims of Scripture—about God, about Christ, about man, about itself. He will compare the biblical way of looking at things with his own way. And if God wills, he will see the wisdom in looking at things Scripture's way. But we must not mislead him about the demand of Scripture. He must not be allowed to think that he can become a Christian and go on thinking the same old way. He must be told that Christ demands a *total* repentance—of heart, mind, will, emotions—the whole man. He must learn that Christ demands a change in "ultimate criterion." And thus he must learn that even the evidentiary procedures he uses to establish biblical authority must be reformed by the Bible. He must learn that "evidence" is at bottom an elaboration of God's self-witness; that "proving" God is the same as hearing and obeying him.

So the question of the biblical self-witness is a momentous one indeed. In a sense it is the *only* question. If by "self-witness" we mean, not merely the texts in which the Bible explicitly claims authority, but the whole character of the Bible as it confronts us, then the question of biblical authority is purely and simply the question of biblical self-witness.

On the other hand, the question is also commonplace: Simply because it is so important, the question has been discussed

over and over again by theologians. Although I feel greatly
honored by the invitation to speak and write on such a basic
question, I must confess also to a slight feeling of numbness.
What can I say that hasn't been said already? What can I
say that Gäussen, Warfield, Kuyper, Murray, Young, Van Til,
Kline, Ridderbos, Pache, Wenham, Packer, Montgomery, Pinnock and Gerstner haven't said? Even in this collection, some
of the other papers will overlap this topic! No doubt, in a collection of papers of this sort, someone ought to summarize the
basic material. But I can't help thinking it might be best just
to quote snatches from other authors whose scholarship and
eloquence is far superior to my own. It *might* be; but I won't
follow that course here, because I do have a few reasons
for attempting an individual, if not independent, study.

Past orthodox Christian discussions of this matter have,
in my opinion, done a very adequate job on the whole. As in
all human endeavors, however, there is room for improvement
here. The improvements I have in mind are chiefly two:

1. There needs to be a greater emphasis upon the *persuasive-
ness* throughout Scripture of the biblical self-witness. As we
suggested earlier, there is a sense in which *all* of the Bible
is self-witness. Whatever the Bible says, in a sense, it says
about itself. Even the genealogies of the kings tell us about
the content, and therefore the character of Scripture. The *way*
in which the Bible speaks of kings and vineyards and wilderness
journeys and God and man and Christ—its *manner* is a testimony
to its character. More specifically: the overall doctrinal structure
of Scripture is an important element of the biblical self-witness.
For when the Bible speaks of atonement, reconciliation, justification, glorification, it speaks of these in such a way as to presuppose a crucial role for itself. Or, to look at redemption from
a more historical perspective, from the beginning of God's
dealings with men God has taught them to give his words a
particular role in their lives, a lesson which is taught again
and again through the thousands of years of redemptive history.
Now when we neglect this emphasis on the pervasiveness of
the biblical self-witness, at least two bad things happen: (a)
People can get the idea that the concept of biblical authority
is based largely on a few texts scattered through the Bible,
texts which may not be very important in the overall biblical
scheme of things. They might even get the idea that the doctrine
of inspiration is based largely upon a *couple* of texts (II Pet.
1:21, II Tim. 3:16) which liberal scholars dismiss as being late

and legalistic. Thus it may seem as though the doctrine of biblical authority is a rather peripheral doctrine, rather easily dispensable for anyone who has even the slightest inclination to dispense with unpalatable doctrines. (b) People can get the idea that Christ and the Bible are separable, that you can believe in and obey Christ without believing in and obeying the Bible. They may think that Scripture is unimportant to the Christian message of redemption.

2. If, as orthodox people maintain, the biblical self-witness to its authority and infallibility is *obvious, clear*—and certainly if it is "pervasive"!—then we must face more squarely the question of why not-so-orthodox people see the matter differently. At one level, of course, it is legitimate to say that they fail to see the truth because of their unbelief: the god of this world has blinded their minds.[3] Sin is "irrational"—it turns away from the obvious. But sinners, when they are scholars, at least, generally do things for a *reason*, perverse as that reason may be. And perverse or not, such reasoning is often highly plausible. If orthodox people can identify that reasoning, explain its surface plausibility, and expose its deeper error, then the orthodox view of the biblical self-witness will be stated much more cogently.

In the remaining portion of this essay, I shall present an essentially traditional argument concerning the character of the biblical self-witness; but I shall structure the discussion in such a way as to implement the above two concerns—not comprehensively, to be sure, probably not adequately—but to greater degree than one might expect in a paper of this length.[4] The first section will examine the role of verbal revelation in the biblical understanding of salvation. The second will discuss the relationship of that verbal revelation to Scripture, and the third will analyse what I take to be the most common and plausible objection to the previous line of reasoning.

I. REVEALED WORDS AND SALVATION

We have suggested that the whole Bible is self-witness; but the Bible is not *only* or *primarily* self-witness. It is first and foremost, not a book about a book, but a book about God, about Christ, about the salvation of man from sin. But that message of salvation includes a message about the Bible. For this salvation requires *verbal revelation*. In saving man, God *speaks* to him.

A. Lord and Servant

God spoke to man even *before* man fell into sin. The first human experience mentioned in Scripture is the hearing of God's word; for immediately after the account of man's creation we read,

> And God blessed them: and God said unto them, Be fruitful, and multiply, and replenish the earth, and subdue it; and have dominion over the fish of the sea, and over the birds of the heavens, and over every living thing that moveth upon the earth.[5]

It is appropriate that the hearing of these words be presented in Scripture as man's first experience. For this was the experience by which the whole course of man's life was determined. When man heard these words of God, he heard his own *definition.* God was telling man who man was, what his task was. Everything else that man did was to be in obedience to this command. Whether a shepherd, a farmer, a miner, a businessman, a teacher, a homemaker—his main job was to replenish and subdue the earth in obedience to this command. The command covered *all* of life, not just some compartments of it. The command was not to be questioned; it was God's sovereign determination of man's responsibility. The command asserted God's claim to *ultimate* authority; for, paradoxically, while the command declared man to have dominion over the earth, it also declared God's dominion over man! Whatever dominion man enjoys, he receives from God; he enjoys it at God's pleasure; he enjoys it out of obedience to God's command.

Why? Simply because God is God and man is man. God is Lord, man is servant. God commands; man must obey. To have a Lord is to be under authority. A servant is one responsible to obey the *commands* of another. What kind of lordship would there be without commands? The very idea is absurd. Without commands, no obedience; without obedience, no responsibility; without responsibility, no authority; without authority, no lordship.

Man was created in obedience; he fell through disobedience—disobedience to another command, this time the command concerning the forbidden tree.[6] The simplest biblical difinition of sin is "lawlessness"[7]—rejection of, disobedience to God's commands. Therefore just as the word of God defines our status as God's creatures and servants, it also defines our status as *fallen* creatures, as sinners.

Redemption, according to Scripture, involves a re-assertion of God's lordship. The fall, of course, did not annul God's lordship; God's lordship over fallen man is vividly expressed in divine judgment against sin. But if man is to be saved, he must be brought to realize again that God is Lord and demands man's unconditional obedience. When God saved Israel from Egypt, He called himself by the mysterious name Jehovah which, though its exact meaning is uncertain, clearly asserts his claim to unconditional lordship.[8] And throughout the history of redemption, God continually asserted this claim by making *absolute demands* upon his people.

God's demands are absolute in at least three senses: (1) They *cannot be questioned.* The Lord God has the right to demand unwavering, unflinching obedience. God blessed Abraham because he "obeyed my voice, and kept my charge, my commandments, my statutes, and my laws." [9] He did not waver[10] even when God commanded him to sacrifice his son Isaac, the son of the promise.[11] To waver—even in that horrible situation!—would have been sin. (2) God's demand is absolute also in the sense that it *transcends all other loyalties*, all other demands. The Lord God will not tolerate competition; he demands *exclusive* loyalty.[12] The servant must love his Lord with all his heart, soul and strength.[13] One cannot serve two masters.[14] One of the most remarkable proofs of the deity of Christ in the New Testament is that there Jesus Christ demands—and receives—precisely this kind of loyalty from his followers, the same sort of loyalty which Jehovah demanded of Israel.[15] The Lord demands *first* place. (3) God's demand is also absolute in that it *governs all areas of life.* In the Old Testament period, God regulated not only Israel's worship, but also the diet, political life, sex life, economic life, family life, travel, calendar of his people. No area of life was immune to God's involvement. To be sure, the New Testament gives us more freedom on a certain sense: the detailed dietary restrictions, uncleanness rituals, animal sacrifices and other elements of the old order are no longer literally binding. But the New Testament, if anything, is *more* explicit than the Old on the comprehensiveness of God's demand: *Whatsoever* we do, even eating and drinking, must be done to the glory of God.[16] We must never shut the Lord out of any compartment of our lives; there must be no areas kept to ourselves. God's lordship involves such *absolute demands*.

B. *Savior and Sinner*

But salvation is more than a reassertion of God's lordship. If God merely reasserted his lordship, we would be without hope, for we have turned against him and deserve death at his hand.[17] If God merely spoke to us absolute demands, we would perish, for we have not obeyed these demands. But our God is not only Lord; he is also *savior*. And he speaks to us not only demands, not only law, but also *gospel*—the good news of Jesus Christ. But we must emphasize that he *speaks* the gospel. The gospel is a *message*, a revelation in words. How can we know that the death of Christ is sufficient to save us from sin? No human wisdom could have figured that out! Only God can declare sinners to be forgiven; only God has the right to promise salvation to those who believe! The same lord who speaks to demand obedience, also speaks to promise salvation. As Abraham,[18] we are called to believe the gospel simply because it is God's own promise. We know that believers in Christ are saved because Jesus has told us they are.[19] Only the Lord can speak the word of forgiveness, that word which declares sinners to be forgiven, and promises eternal life.

Just as there can be no lordship without an absolute demand, so there is no salvation without a gracious and certain promise. Therefore the whole biblical message presupposes the *necessity of verbal revelation*. Without revealed words, there is neither lordship nor salvation. To "accept Christ as Savior and Lord" is to accept from the heart Christ's demand and promise. Let there be no misunderstanding: you *cannot* "accept Christ" without accepting his words! Christ himself emphasizes this point over and over again.[20] If we set aside the words of Christ in favor of a vague, undefined "personal relationship" to Christ, we simply lose the biblical Christ and substitute a Christ of our own imagination.

And not just any words will do! They must be *God's* words— words of divine, and not merely human authority; words which cannot be questioned, transcend all other loyalties, govern all areas of life. They must be words which *cannot* be contradicted by human philosophies or theologies—or even by the "assured results of modern scholarship"! Without words like *that*, we have no Lord and we have no Savior.

But where can we find words like *that*? No mere philosopher or theologian or scholar speaks such words! Many religions, indeed, claim to have such words; but how are we to judge

among these many claims? How do we distinguish the voice
of God from the voice of devils and the imaginations of our
own hearts?

II. REVEALED WORDS AND SCRIPTURE

Scripture tells us to go to Scripture! Or, rather, the *God* of
Scripture tells us in Scripture to go to Scripture!

Of course we must note at the outset that the Bible is not
the *only* word that God has spoken. God has spoken words to
and by his apostles and prophets that are not recorded in
the Bible. He has also spoken, in a sense, to the earth, to the
storms, to the winds and waves.[21] And in a mysterious sense,
the word of God may also be identified with God Himself[22]
and particularly with Jesus Christ.[23] But God does not always
tell us what he says to the winds and waves, and he has not
always provided us with prophets at a handy distance! Rather,
he has directed us to a *book*! That is where we are to go for
daily, regular guidance. That is where we may always find
the demands of the Lord and the promise of the Savior.

Writing goes back a long way in the history of redemption.
The book of Genesis appears to be derived largely from "books
of generations."[24] We don't know much about the origin of
these books, but it is significant that (1) they include inspired prophecies[25] and (2) they were eventually included
among Israel's authoritative writings. From a very early time,
God's people began to *record* the history of redemption for their
posterity. It was important from the beginning that God's covenants, his demands and his promises be written down lest they
be forgotten. The first explicit reference, however, to a divinely
authorized book occurs in connection with the war between
Israel and Amalek shortly after the Exodus:

> And Joshua discomfited Amalek and his people with
> the edge of the sword. And the Lord said unto Moses,
> Write this for a memorial in a book, and rehearse it
> in the ears of Joshua: that I will utterly blot out the
> remembrance of Amalek from under heaven. And Moses
> built an altar, and called the name of it Jehovah-nissi;
> and he said, the Lord hath sworn: the Lord will have
> war with Amalek from generation to generation.[26]

Not only does the Lord authorize the writing of the book; the
content of it is God's own oath, his pledge. It is the word of
God, a word of absolute authority and sure promise. Because
God has spoken it, it will surely happen.

But an even more important example of divine writing occurs a few chapters later. In Exodus 20, God speaks the Ten Commandments to the people of Israel. The people are terrified, and they ask Moses to act as mediator between themselves and God. From Ex. 20:22 to 23:33, God presents to Moses further commandments in addition to the ten, which Moses is to convey to the people. In Ex. 24:4, we learn that Moses wrote down all these words and in verse 7 read them to the people. The people received these words as the word of God himself: "All that the Lord hath spoken will we do, and be obedient." [27] They accepted these *written* words as words of absolute demand! But something even more remarkable occurs a few verses later. The Lord calls Moses alone to ascend the mountain "and I will give thee the tables of stone, and the law and the commandment which I have written, that thou mayest teach them." [28] Note the pronouns in the first person singular! *God* did the writing! In fact, the implication of the tenses is that God had completed the writing before Moses ascended the mountain. Moses was to go up the mountain to receive a completed, divinely written manuscript! Nor is this the only passage that stresses divine authorship of the law. Elsewhere, too, we learn that the tables were "written with the finger of God" [29]; they were "the work of God, and the writing was the writing of God, graven upon the tables." [30]

What was going on here? Why the sustained emphasis upon divine writing? Meredith G. Kline[31] suggests that this emphasis on divine writing arises out of the nature of covenant-making in the ancient near East. When a great king entered a "suzerainty covenant relation" with a lesser king, the great king would produce a *document* setting forth the terms of the covenant. The great king was the author, because he was the lord, the sovereign. He set the terms. The lesser king was to read and obey, for he was the servant, the vassal. The covenant document was the Law; it set forth the commands of the great king, and the servant was bound to obey. To disobey the document was to disobey the great king; to obey it was to obey him. Now in Exodus 20 and succeeding chapters, God is making a kind of "suzerainty treaty" with Israel. As part of the treaty relation, he authors a document which is to serve as the official record of his absolute demand. Without the document there would be no covenant.

Later, more words were added to the document; and we read in Deuteronomy that Moses put all these words in the ark of the covenant, the dwelling place of God, the holiest place in Israel, "that it may be there for a witness against thee." [32] The covenant document is not man's witness concerning God; it is God's witness *against* man. Man may not add to or subtract anything from the document;[33] for the document is God's word, and must not be confused with any mere human authority.

This divine authority takes many forms. In the extra-biblical suzerainty covenants, certain distinct elements have been discovered [34]: the self-identification of the lord (the giving of his name), the "historical prologue" (proclaiming the benevolent acts of the lord to the vassal), the basic demand for exclusive loyalty (called "love"), the detailed demands of the lord, the curses upon the disobedient, the blessings upon the obedient, and finally the details of covenant administration, use of the document, etc. In the law of God, all of these elements are present. God tells who he is,[35] he proclaims his grace through his acts in history,[36] he demands love,[37] he sets forth his detailed demands,[38] he declares the curses and blessings contingent on covenant obedience,[39] and he sets up the machinery for continuing covenant administration, laying particular emphasis on the use of the covenant book.[40] All of these elements of the covenant are authoritative; all are words of God.

Theologians generally oversimplify the concept of biblical authority. To some theologians, it is God's personal self-manifestation (as in the giving of the divine name) which is authoritative. To others, it is the account of historical events. To others, the demand for love is the central thing. To others it is the divine self-commitment to bless. But the covenantal structure of revelation has room for all of these elements, and what's more, places them in proper relation to one another. There is both love and law, both grace and demand, both kerygma and didache, both personal disclosure (stated in "I-thou" form) and objective declarations of facts, both a concept of history and a concept of inspired words. The covenant document contains authoritative *propositions* about history (the servant has no right to contradict the lord's account of the history of the covenant), authoritative *commands* to be obeyed, authoritative *questions* (demanding the vassal's pledge to covenant allegiance), authoritative *performatives* (God's self-commitment to bless and curse).[41] The propositions are infallible; but infallibility is only part of biblical authority. This authority also includes the authority of non-propositional language as well.

We have seen that the idea of a "canon," an authoritative written word of God, goes back to the very beginning of Israel's history, back to its very creation as a nation. The Scripture is the constitution of Israel, the basis for its existence. The idea of a written word of God did *not* arise in twentieth-century fundamentalism, nor in seventeenth-century orthodoxy, nor in the post-apostolic church, nor in II Timothy, nor in post-exilic Judaism. The idea of a written word of God is at the very foundation of biblical faith. Throughout the history of redemption, therefore, God continually calls his people back to the written word. Over and over again he calls them to keep "the commandments of the Lord your God, and his testimonies, and his statutes which he hath commanded thee." [42] These are the words of absolute demand and sure promise, the words of the Lord. These were the words that made the difference between life and death. These were the words which could not be questioned, which transcended all other demands, which governed all areas of life. When Israel sinned and returned to the Lord, she returned also to the law of God. [43]

From time to time there were new words of God. Joshua added to the words which Moses had placed in the ark. [44] How could a mere man add to the words of God in view of the command of Deut. 4:2? The only answer can be that Joshua's words were also recognized as God's words. The prophets also came speaking God's words, [45] and some of them were written down. [46]

Thus the "Old Testament" grew. By the time of Jesus there was a well-defined body of writings which was generally recognized as God's word, and which was quoted as supreme authority, as Holy Scripture. Jesus and the apostles did not challenge, but rather accepted this view. Not only did they accept it, but they actively testified to it by word and deed. The role of Scripture in the life of Jesus is really remarkable: although Jesus was and is the Son of God, the second person of the Trinity, during his earthly ministry he subjected himself completely to the Old Testament Scripture. Over and over again, he performed various actions "so that the Scripture might be fulfilled." [47] The whole point of his life—his sacrificial death and resurrection was determined beforehand by Scripture. [48] Jesus' testimony to Scripture, then, is not occasional, but pervasive. His whole life was a witness to biblical authority! But listen particularly to what Christ and the apostles *say* concerning the Old Testament! Listen to the way in which they cite Scripture, even in the face of Satan, to "clinch"

an argument, to silence objections.[49] Listen to the titles by
which they describe the Old Testament: "Scripture," "holy
Scripture," "law," "prophets," "royal law of liberty," "the
oracles of God." [50] Listen to the formulae by which they
cite Scripture: "It is written"; "it says"; "the Holy Spirit
says"; "Scripture says." [51] All of these phrases and titles
denoted to the people of Jesus' day something far more than
a mere human document. These terms denoted nothing less
than inspired, authoritative words of God. As Warfield pointed
out, "Scripture says" and "God says" are interchangeable! [51]

And consider further the explicit *teaching* of Jesus and the
apostles concerning biblical authority:

> 1. Think not that I am come to destroy the law or the
> prophets: I came not to destroy, but to fulfill. For truly
> I say to you, Till heaven and earth pass away, one jot
> or one tittle shall in no wise pass away from the law;
> until all things are accomplished. Whosoever therefore
> shall break one of the least of these commandments, and
> shall teach men so, shall be called least in the kingdom
> of heaven: but whosoever shall do and teach them, he
> shall be called great in the kingdom of heaven.[52]

Jots and tittles were among the smallest marks used in the
written Hebrew language. Jesus is saying that *everything* in
the law and the prophets (equals the Old Testament) carries
divine authority. And obedience to that law is the criterion
of greatness in the kingdom of heaven.

> 2. Think not that I will accuse you to the Father: there
> is one that accuses you, even Moses, whom you trust.
> For if ye believed Moses, ye would believe me; for he
> wrote of me. But if ye believe not his writings, how shall
> ye believe my words? [53]

The Jews claimed to believe Moses' writings, but they rejected
Christ. Jesus replies that they do not *really* believe Moses;
and he urges them to a *greater* trust in the Old Testament.
He urges them to believe *all* of the law, and thus come to
accept his messiahship. We see here that Jesus did not merely
quote Scripture because it was customary among the Jews.
Rather, he *criticized* the prevailing custom because it was in-
sufficiently loyal to Scripture. Jesus' view of Scripture was
stronger than that of the Pharisees and Scribes. Jesus sees
Moses justly accusing the Jews because of their unbelief in
Scripture. Believing Moses is the prerequisite to believing Christ.

3. The Jews answered him, For a good work we stone thee not, but for blasphemy; even because thou, being a man, makest thyself God. Jesus answered them, Is it not written in your law, I said, Ye are gods? If he called them gods unto whom the word of God came (and the Scripture cannot be broken), say ye of him whom the Father sanctified and sent into the world, Thou blasphemest; because I said, I am the Son of God? [54]

A difficult passage, this; but note the parentheses. Concerning a fairly obscure Psalm, Jesus says that "scripture cannot be broken." It cannot be wrong, it cannot fail, it cannot be rejected as we reject human words.

4. For whatsoever things were written aforetime were written for our learning, that through patience and through comfort of the scriptures we might have hope. [55]

Here, the apostle Paul tells us that the Old Testament is relevant, not only for the people of the Old Testament period, but for us as well. It teaches us, gives us patience, comfort, hope. And most remarkably, the *whole* Old Testament is relevant! None of it is dated, none of it is invalidated by more recent thought. Of what human documents may *that* be said?

5. And we have the word of prophecy made more sure; whereunto ye do well that ye take heed, as unto a lamp shining in a dark place, until the day dawn, and the day star arise in your hearts: knowing this first, that no prophecy of scripture is of private interpretation. For no prophecy ever came by the will of man: but men spake from God, being moved by the Holy Spirit. [56]

Note the context of this passage: Peter expects to die soon, and he wishes to assure his readers of the truth of the gospel. [57] He knows that false teachers will attack the church, deceiving the flock. [58] He insists that the gospel is not myth or legend, but the account of events which he himself had witnessed. [59] Yet even when the eyewitnesses have left the scene, the believers will still have a source of sure truth. They have the "word of prophecy"—the Old Testament Scriptures—a word which is "more sure." [60] They are to "take heed" to that word, and forsake all conflicting teaching; for the word is light, and all the rest is darkness. Moreover, it did not originate through the human interpretative process; it is not a set of human opinions about God; nor did it originate in any human volition. Rather the Holy Spirit carried the biblical writers along, as they spoke for him! The Holy Spirit determined their course and their destination. The Bible consists of human writings, but its authority is no mere human authority!

> 6. All Scripture is God-breathed and profitable for doc-
> trine, reproof, correction, instruction in righteousness:
> that the man of God may be complete, furnished com-
> pletely unto every good work.[61]

Note again the context, for it is similar to that of the last passage. Paul in this chapter paints a gloomy picture of de-
ceivers leading people astray. How shall we know the truth in all this confusion? Paul tells Timothy to hang on to the truth as he learned it from Paul,[62] but also to the "holy scriptures" [63] (which, we note, are available even to us who have not been taught personally by Paul). This Scripture is "inspired of God" as the KJV says, or more literally "God-
breathed"—*breathed out by God.* In less picturesque language, we might say simply "spoken by God"; but the more picturesque language also suggests the activity of the Holy Spirit in the process, the words for "spirit" and "breath" being closely related in the original Greek. Scripture is *spoken* by God; it is *his Word*; and as such it is *all* profitable, and it is *all* that we need to be equipped for good works.

Both Old and New Testaments then pervasively claim author-
ity for the Old Testament scriptures. But what about the New Testament scriptures? Can we say that they, also, are the word of God?

We have seen the importance of verbal revelation in both Old and New Testaments. Both Testaments insist over and over again that such words are a necessity of God's plan of salvation. As we have seen, the concepts of lordship and salva-
tion presuppose the existence of revealed words. And in the New Testament, Jesus Christ is Lord and Savior. It would be surprising indeed if Jehovah, the Lord of the Old Testament people of God, gave a written record of his demand and promise, while Jesus, the Lord incarnate of whom the New Testament speaks, left no such record. Jesus told his disciples over and over again that obedience to *his words* was an absolute necessity for kingdom service and a criterion for true discipleship.[64] We *need* the words of Jesus! But where are they!? If there is no written record, no New Testament "covenant document," then has Jesus simply left us to grope in the dark?

Praise God that He has not! Jesus promised to send the Holy Spirit to lead his disciples into all truth.[65] After the Holy Spirit was poured out on the day of Pentecost, the disciples

192/ God's Inerrant Word

began to preach with great power and conviction.[66] The pattern remains remarkably consistent throughout the Book of Acts: the disciples are filled with the Spirit, and then they speak of Jesus.[67] They do not speak in their own strength. Further, they constantly insist that the source of their message is God, not man.[68] Their words have absolute, not merely relative, authority.[69] And this authority attaches not only to their spoken words, but also to their written words.[70] Peter classes the letters of Paul together with the "other Scriptures"! [71] Paul's letters are "Scripture"; and we recall that "Scripture" is "God-breathed"! [72]

We conclude, then, that the witness of Scripture to its own authority is pervasive: (1) The whole biblical message of salvation presupposes and necessitates the existence of revealed words—words of absolute demand and sure promise; without such words, we have no Lord, no Savior, no hope. (2) Throughout the history of redemption, God directs his people to find these words in written form, in those books which we know as the Old and New Testaments.

III. REVEALED WORDS AND MODERN THEOLOGIANS

Our conclusion, however, raises a serious problem. If the witness of Scripture to its own authority is pervasive, then why have so many biblical scholars and theologians failed to see it?

We are not asking why it is that these theologians fail to believe the claim of Scripture. The unbelief of theologians is at bottom rather uninteresting; it is not much different from the unbelief of anyone else. Yet it is surely possible to disbelieve Scripture's claim while at the same time admitting that Scripture makes such a claim. And some liberal theologians have indeed accepted this option: the Bible claims inspiration and authority, but modern men cannot accept such a claim.[73] But others have refused to admit even that Scripture makes that claim! Or more often: they have recognized this claim in some parts of Scripture, but they have judged this claim to be inconsistent with other, more important Scriptural teachings, and thus have felt that Scripture "as a whole" opposes the notion of authoritative Scripture in our sense.

Putting the same question differently: is it possible to construct a sound biblical argument for biblical fallibility? Some theologians, amazingly enough, have said "yes," despite the evidence to the contrary we and others have adduced. Is this simply a wresting of Scripture in the interest of a heresy? Is it at bottom simply another form of modern unbelief (and therefore as "uninteresting" as the unbelief alluded to earlier)? In the final analysis, I would say, the answer is yes. But some analysis, final or not, is called for. The argument must be scrutinized, lest we miss something important in the biblical self-witness.

We are not here going to argue specific points of exegesis. Some thinkers would question our interpretation of Matt. 5:17-19, arguing that in the Sermon on the Mount and elsewhere Jesus makes "critical distinctions" among the Old Testament precepts. Some, too, would question our reading of the phrase "inspired of God" or "God-breathed" in II Tim. 3:16. And indeed, some would argue from II Pet. 1:21 (but in defiance of II Tim. 3:16!) that inspiration pertains only to the writers of Scripture and not to the books which they have written. For enlightenment on these controversies, see the references in the footnotes. In general, we may say that even if it is possible to question a few points of our exegesis, the evidence is so *massive* that the general conclusion is still difficult to avoid:

> The effort to explain away the Bible's witness to its plenary inspiration reminds one of a man standing safely in his laboratory and elaborately expounding—possibly by the aid of diagrams and mathematical formulae—how every stone in an avalanche has a defined pathway and may easily be dodged by one of some presence of mind. We may fancy such an elaborate trifler's triumph as he would analyze the avalanche into its constituent stones, and demonstrate of stone after stone that its pathway is definite, limited, and may easily be avoided. But avalanches, unfortunately, do not come upon us, stone by stone, one at a time, courteously leaving us opportunity to withdraw from the pathway of each in turn: but all at once, in a roaring mass of destruction. Just so we may explain away a text or two which teach plenary inspiration, to our own closet satisfaction, dealing with them each without reference to the others: but these texts of ours, again, unfortunately do not come upon us in this artificial isolation; neither are they few in number. There are scores, hundreds, of them: and they come bursting upon us in one solid mass. Explain them away? We should have to explain away the whole New Testament. What a pity it is that we cannot see and feel the ava-

lanche of texts beneath which we may lie hopelessly buried, as clearly as we may see and feel an avalanche of
stones! [74]

Not even the cleverest exegete can "explain away" the biblical
concepts of lordship and salvation and the necessary connection
of these concepts with the revealed words of Scripture! No
exegete can explain away *all* the verses which call God's people
to obey "the commandments, statutes, testimonies, ordinances"
of the Lord; *all* the "it is written" formulae; all of the commands
delivered by apostles and prophets in authoritative tone.

Rather than such detailed questions, therefore, we shall con-
fine our attention to broader considerations which have carried
considerable weight in contemporary theological discussion.
For just as we have argued that the biblical concepts of lordship
and salvation *require* the existence of revealed words, so others
have argued that certain basic biblical concepts *exclude the
possibility of* such words!

The primary appeal of these theological views is to the
divine transcendence; as the following quotes from Karl Barth
and Emil Brunner respectively will indicate:

> Again it is quite impossible that there should be a direct
> identity between the human word of Holy Scripture and
> the Word of God, and therefore between the creaturely
> reality in itself and as such and the reality of God the
> creator.[75]

> It is therefore impossible to equate any human words,
> any "speech-about-Him" with the divine self-communi-
> cation.[76]

Such statements have a kind of primitive religious appeal.
God alone is God, and nothing else may be "equated with
him." To "equate" or "directly identify" something else with
God is idolatry. Now surely we must agree that Scripture endorses this sentiment, for Scripture clearly opposes idolatry
and exalts God above all other things! And if this is the case,
then it seems that Scripture requires us to distinguish sharply
between God Himself on the one hand, and language about
him on the other; The transcendence of God is surely a central
biblical concept! And if transcendence requires us to eliminate
all thought of "revealed words," even though other biblical
doctrines suggest otherwise, then perhaps we ought to give
serious thought to this issue.

However, Barth's concept of "direct identity" is a difficult
one, as is Brunner's reference to "equating." What does it

mean to assert—or deny—a "direct identity" or "equation" between God and language? Clearly, no one wants to say that
"God" and "language about God" are synonymous terms! Nor
has anyone in recent memory suggested that we bow down
before words and sentences. Even the most orthodox defenders
of biblical infallibility maintain that there is *some* distinction
to be made between God and language. Further: even the
most orthodox agree that the words of Scripture are in some
sense creaturely, and thus specifically because of their creature-
liness to be distinguished from God. On the other hand, if
such words are *God's* words, and not *merely* human, then
they are closely related to him, at least as closely as my
words are related to me. If God has spoken them, then their
truth is his truth; their authority is his authority; their power
is his power. Barth is willing to say that from time to time
Scripture *becomes* the word of God; therefore he admits that
some close relation between God and Scripture is essential.
The question then becomes: in what way is God "distinct"
from this language, and in what way is he "related" to it?
A pious appeal to God's transcendence, eloquent though it may
be, does not really answer this sort of question. Both the orthodox
and the Barthian would like to avoid being charged with idolatry. But *what kind* of distinction between God and language
is required by the divine transcendence?

Barth is most reluctant to give any positive description of
this relationship. Commenting upon II Tim. 3:16, he says:

> At the centre of the passage a statement is made about
> the relationship between God and Scripture, which can be
> understood only as a disposing act and decision of God
> Himself, which cannot therefore be expanded but to which
> only a—necessarily brief—reference can be made. At the
> decisive point all that we have to say about it can con-
> sist only in an underlining and delimiting of the inacces-
> sible mystery of the free grace in which the Spirit of God
> is present and active before and above and in the Bible.[77]

Inspiration, says Barth, is a mystery, because it is an act
of God's grace. We cannot define what it is; we can only
assert the graciousness of the process. At another point, however, he does venture to describe inspiration, alluding to the
term used in II Tim. 3:16:

> *Theopneustia* in the bounds of biblical thinking cannot
> mean anything but the special attitude of obedience in
> those [biblical writers] who are elected and called to
> this obviously special service. . . . But in nature and bear-

ing their attitude of obedience was of itself—both out-
wardly and inwardly—only that of true and upright men.[78]

Inspiration is an act of God to create in men a special attitude
of human obedience. It does not give them more than ordinary
human powers. Therefore,

> The Bible is not a book of oracles; it is not an instrument
> of direct impartation. It is genuine witness. And how can
> it be witness of divine revelation, if the actual purpose,
> act and decision of God in His only-begotten Son, as
> seen and heard by the prophets and apostles in that Son,
> is dissolved in the Bible into a sum total of truths ab-
> stracted from that decision—and those truths are then
> propounded to us as truths of faith, salvation and revela-
> tion? If it tries to be more than witness, to be direct im-
> partation, will it not keep from us the best, the one
> real thing, which God intends to tell and give us and
> which we ourselves need? [79]

The question, of course, is rhetorical. Barth is appealing to
something he thinks his reader will concede as obvious. And
this much we will concede: that if the Bible tries to be more
than it is, if it exceeds its rightful prerogatives and usurps
those of God Himself, then it will indeed hide from us the
real message of God's transcendence. But what *are* the "rightful
prerogatives" of Scripture? That must be established before
the rhetoric of divine transcendence can have force. The rhetoric
of transcendence does not itself determine what those prerogatives are.

It is clear from the last quoted section at least that Barth
denies to Scripture one particular prerogative—the prerogative
of presenting "truths of revelation in abstraction from" God's
saving act in Christ. But what does "in abstraction from"
mean in this context? An abstraction is always some sort
of distinction or separation, but what kind of distinction or
separation? An orthodox theologian will insist that the biblical
"truths of revelation" are *not* "in abstraction from" God's
act in Christ. On the contrary, we learn about this act, we
come to adore this act, because the Bible gives us a true
account of it.

I think that in the back of Barth's mind—perhaps in the
front of it!—is a concern of many academic people. When we
teachers see students cramming for theological exams, stuffing
truths into their heads, we sometimes wonder what all of this
has to do with the kingdom of God! And the students wonder
too! The whole business of "mastering truths" somehow seems

"abstract." It almost trivializes the message. Often there is here no real sense of the presence of God, no real spirit of prayer and thankfulness; it seems as if we are taking God's word and making a *game* of it!

Well, theology examinations, theological study *can* be a spiritual trial! But surely if we lose touch with God in studying his truths, it is our fault, not his for providing the truths! And sometimes, at least, the study of truths can be downright inspiring; sometimes, even in the academy, the law of the Lord purifies the soul! The evil in Barth's mind (as I understand him) is not an evil that can be remedied by eliminating the concept of revealed truth. It would be nice if such personal sinfulness could be eliminated by such a conceptual shift! But the sin of trivializing God's word is one of which we are all guilty—Barthians as much as anyone! We cannot eliminate that in Barth's way, nor ought we to try to construct a doctrine of Scripture that will make such trivialization impossible. That is the wrong way to go about constructing doctrinal formulations. Doctrines must not be arbitrarily constructed to counteract current abuses; they must be constructed on the basis of God's revelation.

"Abstraction," then, can't be avoided by renouncing the idea of revealed truths or revealed words. Nor can it be avoided by renouncing biblical infallibility. And in the absence of any other clearly stated threat to God's transcendence in the doctrine we have advocated, we are compelled to stand our ground. The orthodox view does *not* "abstract revelation from God's act," and it does not compromise the greatness and majesty of God. On the contrary: the true greatness of God, his Lordship and saviorhood as described in Scripture, *requires* the existence of revealed truths. Without such truths, we have no Lord, no Savior, no basis for piety. Without such truths, all that we say, think and do will be hopelessly "abstracted" from the reality of God. Without such truths, we have no hope. A Barthian or liberal or "neo-liberal" theology can provide no such words; it can locate no words of absolute demands and sure promise. Rather such a theology retains the right to judge the truth or falsity of *all* words with no divinely authorized criterion. Such theologies must be decisively rejected by the church of Christ, if she is to have any power, any saving message for our time. When Scripture speaks for itself, it claims to be no less than God's own word, and the claim is pervasive and unavoidable. Insofar as we deny that claim, we deny the Lord.[80] Insofar as we honor that word, we honor Christ.[81]

NOTES

¹ See my other paper in this collection.

² We shall cite some of the most helpful sources on these questions. The classic nineteenth-century work on the subject, still useful, is L. Gaussen, *The Inspiration of the Holy Scriptures,* trans. D. D. Scott (Chicago: Moody Press, 1949). The most impressive piece of scholarly work in this area to date remains B. B. Warfield, *The Inspiration and Authority of the Bible,* ed. S. G. Craig (Philadelphia: Presbyterian and Reformed Publishing Co., 1948). In relating the doctrine of inspiration to a comprehensive Christian world and life view, Abraham Kuyper's *Principles of Christian Theology,* trans. J. H. De Vries (Grand Rapids, Mich.: Eerdmans, 1965), is unsurpassed. Almost the only new things that have been said in the last few years about the doctrine have been said by Meredith G. Kline in his *Structure of Biblical Authority* (Grand Rapids, Mich.: Eerdmans, 1972). A helpful guide through the issues raised by New Testament biblical scholarship is H. Ridderbos, *The Authority of the New Testament Scriptures,* ed. J. M. Kik, trans. de Jongste (Philadelphia: Presbyterian and Reformed Publishing Co., 1963); The soundest overall guide to the theological controversies (in my opinion) is C. Van Til, *A Christian Theory of Knowledge* (Philadelphia: Presbyterian and Reformed Publishing Co., 1969); cf. his "unpublished" syllabus, "The Doctrine of Scripture" (Ripon, Cal.: Den Dulk Foundation, 1967). For general summaries of the issues, see: *The Infallible Word,* ed. N. R. Stonehouse and P. Woolley (3rd rev. ed.; Philadelphia: Presbyterian and Reformed Publishing Co., 1967) [the article by John Murray is especially helpful]; *Revelation and the Bible,* ed. Carl F. H. Henry (Grand Rapids, Mich.: Baker, 1958); and, on the more popular level, but most eloquent and cogent, E. J. Young, *Thy Word is Truth* (Grand Rapids, Mich.: Eerdmans, 1957). Other recent works useful in resolving the question of the Bible's self-witness are R. Pache, *The Inspiration and Authority of Scripture,* trans. H. Needham (Chicago: Moody Press, 1969); C. Pinnock, *Biblical Revelation* (Chicago: Moody Press, 1971); and J. W. Wenham, *Christ and the Bible* (Chicago: Inter-Varsity Press, 1973).

³ II Cor. 4:4.

⁴ As such, the paper will also *fail* to do justice to *other* legitimate concerns.

⁵ Gen. 1:28.

⁶ Gen. 2:17, 3:6, 11f.

⁷ I John 3:4.

⁸ Ex. 3:14; note context. In later years, when this sacred name was considered too sacred to be pronounced, the Jews read the word *Adonai*, Lord, in its place.

⁹ Gen. 26:5.

¹⁰ Rom. 4:20.

¹¹ Gen. 22:18.

¹² Ex. 20:3, "Thou shalt have no other gods before me."

¹³ Deut. 6:4f; cf. Matt. 22:37ff and parallels in the other Gospels.

¹⁴ Matt. 6:22ff.

¹⁵ Matt. 19:16-30; cf. 8:19-22, 10-37, Phil. 3:8.

¹⁶ I Cor. 10:31—A New Testament dietary law! Cf. Rom. 14:23, II Cor. 10:5, Col. 3:17.

¹⁷ Rom. 3:23, 6:23.

¹⁸ Rom. 4:19f.

¹⁹ John 5:24.

²⁰ Matt. 7:24-29, Mark 8:38, Luke 9:26, 8:21, John 8:31, 47, 51, 10:27, 12:47-50, 14:15, 21, 23f, 15:7, 10, 14, 17:6, 8, 17. The relationship between Christ and his words is essentially the same as that between God and his words in the Old Testament.

²¹ Psm. 119:90f, 147:15-18, 148:5f, Gen. 1:3, Psm. 33:6, 9, cf. Matt. 8:27.

²² John 1:1.

²³ John 1:14.

²⁴ Gen. 5:1; cf. 2:4, 6:9, 10:1, 11:10, 27, 25:12, 19, 36:9, 37:2.

²⁵ Gen. 9:25-27: though Noah is speaking, he is administering a covenantal blessing and curse which can only take effect under divine sanction. The fulfilment of these words at a much later period shows that these words were in essence the words of God. Cf. Gen 25:23, 27:27-29, etc.

²⁶ Ex. 17:13-16. The language here suggests a parallel with the divine "book of life," as though this earthly book were a kind of copy of the divine original.

²⁷ Ex. 24:7.

²⁸ Ex. 24:12.

²⁹ Ex. 31:13.

³⁰ Ex. 32:16; cf. also 34:1, Deut. 4:13, 9:10f, 10:2-4. Moses too is said to have done some

writing in Ex. 34:27f—probably portions of the law other than the ten commandments. And yet the written work of Moses is no less authoritative than that of the Lord himself—cf. Ex. 34:32. Moses was the mediator of the covenant and as such was a prophet conveying God's word to the people. Cf. Ex. 4:10-17, Deut. 18:15-19. The unique "finger of God" writing therefore is not necessary to the authority of the documents; humanly *written* documents may be equally authoritative, as long as the words are God's. But the "finger of God" picture places awesome *emphasis* upon the authority of the words.

[31] Kline, *op. cit.* in note 2 above.

[32] Deut. 31:26.

[33] Deut. 4:2, 12:32; cf. Prov. 30:6, Rev. 22:18f. How, then, could any additions be made to the document? For some additions clearly were made (Josh. 24:26, etc.). Since no man could add or subtract, the addition of a book to the covenant canon carries with it the claim that the addition has *divine* sanction.

[34] Kline, *op. cit.*; we are listing the elements Kline finds in treaties of the second millennium, B.C. He regards the decalogue and the book of Deuteronomy as having this basic structure (thus implying a second millennium date for Deuteronomy!), and he regards the entire Old Testament canon as an outgrowth of these "treaties."

[35] Ex. 20:2, "I am the Lord thy God"; cf. 3:14, etc.

[36] Ex. 20:2, " . . . who brought thee out of the land of Egypt, out of the house of bondage."

[37] Ex. 20:3, "Thou shalt have no other gods before me." Cf. Deut. 6:4f where the term "love" is actually used to denote this exclusive covenant loyalty. The demand for love follows the account of God's gracious acts in history, and is regarded as the vassal's response of gratitude for the Lord's benevolence. Cf. the New Testament emphasis, "We love, because he first loved us," I John 4:19.

[38] Ex. 20:12-17. Though the division cannot be sharply made, the first four commandments might be said to represent the fundamental love-requirement, while the last six describe some of its detailed outworkings.

[39] Ex. 20:5f, 12. We have been tracing these covenant elements through the decalogue, but we could have used many other parts of Scripture as well.

[40] This emphasis is not found in the decalogue, but it is a major emphasis of Deut. (see 31:24-29) which Kline also identifies as a covenant document.

[41] Performatives ("I pronounce you man and wife," "You are under arrest," "Cursed be all who do not obey") do not merely state facts, but "perform" various sorts of actions. When spoken by one in authority, they "accomplish" what they set out to do. Performatives of the Lord in Scripture are uniquely authoritative, but their authority is not *adequately* characterized by the term "infallibility." "Infallibility" is important, but it is only *part* of the meaning of biblical authority. "Infallibility" is, not too strong, but too *weak* a term adequately to characterize biblical authority.

[42] Deut. 6:17; cf. 4:1-8, 5:29-33, 6:24f, 7:9-11, 8:11, 10:12f, 11:1, 13, 18ff, 27f, 12:1, 28, 13:4. In Deuteronomy, almost every page contains exhortations to obey God's commandments and statutes and ordinances! But not only in Deuteronomy! Cf. Josh. 1:8, 8:25-28, Psm. 1:1-3, 12:6f, 19:7-11, 33:4. 11, 119:1-176, Isa. 8:16-20, Dan. 9:3ff, II Kings 18:6. Read over these and the many similar passages and let the message sink into your heart! The conclusion concerning the authority of the written word is simply inescapable.

[43] II Kings 23:2f, 21, 25, Neh. 8. The whole Old Testament history is a history of obedience and disobedience: obedience and disobedience to what? To God's commands; and after Ex. 20, to God's written word! The self-witness of the Old Testament is therefore present on every page. "Pervasive," as we said.

[44] Josh. 24:26.

[45] Deut. 18:15-19, Isa. 59:21, Jer. 1:6-19, Ezek. 13:2f, 17. The mark of the prophet was the phrase "Thus saith the Lord," which is found over and over again in the prophetic literature. Many theologians hostile to the orthodox view of biblical authority recognize that the prophets *claimed* an identity between their words and God's. See, e.g., E. Brunner, *Dogmatics*, Vol. I: *The Christian Doctrine of God*, trans. O. Wyon (Philadelphia: Westminster Press, 1950), pp. 18, 27, 31f.

[46] Isa. 8:1, 30:3ff, 34:16ff, Jer. 25:13, 30:2, 36:1-32, 51:60ff, Dan. 9:1f.

[47] Matt. 4:14, 5:17, 8:17, 12:17, 13:35, 21:4, 26:54-56, Luke 21:22, 24:44, John 19:28.

[48] Luke 24:26: "*Behooved* not. . . . " Scripture imposes a *necessity* upon Christ!

[49] Matt. 4; 22:29-33; etc.

[50] See Warfield, *op. cit.* (in note 2 above), especially pp. 229-241, 351-407.

[51] *Ibid.*, pp. 229-348.

[52] Matt. 5:17-19. For detailed exegesis, see John Murray, *Principles of Conduct* (Grand Rapids, Mich.: Eerdmans, 1957), pp. 149-157. Cf. also his essay, "The Attestation of Scripture," in *The Infallible Word*, (*op. cit.* in note 2 above), pp. 15-17, 20-24.

[53] John 5:45-47.

[54] John 10:33-36; cf. Warfield, *op. cit.*, pp. 138-41.

[55] Rom. 15:4.

[56] II Pet. 1:19-21; cf. Warfield, *op. cit.*, pp. 135-38.

[57] II Pet. 1:12-15.

[58] II Pet. 2.

[59] II Pet. 1:16-18; in the current theological scene it is worth noting that Peter denies any mythological character to the message. It is not *mythos*.

[60] Is the word "more sure" in the sense of being confirmed by eyewitness testimony? Or is it, as Warfield suggests (above reference) "more sure" *than* eyewitness testimony? In either case, the passage places a strong emphasis upon the *certainty* of the word.

[61] II Tim. 3:16f. For detailed exegesis, see Warfield, *op. cit.*, pp. 133-35, and also pp. 245-96 (a comprehensive treatment of the meaning of "God-breathed").

[62] II Tim. 3:14.

[63] II Tim. 3:15.

[64] Matt. 7:21ff, 24, 28f, Mark 8:38, Luke 8:21, 9:26, John 8:47, 10:27, 12:47, 14:15, 21, 23f, 15:7, 10, 14, 17:6, 8, 17, 18:37, cf. I John 2:3-5, 3:22, 5:2f, II John 6, I Tim. 6:3, Rev. 12:17, 14:12. Again: look these up, and allow yourself to be impressed by the *prevasiveness* of this emphasis.

[65] John 16:13, cf. Acts 1:8.

[66] Acts 2.

[67] Acts 2:4, 4:8, 31, 6:10 (cf. 3 and 5), 7:55, 9:17-20, 13:9f, 52ff.

[68] II Thess. 2:2, Gal. 1:1, 11f, 16, 2:2, I Cor. 2:10-13, 4:1, 7:40, II Cor. 4:1-6, 12:1, 7, Eph. 3:3, Rom. 16:25.

[69] Rom. 2:16, I Thess. 4:2, Jude 17f.; and cf. the passages listed in the preceding and following notes.

[70] Col. 4:16, I Thess. 5:27, II Thess. 3:14, I Cor. 14:37.

[71] II Pet. 3:16. Cf. I Tim. 5:18 which appears to couple a quotation from Luke with a quotation from the law of Moses under the heading "Scripture."

[72] The question of what books are to be regarded as New Testament Scripture is beyond the scope of this paper, since no actual list can be found as part of the New Testament's self-witness. We may certainly assume, however, on the basis of what has been said, that if revealed words are a *necessary* ingredient of biblical salvation, and if specifically the words of the incarnate Christ and his apostles have such necessity, our sovereign God will "somehow" find a way to enable us to find those words! And surely he has! Although there have been disputes among different churches concerning the *Old Testament* canon, there have never been any church-dividing disputes over the *New Testament* canon! Through history, of course, some New Testament books have been questioned. But once all the facts have gotten before the Christian public, it seems, the questions have always melted away. This is rather amazing, for the Christian church has always been, to its shame, a very contentious body! And yet no serious contentions have ever arisen over the matter of canonicity, a matter which many have found baffling! Try an experiment: read Paul's letter to the Corinthians (canonical), and then read Clement's (non-canonical). *Think* about it; *pray* about it. Is there not an *obvious* difference? Christ's sheep hear his voice!

[73] Cf. Warfield, *op. cit.*, pp. 115, 175ff, 423f. More recently, F. C. Grant admits that the New Testament writers assume Scripture to be "trustworthy, infallible, and inerrant": *Introduction to New Testament Thought* (Nashville: Abdingdon Press, 1950), p. 75.

[74] Warfield, *op. cit.*, pp. 119f.

[75] Karl Barth, *Church Dogmatics*, Vol. I: *The Doctrine of the Word of God*, ed. G. W. Bromiley and T. F. Torrance; trans. G. T. Thomson and Harold Knight (New York: Scribner, 1956), Pt. 2, p. 499.

[76] Emil Brunner, *op. cit.*, p. 15.

[77] Barth, *op. cit.*, p. 504.

[78] *Ibid.*, p. 505; in my view and Warfield's, Barth offers here a most inadequate exegesis of the "God-breathed" of II Tim. 3:16.

[79] Barth, *op. cit.*, p. 507.

[80] Mark 8:38.

[81] John 8:31, and those passages cited above in our note 64.

9

THE INSPIRATION OF SCRIPTURE AND THE AUTHORITY OF JESUS CHRIST

Clark H. Pinnock

The chief reason why Christians believe in the divine origin and authorship of the Bible is because Jesus Christ himself taught it plainly. This simple and yet massive fact more than any other accounts for the persistently high view of Scripture held by the Apostles and the entire Christian church until quite recently. The attitude characteristic of believers in every age has been one of complete trust in each and every utterance of Holy Writ on the understanding that it is, as no other document can claim to be, the very Word of God. Although it may be fairly argued that several factors are at work bringing about this result, it is our contention that no factor is of greater weight and importance than our Lord's doctrine of inspiration.[1]

The fact that Jesus consistently regarded the biblical text as the utterance of God his Father is a source of constant embarrassment to those Christians who for one reason or another wish to maintain a different and lower view of it. For it is difficult to see what meaning the doctrine of Incarnation could have if it did not at least uphold the *normativeness* of Jesus and his teachings. If Jesus is our only Lord and Light, from whence could we possibly derive the right to set aside or even temper his claim upon us? Such an act in itself amounts to a contrary revelational claim. In preferring an alternate view of Scripture to his, we are in effect setting aside his normativeness, and thereby denying his divine authority as well. Unreserved commitment to Jesus requires us to look at the Bible through his eyes. The indissoluble connection that exists between the inspiration of Scripture and the authority of Jesus Christ should have the greatest possible significance for Christians when they enquire what their view of the Bible should be.

In the realisation of just how deep this issue lies in the bedrock of the Christian faith, let us proceed to examine our Lord's view of Scripture, and consider some of the questions that arise in connection with it.[2]

I. CHRIST'S DOCTRINE OF SCRIPTURE

Jesus lived and breathed in the Old Testament. Joachim Jeremias remarks that his sayings are incomprehensible unless we recognise this fact.[3] His allusions to its teachings, direct and indirect, obvious and subtle, provide unmistakable evidence not only of his comprehensive knowledge of the entire extent of Scripture but of his evaluation of it as divine truth. His mind was evidently soaked in it and his whole career guided, even determined by it. Something which C. H. Spurgeon recommended for us was certainly true of him: "It is blessed to eat into the very soul of the Bible until, at last, you come to talk in scriptural language, and your spirit is flavoured with the words of the Lord, so that your blood is *Bibline* and the very essence of the Bible flows from you." [4]

One good indication of Christ's high regard for the biblical text is found in his complete trust in the literal truth of biblical *history*. He always treats the historical narratives as factually truthful accounts. In the course of his teachings he makes reference to: Abel (Lk. 11:51), Noah (Mt. 24:37), Abraham (Jn. 8:56), Sodom and Gomorrah (Lk. 10:12), Lot (Lk. 17:28), Isaac and Jacob (Mt. 8:11), David eating the shewbread (Mk. 2:25), and many other persons and incidents. It is not too much to say that he accepted without reservation the entire historical fabric of the Old Testament, including those aspects of it most troublesome to modern minds.

Two comments are in order in connection with his regard for biblical history. First, we would not wish to convey the impression that Jesus alludes to these persons and incidents in a disinterested, academic manner. On the contrary each of them possessed deep relevance for the contemporary situation. Jesus interpreted the Old Testament typologically. He could see in pre-messianic revelation the prefigurement of his own life and work. Persons such as David, Solomon, and Jonah were types of himself. The experiences of Israel foreshadowed his own. The prophetic hope was being fulfilled in himself. Nevertheless, it was typology and not allegory which characterized his interpretation, and typology does not involve any denigration of the historical matter being fulfilled. Quite the opposite, it depends on its being true.

Second, in a similar vein, we find no reason to suppose that Jesus was indifferent to the historicity of the Old Testament accounts. Indeed, there are striking examples in which the nature of his appeal requires that historicity be affirmed. Addressing on one occasion the unbelieving Pharisees, Jesus refused to give them a sign to overcome their stubborn disbelief, and instead referred to the experience and preaching of the prophet Jonah (Mt. 12:41). The only way in which this argument would have any weight at all is if the prophet and his converts from Nineveh were real, historical people. If they are not, the warning falls flat. The Pharisees would have had no reason to fear the condemnation of imaginary men on the day of judgment. In a later sermon our Lord connected the historical circumstances that obtained in the days of Noah with those that will prevail at his own advent (Mt. 24:37). It is plain that his warning concerning future events is tied in very closely with the historical record of the great flood. From these two incidents we can see the impossibility of sidestepping the significance of Jesus' confidence in the historical reliability of the Bible. Because these events are recorded in Scripture, he affirms them and appeals to them in an attitude of total trust.

Our Lord displays the selfsame attitude in respect of Old Testament *doctrinal* teachings. In his encounter with the devil just following his baptism Jesus repudiates the three temptations by a decisive appeal to written Scripture. Evidently he believed that what stood written in the Bible was nothing less than God's Word given to guide and instruct him, in this situation as in all others. Our Lord based the whole understanding of his mission and God's will upon the veracity of these biblical statements (Mt. 4:1-11, Lk. 4:1-13).

The same holds true in his various debates with the religious leaders who opposed him. Never did he criticise them for heeding the Old Testament too carefully. Rather he rebuked them for not believing it, over against human traditions, and for not reading it profoundly. He was shocked, for example, by their meticulous concern for the minutiae of the text while neglecting the weightier matters of the law altogether (Mt. 23:23). In particular he disliked the way the Pharisees permitted human tradition to obscure and even falsify God's written Word (Mk. 7:1-13). One of the abuses which he singled out was the tradition which enabled a person to avoid the duty of supporting his parents if he could prove that the money that could be used for that purpose was already *qorban*, "devoted to God" (v. 11). Jesus' antagonism was aroused by such examples of casuistry as this which were superimposed upon the Bible and rendered the reader insensitive to the real claim of God. Obviously Jesus distinguished between Scripture and tradition, between God's written Word and all human interpretations and accretions. To him Scripture was divine in origin, obligatory, supreme; whereas tradition was human in origin, optional and subordinate.

As he set forth his own teaching, Jesus made it plain that his views were based upon the principles of Scripture. When the young man enquired of him how eternal life could be gained, Jesus referred him to God's law in the Bible (Mt. 19:16-22). When a lawyer asked after the great commandment, he gave him two verses out of the Pentateuch as the summary of Old Testament teaching. He was convinced that the divine will with regard to the institution and purpose of marriage was authoritatively defined in the book of Genesis (Mt. 19:4-6). The difficulty that he found with the Sadducean theologians was that they knew neither the Scriptures nor the power of God (Mt. 22:29). He showed himself ready to comply even with relatively minor matters as can be seen in his command to the leper to show himself to the priest (Mk. 18:16), and his payment of the temple tax (Mt. 17:24f). Finally, it is of great importance to observe that after his resurrection when he appeared to his disciples prior to his ascension he occupied himself chiefly with the exposition of Scripture (Lk. 24:25-27, 44-45). Although Luke does not give us a detailed account of the drift of this teaching, it is likely that it was a continuation of the teachings already given in the Gospels and the basis of teachings in the Epistles as well. The easiest way to account for the apostolic use of the Old Testament in reference to Jesus is to regard it as based upon his own interpretation of it.[5] It is most likely that we possess in the Epistles an even more extensive witness to our Lord's understanding of Scripture.

Not only did Jesus believe the truth of biblical history and regard Scripture as his final authority in matters of theology and ethics, he also held and taught an exceedingly high view of the writings themselves. He heard God's voice speaking through the words of Scripture. Although he may refer to something Isaiah or Moses or Daniel said as truly an utterance of theirs, it is obvious that their words do not derive their authority from the fact that these men spoke them, but from the fact God spoke them, through his servants. It was the fact that David spoke by the Spirit which made the utterance so crucial (Mk. 12:36). In the last analysis it was God who gave the words recorded in the book of Genesis (Mt. 19:5). Therefore it is not at all surprising to find in the patristic period the term "author" being applied to God as the ultimate source of the inspired writings.[6]

Jesus' doctrine of inspiration receives expression in the Sermon on the Mount. Before setting forth his ethical instructions, Jesus explained his intention. "Think not that I have come to abolish the law and the prophets; I have not come to abolish them but to fulfill them" (Mt. 5:17). Evidently he does not want us to think that the thrust of his teaching is to violate or even to devalue Old Testament revelation. The saying which is also contained in Luke (16:17) has an entirely genuine ring to it.[7] Jesus' enemies were eager to pin an "antinomian" label on him if they could. Therefore, Jesus made it clear that the object of his criticisms was not the Bible, but the traditions which the Rabbis had built as a fence around it, traditions which in practice enjoyed an authority actually higher than the written Word. He assures us that his confidence in the divine character of Scripture does not stop short even of its smallest elements. "Not an iota, not a dot, will pass" (Mt. 5:18). He issues a stern warning: "Whoever then relaxes one of the least of these commandments and teaches men so, shall be called least in the kingdom of heaven; but he who does them and teaches them shall be called great in the kingdom of heaven" (v. 19).

At the same time Jesus speaks of *fulfilling* Scripture (v. 17). One aspect of his meaning can be discerned in the teaching which follows, where Jesus disentangles God's intention in the law from the weight of Rabbinic interpretation (5:21-22). We see what "fulfilment" involves when he summarises the law and the prophets in a single ethical maxim, "So whatever you wish that men would do to you, do so to them" (Mt. 7:12). But there is even more to the meaning of "fulfilment" than that. In the light of Aramaic backgrounds some scholars find his meaning to be a filling out of the full measure of the text.[8] As the Messiah, who according to the Old Testament would bring his own *torah* to the people (Is. 42:4), it was imperative for Jesus to define his relation to the already existing Scriptures and to announce the *final* revelation toward which they pointed. Thus in the Sermon on the Mount we find a radical deepening of God's requirements, not in violation of what was given, but in the direction set by the ancient rules.

Jesus' high doctrine of Scripture comes to the surface in an unusual discussion with unbelieving Jews late in his ministry (Jn. 10:31-39).[9] The manner in which he had been speaking of the Father had convinced them that he was blaspheming. In reply Jesus appealed to Scripture, calling it "the law" even though the text came from the Psalms (82:6). No doubt this was because all Scripture possessed binding, legal force for him. He asked, "Is it not written in your law, 'I said, ye are gods'?" He called their attention to a casual phrase, "gods." In the phrase the writer referred to the judges of Israel as "gods" in the exercise of their God-given office. It was an argument *a minori ad maius*. If these men could be called "gods" because they served as vehicles of God's Word, all the more does the one whom the Father consecrated and sent into the world deserve that title (v. 36). The underlying assumption in this passage is that God is the author of Scripture and that consequently its teaching, even in an unassuming phrase, is inviolable. The importance of the phrase "Scripture cannot be broken" does not lie in its being an isolated proof text for Jesus' view of inspiration, but in the fact that it is entirely representative of his constant approach to the Bible. This document is for him God's written Word to man.[10]

In an earlier discussion recorded in the Fourth Gospel, Jesus is explaining the accreditation which made possible the divine claims he had been making (Jn. 5:30-47). He insists that he is acting and speaking on the Father's authority. To this fact, he observed, John the Baptist and the miracles bear witness. But even more than that, the Father bears witness to him in the words of Scripture, his written Word. Unfortunately, his unbelieving audience did not let the witness of the Father abide in them, because although they read his Word they rejected it (v. 38f). Jesus' point is that Scripture is the witness which God himself has born and to it man owes unconditional obedience.

Another emphatic piece of evidence as to our Lord's view of Scripture lies in his understanding of promise and fulfilment. It is safe to say that his whole life was conditioned by what he understood biblical prophecy to be saying about the coming messiah. Time and again he uses a phrase such as, "the "scripture must be fulfilled" (Lk. 22:37, Mt. 26:56, Lk. 4:21, etc.).

The reason why these prophecies had to occur by a kind of divine necessity was because they were God-given utterances recorded in God-inspired Scriptures. How could it be otherwise? These things must assuredly come to pass in order that God's Word may prove true. In his attitude to prophecy Jesus reveals his conviction concerning the divine character of the Scriptures.[11] In summary we can say that Jesus everywhere and always regards Scripture as an authoritative document whose ultimate author is God himself. There is, as Warfield said, an avalanche of cumulative evidence on behalf of his doctrine of inspiration which cannot be denied and which for a Christian possess a binding character.

A convenient way to dodge this evidence is to attempt to attribute to the *writers* of the Gospels the view of Scripture Jesus is represented as having held. T. F. Torrence in his review of Warfield's book on inspiration stated that biblical studies have advanced since his day, making an appeal to Jesus' actual views impossible.[12] This statement, accompanied by no exegetical or critical evidence of any kind, reflects a negative view of the historicity of the Gospels widely held today.[13] In reply, let two points be made. The logical consequence of denying the authenticity of Jesus' doctrine of Scripture which pervades all our channels of information about him leads a person to total pessimism regarding any historical knowledge about Jesus of Nazareth, a view completely unacceptable on critical grounds.[14] And, furthermore, it is far more likely that Jesus' understanding and use of the Scriptures conditioned the writers' understanding and use rather than the reverse. The originality with which the Old Testament is interpreted with respect to the person and work of Jesus is too coherent and impressive to be secondary. Certainly this question deserves a fuller treatment than can be attempted here. Nevertheless, there can be little doubt as to what the results of such a study would be.[15]

An older, and even less convincing, attempt to evade the force of Christ's evident high regard for Scripture is the theory of accommodation; as if our Lord adopted the view of his contemporaries without committing himself to the correctness of their position. There are at least two decisive objections to this theory. In the first place, Jesus was no conformist in theology. He openly contradicted views of his time which he considered false. He was not unduly sensitive about undermining current beliefs, a quality of his which must have contributed in part to his being arrested and executed. Secondly, his doctrine of Scripture lay too close to the heart of his vocational consciousness to have been assumed for the sake of argument. Later on we will consider the contention that he was mistaken in his view of inspiration, a serious objection indeed. An error on his part might account for it, but not accommodation.[16]

J. I. Packer expresses our conclusion exactly:

> The fact we have to face is that Jesus Christ, the Son of God incarnate, who claimed divine authority for all that he did and taught, both confirmed the absolute authority of the Old Testament for others and submitted to it unreservedly himself.[17]

II. WAS JESUS A NEGATIVE BIBLICAL CRITIC?

Many interpreters have attempted to evade the force of this evidence by maintaining that Jesus himself qualified, even abrogated, some Old Testament teachings, and could not have held to the high doctrine of inspiration we have described. It will be necessary, therefore, for us to examine his use of Scripture with this objection in mind. Did our Lord differentiate in the biblical teaching that which came from God and that which did not? [18]

It is certainly true that Jesus at times employed the biblical text in a potentially scandalising way in order to drive home his own message. In Mt. 11:5f, for example, he passes over God's judgment on the Gentiles, even though it is announced in the Old Testament texts which he cites (Is. 35:5, 6; 61:1). Similarly, in his inaugural sermon at Nazareth, he breaks his text off in mid-sentence, and drops out the phrase "the day of vengeance of our God" (Lk. 4:19). Often he will deliberately contrast the significance of his mission with leading figures in the Old Testament such as Solomon and Jonah, his own having the greater importance (Mt. 12:41, 42). He let it be known in no uncertain terms that because his message is of greater weight than anything previously, the judgment for refusing it will be correspondingly greater (Mk. 13:19). In these instances, however, we do not detect a low view of Scripture, but rather a radical interpretation at work which cuts across the traditional, domesticated readings to which the text was at that time being subjected. Jesus found it necessary to use shock tactics to get people to hear the underlying divine message which had been so overlaid and subverted by human tradition. He was angered by the approach to the text which blinded men to the inner principles of divine revelation and its messianic fulfilment.

There are, however, some sayings of Jesus in which he appears to repudiate certain Old Testament provisions and replace them with his own seemingly novel instructions. It is crucial for our purpose that we give careful attention to some of these. We must ask, did Jesus employ critical methods of interpretation which would have the effect of undermining the divine authority of the text of Scripture?

Several examples need to be examined which occur in the Sermon on the Mount. We must emphasise the importance of Mt. 5:17 in this connection. Jesus declared emphatically that his purpose was *not* to correct, or deny, or set aside Scripture. He made it perfectly clear that the Old Testament stood on the highest pinnacle of authority. It would be perverse to go ahead and interpret the teaching which follows this saying as if Jesus meant to overthrow and replace it.

Jesus expresses the purpose of his mission in terms of the fulfilment and accomplishment of the Scriptures. His conviction as to the validity of the Old Testament as the Word of God is obvious. David Daube has helped to explain the form of teaching which Jesus is using in the Sermon on the Mount. Our Lord wishes to show the full scope of the Old Testament commands and to strip away current misinterpretations of them. In none of the antitheses is there an intention to annul the provisions of the law but only to carry them to their ultimate extent and meaning. The teaching, Daube observes, is far milder, less revolutionary, than seems at first sight. Jesus is actually upholding the law by unfolding its deeper meaning for the new age. If there is change involved, it is change in accordance with its own intention. It is doubtful whether at any point Jesus negates God's Word. Certainly it was not his intention to do so.[19]

The "eye for an eye" principle of the Old Testament for example was ennacted in the first instance to *limit* vengeance. By means of it the practice of private revenge and family feud was replaced by a fairer and more impartial system of public justice. Our Lord saw how in his day this principle was being utilised for the very thing it was meant to abolish, namely, personal revenge. Therefore, he declares God's demand in that connection. Even if he pushes the renunciation of vengeance a step further, it is in the *direction* set by the ancient rules (Mt. 5:38-42).

The situation is even clearer with regard to Jesus' rejection of hating the enemy. The Old Testament gave the command, "you shall love your neighbour," but does not contain the corollary which tradition had added to it, "and hate your enemy" (Mt. 5:43). Jesus repudiated clearly in this case, not what the Scriptures taught, but the popular interpretation that had been placed upon them. Indeed, the text in Leviticus which was being abused goes on to enjoin love for the stranger, implying something of the principle which Jesus proceeds to expound (Lev. 19:34).

In connection with marriage and divorce Jesus is often thought to advocate the repudiation of an Old Testament ordinance found in Deuteronomy which permitted divorce under certain circumstances (Deut. 24:1-4). His teaching is not, however, a radical departure from the law, but a radical interpretation of it (Mt. 19:3-9). In fact Jesus appeals to another text in the law (Gen. 2:24) as the basis for interpreting Deuteronomy. What he objected to was the deductions people were drawing from the Bible to the effect that God *approves* of divorce. Undoubtedly God gave civil permission for divorce in his law; but that is not to say he gave his moral approval to it. He gave his permission for divorce to a very imperfect people. But the divine ideal was then, and still is, the indissolubility of marriage.

The same pattern is clear in Jesus' attitude to the sabbath. He believed that God ordained the sabbath for man's sake (Mk. 2:27). The sabbath was God's gift to man to bring him rest and blessing. Therefore, Jesus opposed the perversion of this gift which had the effect of making man a slave to the sabbath. He objected, not to the scriptural ordinance, but to the Rabbinic "halakah" which severely restricted the actions permitted on the sabbath day. Thus Jesus not only tolerated the way in which his disciples rubbed together ears of corn on the sabbath day, but also healed repeatedly on the sabbath even when human life was not in danger (Mk. 3:1-6). He justified his approach on his understanding of God's intention in giving man this gift. In addition, he saw clearly that the effect of the "halakah" was to prevent the fulfilling of the command to love the neighbour in need even on the sabbath day.

Jesus collided with the "halakah" on the issue of ritual purity also. The Pharisees had a regulation about washing their hands in a certain way before eating, and many other traditions as well (Mk. 7:3f). Jesus saw in this a clear example where ceremonial customs crowded out really ethical concerns. Therefore, he opposed these Rabbinic prescriptions which had no foundation in the law, and stressed the danger of sins that originate in the heart (7:14-22). Even in the case of clean and unclean foods in that same discussion, it is possible that his purpose was not to declare all such distinctions passé, but only to emphasise God's ethical demands. Had he actually abolished the distinction it is difficult to explain why the early church experienced such difficulty getting over that hurdle (cf. Acts 10:14, 15, 28f).

In the Old Testament oaths were permitted as a concession to dishonesty and to limit abuse of the name of God. But in Jesus' time this right was being badly abused so that the oaths meant nothing and truth was not being protected by them. Therefore, Jesus said, "Swear not at all!" (Mt. 5:34). The command had been given in the first place to preserve truthfulness, so Jesus carries the intent on to its full accomplishment. What God desires is truth, and if we must forbid oaths to achieve it, so be it. The prohibition is easily understandable in the light of contemporary misuse of the practice.[20]

Now we are in a position to get at the heart of what it was about Jesus' use of the Old Testament that shocked people. It was something other than negative biblical criticism. It was rather the extraordinary authority which he assumed for himself in contradicting traditional interpretations and setting forth in no uncertain terms the correct, divine meaning. Without having gone through the prescribed scribal training for Rabbis, Jesus taught "with authority" (Mt. 7:29). Jews of his day believed the age of the Spirit and of prophecy had passed (cf. Ps. 74:9). Yet Jesus came along claiming the anointing of the Spirit and the right to declare God's Word afresh (Lk. 4:18-21). What offended them was his claim to be God's last and most eminent messenger, the one whose life and teachings constituted a new and final revelation to consummate the old.[21]

R. T. France sums it up well:

> While second to none in his reverence for the Scriptures, his diligent study of them and his acceptance of their teaching, and while employing an exegesis that differed from that of his contemporaries generally only in a closer adherence to the original sense where misunderstanding or misuse was the rule, he yet applied the Old Testament in a way which was quite unparalleled. The essence of his new application was that he saw the fulfilment of the predictions and foreshadowings of the Old Testament in himself and his work.[22]

To those who did not accept Jesus' claim to possess an authority equal to the Old Testament and to be the goal toward which the earlier divine revelation was moving, his use of the Scripture was revolutionary and shocking indeed. So strongly did our Lord lay emphasis upon his own authority that it seemed to those outside his circle to be an impingement on the divine authority of the law. Implied in Jesus' teaching about the kingdom of God, for example, was a new definition of the role of the law. The law and the prophets were until John; after John is the time of messianic salvation (Mt. 11:13). From now on a man's relation with the Father is not determined by reference to the law but through the person of Jesus himself. When we realise the magnitude of Jesus' claims, we can begin to appreciate something of what was involved in his reinterpretation of the law in the light of the new age that was dawning.[23] So even if, as some believe, Jesus laid aside some Old Testament ordinance such as the distinction between clean and unclean foods, as Wenham for example contends, it would be as Messiah that he did so, not as a negative biblical critic. It would simply mean that an ordinance whose divine origin he never doubted and which was valid for the pre-messianic period was now no longer in effect. Even this is quite a different matter from what we refer to today as negative biblical criticism.

In conclusion then, we find no evidence to suggest that Jesus' *use* of the Bible contradicted his *doctrine* of it. In both, his witness comes clearly across that Scripture is God's written Word to man, and cannot be broken or laid aside.

III. SHALL WE FOLLOW JESUS CHRIST?

Having considered what Jesus' doctrine of inspiration was, and dealt with a basic objection to it, it is time to assess more fully its bearing upon his followers. How did our Lord understand the nature and force of his own teachings? Does our commitment require that we adopt a certain view of Scripture on the basis of his authority?

In countless ways Jesus indicated that he spoke with the authority of God, and that men would be judged on the basis of whether or not they received his testimony. Jesus explains the basis of this astonishing claim in Mt. 11:27: "All things have been delivered to me by my Father; and no one knows the Son except the Father, and no one knows the Father except the Son and anyone to whom the Son chooses to reveal him." Critics have frequently rejected the authenticity of this *logion*, calling it a thunderbolt fallen from the Johannine sky (Karl von Hase). However, the semitic character of the saying is clear from its language and style, making it most unlikely that it is a late product of hellenistic Christianity. (Notice, for example, the Hebraic use of "know" in the sense of election, as at Qumran.) The saying certainly originates in a semitic milieu.[24] Indeed, we should turn the whole matter around and say that this saying is yet another piece of evidence for taking the Johannine tradition with utmost seriousness. In any case, the meaning of the saying is this: Jesus is the recipient of a divine revelation as complete as only a father can disclose to his son. He is the mediator of the knowledge of God which is intimate, reliable, and true. In this context, with this claim in view, we must assess the bearing of his doctrine of inspiration upon our minds.

This awareness of having received true revelation from the Father is powerfully expressed in Mk. 13:31: "Heaven and earth will pass away, but my words will not pass away." This saying which is recorded in all three Synoptic Gospels is most emphatic. As Wenham puts it, in a paraphrase, "Heaven and earth —the most durable things of time—will pass away, but my words—the eternal truth of God—will never pass away." [25] This text is immediately followed by another which sheds light on our subject. "But of that day and that hour no one knows, not even the angels in heaven, nor the Son, but only the Father" (v. 32).

Two remarks are in order. First, we should notice the claim to authority implicit here. The time of the *parousia* is known only to the Father. It is not known by the angels, and *not even* by the Son. The Son's knowledge is placed second only to the Father's. Second, there is a clear admission by Jesus that his knowledge is limited, at least in respect of this fact. Evidently he does not claim that his knowledge is omniscient in its extent. At the same time, he was not ignorant of his ignorance so to speak, and claimed for the matters he did know and did teach absolute divine authority. On that basis we can understand Jesus' stern warning, "For whoever is ashamed of me and of my words in this adulterous and sinful generation, of him will the Son of man also be ashamed, when he comes in the glory of his Father with the holy angels" (Mk. 8:38).

This sense of divine authority pervades his entire teaching ministry. Over against the entire weight of traditional interpretation, Jesus utters the lofty "verily, verily I say unto you" or "but I say unto you" (Mt. 5:22, 28, 32). Without prefacing his remarks with the prophetic "Thus saith the Lord," Jesus delivers his utterances with a note of unmistakable divine authority.[26] The implication was not lost on his Jewish audience: he was either speaking as God or he was blaspheming. This sense of unqualified assurance in the truth of what he was teaching made a deep impression on his hearers. Just the way Jesus prefaces his sayings with "verily" indicates his messianic consciousness as speaking utterly reliable truth.[27] Unlike an ordinary teacher ever conscious of his limitations and fallibility,

Jesus never betrayed the slightest hesitation concerning the divine authority of what he taught. Wenham cites the forceful comments of the late N. B. Stonehouse:

> Matthew presents Christ as constituting a new authority alongside that of the Old Testament. While he affirms the revelation of the law and the prophets, and is even subservient to it, yet paradoxically his own authority is not derived from the revelation that had gone before, and even completes and transcends it. As not derived from the Old Testament or from any other extraneous source, his authority is seen to inhere in his own person, that is, in his sheer right, simply because of who and what he is, to speak as he spoke. Consequently, not his words only but his person and life also come as a new revelation . . . to fail to comprehend him as constituting a divine disclosure is to fail utterly to understand him at all.[28]

Just how seriously we are expected to take Jesus' teachings is indicated by his remarks at the end of the Sermon on the Mount. He warns us not to think that entrance to the kingdom will be gained simply by saying "Lord, Lord." The condition of approval and admittance is the doing of God's will. We are not merely to listen to his teaching with interest and admiration. We are expected to dedicate ourselves to carry them out in our lives. The wise man, according to Jesus, is the one who hears his words and does them.

Jesus' claim in the Synoptic Gospels to be teaching divine truth on which the salvation of man depends is strongly reinforced by his words recorded in John: "Truly, truly, I say to you, he who hears my word and believes in him who sent me, has eternal life" (5:24f). "My teaching is not mine, but his who sent me" (7:16). He told the Jews who were seeking to kill him that he was "a man who has told you the truth which I heard from God" (8:40). "He who rejects me and does not receive my sayings has a judge; the word that I have spoken will be his judge on the last day. For I have not spoken on my own authority; the Father who sent me has given me commandment what to say and what to speak. And I know that his commandment is eternal life. What I say, therefore, I say as the Father has bidden me" (12:48-50). "For this I have come into the world, to bear witness to the truth. Every one who is of the truth hears my voice" (18:37). The force of these claims is inescapable, and in this connection we should recall the words of the risen Lord: "All authority in heaven and on earth has been given to me" (Mt. 28:18). We are to accept the veracity of his commandments because he is the Lord of all creation.

Shall we follow Jesus in his view of Scripture? In the light of this evidence the question calls for another. How can a Christian even consider *not* doing so? Our Lord's view of inspiration was not an incidental tenet on the border of his theology. His belief in the truthfulness of the Old Testament was the rock on which he based his own sense of vocation and the validity of much of his teachings. Tasker writes:

> Here, if anywhere, we should expect our Lord to speak with divine authority and absolute truth. Indeed, if he could be mistaken on matters which he regarded as of the strictest relevance to his own person and ministry, it is difficult to see exactly how or why he either can or should be trusted anywhere else.[29]

How is it possible to receive Jesus in the unqualified way required by the gospel if the suspicion exists in our mind that he failed to understand himself and his mission at such an important point? Surely it is not possible.

The question about the inspiration of Scripture then really boils down to the issue of Christology. It is impossible to affirm his authority while at the same time seeking to evade his teachings regarding the divine authority of the Bible. If Christ's claim to be the Son of God is true, his person guarantees the truth of all the rest of his teachings as well. Accepting his claims, Christians are committed to believe all that he taught— on his authority. As Packer writes:

> If we accept Christ's claims, therefore, we commit ourselves to believe all that he taught—on his authority. If we refuse to believe some part of what he taught, we are in effect denying him to be the divine messiah—on our own authority. The question, "What think ye of the Old Testament?" resolves into the question, "What think ye of Christ?" And our answer to the first proclaims our answer to the second.[30]

So long as Jesus Christ is confessed, honored, and adored, we may confidently expect a high view of Scripture to persist in the church. And in the light of a considerable defection from that view amongst professed Christians today we boldly appeal for a return to a proper view of the Bible on the basis of the massive fact of our Lord's doctrine of inspiration.

CONCLUSIONS

1. We are fully justified in concluding, having surveyed the evidence, that, according to Jesus Christ, Scripture is the Word of God written. He continually appealed to it as completely authoritative to back up his claims, vindicate his authority, and substantiate his judgments. We consider this conclusion *historically* and *critically* certain regardless of theological presuppositions. In fact, the leading liberal biblical critics readily acknowledge that Jesus was committed to the infallible authority of the Bible.[31]

Furthermore, the doctrine of inspiration is not seldom or weakly taught by our Lord, but repeatedly, emphatically, and with the utmost seriousness set forth. The teaching on this subject is equal in weight and amount to that which can be adduced for any other major doctrine that he taught. We are driven to acknowledge that, according to Jesus' own conviction, the Scriptures are of divine origin, and therefore completely trustworthy, inerrant and infallible.

The point is sometimes made that God could use fallible writings to convey his Word, even as he uses fallible preachers to proclaim it today. Of course he could. But the real issue is not whether he *could* but whether he *did* so. It seems plain according to the testimony of Jesus that God took greater care of his Word than that, seeing to it in his providence that it came to us possessed of his own infallibility, a wholly trustworthy communication to us in writing.

2. The real issue for us in the matter of inspiration then is the authority of Jesus as a doctrinal teacher. If we abandon the high view of Scripture, we are in effect abandoning *Him* in his authority over us. Evangelicals must insist on keeping this issue squarely at the forefront of the discussion. Simply because Jesus Christ is the Lord and Light of Christians, they are bound to acknowledge in turn the authority of the Bible. Jesus teaches them to do so. In his first epistle John offers several tests for determining the genuineness of a person's professed relationship with God. One of them is obedience, or the moral test (2:3-6). Only if we obey Christ can we claim to have a true knowledge of him. Although none of us can claim to obey him perfectly, all of us can strive to conform our thought and life to the will of God. Our love for God is evidenced in our keeping of his commandments.

3. This leads us to an exhortation for those historic Christians who do tremble at God's Word and wish to keep it. Let us take our own argument very seriously. After all, the normative-

ness of Jesus Christ applies much further afield than the doctrine of inspiration. The Pharisees, we should recall, believed in the infallible authority of Scripture, but did not believe and obey it. Let us not invoke the authority of our Lord selectively, to confirm one doctrine precious to us, while disregarding the relevance of his teaching on other subjects. For example, the bearing of Jesus' life and teachings on the questions of political and social ethics are very direct and forceful. We evangelicals should be at the forefront of those who desire to see his authority fully acknowledged and realised in each and every realm.[32]

Finally, let us state, as evangelical Christians, that we do not find it oppressive to submit to the authority of Jesus and his Word as if we secretly envied those who are free of it. All men live and move under the press of some authority or another. What *is* dangerous and oppressive is the acceptance of finite authorities, which do indeed stultify man's freedom and become a source of evil in human affairs.[33]

The apostle John wrote, "This is the love of [for] God, that we keep his commandments. And his commandments are *not* burdensome" (5:3). Jesus' yoke on us is "easy" and his burden is light (Mt. 11:30). God's will for us is "good, acceptable, and perfect" (Rom. 12:2). It is the will of an all-wise, all-loving Father who seeks our highest welfare. Paul wrote in respect of Scripture: "For whatever was written in former days was written for our instruction, that by steadfastness and by the encouragement of the scriptures we might have hope" (Rom. 15:4). We do not feel burdened in having to accept our Lord's commandment with regard to divine inspiration. On the contrary, we are glad to be liberated from the uncertainty and tyranny of merely human opinions, and possessed of the authoritative written Word of God.

NOTES

[1] B. B. Warfield sets forth the evidence pertaining to the view of inspiration held by our Lord, his apostles, and the historic church in *The Inspiration and Authority of the Bible.* (Philadelphia: Presbyterian and Reformed Publishing Co., 1948), pp. 71-166. A fuller treatment of the doctrine in the history of Christian thought is to be found in J. F. Walvoord (ed.), *Inspiration and Interpretation* (Grand Rapids, Mich.: Eerdmans, 1957), and in Clark H. Pinnock, *Biblical Revelation: Foundation of Christian Theology* (Chicago: Moody Press, 1971), pp. 147-74.

[2] The latest and best treatment of our theme is J. W. Wenham, *Christ and the Bible* (Chicago: Inter-Varsity Press, 1973), to which we gladly acknowledge our indebtedness in this essay. R. P. Lightner prepared a similar study entitled *The Saviour and the Scriptures* (Philadelphia: Presbyterian and Reformed Publishing Co., 1966). The subject has been explored on numerous occasions from nonevangelical points of view: e.g., M. Goguel, "Autorité de Christ et autorité de l'Ecriture," *Revue d'Histoire et de Philosophie Religieuses,* XVIII (1938),

218 / God's Inerrant Word

101-125; W. Dantine, "Christologische Grundlegung einer Lehre vom Worte Gottes," *Theologische Zeitschrift*, XII (1956), pp. 471-78; Ch. Hauter, "Christologie et inspiration des Ecritures," *Revue d'Histoire et de Philosophie Religieuses*, XXXIX (1959), pp. 83-96.

³ J. Jeremias, *New Testament Theology. The Proclamation of Jesus* (New York: Scribner 1971), p. 205.

⁴ Cited by J. R. W. S+ott, *The Preacher's Portrait* (London: Tyndale Press, 1961), p. 27.

⁵ Cf. C. H. Dodd, *According to the Scriptures* (London: Nisbet, 1952), pp. 109f.

⁶ Cf. Bruce Vawter, *Biblical Inspiration* (Philadelphia: Westminster, 1972), pp. 22-28.

⁷ W. D. Davies defends the authenticity of this saying against Bultmann in his essay "Matthew 5:17, 18," in *Christian Origins and Judaism* (Philadelphia: Westminster, 1962), pp. 31-66.

⁸ Jeremias presents the Aramaic backgrounds to the expression *op. cit.*, pp. 83f.

⁹ Cf. E. D. Freed, *Old Testament Quotations in the Gospel of John* (Leiden: Brill, 1965), pp. 60-65.

¹⁰ For detailed analysis of this passage, cf. the major commentaries on John by R. E. Brown, L. Morris, C. K. Barrett, and R. Bultmann.

¹¹ On the use Jesus made of Old Testament predictions, cf. R. T. France, *Jesus and the Old Testament* (Chicago: Inter-Varsity Press, 1971), pp. 83-163.

¹² Torrence, *Scottish Journal of Theology*, VII (1954), p. 105.

¹³ J. W. Wenham gives ample reasons for not subjecting the Gospels to radical criticism (*op, cit.*, pp. 38-42). It is more reasonable to suppose that Jesus created the community than that the community created Jesus.

¹⁴ Jeremias is now prepared to say, on the basis of his investigations, that "in the synoptic tradition it is the inauthenticity, and not the authenticity, of the sayings of Jesus that must be demonstrated" (*op. cit.*, p. 37).

¹⁵ Cf. the impressive work of R. T. France, *op. cit.*

¹⁶ R. V. G. Tasker, *The Old Testament in the New Testament* (rev. ed.: London: SCM 1954), pp. 36f.; J. I. Packer, *"Fundamentalism" and the Word of God* (London: Inter-Varsity, 1958), pp. 60f.

¹⁷ *Ibid.*, p. 55.

¹⁸ For an overview of Jesus' use of the Bible, see E. E. Tilden, "The Study of Jesus' Interpretive Methods," *Interpretation*, VII (1953), pp. 45-61; A. H. McNeile, "Our Lord's Use of the Old Testament," in H. B. Swete. (ed.), *Essays on Some Biblical Questions of the Day* (London: Macmillan, 1909), pp. 215-50; R. T. France, *op. cit.*

¹⁹ Daube, *The New Testament and Rabbinic Judaism* (London: Oxford University Press, 1956), pp. 55-62.

²⁰ Cf. W. D. Davies, *The Setting of the Sermon on the Mount* (Cambridge: Cambridge University Press, 1964), pp. 239-45.

²¹ Jeremias, *op.cit.*, pp. 76-85.

²² R. T. France, *op. cit.*, p. 223.

²³ Cf. G. E. Ladd, *Jesus and the Kingdom* (New York: Harper & Row, 1964), pp. 280f.

²⁴ Jeremias discusses this *logion*, defending its authenticity, *op. cit.*, pp. 56-61.

²⁵ Wenham *op. cit.*, p. 47. Recognising the problem implicit in the eschatological discourse in which this saying is lodged, Wenham includes an extensive discussion on the so-called "delay of the Parousia" (pp. 64-73).

²⁶ Cf. N. Geldenhys, *Supreme Authority* (London: Marshall, Morgan and Scott, 1953).

²⁷ Article "Amen," *Theological Dictionary of the New Testament*, ed. G. Kittel, trans. G. W. Bromiley, I (Grand Rapids, Mich.: Eerdmans, 1964), pp. 337-38.

²⁸ Wenham, *op. cit.*, p. 51.

²⁹ Tasker, *op. cit.*, p. 37.

³⁰ Packer, *op. cit.*, p. 59.

³¹ Kenneth S. Kantzer documents this fact in an article, "Christ and Scripture," *HIS* Magazine, [Inter-Varsity Christian Fellowship], January, 1966.

³² John H. Yoder's work in this field deserves careful attention. See *The Original Revolution* (Scottdale, Pa: Herald, 1971) and *The Politics of Jesus* (Grand Rapids, Mich.: Eerdmans, 1972).

³³ Cf. G. D. Kaufman, "The Ground of Biblical Authority: Six Theses," *Journal of Bible and Religion*, XXIV (1956), pp. 25-30.

10

THE APOSTLE PAUL: SECOND MOSES TO THE NEW COVENANT COMMUNITY

A Study in Pauline Apostolic Authority

Peter R. Jones

In 1896, after a century of critical study of the New Testament apostolate, E. Haupt observed: "The question of the origin and the concept of the apostolate currently belongs to the most complicated and the most difficult problems of New Testament scholarship."[1] Some seventy-six years later, in 1970, Rudolf Schnackenburg is forced to admit: "In spite of the strenuous efforts of the past few decades, the origin and early history of the apostolate remain still quite obscure."[2] The Jewish *shaliach* theory[3] has been unable to account in itself for the prophetic nature of Paul's call and mission,[4] and Harnack's theory of the wandering charismatic missionary[5] (which still persists today in many circles[6]), cannot begin to explain the eschatological and foundational role that Paul seems clearly to play. Happily the eschatological interpretation has lately received some attention by a few recognized scholars. However, the most recent attempt, by the radical critic Walter Schmithals,[7] explaining Paul's apostolate by means of Gnosticism, "de-eschatologizes" him and makes him a member of a numberless band of timeless "gnostic envoys." Thus Paul and his words are reduced to the level of just another Christian person and opinion, in accordance with the gnostic (and existentialist) rejection of "office" and deification of every knowing soul. The unmistakable New Testament notion of the apostle *extra nos*, standing over-against the church, has been destroyed.[8]

In the opinion of the present writer, the above solutions fail to account for the essence of Paul's apostolate, and hence his authority. Thus this essay[9] makes a different and somewhat novel proposal. Paul's apostolate should be seen as the eschatological fulfillment of Old Testament and Jewish expectations concerning the coming of a second Moses. Paul's authority consists in the exercise of this unrepeatable role, specifically as the recipient of the eschatological revelation of the New Covenant. This revelation is the foundation which he lays for the new people of God. It has abiding normative significance for them throughout the period of the last days.

PAUL AS FOUNDATION-LAYER

The obvious starting point in the *corpus Paulinium* for Paul's role as foundation-layer is I Corinthians 3:5-16. Here Paul makes some remarkable claims. He "plants" (ἐγὼ ἐφύτευσα, v. 6), "lays a foundation" (θεμέλιον ἔθηκα, v. 10), and the latter he does "as a wise master-builder" (ὡς σοφὸς ἀρχιτέκτων, v. 10). In the first place, it should be noted that God's work of creation, the divine foundational activity which establishes the physical cosmos, can be expressed as "planting the heavens and laying the foundations of the earth" (*linto'a šamayim v*e*liṣodh 'arets*, Isa. 51:16.[10] God also "plants" his people. This is expressed in the form of a promise in Exodus 15:17: "Thou wilt bring them in, and plant (*nata'*; cf. καταφυτεύειν, LXX) them on thy own mountain," and became a reality according to Jeremiah 11:17,[11] so that Israel is known as God's "planting" (Isa. 5:7, *n*e*ta'*; LXX, νεόφυτον).[12] The verb *yaṣadh*, "to found or lay a foundation," is many times used by itself to describe God's creation of the world.[13] In particular it is used of the creating work of Wisdom according to Proverbs 3:19: *YHVH b*e*hakhmah yasadh-'arets* ("The Lord by Wisdom founded the earth"). But again, God also "lays the foundation" of His people[14] and of the Temple, where He dwells in the midst of His people.[15] Thus with the terms "planting" and "founding" the Old Testament presents God's creation both of the world and of the people of His own choosing.

However, the eschatological aspect of these notions ought

not to be overlooked. For the Old Testament Scriptures look forward to a day when God will do a new thing, and establish a New Covenant with His people. The *loci classici* for the expectation of a New Covenant are Ezekiel 36-37 and Jeremiah 31:27-34. Significantly in both places this new work of God is spoken of as "building" and "planting." Thus the Lord says through Jeremiah:

> Behold, the days are coming, says the Lord, when I will sow the house of Israel and the house of Judah with the seed of Man and the seed of beast. And it shall come to pass that as I have watched over them to pluck up and break down, to overthrow, destroy and bring evil, so I will watch over them to build and to plant, says the Lord. (Jer. 31:27-28; cf. Ezek. 36:36) [16]

Significantly, the Qumran Community, who believed itself to be the community of the New Covenant, is also described in the Community Rule as *l°sòdh mabhnîth qòdhes l°matta'ath 'olam* ("a foundation to the Building of Holiness, an eternal plantation:" 1QS 11:8; cf. 8:5).[17]

On the basis of this Old Testament and Jewish background, the statements of Paul in I Cor. 3:6 about his apostolic task would indicate that he is claiming more than simply the honor of being the first missionary at Corinth,[18] or a successful church-planter as we moderns understand that term. Rather Paul is affirming his eschatological role in establishing the terms and content of the *New Covenant*. In his second letter to the Corinthians he explicitly refers to himself as a minister of the New Covenant (II Cor. 3:5—$\iota\kappa\acute{\alpha}\nu\omega\sigma\epsilon\nu$ $\dot{\eta}\mu\tilde{\alpha}\varsigma$ $\delta\iota\alpha\kappa\acute{o}\nu o\nu\varsigma$ $\kappa\alpha\iota\nu\tilde{\eta}\varsigma$ $\delta\iota\alpha\vartheta\acute{\eta}\kappa\eta\varsigma$), and then further describes this New Covenant ministry in II Cor. 13:10 with terms taken directly from the New Covenant prophecy already quoted, Jer. 31:28. He speaks of his authority($\dot{\epsilon}\xi o\upsilon\sigma\acute{\iota}\alpha$) for building ($\epsilon\dot{\iota}\varsigma$ $o\dot{\iota}\kappa o\delta o\mu\acute{\eta}\nu$) and not for destroying ($\epsilon\dot{\iota}\varsigma$ $\kappa\alpha\vartheta\alpha\acute{\iota}\rho\epsilon\sigma\iota\nu$).[19] In other words, Paul shows by his explicit reference to Jer. 31:28 that he understands his own task of planting[20] and building/founding as an eschatological ministry of establishing the New Covenant, an act of God prophesied in the Old Testament and realized through him as an apostle. In the words of J. Roloff, commenting on these images, Paul is employing "eine grundsätzliche Aussage über den heilsgeschichtlichen Ort des Apostels in Volk Gottes." [21]

The Old Testament states that God by wisdom, understood as impersonal principle, laid the foundations of the earth (*yāṣadh*, Prov. 3:19; LXX, $\dot{\epsilon}\vartheta\epsilon\mu\epsilon\lambda\acute{\iota}\omega\sigma\epsilon\nu$), and that Wisdom, now personified, was beside Him as He marked out the foundations (*mosdey*; LXX, τὰ θεμέλια) of the earth like a master workman ('*āmōn*; LXX, ἁρμόζουσα; i.e. a "joiner" or "artificer," Prov. 8:29-30). Can this Scriptural background throw any light on Paul's claim to be a σοφὸς ἀρχιτέκτων? It has already been established that Paul by his images of planting and foundation-laying is dependent upon the Old Testament notions of divine creation of the cosmos and the eschatological creation of a new people or new humanity. Indeed, Paul goes so far as to call the Church a "new creation"—καινὴ κτίσις (ἐν Χριστῷ-II Cor. 5:17). One should note the remarkable fact that Prov. 8:29-30 and I Cor. 3:10 both contain two identical notions which to my knowledge occur nowhere else in the Scriptures. There is a terminological correspondence between ἐποίει τὰ θεμέλια (Prov. 8:29) and θεμέλιον ἔθηκα (I Cor. 3:10). '*āmōn*, master worker, though not translated as ἀρχιτέκτων in the Septuagint, expresses the very same notion as ἀρχιτέκτων, and already in the Rabbis is understood to mean an "architect." [22] This identification suggests that Paul saw an analogy between the founding of the old and the new creations and that as Christ, the Wisdom of God (incidentally, an important Christological motif in the early chapters of I Corinthians), had laid the foundations of the earth, so Paul, the apostle of Christ, with Christ's authority was laying the foundation of the new creation understood as the people of God. It is in his *office* as apostolic ambassador for Christ (II Cor. 5:20 f.) that Paul could dare to draw such an analogy without any suggestion of innate ontic superiority or semi-divinity. Nevertheless, I do argue that such a lofty conception of his calling is the way Paul intended his apostolic office to be understood in the Church. Perhaps this is how we should understand his statement to the Galatians that they received him "as an angel of God, as Christ Jesus" (Gal. 4:14). Furthermore, such a conception of his office makes sense out of his apostolic claim associating himself so closely with Wisdom as to "impart a secret and hidden wisdom of God" (I Cor. 2:7), to "have the mind of Christ" [23] (I Cor. 2:16) who is the "Wisdom of God" (I Cor. 1:24, 30) and to know that Christ is speaking in him (II Cor. 13:3) so that he "cannot do anything against the truth but only for the truth" (II Cor. 13:8). But the force of these claims is to stress the essential nature of Paul's apostolic office as a unique spokesman for the Lord, empowered with all the divine authority for laying the foundation of God's new creation, kingdom, and covenant people.

Primarily the content of the foundation that Paul lays is Jesus Christ (I Cor. 3:11). And Paul is unambiguously clear that he does this on the basis of the theophanic revelation of the Son to him (Galatians 1:15 f.). The Damascus Road is both revelation and vocation. Paul saw God the Son, and at the moment when he saw "the glory of God in the face of Christ" (II Cor. 4:6) he received the Gospel (Gal. 1:12). This is revelation. But the experience was also one of prophetic vocation containing all the traditional elements of the Old Testament prophetic calls. In other words, Paul is called to a life of prophecy in which he not only proclaims the word of the Lord, the Gospel, to the Gentiles (Gal. 1:16; cf. Acts 9:15, 26:17-18) but also receives an "abundance of revelations"— $ὑπερβολὴ τῶν ἀποκαλύψεων$ (II Cor. 12:7). This "abundance" indicates that Paul was competent to speak as a prophet of God on subjects other than the Gospel narrowly defined in the terms of I Cor. 15:3 f. Moreover, if the foundation of the living eschatological temple of God is Jesus Christ, God's mystery in whom are hid all the treasures of wisdom and knowledge (Col. 2:3),[24] then it will be seen that the content of Paul's foundational revelation is broader than soteriological missionary proclamation. This is not to suggest that whenever Paul spoke he uttered prophetic words. The Old Testament prophets were presumably able to make a distinction between their prophecies and the rest of their speech. But Paul gives evidence through the solemn appeal to his apostolicity in the praescripts of his letters[25] that he was conscious of laying the apostolic foundation of the Church when he put pen to parchment in this way. This is said explicitly in the only Pauline letter which does not contain the term "apostle" or a synonym for it, namely II Thessalonians. Here Paul says: "Hold to the traditions which you were taught by us, either by word of mouth or *by letter*" (II Thes. 2:15).

The argument emerging here is that Paul implies that the foundation which he lays for the Church is his prophetically inspired words and letters consciously issued from an unmistakable sense of eschatological apostolic authority. Thus, his letters can act as a perfectly adequate substitute for his apostolic presence (II Cor. 13:10). This he states immediately before defining his apostolic authority as "building" and "planting," a clear reference to the Old Testament grounds for his office as foundation-layer. In other words, his letters "build and plant" and make up the foundation. Thus Paul insists that they be read in the gatherings of worship along with and just as the Old Testament Scriptures.[26]

Paul gives additional evidence that he conceived of his letters as the foundation on which the Church is built when in II Thes.

2:15 he clearly identifies them with "the traditions." By the use of this term the apostle places his writings in the category of the permanently significant in which the believers must stand firm—$\kappa\rho\alpha\tau\epsilon\tilde{\iota}\nu$ (cf. Romans 6:17) [27]—and which, of course, they must obey and preserve. Similarly, Paul refers to his teaching as "my ways," my $h^a likhah$, which he teaches "everywhere in every church" (I Cor. 4:17-18),[28] so that the extent of his authority is "all the churches" (II Cor. 11:28; cf. I Cor. 14:34). Now with this awareness of "traditional" and "foundational" activity already apparent in Paul's early letters, it comes as no surprise to find the same emphasis on "guarding what has been entrusted" in the pastoral epistles.[29] Paul is simply insisting that the foundation he lays be recognized for what it is—the indispensable foundation of the Church.

The eschatological foundation-laying activity of the apostle, promised beforehand in the Scriptures, is neither a ministry of temporary significance to be replaced by further revelation, because the apostolic tradition must be kept and guarded; nor is it a ministry to be repeated from generation to generation, for it is, according to Ephesians 2:20 and Jude 3 a foundation of apostolic tradition "once delivered" ($\ddot{\alpha}\pi\alpha\xi\ \pi\alpha\rho\alpha\delta o\vartheta\epsilon\acute{\iota}\sigma\eta$) upon which the Church is built. Moreover, in terms of the metaphor, a building requires but one foundation.

Nevertheless, it is necessary to fit this notion of foundation-laying into other elements of Paul's thought which express a heightened sense of the apocalyptic significance of his apostolate. According to Rom. 11 the revelation to Paul of the Gospel to the Gentiles completes the foundation of the Church, and the last act of world history begins.[30] Thus the advent of Paul's Gentile mission means that Paul, in a very real sense, is the prophetic forerunner of the end of the world.[31] For many scholars the tension which these two notions produce is so great that in general Paul the "establisher" is jettisoned as deutero-Pauline, in favor of Paul the apocalyptic who was nevertheless wrong about the end of the world. It seems to this present author that Paul himself indicates the solution to this apparent dilemma by presenting himself as an eschatological or second Moses, for the second Moses in Judaism was expected to be *both* the last prophet before the consummation and the founder of the New Covenant community whose teaching would guide it until the end came. The evidence for this will now be discussed.

THE APOSTLE PAUL—A SECOND MOSES

Again the starting point is a text in the Corinthian correspondence, II Cor. 3:1-4:6. This epistle is significant for present purposes because in it Paul meets head on the claims to apostolicity from so-called ψευδαπόστολοι with his own apostolic claims and criteria in order to convince a confused and disloyal Church. II Cor. 3:1-4:6 stands at the very heart of what scholars call the "Great (Apostolic) Apology," II Cor. 2:14-7:4.[32]

The argumentation is as follows: (*A*) Paul in II Corinthians 3 compares himself with Moses. (*B*) Because of the presence of the eschatological glory, Paul's ministry is superior to and different than the ministry of Moses. This superiority suggests that Paul is claiming the ministry of the second Moses. (*C*) What Paul says about the second Moses can be checked against the second Moses of the Qumran Scrolls. We shall now take up each of the three points of this argument in detail.

A.

It is immediately apparent that Paul sets his understanding of the apostolate in the context of Old Testament *Heilsgeschichte*. In II Cor. 3:4 he makes the remarkable claim of being a "minister of the New Covenant" διάκονοι καινῆς διαθήκης.[33] Moreover, this apostolic New Covenant ministry is compared with Moses' Old Covenant ministry, as II Cor. 3:12 clearly states.[34] In other words, Paul is not thinking at random about any of the Old Covenant ministries of kings, priests, and prophets.[35] Rather he has in view the specific ministry of Moses, the Old Covenant mediator, whose task it was to receive and establish in written form and practice the Sinaitic Covenant between Jahweh and his people.[36] Now beyond the obvious force of the passage, there are two other items that would indicate Paul's intention to compare his and Moses' "founding" ministries, namely the allusion which Paul makes here to the reception of the Gospel, and an implied comparison with the call of Moses.

1. The ministry of the New Covenant in II Cor. 3:6 is introduced by the phrase ἡ ἱκανότης ἡμῶν ἐκ τοῦ θεοῦ ὃς καὶ ἱκανώσεν ἡμᾶς κ.τ.λ. Paul is referring to the experience of conversion and commission as an apostle whereby God made him worthy to exercise the New Covenant ministry. He uses a similar phrase in I Thes. 2:4– δεδοκιμάσμεθα ὑπὸ τοῦ θεοῦ πιστευθῆναι τὸ εὐαγγέλιον ("we have been approved by God to be entrusted with the gospel"). In both cases it is God who makes Paul worthy or approves him just as it is God who reveals His Son to Paul in Gal. 1:15, while the New Covenant ministry of II Cor. 3 and the gospel of I Thes. 2:4 are clearly in parallel (cf. the gospel in Gal. 1:11-12, and 16—εὐαγγελίζωμαι) as the purpose and result of the divine activity.[37] Clearly then, Paul is referring to his reception of "the gospel" when he uses the term ἱκανόω. More-

over, the aorist tense of the verb indicates this, as a number
of scholars have argued.[38] Baird establishes this in reference to the aorist tense employed in the case of Moses. He
comments: "The latter [Moses' ministry] which is 'a ministry
of death, carved in letters of stone, came (ἐγενήθη—aorist) in
glory.' Thus, the apostle, by way of contrast, is stressing the
receiving of the ministry or the commission to his apostolic
calling." [39] However, the contrast with the *"coming"* of the
Old Covenant through Moses means that Paul is speaking of
the New Covenant *coming* through him as an apostle of Christ.
In other words, Paul implies that he is a mediator of the New
Covenant. The term διάκονος was a very general reference as
I Cor. 3:5 shows. Both Paul and Apollos are διάκονοι. But Paul
shows that in each particular case it has a specific content—
καὶ ἑκάστῳ ὡς ὁ κύριος ἔδωκεν (v. 5). In I Cor. 3:5, Paul describes
his διακονία as planting and foundation-laying. And it is now
evident that this is consistent with his usage of διακονία in II Cor.
3:5.

2. One should note the further comparison of Paul's and
Moses' call and commission in the employment of the terminology in II Cor. 3. It is significant, and perhaps more than
coincidental, that the account of Moses' own vocation at the
burning bush contains the pregnant term ἱκανός. To my knowledge only Austin Farrer makes this connection, and it will suffice to quote him. Moses, when faced by the divine majesty
and awesomeness of the task to which God had called him, ex-
claimed: οὐχ ἱκανός εἰμι (Ex. 4:10). But, says Farrer, Moses
"was made sufficient by the All-Sufficing One (*El Shaddai*, interpreted as *Theos ho hikanos*). For God said to him, 'Who hath
made man's mouth: or who maketh dumb or deaf or seeing or
blind? Do not I the Lord? Now, therefore, go, and I will be
with thy mouth, and teach thee what thou shalt speak.' [40] Who
then, says the apostle, is sufficient (*hikanos*) for the second
and greater ministry? We are; but our sufficiency also is in-
fused by grace." [41]

Establishing the comparison between the covenantal ministries of Moses and Paul helps elucidate the meaning of the
enigmatic images of "letters of recommendation" and the "New
Covenant" in vv. 1-3 of chapter 3. For clarity's sake I will
first state my conclusion: Paul as an apostle claims to have
been entrusted with the New Covenant, just as Moses was given
the Old, but this time it is written on his heart, not on stone
tablets. How do we demonstrate this?

Paul answers the charge, no doubt instigated by the false

apostles,[42] that he carries no letters of recommendation by identifying the Corinthian believers as such a letter. There is an important textual problem in II Cor. 3:2, but the preferred reading must certainly be "our hearts." [43] Thus the letter is written on Paul's heart. In support of this interpretation is the ancient usage of letters of recommendation, since this requires that the one introduced *carries the letter with him*. [44] Paul goes on then to define this letter as written by the Holy Spirit, from Christ delivered by Paul and written on his "fleshly heart." But he moves quickly to the New Covenant imagery.[45]

Moses' letter of recommendation one might say, was the Old Covenant represented by the two stone tablets (v. 6). His authentication before the children of Israel was the Covenant entrusted to him. Similarly Paul's letter of recommendation was the New Covenant, represented by the new people of God, written on his heart.[46] Moreover, that the fleshly heart of the apostle is the *locus* of God's latest revelation of the New Covenant in Christ is shown by the subsequent context, II Cor. 4:6. Here alluding to his vocation, Paul claims that through the face of Christ God has shone *in his heart*. The statement in Gal. 1:16 regarding the Damascus Road event is virtually the same: "God revealed His Son in me ($\dot{\epsilon}\nu$ $\dot{\epsilon}\mu o \iota$)." [47] In other words, the *contents* of the New Covenant, God's Son and the new universalized people of God, are written on Paul's heart. This then is the ministry of the New Covenant of which Paul speaks. Little wonder he can speak so possessively of "my gospel." [48]

B.

The words $o\dot{\upsilon}$ $\kappa\alpha\vartheta\acute{\alpha}\pi\epsilon\rho$ $M\omega\upsilon\sigma\tilde{\eta}s$ ("not like Moses") characterize the remainder of the Moses/Paul discussion. If there is a formal comparison between Moses and Paul being entrusted with Covenants, there are elements of contrast between the "dispensation of righteousness" or, one could say, between the ministry of Moses and the ministry of the second Moses. According to II Cor. 3 the new features are threefold.

1. There is a democratization of the Spirit and knowledge in the new such as there never was in the old. Moses had to veil his face because the people were unable to share his vision of God (II Cor. 3:12).[49] This is not the case in the New Covenant. The apostle as a second Moses is "very bold" (3:12) since his vision of God's glory in the face of Christ may be shared with all so that "we all with unveiled face" can behold the glory of God (3:18).

2. The second new element suggests that the second Moses is the source of true saving knowledge of God *via* his inspired exegesis of the Old Testament. Moses was the source of true knowledge about God in the Old Covenant and this knowledge theoretically could give life. And it appears that a unique experience of God is allowed to Moses, according to Num. 12:6-8: "If there is a prophet among you, I the Lord make myself known to him in a vision, I speak with him in a dream. Not so with my servant Moses; he is entrusted with all my house. With him I speak mouth to mouth, clearly and not in dark speech; and he beholds the form of the Lord." However, the difference between Moses and the apostle, the second Moses, is that God's final revelation also comes through a divinely inspired exegesis of the Old Testament. This is true for the other apostles according to Luke 24,[50] and it is certainly true of Paul. II Cor. 3:12ff must be read in the light of Rom. 1:1 where Paul states that the Gospel was "promised beforehand through His [God's] prophets in the Holy Scriptures," and in the light of Rom. 16:25f where Paul speaks of "my gospel" and, synonymously, "the revelation of the mystery" which "is now disclosed and through the prophetic writings is made known." [51]

Of course, on closer observation, II Cor. 3:12 ff clearly says the same thing, though with different terms.[52] Notice a certain parallelism. There is a veil over the Old Covenant when it is read (3:14-15) and there is also a veil over "our gospel" (4:3). Paul's gospel is on a par with the written Old Covenant. Moreover, it removes the veil from the Old Covenant. In 3:14 it is true that Christ is the one who removes this veil, but in 4:4 the Gospel and Christ are identified. What the Gospel permits to be seen is the glory of Christ who is the likeness of God. And of course it is the divine glory in the Scriptures that cannot be seen because of the veil. In other words, the gospel is the key, deriving from the Scriptures, which unlocks the Scriptures and permits God's glory to be seen. Thus the statement of Paul "When a man turns to the Lord the veil (over the Scriptures) is removed" means that when a man believes the apostolic Gospel he is able to understand the Scriptures/Moses.[53] This apostolic Gospel is the source of saving knowledge. Therefore not to believe the Gospel is to perish.[54] To be charged with this apostolic task is to be "to one a fragrance from death to death, to the other a fragrance from life to life." [55]

3. In the New Covenant ministry, the role of the Servant of

the Lord, the 'ebhedh YHVH of the Isaianic Servant Songs, qualifies the second Moses' mission. A number of recognized scholars have noted the existence and importance of servant traditions in Paul's own apostolic self-understanding.[56] Jesus is presented as the Servant on only three occasions in Paul's writings, clearly because the focus is now on Christ as the κύριος.[57] Paul on significant occasions uses Servant traditions to characterize his own ministry. In Paul's description of his call in Gal. 1 he not only employs the term for the Servant in the Servant Songs, i.e. δοῦλος (Gal. 1:10),[58] but describes his call with terms and concepts common to the call of the Servant. Paul says: "ὅτε δὲ εὐδόκησεν ὁ ἀφορίσας με ἐκ κοιλίας μητρός μου καὶ καλέσας (Gal. 1:15). The Servant says: κύριος ὁ πλάσας με ἐκ κοιλίας δοῦλον ἑαυτῷ (Isa. 49:5), and ἐκ κοιλίας μητρός μου ἐκάλεσεν τὸ ὄνομα μου (Isa. 49:1).[59] Paul's task ("to preach the gospel to the Gentiles," Gal. 1:16) is the same as the Servant's to whom the Lord says, "I will give you as a light to the nations that my salvation may reach the ends of the earth." Indeed, Paul quotes this very passage, according to Acts 13:47, at the decisive moment of turning from the unbelieving Jews in pursuit of the call of the Risen Lord. Luke's account again agrees with Paul's in Gal. 1:15-16, for the Lord commissions Paul with terms taken from the First and Second Servant Songs (Acts 26:17-18).[60] Also Paul fears to have "run in vain"—κενὸν ἐκοπίασα (Phil. 2:16), as did the Servant, who says, "I have laboured in vain" —κενῶν ἐκοπίασα (Isa. 49:4).[61] Paul also entreats the Corinthians not to accept the grace of God in vain (κενός), and then goes on to quote from the Second Servant Song, "At the acceptable time I have listened to you, and helped you on the day of salvation" (II Cor. 6:1-2).[62] Paul identifies the present as the time of eschatological fulfilment of this prophecy, and calls upon the Corinthians, as he argues for his apostolic authority, to accept his New Covenant διακονία (v. 3). Now the "original reference (Isa. 49:8) is to the help which would give his Servant in the day when salvation would be offered to the Gentiles,"[63] and since there is no indication that Paul would speak to the Corinthians as if they were the Servant who should offer salvation to the Gentiles (they *are* the Gentiles!) one is led to conclude that Paul is referring to his own eschatological Servant role.

The presence of Servant traditions qualifying Paul's ministry in II Cor. 6:1 f. helps to clarify the Servant allusions in II Cor. 4:6. Here Paul, as he concludes his apostolic apology, refers again to his own call and commission, now by alluding to the call of the Servant. Christ Jesus is the Lord— κύριος (4:5); Paul is the Servant— δοῦλος; and God through Christ has shone in Paul's heart in calling and commissioning him. This calling is otherwise represented as being promised beforehand in the Scriptures where God said: "Let light shine out of darkness." This is hardly the command of God at creation[64] and may safely be seen as an allusion to the mission of the Servant in Isaiah.[65] Now the importance of seeing this allusion lies, for present purposes, in the fact that Paul has apparently juxtaposed second Moses and ʿebhedh YHVH traditions in his apostolic apology in II Cor. 3 f.

C.

In order to show conclusively that Paul is presenting himself as a second Moses in II Cor. 3, these three features of newness and contrast—democratization, inspired exegesis, and servant traditions—will have to be established as essential features of the second Moses figure in pre-Pauline Judaism. Remarkably, they are so.

The traditions of a second Moses expectation are many and varied, to be found in the Old Testament,[66] at Qumran, in Samaritan eschatology, in Philo and Josephus, the New Testament and the Rabbis. They divide into two major forms, the messianic and the non-messianic. Our Lord appeared as a messianic/kingly second Moses[67] as did those about whom he warned in Matthew 24:24 f. These did Mosaic "signs and wonders" in "the wilderness," and, according to Josephus, promised to conquer the Romans and establish their own thrones.[68] But there is evidence for the expectation of a non-messianic Mosaic eschatological Prophet, for instance in John 1:21, where "Christ" and "the Prophet" are distinguished. The best example of this type is the Teacher of Righteousness of the Qumran Scrolls: and this figure offers some remarkable comparisons with the Apostle Paul.

The Qumran Community believed itself to be the people of God of the last days, the "members of the New Covenant" (habbᵉrith hahᵃdhasah),[69] who typologically re-enacted the second Exodus and the wilderness sojourn of the first wilderness generation in order to be proved by God,[70] though now with the presence of the eschatological Spirit,[71] awaiting the "New Conquest" of the kingdom of God.[72] Similarly Paul represents the Christian community as those "upon whom the ends of the ages has come," [73] who are indeed the community of the New Covenant.[74] "Christ, the paschal lamb has been

sacrificed," [75] thus making possible the second Exodus, and
the present life of the Church, though empowered by the Spirit,
is in effect a wilderness sojourn,[76] the way of the Cross,
awaiting the final consummation. These convictions of the
Qumran community were based upon the revelation given to
their founder, the Teacher of Righteousness.[77] He is everywhere in the Scrolls portrayed as a second Moses.[78] Deuteronomy 18:15 f., the key passage of second Moses expectations,
is applied to him.[79] In the Damascus Document he is called
"The Stave" (*hamm^{e}hôqēq*), a title given to Moses in Jewish
and Samaritan traditions,[80] and "The Interpreter of the
Law" *(dhōreš hattôràh)*, which is synonymous with the epithet
given to Moses by Philo—$\dot{\epsilon}\rho\mu\eta\nu\epsilon\omega\varsigma$ $\nu\acute{o}\mu\omega\nu$ $\dot{\iota}\epsilon\rho\tilde{\omega}\nu$. [81] Over and over
his role in the New Israel recalls the Pentateuchal account of
Moses' life. The Teacher of Righteousness and his teachings
are compared with Moses holding up the brass Serpent.[82]
As Moses provided water for the wilderness generation, so the
Teacher of Righteousness opens up a Spring (albeit spiritual
in nature) for the Qumran community.[83] The parallels could
be multiplied, but there are some also shared by Paul which
should be noted.

The Teacher of Righteousness complains, "The members
of my Covenant have rebelled and have murmured round about
me," [84] recalling the murmuring against Moses. Indeed, the
pentateuchal terms *ràghal* (Deut. 1:27, Ps. 104:25) and *t^{e}lun-
noth* (Ex. 16:7, 8, 9, 12: Num. 17:25) occur in 1QH 8:22-23.
Interestingly, Paul also employs the Septuagint equivalent
$\gamma o\gamma\gamma\acute{\upsilon}\zeta\epsilon\iota\nu$ in I Cor. 10:10 and Phil. 2:14 in warning against opposition in his own community. Further, the Teacher of Righ-
teousness describes himself as a father, and nurse, and the one
who gives birth to his own community.[85] With strikingly identical images, Paul speaks of the Corinthians and Galatians as
his "children" [86] whom he "begot" ($\dot{\upsilon}\mu\tilde{a}\varsigma$ $\dot{\epsilon}\gamma\acute{\epsilon}\nu\nu\eta\sigma\alpha$) [87] or with
whom he is in the throes of childbirth($\dot{\omega}\delta\acute{\iota}\nu\omega$).[88] To the Thes-
salonians Paul was like a "father" and a "nurse taking care
of her children" (I Thes. 2:7, 11). Needless to say, these are
the very images used by Moses to describe his relation to the
Old Covenant community.[89] Gert Jeremias, who has written
the definitive study on the Teacher of Righteousness, notes
this correspondence between Paul and the Teacher of Righteousness over the fathering and nursing of a community when
he says: "So tritt der Lehrer mit seinem Ausspruch durchaus
in eine Reihe mit Paulus." [90] But Jeremias is unable to account
for this "Reihe" whereas the present interpretation of Paul
as a second Moses can. Accordingly, the Teacher of Righteous-

ness is able to clarify the Moses/Paul comparisons in II Cor. 3, and especially the features of newness which characterize the second Moses.

1. Like Paul, the Teacher of Righteousness is the means of the democratization of the New Covenant, for unlike Moses, the second Moses receives the end-time revelation of God to share it fully with the eschatological community. The Teacher of Righteousness speaks of his reception and mediation of the glory of the New Covenant in a fashion very similar to Paul. He says: "I thank Thee, O Lord, for Thou has illumined my face by Thy Covenant." [91] And then, alluding to the veil and implicit "shame" on Moses because of the unworthiness of the people, he says: "Thou hast not covered my face with shame." [92] Indeed he is able to claim, as Paul does: "Through me Thou has illumined the face of the Congregation." [93]

2. Paul's gospel came in part through an inspired exegesis of the Old Testament. This is also true for the Teacher of Righteousness. The Habakkuk Commentary claims for him that God made known to him "all the mysteries of the words of His Servants the Prophets"—*qôl rāzèy dhibhrèy 'ᵃbhādāyv hannᵉbhi'ym* (1QHab. 7:4-5). Similarly with the image of the "Stave" which digs in the "well," a figure for the law, the Damascus Document presents the Teacher of Righteousness as an inspired exegete whose teaching is authoritative for the sect "in all the age of wickedness." [94] Paul and his gospel are decisive for salvation since they are a fragrance of life unto life and death to death to those who are being saved and those who are perishing. Further, his gospel will be the criterion at the final judgment. [95] This is true also of the Teacher of Righteousness, who claims: "For Thou wilt condemn in Judgment all those who assail me distinguishing through me between the just and the wicked" (1QH 7:12).

3. Finally, it should be noted that essential elements of the Teacher of Righteousness' second Moses role, like Paul's, are expressed through the adoption of the Servant of the Lord traditions. [96] Space does not permit a full exposition of this. It must suffice to note a few pieces of evidence. The Teacher of Righteousness rejoices that "Thou [God] . . . hast chosen me from the womb" (1QH 9:29), recalling Isa. 49:1; he describes his ministry to the community in words taken from the third Servant Song (1QH 7:10, 1QH 8:36; cf. Isa. 50:4); 1QH 18, written about the Teacher of Righteousness, acknowledges him to be "Thy Servant" whose work is described with expressions from Isa. 61:1-2. However, like Paul, the Teacher

of Righteousness is not a soteriological figure.[97] This part of the Servant's mission is notably lacking in both their appropriations of the *'ebhedh YHVH's* role. However, it should not appear surprising that both take on the mission of the Servant since in many circles of ancient Judaism the Servant was thought of as the second Moses.[98] Indeed, there are good internal reasons for believing that the *'ebhedh YHVH* of Isaiah is presented as a second Moses.[99]

CONCLUSION

In sum, it is argued here that the external control of the Essenes' second Moses demonstrates the correctness of the present exegesis of II Cor. 3:1 ff. The consequences of this should not be missed. The descriptions of apostleship alluded to at the beginning of the essay are clearly inadequate for, with eschatological qualifications, the model for Paul's apostolic authority over the Church is *Moses*. J. Munck has seen it in his own way when he comments on II Cor. 3: "The greatest man in the history of Israel is put beneath the travelling tentmaker." [100] This is not to imply some ontological superiority in Paul himself, only the superiority of the office and mission to which in grace he is called (Rom. 1:5; I Cor. 15:10). But the comparison with Moses authorizes us to see the continuity and analogy between the two Covenant ministrations.[101] Moses, the greatest prophet of the Old Covenant,[102] who received and mediated that Covenant to Israel, and also, in accordance with ancient treaty patterns, set it down in inscripturated and canonical form,[103] is the prototype of the apostle. Is it not, then, to be expected that Paul would be concerned for the preservation of the New Covenant foundation entrusted to him, even, may one say, in inscripturated and canonical form, as II Thes. 2:15 suggests? The books of Moses were canonical throughout Israel's history. The teachings of the Qumran community's second Moses were to be preserved and obeyed "throughout the age of wickedness." [104] Surely, therefore, the same would be the case with the παράδοσις of the Apostle, the second Moses of the Church. Thus the stress on preserving the apostolic doctrine or deposit (ἡ παραθήκη) in the Pastorals is hardly to be taken, as most modern critics do, as convincing evidence for the post-Pauline defensive theologizing of *Fruhkatholizismus*,[105] but rather as a fundamental part of the apostle's second-Moses role.

The apostolic authority of Paul over the Church resides, then,

[22] According to A. Cohen, *Proverbs* (Surrey: Socino Press, 1945), p. 50, who quotes Bereshith Rabb 1.1, where Wisdom is identified with the Torah. It reads as follows: "The Torah said, "I was the architectural instrument of the Holy One, blessed be He. It is customary when a human king erects a palace he does not build it according to his own ideas, but according to the ideas of an architect. . . . So did the Holy One, blessed be He, look into the Torah and created the universe accordingly" (p. 48). Cohen also notes that a number of scholars regard *amon* in Proverbs in the same way as it appears in Song of Solomon 7:2, namely as ʹτεχνῖτις . In the Wisdom of Solomon, the personified Wisdom of Proverbs 8 is also described as a τεχνῖτις. This is the feminine form of and means artificer, craftsman, or skilled workman. The closeness to ἀρχιτέκτων, "chief artificer," "master builder," is obvious—see Liddell and Scott, *A Greek-English Lexicon*, ed. Henry Jones (Oxford: Clarendon Press, 1961), *ad. loc.*, which shows that both terms derive from τίκτω and the root τεκ, to beget.

[23] Some commentators, e.g. Grosheide, Leon Morris, Robertson and Plummer, Barrett, and Conzelmann, see in the phrase οἱ πνευμάτικοι the inclusion of all believers. However, I agree with Calvin and Moffatt, *ad. loc.* that it is the apostle who is meant, since in the context Paul distinguishes himself from the mature, οἱ τελείοι. These are also the πνευμάτικοι in view of vs. 14 and 3:1 where the spiritual men are opposed to the babes. Paul is imparting wisdom to the mature (2:6) who, because they are spiritual, can be addressed. But the imparting of secret, hidden wisdom belongs to the apostolic office. See 4:1, Rom. 16:25-26. Most explicitly does this appear in Col. 1:25 where Paul says that his divine office was given to him to make known the mystery hidden for ages and generations.

[24] Note Paul's claim to have been entrusted with this "mystery," e.g. Rom. 16:25f.

[25] Of the thirteen books in the Pauline corpus, all but four (Philippians, I and II Thessalonians, and Philemon) begin, "Paul, an apostle of Jesus Christ." In Philippians Paul uses a title, "servant," which may rightly be considered a synonym for apostle (see below, and David P. Scaer, *The Apostolic Scriptures* [St. Louis, Mo.: Concordia, 1971], p. 58). In I Thessalonians Paul does use the term "apostle," though not in the praescript (2:6, cf. 2:4), and in Philemon employs the term "ambassador," a conceptually analogous notion to apostle, as the basis of his appeal to Philemon. See below, on II Thessalonians.

[26] See I Thes. 5:27, Col. 4:16 and George E. Ladd, *The New Testament and Criticism* (Grand Rapids, Mich.: Eerdmans, 1967), p. 110.

[27] Calvin argues that Paul must be including all doctrine because believers must stand firm in it. On the subject of tradition, see F. F. Bruce, *Tradition Old and New (Contemporary Evangelical Perspectives*; Grand Rapids, Mich.: Zondervan, 1970). Bruce argues that Paul's use of the term is inclusive both of doctrine and practice (p. 36). See also N. B. Stonehouse, "Special Revelation as Scriptural," in *Revelation and the Bible*, ed. Carl F. H. Henry (Grand Rapids, Mich.: Baker Book House, 1959), p. 83. Bruce also cogently demonstrates that while Paul was in some sense dependent on prior tradition, he was an independent source of divine tradition since he includes his own experience of the Risen Lord in the body of tradition. Paul does not "receive" this from men but from the Lord (Gal. 1:11) but he does "deliver" it to others (I Cor. 15:3f.; p. 30). This, incidentally, demonstrates how misleading is the comment of Conzelmann/Dibelius—"In the pastorals the apostle himself never stands on the level of the recipient within a chain of tradition—in contrast to I Cor. 11:23, 15:3" *The Pastoral Epistles* (*Hermeneia*; Philadelphia: Fortress Press, 1972), p. 1. It is true that Paul does recognize his indebtedness to other apostolic tradition, but he also asserts his independence and the divine source of his tradition, which in the Pastorals he chooses to stress.

[28] H. Conzelmann, *Der erste Brief an die Korinther* (Meyer Kommentar; Göttingen: Vandenhoeck & Ruprecht, 1969), p. 112, shows that by this term Paul is referring to his teaching. See also Moffatt and Grosheide, *ad. loc.*

[29] See I Tim. 6:20; II Tim. 1:12, 14, 2:1; cf. Titus 1:1f.

[30] According to Paul the Gentile mission, by provoking the Jews to jealousy, precipitates their salvation and the coming of the consummation. See J. Munck, *op. cit.*, pp. 40f.

[31] See E. Käsemann, *New Testament Questions of Today* (London: Student Christian Movement, 1969), p. 241, who says: "The mission of the apostle is a colossal detour to the salvation of Israel . . . On this . . . detour . . . Paul is nothing other than . . . the forerunner of the end of the world." See also O. Cullmann, "Le caractère eschatologique du devoir missionaire et de la conscience apostolique de S. Paul. Etude sur le κατέχον(-ων) de II Thes. 2:6-7," *Revue d-Histoire et de Philosophie Religieuses*, XVI (1936), pp. 210-45, who argues that Paul is ὁ κατέχων, the one who restrains the man of lawlessness, just as the preaching of

the gospel to the Gentiles also extends the time of grace. This is *prima facie* plausible and Paul's death would not necessarily mean that he was wrong since the death of the Teacher of Righteousness did not mean that he was not considered still as the eschatological Prophet.

[32] So, for instance, Rudolf Bultmann, *Exegetische Probleme des zweiten Korintherbriefes* (*Symbolae Biblicae Upsaliensis*, 9; Supplementhaften till *Svensk Exegetisk Årsbok*; Uppsala: Wretmans Boktryckeri, 1947), p. 3. Most scholars would not include the section 6:14 - 7:1, since it is considered a misplaced fragment (see even Ladd, *op. cit.*, p. 113), but this is not necessarily the case as my dissertation (pp. 368ff.) shows. On the literary, critical problems of II Corinthians, see the recent discussion by G. Bornkamm, "The History of the Origin of the So-Called Second Letter to the Corinthians," in *The Authorship and Integrity of the New Testament* (London: SPCK, 1965), pp. 73-81, and in the same volume, espousing an opposite position, A. M. G. Stephenson, "A Defense of the Integrity of II Corinthians" (pp. 82-91). Exegesis of the epistle is not materially affected by the source problem, however, so long as one assumes dependency, as the overwhelming majority of scholars does.

[33] The plural "we are ministers, etc." indicates a major problem in interpreting II Corinthians, namely Paul's ambiguous use of the first person plural pronoun. There are a number of possible solutions. Paul may be obliged to employ ἡμεῖς as often as possible because for the sake of his apostolic mission which embraces fellow-workers, he has chosen to write this epistle including Timothy. The "we" may also refer to all the apostles, and sometimes to all believers, though when this is the case it is much clearer, or just to Paul himself, as R. H. Strachan, *The Second Epistle of Paul to the Corinthians* (*Moffatt Series*; London: Hodder and Stoughton, 1935), p. 80, and A. Denis, O.P., "L'Apôtre Paul, 'prophète messianique' des Gentils," *Ephemerides Theologicae Lovanienses*, XXXIII (1957), p. 295, argue. See also W. H. Isaacs, *The Second Epistle of Paul to the Corinthians* (Oxford: Oxford University Press, 1921), pp. 6f. In this latter case Paul is seen to be using the authorial plural, as he does in I Thes. 2:6 and II Cor. 10:1ff. But whatever the case, at the very least Paul is referring to himself in his apostolic office.

[34] Needless to say, therefore, the ministries of Moses and Christ are not compared, as a number of commentators have suggested.

[35] This is clearly the mistake Plummer (*A Critical and Exegetical Commentary on the Second Epistle of Paul to the Corinthians* [*International Critical Commentary*; New York: Scribner, 1915], p. 85) makes in his exegesis. He states: "To be ministers of the Old Covenant was no great distinction; there were large numbers of them, and their duties were largely matters of routine. But to be made competent ministers of a New Covenant with God was an extraordinary grace."

[36] See M. G. Kline, *The Structure of Biblical Authority* (Grand Rapids, Mich.: Eerdmans, 1972), p. 35, who describes Moses' role as "covenant mediator" as follows: "At Sinai, and again in the plains of Moab, the administration of Jahweh's lordship over Israel was solemnized in ceremonies of covenant ratification. Through Moses, his covenant mediator, the Lord God addressed to his earthly vassals the law of his kingdom. His authoritative treaty words, regulative of Israel's faith and conduct, were inscripturated on tables of stone and in 'the book.' " Already one can see the similarity with Paul's apostolic ministry, which Kline implies on p. 71.

[37] See also I Tim. 1:12 where Paul is "strengthened" for his task by Christ, and "appointed" to "his service."

[38] E.g., J.-F. Collange, *Enigmes de la deuxième Epître de Paul aux Corinthiens* (*Society for New Testament Studies Monograph Series*; Cambridge: Cambridge University Press, 1972), p. 60; P. E. Hughes, *Paul's Second Epistle to the Corinthians* (*New International Commentary on the New Testament*; Grand Rapids, Mich.: Eerdmans, 1962), p. 93; A. Plummer, *op. cit.*, p. 85; and William Baird, "Letters of Recommendation: II Cor. 3:1-3," *Journal of Biblical Literature*, LXXX (1961), p. 172.

[39] *Ibid.*

[40] One may note that the Risen Lord in Acts 9:16 promises future teaching to Paul.

[41] A. Farrer, "The Apostolic Ministry in the New Testament," *The Apostolic Ministry*, ed. K. E. Kirk (London: Hodder and Stoughton, 1946), p. 173. I have argued elsewhere (*op. cit.*, pp. 60-79) that of all the Old Testament calls, the one which most closely parallels the call of Paul is the vocation of Moses.

[42] See Dieter Georgi, *op. cit.*, p. 241, esp. n. 6. These letters, according to Georgi, are "eine unmittelbare Fortsetzung der Diskussion des Paulus met dem Gegner" (an immediate continuation of the discussion between Paul and the opponents).

[43] In spite of the R.S.V. preference for "your" the reading "our" is supported by P46, A, B, C, D, G, K, P, Ψ and many others, and is given a "B" rating in the United Bible Societies' Greek New Testament. B. M. Metzger, *A Textual Commentary on the Greek New Testament* (New York: United Bible Societies, 1973), p. 577, speaks of "the overwhelming support for ἡμεῖς, and refers to Paul's statement in 7:3, "You are in our hearts." For some reason the second edition of the Bible Societies' Greek New Testament reduces the rating to a "C". See Baird, *op. cit.*, p. 168, who enumerates the modern editors and commentators who support ἡμεῖς.

[44] See Clinton W. Keyes, "The Greek Letter of Introduction," *American Journal of Philology*, LVI (1935), pp. 28ff. Referred to in Baird, *op. cit.*, p. 168. Baird also argues that διακονέω is used elsewhere in Paul and in Josephus to mean "deliver" (Rom. 15:25; II Cor. 8:19-20; Josephus, *Antiquities*, VI, 298).

[45] See Jer. 31:33; Ezek. 11:19, 36:26.

[46] Cf. the two phrases· ἡ ἐπιστολὴ ἡμῶν ὑμεῖς ἐστε (II Cor. 3:2) ἡ σφραγίς μου τῆς ἀποστολῆς ὑμεῖς ἐστε (I Cor. 9:2) Cf. also II Cor. 1:22.

[47] See also Baird, *op. cit.*, p. 172.

[48] See also Rom. 2:16, 16:25; II Tim. 2:8; Gal. 1:11, 2:2. Cf. II Cor. 4:3; I Thes. 1:5; II Thes. 2:14.

[49] W. C. van Unnik, "With Unveiled Face," *Novum Testamentum*, VI (1963), pp. 160f. has ably shown that the contrast with Moses is carried on *via* the notions of "covering the head" and "boldness" since in Aramaic *GLH 'PYR or GLH R'S*, "to uncover the face or head," are idioms which mean "to have confidence" or "freedom."

[50] B. Gerhardsson, *Memory and Manuscript (Acta Seminarii Neotestamentlici Upsaliensis*, XXII; Lund: C. W. K. Gleerup, 1961), pp. 285-86, and J. Roloff, *op. cit.*, p. 103, both draw some significant parallels between Luke 24:13ff., 36ff. and II Cor. 3:4f. in seeing the apostle as the one who is given the inspired ability to read the Old Testament.

[51] See also Rom. 15:4; I Cor. 9:10, 10:11, and everywhere where Paul refers to the "mystery."

[52] Roloff, *op. cit.*, understands II Cor. 3:4ff. in this manner. Indeed, this section of his treatment of Paul's apostolate in II Cor. 3 is entitled, "Der Apostel als bevollmächtigter Ausleger der Schrift."

[53] *Ibid.*, p. 102, agrees with this interpretation when he says: "Das Wesen der διακονία τῆς δικαιοσύνης die Paulus vertritt, ist es, die Decke Wegzunehmen—von der Schrift *und* den 'alten Bund' so darzustellen, wie ihn Gott gemeint hat: *und genau dies fut Paulus in II Kor. 3:4-18!*" (italics mine).

[54] II Cor. 2:15, 4:3.

[55] II Cor. 2:16.

[56] See, for instance, G. Sass, "Zur Bedeutung von δοῦλος bei Paulus," *Zeitschrift für* die neutestamentliche Wissenschaft (1941), pp. 24-32; K. H. Rengstorf, *art.* " δοῦλος, κ.τ.λ.," *Theological Dictonary of the New Testament*, II (1935), p. 277; L. Cerfaux, "St. Paul et le 'serviteur de Dieu' d'Isaïe," *Recueil L.Cerfaux*, II (Gembloux, 1954), pp. 439-54; C. M. Martini, "Alcuni termi letterari di II Cor. 4:6 e i racconti della conversione di san Paolo negli Atti," *Analecta Biblica*, XVII-XVIII (1963), Pt. 1, pp. 461-74; A. Kerrigan, "Echoes of Themes from the Servant Songs in Pauline Theology," *ibid.*, pp. 217-28; D. M. Stanley, S. J., "The Theme of the Servant of Jahweh in Primitive Christian Soteriology and its Transposition by St. Paul," *Catholic Biblical Quarterly*, XVI (1964), pp. 385-425; K. L. Fitzgerald, "A Study of the Servant Concept in the Writings of Paul" (unpublished Th.D. dissertation, Southern Baptist Theological Seminary, 1960); A. Bertrangs, "La vocation des Gentils chez St. Paul: Exégèse et herméneutique Pauliniennes des citations vetero-testamentaire," *Ephem. Theol. Lov.*, XXX (1954), pp. 391-415; J. Giblet, "St. Paul, serviteur de Dieu et apôtre de Jésus Christ." *Vie Spirituelle*, CCCLXXXVIII (1953), pp. 244-65; Traugott Holtz, "Zum Selbstverständnis des Apostels Paulus," *Theologische Literaturzeitung*, XCI (1966), pp. 320-30; J.-F. Collange, *op. cit.*, p. 137; F. F. Bruce, "Paul and Paulinism," *Vox Evangelica*, VII (1971), p. 11.

[57] On the three occasions when Servant Christology can be discerned in Paul, namely I Cor. 15:1-4; Rom. 4:25; and Phil. 2: 5-11, these texts bear the marks of pre-Pauline tradition—though this is not to suggest a tension between Paul and this incorporated material.

[58] Isa. 49:3, 5; cf. 42:19. Note that the synonym παῖς also translates *'ebhedh* in the Servant Songs—see 42:1; 50:10. παῖς and δοῦλος are interchangeable in the Second Song (Is. 49:1-6).

[59] Such correspondences led P.-E. Langevin, S. J., "Saint Paul, prophète des Gentils,"

Laval Theologique et Philosophique, XXVI (1970), 8, to conclude: "Les lieux nous paraissent assez étroits entre Gal. 1:15-16 et le second chant du serviteur (Isa. 49) pour que nous parlions de contact littéraire."

[60] See Isa. 42:6, 49:6. See D. M. Stanley, *op. cit.*, p. 415, and the notes in the Bible Societies' Greek New Testament, *ad. loc.*

[61] Stanley, *op. cit.*, p. 416.

[62] Isa. 49:8. Strictly speaking, the Song ends at 6, though Stanley (*ibid.*) includes v. 8 in the Song.

[63] R. V. G. Tasker, *The Second Epistle of Paul to the Corinthians* (*The Tyndale New Testament Commentaries*; Grand Rapids, Mich.: Eerdmans, 1968), p. 92; also P. E. Hughes, *op. cit.*, p. 219.

[64] See Collange, *op. cit.*, p. 138, who opposes the Genesis background by asking what average Christian would not have known that God said "Que la lumière soit" and not "la lumière brillera." If Paul was quoting the Septuagint of Gen. 1:3, he has changed γίνομαι to λάμπω and the imperative form γενηθήτω to the future form λάμψει. On this, see also D. W. Oostendorp, *Another Jesus: A Gospel of Jewish-Christian Superiority in II Corinthians* (*Academisch Proefschrift: Vrije Universiteit te Amsterdam*; Kampen: J. G. Kok, 1967), p. 48.

[65] While this is by no means a verbatim quotation, it seems that the most plausible source for the terms and conception is the Servant Songs, esp. Isa. 49:6, 42:6, 16; cf. 60:1-2—so Collange, *op. cit.*, p. 139 and Oostendorp, *op. cit.*, p. 48.
There are other servant traditions in Paul which cannot be touched upon here, but the appropriateness of the servant's role for Paul's mission is clearly seen in the servant's commission *both* to go to the Gentiles *and* to raise up the tribes of Israel, for Paul's mission certainly is, in Käsemann's words, a "colossal detour for the salvation of Israel."

[66] Deut. 18:15ff., and the Servant Songs (see below).

[67] Jesus is presented as a second Moses in Acts 3:22 and 7:27, the Gospels of Matthew and John, and the Epistle to the Hebrews 3:1-6. On Jesus as the second Moses in Matthew, see W. D. Davies, *Paul and Rabbinic Judaism* (New York: Harper, 1948), p. 72, and *The Setting of the Sermon on the Mount* (Cambridge: Cambridge University Press, 1964), *passim*. On Jesus as a second Moses in John, see T. F. Glasson, *Moses in the Fourth Gospel* (*Studies in Biblical Theology*; London: SCM, SCM, 1963).

[68] In Josephus' *Antiquities*, XX, pp. 97-99, a certain Theudas led his followers to the Jordan in anticipation of performing the miracle of dividing the waters, to be followed by a wilderness march. In Josephus' *Jewish War*, II, pp. 261f. and *Antiquities*, XX, pp. 169-172 an Egyptian Jew (cf. Acts 21:38) led a group of followers through the desert to the Mount of Olives in order to overthrow the Romans and set up his own rule in Jerusalem.

[69] The Damascus Document (*CD*) 6:19, 8:21, 19:33, 20:12. For the Hebrew text of the Scrolls, I am using Eduard Lohse, *Die Texte aus Qumran* (München: Kösel-Verlag, 1964).

[70] See especially W. R. Stegner, "The Self-Understanding of the Qumran Community Compared with the Self-Understanding of the Early Church" (unpublished Ph.D. dissertation, Drew University, 1960). See also F. M. Cross, Jr.; *The Ancient Library of Qumran* (rev. ed.; New York: Doubleday Anchor Books, 1961), p. 78, who says: "They go into the desert for a season, to be born again as the New Israel, to enter into the New Covenant of the last days. They await in the desert the Second Exodus (or Conquest). . . . [They are] a *Heilsgemeinschaft*, imitating the ancient desert sojourn of Mosaic times in anticipation of the dawning Kingdom of God."

[71] See O. Betz, "Die Geburt der Gemeinde durch den Lehrer," *New Testament Studies*, III (1956-1957), pp. 320f.

[72] Cross, *op. cit.*, p. 78. See the War Scroll (1 QM), *passim*.

[73] I Cor. 10:11.

[74] II Cor. 3:6; I Cor. 11:25.

[75] I Cor. 5:7.

[76] I Cor. 10:1-13. Note here the same emphasis as Qumran on the eschatological community being analogous to the first wilderness generation. See also the wilderness motif in II Cor. 5:1 (so W. D. Davies, *op. cit.*, pp. 313f.) and Phil. 2:12-15.

[77] See, for instance, Hodayoth (1 QH) 18.

[78] See my own work (*op. cit.*, p. 186, n. 1) where I list a score of leading scholars who argue that the Teacher of Righteousness was a second Moses. I quote Wayne A. Meeks,

240 / God's Inerrant Word

The Prophet-King: Moses Traditions and the Johannine Christology (Supplements to Novum Testamentum; Leiden: E. J. Brill, 1967), p. 175 as an example: "The importance of the typology of the wilderness sojourn under Moses' leadership . . . emerges with exceptional clarity in the scrolls. Within this typological framework the sect's principal midrashic teacher and lawgiver functioned as a new Moses, although he is never called by that name."

[79] There is a fair amount of debate over the interpretation of 4QTestimonia. See my argumentation, *op. cit.*, pp. 202-206.

[80] *CD* 6:3. See the important article by N. Wieder, "The Law-Interpreter of the Sect of the Dead Sea Scrolls," *Journal of Jewish Studies*, IV (1953), pp. 158-75.

[81] *De Vita Mosis* 1:1.

[82] 1QH 2:1f. M. Delcor, *Les Hymnes de Qumran* (Paris: Letouzey et Ané, 1962), p. 64, argues for this.

[83] 1QH 8:21 (*ibid.*). For more on the Moses/Teacher of Righteousness analogies, see O. Betz, *op. cit.*, p. 163.

[84] 1QH 5:22-23. For the English quotations of the Scrolls, I use the translation by G. Vermès, *The Dead Sea Scrolls in English* (London: Penguin Books, 1965).

[85] 1QH 3:1-18 and 7:20-22. See Betz, *op. cit.*, p. 65, who argues that "Der Lehrer der Sekte spielt in den Hodayoth auf Moses vorwurfsvolle Rede Nu. 11:11f. an." Betz persuasively shows that Hymn 3 is describing the birth of "die geistlichen kinder der Heilsgemeinde" through the labours of the Teacher of Righteousness, and not the birth of the Messiah.

[86] I Cor. 4:14; Gal. 4:19.

[87] I Cor. 4:15.

[88] Ὠδίνω may mean great pain or travail as such, but the presence of τεκνία as the object of the verb makes the allusion to childbirth certain. It recalls most readily the Teacher of Righteousness' vivid expressions in 1QH3:

> They caused me to be
>> like a ship on the deeps of the sea
> and like a fortified city
>> before the aggressor,
> and like a woman in travail
>> with her first born
> upon whose belly pangs have come
>> and grievous pain. . . .

[89] Num. 11:11f.

[90] G. Jeremias, *Der Lehrer der Gerechtigkeit* (*Studien zur Umwelt des Neuen Testaments*, 2; Göttingen: Vandenhoeck & Ruprecht, 1963), p. 190.

[91] 1QH 4:5.

[92] 1 QH 4:23.

[93] 1 QH 4:27.

[94] *CD* 6:10.

[95] Rom. 2:16.

[96] A number of scholars besides Dupont-Sommer argue for this. They include Matthew Black. W. H. Brownlee, H. Bardtke, F. F. Bruce, P. Benoit, O. Cullmann, M. Delcor, R. H. Fuller, and A. S. Van der Woude. For bibliographical details, see my dissertation (*op. cit.*), p. 237, n. 1.

[97] R. H. Fuller, *The Foundations of New Testament Christology* (New York: Scribner, 1965), p. 53, notes this fact about the Teacher of Righteousness's appropriation of the Servant role, as does F. Hahn, *The Titles of Jesus in Christology* (New York: World, 1969), p. 362. Neither scholar sees the same remarkable qualification in Paul's appropriation of the Servant's task.

[98] In the Rabbis, Moses was identified with the Servant—see Renée Bloch, "Quelques aspects de la figure de Moïse dans la tradition rabbinique," in *Moïse: l'homme de l'Alliance*, ed H. Cazelles, *et al.* (special issue of *Cahier Sioniens*; Paris: Desclée, 1955), p. 155; and H. M. Teeple, *The Mosaic Eschatological Prophet* (*Journal of Biblical Literature Monograph Series*, 10; Philadelphia, 1957), p. 63. This also is the case in Samaritan theology—see John McDonald, *The Theology of the Samaritans* (London: SCM, 1964), p. 211, and my own work, *op. cit.*, pp. 129 ff.—and in the early chapters of Acts—see R. H. Fuller, *op. cit.*, p. 47.

[99] This is argued by Old Testament scholars such as Aage Bentzen, G. von Rad, and Claus Westermann. On the internal evidence, see my dissertation, pp. 123ff.

[100] J. Munck, *op. cit.*, pp. 60f.

[101] On the analogy of the two testaments, see N. B. Stonehouse, *op. cit.*, pp. 79-81; and C. H. Pinnock, *Biblical Revelation* (Chicago: Moody Press, 1971), pp. 62f. and "The Inspiration of the New Testament," *The Bible—The Living Word of Revelation*, ed. M. C. Tenney (*An Evangelical Theological Society Publication Monograph*, 6; Grand Rapids, Mich.: Zondervan, 1968), pp. 146f.

[102] Deut. 34:10; Num. 12:6-8; cf. Deut. 18:15f. (where Moses is the paradigm for the eschatological Prophet); Heb. 3:1:1-5. See N. B. Stonehouse, *op. cit.*, p. 77, who says of Moses: "He was preeminently the prophet of the old covenant, the prototype of the Great Prophet to come . . . with whom the Lord spoke face to face."

[103] M. Kline, *op. cit.*, pp. 27ff.

[104] *CD* 6:10.

[105] This term is taken from Käsemann, *op. cit.*, who ably and programmatically draws the lines between Paul and the later ecclesiastical developments in the Pastorals and Acts, as the modern critic sees them. See also Martin Dibelius and Hans Conzelmann, *The Pastoral Epistles*, ed. Helmut Koester (Philadelphia: Fortress Press, 1972), p. 1, where the sign of the post-Pauline character of the Pastorals is that "the kerygma of the apostles, during the course of transmission, becomes doctrinal authority." Some non-evangelical scholars who hold to the authenticity of the Pastorals are J. Jeremias, *Die Briefe an Timotheus und Titus* (*Das Neue Testament Deutsch*, 9; Gottingen: Vandenhoeck & Ruprecht, 1954), and J. N. D. Kelly, *A Commentary on the Pastoral Epistles* (*Harper's New Testament Commentaries*; New York: Harper, 1963).

[106] On this, see Stonehouse, *op. cit.*, p. 78.

11

THE CASE
FOR INERRANCY:
A METHODOLOGICAL
ANALYSIS

R. C. Sproul

The church of the 20th century not only demands an apologia for the authority of her Sacred Scriptures but an apologia for the apologia. In these times not only an adequate defense of inerrancy is necessary, but such a defense needs to be defended. The reason for this proliferation of apologies is clear. Not only do we face the viewpoint of those who maintain that the Bible is full of errors and consequently no cogent case for its inspiration or infallibility *can* be made, but many who maintain a high view of Scripture contend that a rational defense of inerrancy *ought not* to be made even if it could be made.

The position of this essay is to maintain that not only can a defense of inerrancy be presented, but that such a defense *ought* to be made. The purpose of this paper is not to provide a comprehensive apology for the case for inerrancy but rather to provide a methodological framework for such a defense. This will involve a brief rehearsal and analysis of methodological options that are before us.

THE CONFESSIONAL METHOD

The confessional method may be defined as that method by which the Scriptures are confessed to be the Word of God (being inspired, trustworthy, reliable, etc.) and this is recognized by faith alone. No rational defense for infallibility or inerrancy is given. On the contrary this method eschews such a defense for introducing foreign rationalistic elements into a purely fideistic approach. A major exponent of this method would be G. C. Berkouwer of the Netherlands. In his two-volume work on Holy Scripture (part of the larger series, *Dogmatische Studiën*) Berkouwer celebrates the Scriptures as the Word of God, as being inspired, sufficient, trustworthy, etc., but shrinks from the notion of *verbal* inspiration or inerrancy. Berkouwer sees the doctrine of inerrancy and/or verbal inspiration as involving a formalistic view of Scripture that isolates itself from the "message" of the Scripture itself. He directs his critique primarily against Roman Catholic views (particularly those arising out of the modernist controversy at the turn of the century)[1] and against positions articulated by American fundamentalism of the same period. He sees verbal inspiration as a product of a post-reformation quest for rational certainty. He warns of the danger of a speculatively constructed theory of inspiration that provides an apriori escape hatch from all uncertainty. He sees in this theory an intrusion of foreign Aristotelian elements into the Christian faith.[2]

Berkouwer speaks of a "confidence" (*vertrouwen*) in the trustworthiness of Scripture that is inseparably related to the contents of the message.[3]

> Zo kan ook blijken, dat het in de Schrift niet gaat om een door ons geconstrueerd zekerheidspunt, dat door ons wordt aangegrepen, omdat we in de crisis der zekerheden toch een vast, onaantastbaar oriëntering spunt nodig hebben. Zulk een verklaring heeft men meermalen gegeven, b.v. toen men in de belijdenis van het Schriftgezag een protestantse parallel meende te zien van het vaste punt in het rooms-katholieke denken nl. de onfeilbaarheid van de paus. Van de protestantse visie op het Schriftgezag gaf men dan een psychologische verklaring—vanuit de behoefte aan een tastbare onwrikbare zekerheidsgrond—en sprak van een papieren paus, een door Lessing gebruikte uitdrukking.[4]

H. Berkof accurately traces the development of Berkouwer's method in terms of a method of "*correlatie.*" This method of correlation can be traced throughout Berkouwer's *Dogmatische Studiën* and involves a decisive shift in Berkouwer's view of Scripture. Berkof sees Berkouwer moving through three different *stages* of Biblical views. The first stage involves a view of the "complete authority of Scripture." This stage (directed against the movement toward subjectivism of German theology) is detected in Berkouwer's earlier writings including his doctoral dissertation of 1932, *Geloof en Openbaring in de nieuwere duitse theologie*, his book *Karl Barth* (1936) and especially his major volume of 1938, *Het probleem der Schrift-kritiek*. The second phase which Berkof delineates is that one which emphasizes the "Redemptive Content of Scripture" which he sees beginning in 1949 and manifesting itself clearly in *Geloof in volharding*. The third and final phase is what Berkof calls the "existential tendency of Scripture." [5] In the third phase Berkouwer seeks to steer a course between subjectivism and objectivism in which the accent is found on the personal involvement of the believer with the life-transforming message of the Scripture. This approach, which Van Til calls "activistic" [6] seeks to avoid a "causal approach" to the Word of God that would build an apologetic from the perspective of the believer who responds to God *ex auditu verbi*.

The strength of the method of confession as advocated by Berkouwer consists in the following: 1. This method escapes the pejorative, emotive categories so often identified with fundamentalism and orthodoxy. It is "organic" and open-ended enough to escape the appellations of "rigid," "dogmatic," "obscurantist," etc. 2. This method takes seriously the human element of Scripture and allows for a thorough-going analysis of the cultural, linguistic, and historical framework of the Scripture. This method can make abundant use of higher critical tools of Biblical studies without abandoning a confidence of the trustworthiness of Scripture. 3. This method is free from any charge of a "docetic" view of Scripture such as that leveled by Karl Barth against orthodoxy. 4. This method provides liberation from any need to define and redefine such terms as "inerrancy" or "infallibility." The believer is freed from any need to "harmonize" difficult passages into a coherent, "systematic" form. Berkouwer is in no danger of being accused of holding to a "mechanical" or "dictation" theory of inspiration.

The weaknesses of this method include the following: 1. Berkouwer's method leaves us without a rational apologetic. His method never takes us away from fideism. Consequently the Christian has no better argument to offer the unbeliever than does the Muslim with his Koran. 2. Berkouwer's method leaves us no way to solve the subject-object dilemma and offers no escape from an arbitrary subjectivism. Van Til says:

> If Berkouwer thinks that an activistic pattern of thinking
> is a better means of expressing the doctrines of grace

than the traditional one, he would oblige us by showing how he can, by using his method, avoid slipping into neo-orthodoxy altogether. So far, every time he uses the activist pattern of thought, his theology also becomes activist. When Berkouwer is most activist in his thinking he first starts off with causal thinking as though it were an intelligible way of thinking without the biblical presuppositions of creation and redemption, then he takes off into the realm of the unspeakable, the realm of praise without words, in order to finally return and speak of that realm in the language of causality.[7]

3. Berkouwer's method leaves us without an answer to the crucial issue of our day concerning Scripture, namely the question of the *degree* of Biblical trustworthiness. Is the Bible altogether and completely trustworthy? If so, then what is wrong with the categories of verbal inspiration and inerrancy? If not, then to what degree is the Bible *un*-trustworthy? How do we deal with the Biblical writers' claims for themselves? To what extent is the Bible the Word of God as well as the Word of man? Does God inspire error? 4. Berkouwer's method is weak with respect to the one who is a spectator, namely, the unbeliever. Berkof says: "Ik geloof dat the Schrift minder bang is voor toeschouwers-elementen dan Berkouwer" (I believe that the Scripture is less afraid of spectator-elements than Berkouwer).[8] To be sure, a believer's confidence in the Biblical text is closely linked to the content of Scripture. We know that "faith comes by hearing and hearing from the Word of God." We respect the importance of faith that comes *ex auditu verbi* but it seems that in the final analysis the only apologia Berkouwer leaves us is the plea *Tolle lege, tolle lege.*

THE PRESUPPOSITIONAL METHOD

The presuppositional method of apologetics follows closely the Dutch Calvinistic school that has been influenced heavily by Abraham Kuyper. The leading exponent of this methodology in the 20th century has been Cornelius Van Til. Van Til's defense of Scripture follows closely his general method of apologetics which is presuppositional. He says: "In fact it then appears that the argument for the Scripture as the infallible revelation of God is, to all intents and purposes, the same as the argument for the existence of God."[9] The starting point of all apologetics is clearly stated by Van Til: "A truly Protestant apologetic must therefore make its beginning from

the presupposition that the triune God, Father, Son and Holy
Spirit, speaks to him with absolute authority in Scripture." [10]
Thus, according to Van Til, the proper method of defending
the absolute authority of the Scripture is that method which
incorporates the notion of the absolute authority of the Scripture
in its foundational premise. Any method which does not proceed
from the presuppositional basis of the absolute authority of
the Scripture involves a presupposition of human autonomy.
Scripture must be taken as "self-attesting" if we are to avoid
autonomous thinking. [11] Autonomous thinking or reasoning
on "neutral ground" with unbelievers can only lead to conclusions that are at best "probably true." For the Christian to
say that God's Word is "probably true" is to do violence
to the integrity of God's self-revelation.

The presuppositional method of apologetics follows closely
in the following way:

Premise A — The Bible is the infallible Word of God
Premise B — The Bible attests to its own infallibility
Premise C — The self-attestation of Scripture is an in-
              fallible attestation.
Conclusion — The Bible is the infallible Word of God.

Here we have a line of reasoning where the conclusion is
explicitly stated in the opening premise. This approach has
been and may fairly be called circular reasoning. The classical
problem with circular reasoning is that it "begs the question."

> Circular definitions are a rather obvious instance of
> of question begging. In its full-blown maturity question
> begging can go on for volumes, even through whole
> systems of thought. As can be guessed, the mature fallacy
> is not easy to handle. There it is, big as the universe
> (in Hegel, for example), but just how it operates is hard
> to show in a simple instance. [12]

Van Til and others within the presuppositional school are
not particularly bothered by the circularity of their approach. [13] Van Til, of course, recognizes circularity and goes
on at great length to defend it. He maintains that all reasoning
is circular in the final analysis. He says:

> To admit one's own presuppositions and to point out the
> presuppositions of others is therefore to maintain that all
> reasoning is, in the nature of the case, *circular reason-
> ing.* The starting point, the method, and the conclusions
> are always involved in one another. [14]

Van Til has written extensively in an attempt to show that

non-Christian presuppositional thinking is self-destructive. He maintains that any presupposition apart from the Christian one leads inevitably to irrationalism.[15] Only if one begins with the existence of God can reason be ultimately rational and coherent and empirical data be intelligible.

That Christianity alone provides an ultimately coherent world-view is not in dispute among Christian thinkers. That the presupposition of autonomy will lead inevitably to the denial of theism is not in dispute. That there is no higher authority possible than the testimony of God is not in dispute. That all men *ought* to recognize the Scripture as being the Word of God is not in dispute. That a Christian cannot abandon his conviction of the existence of God when he enters into debate with the unbeliever is not in dispute. That all reasoning is ultimately circular in the sense that conclusions are inseparably related to presuppositions is not in dispute. What is in dispute is the form of argument for Scripture.

When the classical method argues from historical reliability to infallibility, the existence of God is presupposed in a certain sense. (That is, the category of history has no meaningful basis apart from the existence of God.) But the argument is not explicitly circular. The progression is from general reliability to infallibility, not infallibility to infallibility. The issue is, of course, the issue of common ground. If we are to choose between two possible presuppositions, namely the existence of God or the autonomy of man, then by all means let us choose the former! But this is a false dilemma involving the either/or informal fallacy when there is in fact a *tertium quid* (self-consciousness). If the presupposition of the existence of God leads inevitably to the affirmation of the existence of God because it begins there and the presupposition of autonomy ends in autonomy (excluding God) because it begins there, how do we decide which presupposition to begin with? This leaves us with a choice between presuppositions that can only be made by pure subjectivism which is a pre-pre-supposition. To avoid this impass of subjectivism classical apologists have sought a *tertium quid* that would provide a point of contact with the unbeliever: a presupposition shared by all. This presupposition which is first in the order of knowing, though not first in the order of being, is self-consciousness. By working with this presupposition, apologists have been able to reason *directly* rather than indirectly to the existence of God and the infallibility of Scripture. Though unbelievers may *assume* autonomy along with self-consciousness, the notion of autonomy is not analytically contained in the premise of self-consciousness. Apologists can and have shown that self-consciousness does not lead to or demand autonomy and that autonomy is a false assumption.

The strengths of the presuppositional method involve the exposure of the existence of, and poverty of pagan presuppositions. In Dooeyweerd's categories autonomy has been exposed as a "pretense." Van Til's method is rich in its critique-value of alternate systems of truth. His method exerts a restraining influence on those who would exalt reason to the primary place in order of *being* rather than knowing. He forces us to be careful about viewing epistemological systems such as rationalism or empiricism as being more authoritative than revelation.

The weaknesses of this method are focused in its dependence upon circularity in argument. The clear and present danger of this approach is subjectivism. As Warfield detected a strong element of mysticism and subjectivism in Kuyper, so not a few contemporary evangelical scholars detect these elements in Van Til. The debate is an intermural one between men who agree as to the nature of Scripture but differ with respect to apologetic methodology. The debate continues as indicated in the compilation of essays found in Van Til's Festschrift, *Jerusalem and Athens.*

THE CLASSICAL METHOD

The classical approach to the defense of Scripture is one that concerns itself both with deduction and induction, external and internal evidence. The approach proceeds on the basis of a progression from the premise of basic or general trustworthiness of Scripture to the conclusion of inerrancy or infallibility. The reasoning proceeds as follows:

Premise A — The Bible is a basically reliable and trustworthy document.

Premise B — On the basis of this reliable document we have sufficient evidence to believe confidently that Jesus Christ is the Son of God.

Premise C— Jesus Christ being the Son of God is an infallible authority.

Premise D — Jesus Christ teaches that the Bible is more than generally trustworthy: it is the very Word of God.

Premise E — That the word, in that it comes from God, is utterly trustworthy because God is utterly trustworthy.

Conclusion — On the basis of the infallible authority of Jesus Christ, the Church believes the Bible to be utterly trustworthy, i.e., infallible.

It is important to note at this point that this method does not involve circular reasoning. Circular reasoning occurs when the conclusion is already present in the first premise. The argument itself is not an infallible argument as each premise involves matters of inductive or deductive reasoning by fallible rational creatures. There is neither a formal apriori assumption nor a subjective leap of faith in the method. Rather, the method is involved with careful historical, empirical investigation as well as with logical inferences.

Premise A — The argument, of course, stands or falls on the basis of the premise. If the Biblical documents are not at least basically trustworthy then we have no historical basis for knowledge of Jesus at all. Without a reliable historical witness to Jesus the Christian faith would be reduced to an esoteric-gnostic religion. That the Bultmannian approach to faith has been called neo-gnostic is inseparably related to its un-historical methodology.

It is not within the scope of this essay to give a detailed defense of the general reliability of the Biblical documents. Such a defense, at this point in history, should not be necessary in light of the overwhelming abundance of evidence and testimony confirming the historical reliability of the Scripture.[16] Only the most radical higher critics would deny the premise of basic or general reliability. One testimony, however, will be added. Consider the following passage from a joint statement issued by William Foxwell Albright, the dean of twentieth century archaeologists, and C. S. Mann:

> For much too long a time the course of New Testament scholarship has been dictated by theological, quasi-theological, and philosophical presuppositions. In far too many cases commentaries on NT books have neglected such basic requirements as up-to-date historical and philological analysis of the text itself. In many ways this preoccupation with theological and metaphysical interpretation is the unacknowledged child of Hegelianism. To this should be added the continuing and baleful influence of Schleiermacher and his successors on the whole treatment of historical material. The result has often been steadfast refusal to take seriously the findings of archaeological and linguistic research. We believe that there is less and less excuse for the resulting confusion in this latter half of the twentieth century.

Closely allied with these presuppositions is the ever present fog of existentialism, casting ghostly shadows over an already confused landscape. Existentialism as a method of interpreting the New Testament is based upon a whole series of undemonstrable postulates of Platonic, Neo-Platonic, left-wing scholastic, and relativistic origins. So anti-historical is this approach that it fascinates speculative minds which prefer clichés to factual data, and shifting ideology to empirical research and logical demonstration.[17]

That the case for the infallibility of Scripture rests on a premise that can only be established on the inductive basis of historical-empirical evidence should not be a problem to the Christian. It is on the historical-empirical plane that our redemption has been accomplished. The Biblical witnesses are "eye" witnesses. If the eye witnesses are not reliable we are left with a subjectivistic arbitrary claim of unconditional importance of Jesus of Nazareth. If the Christian faith is indeed established on an historical foundation then it is essential that we have a reliable knowledge of that history. Without it, the subject-object polarity is reduced to one pole, namely the former.[18]

The basic reliability of the Biblical witnesses provides a crucial point of contact for the Christian believer engaged in apologetics. Without it we must opt for fideism.

Premise B — If the Biblical data concerning the person and work of Christ is reliable we have sufficient evidence for any reasonable man to come to the conclusion that Jesus of Nazareth is God Incarnate. Again, it is beyond the scope of this essay to demonstrate that the New Testament does in fact clearly manifest the deity of Christ. I am aware, of course, that many people have indeed read the New Testament and have not been persuaded of the truth of its claims about Jesus. Many have endeavored to explain this by pointing to the sinful disposition of natural man that makes it impossible for him to acquiesce to the Biblical claims without experiencing the internal testimony of the Holy Spirit. Unfortunately, we are often left with the impression that the Biblical data, apart from the internal testimony, is insufficient to provide a rational-evidential basis for faith in Christ and that the Holy Spirit either provides new internal evidence for the believer that is unavailable to all, or that He gives the Christian the ability to leap over the evidence (being either insufficient or contrary) by an act of faith. Such a view of the internal tes-

timony of the Spirit would involve a serious distortion of its
classical meaning. For example, Calvin points out:

> Let it therefore be held as fixed, that those who are
> inwardly taught by the Holy Spirit acquiesce implicitly
> in Scripture; that Scripture, carrying its own evidence
> along with it, deigns not to submit to proofs and argu-
> ments, but owes the full conviction with which we ought
> to receive it to the testimony of the Spirit.[19]

Again Calvin says:

> If then, we would consult most effectually for our con-
> sciences, and save them from being driven about in a whirl
> of uncertainty, from wavering, and even stumbling at the
> smallest obstacle, our conviction of the truth of Scripture
> must be derived from a higher source than human con-
> jectures, judgments, or reasons; namely, the secret tes-
> timony of the Spirit. It is true, indeed, that if we choose
> to proceed in the way of argument, it is easy to establish,
> by evidence of various kinds, that if there is a God in
> heaven, the Law, the Prophesies, and the Gospel pro-
> ceeded from him. Nay, although learned men, and men
> of the greatest talent, should take the opposite side, sum-
> moning and ostentatiously displaying all the powers of
> their genius in the discussion, if they are not possessed
> of shameless effrontery, they will be compelled to con-
> fess that the Scripture exhibits clear evidence of its be-
> ing spoken by God, and consequently, of its containing
> his heavenly doctrine.[20]

Thus, for Calvin, the testimony of the Spirit does not cause
men to *acquiesce* contrary to the evidence but into the evidence
of Scripture. The evidence of the Scripture for the deity of
Christ is compelling. To refuse to acknowledge what is plainly
manifest must be motivated by a sinful disposition that refuses
to submit to what is plainly evident. If the Biblical documents
are a reliable historical source of information and their testimony of Jesus' activity is reliable we are left with no rational
alternative to a bold declaration of his deity. If in fact he
performed miracles, raised people from the dead, walked on
water, was himself victorious over the grave, and claimed
to be God, who can gainsay that claim?

Premise C — The content and ramifications of this premise
are so crucial and far-reaching to the whole argument that
they are the subject of a complete essay in this volume. Rather
than a detailed reiteration of the whole matter, I will touch
lightly in the issues involved. The basic question raised in

Premise C is not the fact of Jesus' authority but the *scope* of it. It is fair to assume a consensus among Christians that Jesus Christ is the supreme authority of the Church. This is acknowledged not only by Protestantism but by the Roman Catholic Church as well. Where Papal authority is maintained at a human level of primacy it is still viewed as being a derived authority from the authority of Christ.

A classical point of dispute betweeen Protestant Christology and Roman Catholic Christology has to do with the issue of the scope of Christ's knowledge. In Roman Catholic thought the infallibility of Christ is inseparably related to his omniscience. That is, because of the hypostatic union of divine and human natures Jesus' infallibility is rooted in the omniscience of the divine nature which exists in perfect unity with the human nature. This approach to Jesus' infallibility has been sharply criticized by Protestant theologians as being docetic, monophysite, and eutychian inasmuch as it involves a violation of Chalcedonian Christology by confusing or mixing the two natures. The issue centers on the exegesis of Mark 13:32. In this text Jesus claims ignorance concerning the day and the hour of his coming. Traditional Roman Catholic exegesis has maintained that this text could not possibly reflect a limitation of the knowledge of Jesus. This view was made popular by Thomas Aquinas who provided a kind of "accommodation theory" to avoid the inference of limited knowledge. Aquinas maintained that Christ did in fact know the day and the hour but the knowledge was incommunicable.[21] This view reflected the earlier exegesis of Gregory I and was ratified by a decree of 1918.[22] This accommodation view preserves the notion of an infallible Jesus but only by raising serious question about the *integrity* of Jesus.

Protestant Christology has traditionally maintained that, touching Christ's human nature (which can be distinguished from though not separated from the divine nature), he had limited knowledge and in fact did not know the time of his parousia. Thus the issue for Protestantism is not, was the human Jesus *omniscient*, but was he *infallible*?

In recent times, it has been fashionable among Protestant thinkers to deny both omniscience and infallibility in Jesus. C. H. Dodd comments:

> We need not doubt that Jesus, as He is represented, shared the views of His contemporaries regarding the authorship of books in the Old Testament, or the phenomena of "demon-possession"—views which we could not accept without violence to our sense of truth.[23]

Emil Brunner confesses that Jesus shared the high view of Scripture of his Jewish contemporaries: "The Scriptures are to Him the revelation of God." [24] Yet Brunner has no problem criticizing Jesus' understanding and use of the Old Testament saying that "the Bible is full of errors, contradictions, erroneous opinions concerning all kinds of human, natural, historical situations." [25]

Such attitudes toward the authority of the historical Jesus are justified by seeing a limitation to the knowledge of Jesus as part of his culturally conditioned humanness. Jesus could no more be expected to know that Moses did not write the Pentateuch than he could be expected to know the world was round. Being human, he participated in knowledge-gaps, and erroneous views of the Old Testament common to his day.

This approach to the knowledge and authority of Jesus raises even more serious questions than the Roman Catholic view. Not only does this impugn the integrity of Jesus' understanding of the relationship of the Old Testament Scriptures to his own mission and identity,[26] but it casts a shadow over his sinlessness. *Jesus does not have to be omniscient to be infallible. But he must be infallible to be sinless.* That is to say, if Jesus, claiming to be sent from God and invoking the authority of God in his teaching errs in that teaching, he is guilty of sin. The one who claims to be the truth cannot err and be consistent with that claim. Anyone claiming absolute authority in his teaching must be absolutely trustworthy in what he teaches in order to merit absolute authority. In light of his claims, Jesus cannot plead "invincible ignorance" as an excuse for error.

James Orr summarized the matter as follows:

> Does this acknowledged limitation of the human knowledge of Christ, and ignorance of earthly science, imply *error* on the part of Jesus? This is a position which must as strongly be contested. Ignorance is not error, nor does the one thing necessarily imply the other. That Jesus should use the language of His time on things indifferent, where no judgment or pronouncement of His own was involved, is readily understood; that He should be the victim of illusion, or false judgment, on any subject on which He was called to pronounce, is a perilous assertion. If the matter be carefully considered, it may be felt that even sinlessness is hardly compatible with liability of the judgment to error. False judgment, where moral questions are involved, can hardly fail to issue in wrong action.[27]

Premise D — Jesus' view of Scripture is not a hotly disputed issue. This question has been discussed in this volume both

by John Frame in his essay on the *autopiste* and by Clark
Pinnock in his paper on the authority of Christ. A multitude
of writers have demonstrated clearly that Jesus held a very
high view of Scripture. In addition to Dodd and Brunner (cited
earlier), we could mention the word of Murray, Young, Warfield,
Orr, Nicole, Packer, Pinnock, and a host of other scholars
who have demonstrated the high view of Scripture held by
Jesus.

To be sure, questions have arisen concerning Jesus' view
of Scripture, especially in light of Jesus' teaching in the Sermon
on the Mount vis-à-vis the Old Testament. Jeremias maintains
that Jesus exercises a positive criticism of the Old Testament
Law by repealing the Mosaic permission for divorce and implicitly by "Criticizing the Torah primarily by omitting elements
of it." [28] Nevertheless Jeremias agrees that to charge Jesus
with antinomianism is a misinterpretation: "Jesus is not concerned with destroying the law but with filling it to its full
eschatological measure." [29] Though Jeremias sees a radical
rejection by Jesus of the Rabbinic Halakah (the oral tradition),
the same kind of attitude is not demonstrated toward the Torah.

> Jesus lived in the Old Testament. His sayings are incom-
> prehensible unless we recognize this. His last word, ac-
> cording to Mark, was the beginning of Psalm 22, prayed
> in his Aramaic mother tongue (Mark 15:34). He was
> particularly fond of the prophet Isaiah, and above all of
> the promises and statements about the servant of God
> in Deutero-Isaiah. The apocalyptic sayings of Daniel
> were also extremely significant for him. Numerically,
> literal and free quotations from the Psalter predominate
> on the lips of Jesus, and this was evidently his prayer book.
> The twelve prophets are also quoted frequently, and there
> are repeated allusions to the prophet Jeremiah. The nu-
> merous references to the Pentateuch, in which Jesus found
> inscribed the basic norms of the will of God occur es-
> pecially in the controversy sayings.[30]

That Jesus' view of Scripture was high is beyond dispute. That
he regarded the Scriptures as being utterly trustworthy can be
seen from the following examples summarized by J. I. Packer:

> There is no lack of evidence for our Lord's attitude to the
> Old Testament. He prefaces with his regular formula of
> solemn assertion ("Verily (amen) I say unto you") the fol-
> lowing emphatic assurance: "till heaven and earth pass,
> one jot or one tittle shall in no wise pass from the law."
> He quotes Gn. ii. 24—in its context a comment passed
> by Adam or (more likely) the narrator—as an utterance

of God: "have ye not read, that he which made them at the beginning . . . said . . . ?" He treats argument from Scripture as having clinching force. When he says "it is written," that is final. There is no appeal against Scripture, for "the Scripture cannot be broken." God's Word holds good forever.[31]

Thus, even a cursory view of Jesus' use of Scripture in debate, discussion and rebuke of his own disciples, added to an examination of Jesus' own submission to the authority of Scripture, makes clear that the formula *Sacra Scriptura est Verbum Dei* was as vital for him as it would be for the Reformers. That Jesus considered and treated the Old Testament as of divine authority is clear.[32]

Premise E — If God is utterly trustworthy, then his Word carries the trustworthiness of himself. This premise has been subjected to rigorous criticism. What is at issue of course is not that God himself is utterly trustworthy or infallible but that a book which comes to us through human means can bear that degree of trustworthiness. The church has recognized that although the Bible is the *Vox Dei* or the *Verbum Dei*, it is at the same time, the word of man. The controversial confessional statement issued by the United Presbyterian Church in the U.S.A. states the matter as follows:

> The Scriptures, given under the guidance of the Holy Spirit, are nevertheless the words of men, conditioned by the language, thought forms, and literary fashions of the places and times at which they were written. They reflect views of life, history, and cosmos which were then current. The church, therefore, has an obligation to approach the Scriptures with literary and historical understanding.[33]

The Confession elsewhere calls the Bible the "Word of God written." Here the Scriptures are viewed as being both the Word of God and the word of man. The question arises then, can the Bible being the word of man, be utterly trustworthy in light of the propensity of man for error and human fallibility? Can we take the proverbial maxim, "To err is human" and treat it as a tautology which can be reversed to say "To be human is to err?" Though we grant that God is incapable of error must we also admit that man is incapable of being free from error?

Karl Barth has described the view of verbal inspiration or inerrancy of the Bible as one that involves a kind of Biblical docetism. He draws the conclusion that the Bible is fallible because humans are fallible and the Bible is a human document.

The men whom we hear as witnesses speak as fallible, erring men like ourselves. What they say, and what we read as their word, can of itself lay claim to be the word of God, but never sustain that claim. We can read and try to assess their word as a purely human word. It can be subjected to all kinds of immanent criticism, not only in respect of its philosophical, historical and ethical content, but even of its religious and theological. We can establish lacunae, inconsistencies and over-emphases. We may be alienated by a figure like that of Moses. We may quarrel with James or with Paul. We may have to admit that we can make little or nothing of large tracts of the Bible, as is often the case with the records of other men. We can take offence at the Bible.[34]

Again Barth adds:

The prophets and apostles as such, even in their office, even in their function as witnesses, even in the act of writing down their witness, were real, historical men as we are, and therefore sinful in their action, and capable and actually guilty of error in their spoken and written word.[35]

For Barth, failure to confess such errors and contradictions would be to be guilty of docetism.[36] Barth draws a parallel between Biblical docetism and Christological docetism which is indeed a strange one. Christological docetism involves a failure to take the human nature of Christ seriously. As the ancient docetists were scandalized by the notion of incarnation so orthodox thinkers are scandalized by Biblical fallibility. The docetists were guilty of allowing the deity of Christ to swallow up his humanity and leave us with only an "apparent" or "phantom" human nature. So, according to Barth, orthodoxy has allowed the human aspect of the Bible to be swallowed up by the divine when it fails to leave room for human error.

This is a strange analogy indeed! Barth misses the issue completely and produces an argument so fallacious that one wonders how anyone can take it seriously. If we push the analogy we would be forced to ask if Christ could be sinless and still be a man? If being human demands error, is a man not a man when he speaks the truth? The term "fallible" describes an *ability*, not an *act*. To say that men are fallible is to say they are *capable* of error, not that they *must* err or that they *always* err. In theological terms, Christ's sinlessness no more cancels his humanity than does inerrancy cancel the Biblical writers' humanity.

What is at issue is not the question whether or not human beings *can* err. What is at issue is the question whether or not God inspires error or the Holy Spirit guides into error. When Orthodoxy confesses the infallibility of Scripture it is not confessing anything about the intrinsic infallibility of men. Rather the confession rests its confidence on the integrity of God. On numerous occasions I have queried several Biblical and theological scholars in the following manner.—"Do you maintain the inerrancy of Scripture?"—"No"—"Do you believe the Bible to be inspired of God?"—"Yes"—"Do you think God inspires error?"—"No"—"Is all of the Bible inspired by God?" —"Yes"—"Is the Bible errant?"—"No!" "Is it inerrant?" —"No!"—At that point I usually acquire an Excedrin headache. The above dialogue is not a construction of my fancy but a verbatim reproduction of a dialogue I have encountered on numerous occasions. To be sure, there are numerous ways of setting up false dilemmas and committing the either/or informal fallacy when there may be a *tertium quid*. But where is the *tertium quid* between errancy and inerrancy? *In*-errancy is a category that incorporates everything outside of the category of errancy. To affirm or deny both categories is to be involved in logical absurdity. Logical absurdity, however, does not bother some thinkers who see in absurdity the hallmark of truth.

Unless we want to join the ranks of the absurd, or unless we confess that God inspires error and join the ranks of the impious, or unless we confess that the Bible as a whole is not inspired then we are forced by what Luther called "resistless logic" to the conclusion that the Bible is inerrant.

The "resistless logic" of which Luther speaks is not a logic of isolated abstract speculations. It is a logic that is driven to a conclusion drawn from the premise of the integrity of Christ. The Bible is not claimed to be inerrant because of confidence in human ability. Rather the claim rests upon the foundation of the integrity of Christ. As Kähler pointed out in the 19th century: "We do not believe in Christ because we believe in the Bible, but we believe in the Bible because we believe in Christ." [37]

That orthodoxy moves from confidence in Christ's infallibility to confidence in the Scripture has not always been clearly understood. For example, Bernard Zylstra has criticized "orthodox theological circles" for viewing the Bible as the Word of God *because* it contains "propositional truth." [38] This, however, is a caricature in that it reverses the order. Orthodoxy does not believe the Bible to be the Word of God because it contains propositional truth—but believes the Bible to contain propositional *truth* because it is the Word of God.

It is important to add at this point that terms like "inerrant" or "infallible" must gain their content from a Biblical understanding of Truth. The protests of Berkouwer and others against "inerrancy" are often rightly directed against an imposition on the Biblical text of a notion of truth that is foreign to the Bible itself. Much unfair criticism has been leveled at orthodox thinkers at this point inasmuch as many have labored to clarify the notion of inerrancy along Biblical lines.

The late E. J. Young provides us with an excellent treatment of the question of the meaning of inerrancy and infallibility. He says:

> In present discussions of the Bible, both the words infallibility and inerrancy are often used without attempt at definition. The result is that much confusion has adhered and does adhere to current discussions of inspiration. There is not much point in talking of an infallible and inerrant Bible, unless we know what the words mean.[39]

Young goes on to define the terms by saying:

> By the term infallible as applied to the Bible, we mean simply that the Scripture possesses an indefectible authority. As our Lord himself said "it cannot be broken" (John 10:31). It can never fail in its judgments and statements. All that it teaches is of unimpeachable, absolute authority, and cannot be contravened, contradicted, or gainsaid. Scripture is unfailing, incapable of proving false, erroneous, or mistaken.[40]

He defines the term "inerrant" in similar categories: "By this word we mean that the Scriptures possess the quality of freedom from error. They are exempt from the liability to mistake, incapable of error. In all their teachings they are in perfect accord with the truth." [41]

Thus for Young, terms like infallible and inerrant are terms inseparably related to the notion of *truth*. To confess inerrancy is to confess the utter truthfulness of the Scripture. At this point Young, like Warfield before him and Berkouwer after him, warns against imposing an apriori notion of truth upon the Scripture which is at variance with the Bible's own view of truth. If the Biblical writers and/or Jesus claimed "truth" for their writings we should test their claim by an analysis of their writings in terms of consistency to their own view of truth.

Young demonstrates that within the context of a Biblical view of truth there is room for crudity and roughness of literary style, including improper grammatical structure, variations of parallel accounts of events, discourses, etc., but not room for contradiction or deception. Phenomenological, anthropomorphical, hyperbolic, etc. forms of language do not negate or falsify truth.

Hans Küng has commented on the relationship of the word "infallible" to the notion of deception:

> Bearing in mind the root of the word *infallibilitas (fallere*—put wrong, make a false step, lead into error, deceive, delude), I later translated *infallibilitas* more precisely and perhaps also more felicitously as "indeceivability" (*Untrüglichkeit*), which certainly has a more general meaning. *Infallibilitas* can then be understood as a sharing in the truth of God himself who, according to Vatican I, "can neither deceive nor be deceived" (*Deus revelans, qui nec falli nec fallere potest*—DS 3008). *Infallibilitas* would then mean being free from what is deceptive, from lying and fraud.[42]

Küng's definition of infallibility drawn by etymological derivation and customary usage within the Roman Catholic Tradition is not far removed from the New Testament concept of "truth."

Rudolf Bultmann properly analyzes the New Testament meaning of ἀλήθεια in his article on that term in Kittel's *Wörterbuch.* Truth in the New Testament is that which has "certainty and force," which is a "valid norm," "genuine," "proper" and "honest." Bultmann also indicates that ἀλήθεια is "that on which one can rely." The truth involves sincerity and honesty and is concerned with the "real state of affairs."[43]

When we confess that the Scriptures are inerrant and infallible we mean that they are *true* according to the categories mentioned above.

In summary, the Christian's case for the infallibility rests in the reliable trustworthiness of the Biblical documents which provide knowledge of the infallible Christ. The authority we give to Scripture ought to be no more and no less than that given to them by Christ. The Church cannot submit to the authority of Christ without at the same time submitting to the authority of the Scripture. The apologist of the 20th century must echo the argument of Iraeneus against the gnostics of his day:

> If anyone does not agree with them [the apostles] he despises the companions of the Lord himself—he even de-

spises the Father, and he is self-condemned, resisting and refusing his own salvation, as all the heretics do. . . . The apostles, being disciples of the truth, are apart from every lie. For a lie has no fellowship with the truth, anymore than light with darkness, but the presence of one excludes the other.[44]

NOTES

[1] Berkouwer gives particular attention to the Papal Encyclicals *Providentissimus Deus* (1893—Leo XIII) and *Spiritus Paraclitus* (1920—Benedictus XV); see *De Heilige Schrift* (2 vols.; Kampen: Kok, 1966), I, pp. 33-36.

[2] *Ibid.*, I, pp. 32-37.

[3] *Ibid.*, p. 190.

[4] G. C. Berkouwer, "Het Schrifgezag, in *De Bijbel in het Geding*, ed. G. C. Berkouwer and A. S. Van der Woude (Nijkerk: G. F. Callenbach, 1968), p. 14.

[5] H. Berkhof, "De methode van Berkouwer's theologie," in *EX AUDITU VERBI*, ed. R. Schippers, G. E. Meuleman, J. T. Bakker, and H. M. Kuitert (Kampen: Kok, 1965), pp. 44-48.

[6] Cornelius Van Til, *in Defense of the Faith*, Vol. I: *The Doctrine of Scripture* (Ripon: Den Dulk Christian Foundation, 1967), p. 148.

[7] *Ibid.*, p. 155.

[8] Berkhof, *op.cit.*, p. 55.

[9] Cornelius Van Til, *The Defense of the Faith* (Philadelphia: Presbyterian and Reformed Publishing Co., 1955), p. 109.

[10] *Ibid.*, p. 179.

[11] *Ibid.*, p. 285.

[12] W. Ward Fearnside and William B. Hoether, *Fallacy: The Counterfeit of Argument* (Englewood Cliffs, N. J.: Prentice-Hall, 1959), p. 166.

[13] Klass Runia cites Karl Barth's use of circularity in a favorable way: "The doctrine of Holy Scripture in the Evangelical Church is that this logical circle is the circle of self-asserting, self-attesting truth, into which it is equally impossible to enter as it is to emerge from it: The circle of our freedom, which as such is also the circle of our captivity" (*Karl Barth's Doctrine of Holy Scripture* [Grand Rapids, Mich.: Eerdmans, 1962], p. 7).

[14] Van Til, *The Defense of the Faith*, p. 101.

[15] "It is wholly irrational to hold to any other position than that of Christianity" (*ibid., The Defense of the Faith*, p. 298).

[16] See further: C. K. Barrett, *Luke the Historian in Recent Study* (London: Epworth Press, 1961); James Martin, *The Reliability of the Gospels* (London: Hodder and Stoughton, 1959); and F. F. Bruce, *The New Testament Documents: Are They Reliable?* (Chicago: Inter-Varsity Press, 1943).

[17] W. F. Albright and C. S. Mann, *Matthew* ("Anchor Bible"; New York: Doubleday, 1971), pp. v-vi.

[18] See Helmut Gollwitzer, *The Existence of God as Confessed By Faith*, trans. James W. Leitch (Philadelphia: Westminster, 1965), pp. 146-54.

[19] John Calvin, *Institutes of the Christian Religion*, trans. Henry Beveridge, I (Grand Rapids, Mich.: Eerdmans, 1964), p. 72.

[20] *Ibid.*, p. 71.

[21] See G. C. Berkouwer, *De Persoon van Christus: Dogmatische Studiën* (Kampen: Kok, 1952), pp. 178-84.

[22] Heinrich Denzinger (ed.), *Enchiridion Symbolorum* (Rome: Herder, 1965), para. 2183-85.

[23] C. H. Dodd, *The Authority of the Bible* (New York: Harper, 1960), pp. 222-23.

[24] Emil Brunner, *The Mediator*, trans. Olive Wyon (Philadelphia: Westminster, 1948), p. 368.

[25] Emil Brunner, *Religionsphilosophie* (München, 1927), pp. 77-78; cited by Paul King Jewett in *Inspiration and Interpretation*, ed. John F. Walvoord (Grand Rapids, Mich.: Eerdmans, 1957), p. 211.

[26] See J. I. Packer, *"Fundamentalism" and the Word of God* (Grand Rapids, Mich.: Eerdmans, 1958), pp. 54-62.

[27] James Orr. *Revelation and Inspiration* (reprint ed.; Grand Rapids, Mich.: Baker, 1969), p. 151.

[28] Joachim Jeremias, *New Testament Theology: The Proclamation of Jesus*, trans. John Bowden (New York: Scribners, 1971), p. 206.

[29] *Ibid.*, p. 207.

[30] *Ibid.*, p. 206.

[31] Packer, *op. cit.*, p. 55.

[32] Herman Bavinck writes: "Deze canon des Ouden Testaments bezat voor Jezus en de apostelen, evanals voor hunne tijdgenooten, goddelijke autoriteit" (*Gereformeerde Dogmatiek*, I [Kampen: Bos, 1906], p. 412).

[33] *The Constitution of the United Presbyterian Church in the United States of America.* Part I: *Book of Confessions* (Philadelphia: General Assembly Office, 1966), para. 9.26-9.31.

[34] Karl Barth, *Kirchliche Dogmatik*, I, 2, p. 507; cited by Klaas Runia, *op.cit.*, p. 59.

[35] *Ibid.*, p. 60.

[36] *Ibid.*

[37] Martin Kähler, *The So-Called Historical Jesus and the Historic Biblical Christ*, trans. Carl E. Braaten (Philadelphia: Fortress, 1964), p. 75.

[38] James H. Oethius, *et al., Will All the Kings Men....* (Toronto: Wedge Publishing Foundation, 1972), p. 183.

[39] Edward J. Young, *Thy Word is Truth* (Grand Rapids, Mich.: Eerdmans, 1957), p. 113.

[40] *Ibid.*

[41] *Ibid.*

[42] Hans Küng, *Infallible? An Inquiry*, trans. Edward Quinn (New York: Doubleday, 1971), p. 140.

[43] Rudolf Bultmann, " αλήθεια," *Theological Dictionary of the New Testament*, ed. Gerhard Kittel: trans. G. W. Bromiley, Vol. I (Grand Rapids, Mich.: Eerdmans, 1964).

[44] Cyril C. Richardson (ed.), *Early Christian Fathers* ("Library of Christian Classics," Vol. I; Philadelphia: Westminster, 1953), pp. 370-76.

Appendix:

THE APPROACH OF NEW SHAPE ROMAN CATHOLICISM TO SCRIPTURAL INERRANCY: A CASE STUDY*

John Warwick Montgomery

At the beginning of each meeting of the Second Vatican Council, participants and observers witnessed an ancient oriental custom, newly reintroduced at the Council: the enthroning of the Book of the Gospels. This rite well symbolized the powerful Biblical revival in twentieth-century Roman Catholicism and reminded Protestants that Holy Scripture is not the private domain of the heirs of the Reformation. Indeed, Vatican II displayed at its very heart the concern for biblical understanding characteristic of Roman Catholic scholarship since the founding of the Ecole Biblique at Jerusalem by Père Marie-Joseph Lagrange;[1] as Jesuit R. A. F. MacKenzie has recently said of the Council's work: "Important as the Constitution on the Church is generally agreed to be, it is equaled in stature by the Constitution on Divine Revelation; the two are the most fundamental documents produced by the Second Vatican Council."[2] This laudable stress on the doctrine of revelation should goad contemporary Protestantism—too often preoccupied with achieving vaster ecclesiastical unions and non-theological goals—to re-examine its own biblical foundations. More particularly, the current Roman Catholic emphasis on revelation

* An invitational presentation at the Seminar on the Authority of Scripture (Harold John Ockenga, chairman), held at Gordon College, Wenham, Massachusetts, June 20-29, 1966, and subsequently published in the *Evangelical Theological Society Bulletin* [now *Journal*], X (Fall, 1967), pp. 209-25, and in the author's *Ecumenicity, Evangelicals, and Rome* (Grand Rapids, Mich.: Zondervan, 1969), pp. 71-93.

should receive the closest attention from evangelical Protestants who are endeavoring to clarify their historic position on the absolute authority, infallibility, and inerrancy of Holy Writ. It is the judgment of the present essayist that recent developments in Roman Catholic thinking on the revelational issue can provide an invaluable case study for evangelicals facing similar problems. No apology is offered for the negative thrust of later sections of the paper: I praise the Lord of the Church for all genuine enthronements of His scriptural Word, but I must also seek to distinguish what is truly honoring to His Word from what is not. And a valuable lesson can have a negative moral; as a very wise man once said, "Those who refuse to learn by history are forced to repeat its mistakes."

THE CLASSICAL ROMAN CATHOLIC POSITION ON BIBLICAL INERRANCY

Rome's position on the inspiration of Holy Scripture has, through the generations preceding our own, seemed exceedingly clear-cut and unambiguous both to her friends and to her enemies. The Council of Trent, though reacting strongly against the Reformation's formal principle of Sola Scriptura, stated in no uncertain terms the full inspiration of the Bible. In the Fourth Session of the Council (8 April 1546) a "Decree Concerning the Canonical Scriptures" was set forth, describing the Holy Writings as "vel oretenus a Christo, vel a Spiritu Sancto dictatas":

> The holy, ecumenical and general Council of Trent, lawfully assembled in the Holy Ghost, the same three legates of the Apostolic See presiding, keeps this constantly in view, namely, that the purity of the Gospel may be preserved in the Church after the errors have been removed. This [Gospel], of old promised through the Prophets in the Holy Scriptures, our Lord Jesus Christ, the Son of God, promulgated first with His own mouth, and then commanded it to be preached by His Apostles to every creature as the source at once of all saving truth and rules of conduct. It also clearly perceives that these truths and rules are contained in the written books and in the unwritten traditions, which, received by the Apostles themselves, the Holy Ghost dictating, have come down to us, transmitted as it were from hand to hand. Following, then, the examples of the orthodox Fathers, it receives and venerates with a feeling of piety and reverence all the books both of the Old and of the New Testaments, since one God is the author of both, and also the traditions,

whether they relate to faith or to morals, as having been dictated either orally by Christ or by the Holy Ghost, and preserved in the Catholic Church in unbroken succession.[3]

The subsequent centuries display the reinforcement of this strong biblical position over against heresies of various kinds.[4] Pius IX (1846-1878) condemned the pantheists, naturalists, and rationalists of his day for holding that "prophetiae et miracula in sacris Litteris exposita et narrata sunt poetarum commenta" and that "utriusque Testamenti libris mythica continentur inventa" (Denzinger, 1707). By the turn of the present century the Roman Church faced the Modernist controversy, and advocates (such as Loisy) of a partially inspired Scripture or of a Scripture erroneous in "non-theological" matters were condemned in no uncertain terms. In the Holy Office decree of 3 July 1907 ("Lamentabili"), Pius X (1903-1914) labeled as illegitimate the Modernist claim that "inspiratio divina non ita ad totam Scripturam sacram extenditur, ut omnes et singulas eius partes ab omni errore praemuniat" (Denzinger, 2011). Pius X's famous Encyclical "Pascendi dominici gregis" (8 September 1907) warrants extended quotation to show how firmly the Church rejected non-inerrancy views of Holy Writ:

> The result of [the Modernist] dismembering of the records, and this partition of them throughout the centuries, is naturally that the Scripture can no longer be attributed to the authors whose names they bear. The Modernists have no hesitation in affirming generally that these books, and especially the Pentateuch and the first three Gospels, have been gradually formed from a primitive brief narration, by additions, by interpolations of theological or allegorical interpretations, or by parts introduced only for the purpose of joining different passages together. . . .
>
> In the Sacred Books there are many passages referring to science or history where, according to them, manifest errors are to be found. But, they say, the subject of these books is not science or history, but only religion and morals. In them history and science serve only as species of covering to enable the religious and moral experiences wrapped up in them to penetrate more readily among ancient people. The common people understood science and history as they are expressed in these books, and it is clear that the expression of science and history in a more perfect form would have proved not so much a help as a hindrance. Moreover, they add, the Sacred Books, being essentially religious, are necessarily pulsating with life. Now life has its own truth and its own logic—quite different from rational truth and logic, be-

longing as they do to a different order, viz., the truth of adaptation and of proportion to what they call its living medium and living purpose. Finally, the Modernists, losing all sense of control go so far as to proclaim as true and legitimate whatever is explained by life.

We, Venerable Brethren, for whom there is but one and only truth, and who hold that the Sacred Books, "written under the inspiration of the Holy Ghost, have God for their author," [5] declare that this is equivalent to attributing to God Himself the lie of expediency or the officious lie, and We say with St. Augustine: "In an authority so high, admit but one officious lie, and there will not remain a single passage of those apparently difficult to practise or to believe, which on the same most pernicious rule may not be explained as a lie uttered by the author willfully and to serve some higher end." [6] And thus it will come about, the holy Doctor continues, that "everybody will believe and refuse to believe what he likes or dislikes in them," namely, the Scriptures. . . . In short, to maintain and defend these theories they [the Modernists] do not hesitate to declare that the noblest homage that can be paid to the Infinite is to make it the object of contradictory statements! But when they justify even contradictions, what is it that they will refuse to justify? [7]

Loisy was excommunicated, and Pius X's successor, Benedict XV (1914-22), underscored the inerrancy position of "Pascendi gregis" in his Encyclical "Spiritus Paraclitus" (15 September 1920).[8] To all intents and purposes, the partial and limited inspiration views of Catholic Modernism had been dealt the death blow. In point of fact, as George Lindbeck of Yale has correctly noted, Modernism went underground in the Roman communion, only to surface decades later after men sympathetic to a more radical biblical approach had attained positions of authority and influence in the Church.[9]

BIBLICAL CRITICISM IN NEW
SHAPE ROMAN CATHOLIC SCHOLARSHIP

With the classic Roman Catholic stance on inerrancy before us, let us now observe the way in which representative scholars of the Church are presently approaching Holy Writ. The contrast will be instructive.

In 1958, Belgian Jesuit Jean Levie published a work which offers a synoptic view of the New Shape in Roman Catholic biblical scholarship. Its original title is significant (*La Bible, parole humaine et message de Dieu*) [10] for, unlike the title of the 1961 English translation (*The Bible, Word of God in Words of Men*), it well represents its author's major stress: the human rather than the divine aspects of the biblical writings. The book has two major sections, an overview of what Levie calls "progress in history and biblical exegesis" in recent Roman Catholicism, and a hermeneutic examination of Scripture problems, most of which display for him "the human traits in the inspired book." Here are some of his representative conclusions:

> Scientific ideas current in those [biblical] days, but which have now been abandoned, may enter into the formulation of teaching which alone the inspired writer wishes to assert. It is, moreover of little consequence whether he did or did not believe in the ideas current in his time, for they are not what he is claiming to assert.[11]
> It has been possible to discover in the Pentateuch a certain number of doublets—two accounts of the same events, but derived from different sources. There are divergencies in these accounts, since the two traditions are themselves divergent, but they have been combined in a single text by the inspired writer. . . . In J, the deluge lasts for forty days and Noe then opens the window to release the birds (8.6) and fourteen days later, he leaves the ark. In P, the period between the beginning of the Flood to the exit from the ark lasts for more than a year (7.11 and 8.15).[12]
> There may be [in Scripture] fictional historical forms . . . books which though apparently historical in form, seem in fact to be didactic writings, philosophical and religious discussions or theses.[13] In the last days of Judaism, we meet a special literary form, the . . . Haggadic Midrash. . . . It often became a list of marvels full of extraordinary or even fantastic events. . . . The hypothesis of an "inspired Haggadah" here and there (that is, an existing literary form used, under the inspiration of the Holy Spirit, for nobler ends), should not be necessarily excluded *a priori* by Catholic exegesis.[14]
> Every nation writes the history of ancient times with the help of ancestral traditions, accounts that are partly historical, partly poetical, which in their passage from one generation to another, gradually simplify the facts, group them around some more outstanding personality, and artificially link stories which are independent of one another. . . . It is easy to discover significant concrete examples of this literary form in many of the Pentateuch narratives, for instance in the story of the patriarchs (Gen. chapters 11-50), and to throw into relief their character as collective, popular accounts, as ancestral traditions.

In fact it was the study of these accounts which gave rise to the earliest applications of *Formgeschichte* (with H. Gunkel).[15]

The perspective on biblical truth expressed in these quotations from Levie is shared by his British confrère R. A. F. Mac-Kenzie, S. J., whose 1963 publications, *Faith and History in the Old Testament,* has acquired considerable popularity both in England and in the United States. In the author's summation of his key chapter on "the Problem of Myth and History," one reads:

> For them [the Israelite historians], what really happened was what God did, and the material phenomena on the level of sense perception could be freely heightened and colored in their accounts, the better to express the reality that lay behind them.
>
> But when they had no history and traditions of their own, namely, for the period preceding the call of Abraham, then they were of necessity driven to take their materials where they could find them, and that meant only in the tradition and mythology that had originated among other peoples.[16]

American Jesuit John L. McKenzie, the first Roman Catholic to hold a chair at the University of Chicago Divinity School, offers a more generalized account of the same view, employing the personalistic-existential imagery of Martin Buber:

> Surely there now ought to be little room for timidity and misunderstanding if we call Hebrew literature in some passages mythical, or wisdom discourses couched in mythopoeic patterns. Even if the rigorous ethics of scholarship do not clearly demand the adoption of this terminology, they do demand the recognition of Israel's community with the ancient Near East in patterns of thought and language. . . . The Hebrew intuition of the ineffable reality which revealed itself to man as the personal reality behind the succession of phenomena, the agent of the great cosmic event which we call creation, the reality from which all things came, in which they exist, and to which they must return, was not the creation of mythical form or of logical discourse, but a direct and personal experience of God as the "Thou" to whom the human "I" must respond. But they had no media through which they could enunciate the ineffable reality except the patterns of thought and speech which they inherited from their civilization.[17]

In a strictly analogous way, Roman Catholic scholars in the

New Testament field have been re-evaluating their materials. Myles M. Bourke's paper on "The Literary Genus of Matthew 1-2" is characteristic; in a matter strongly reminiscent of Loisy, he uses the fact that the infancy narrative parallels in literary genre a haggadic commentary to dispense with the historicity of many details of the biblical account.[18] The door had been opened for such an orientation by the Encyclical *Divino afflante Spiritu* (1943), which though it did not advocate a radical approach to Scripture, clearly allowed the use of the *formgeschichtliche Methode* and made it possible for Roman Catholic scholars to doubt, for example, that given biblical miracles occurred historically if their doubt stemmed from conviction that the miracles were included as literary devices to illustrate theological points. Indeed, Roger Aubert has stated that Catholic exegetes could theoretically on this basis remain in full fellowship with the Church while denying all biblical miracles but the Virgin Birth and the Resurrection.[19]

Thus we arrive at the most recent official Roman Catholic statements on the nature of Scripture: the 1964 Instruction of the Biblical Commission on the historical truth of the Gospels, and Vatican II's Constitution on Divine Revelation. The Biblical Commission implicitly countenances Gospel interpretation by literary forms—not excluding miracle stories and midrash—and allows for *Redaktionsgeschichte*; and in this connection the Instruction "speaks of 'truth' only, and does not specify it as 'historical truth.'"[20] Vatican II, in its Dogmatic Constitution on Divine Revelation, affirms that "the books of Scripture must be acknowledged as teaching firmly, faithfully, and without error that truth which God wanted put into the sacred writings for the sake of our salvation."[21] Explains the commentator:

> An earlier draft of the Constitution had joined the adjective *salutaris* ("tending to salvation") to the word "truth." Another last-minute change substituted the phrase "for the sake of our salvation," to avoid seeming to limit the truth itself. The point remains the same. . . .
>
> The Bible was not written in order to teach the natural sciences, nor to give information on merely political history. It treats of these (and all other subjects) only insofar as they are involved in matters concerning salvation. It is only in this respect that the veracity of God and the inerrancy of the inspired writers are engaged. This is not a quantitative distinction. . . . It is formal, and applies to the whole text. The latter is authoritative and inerrant in

what it affirms about the revelation of God and the history of salvation. According to the intentions of its authors, divine and human, it makes no other affirmations.[22]

That this interpretation of the Constitution is eminently just can be seen from the history of the schema on revelation. "It is no secret that the first draft of the schema *De fontibus revelationis* contained two paragraphs which incorporated the terminology of the *Monitum* of June, 1961, and leveled anathemas against those who would call in question the genuine historical and objective truth of the words and deeds of Jesus *prouti narrantur*. Thus was rejected along with the rest of the schema." [23] Conservatives had attempted, unsuccessfully, to stem the tide; a recent article describes their views in the following terms:

> There exists a numerous and fairly articulate group convinced that the four Gospels and the Acts of the Apostles are genuine and objectively accurate historical documents, which can be used as such legitimately in the science of apologetics. These individuals insist that they have reason to hold and to teach that these events set forth in these books took place in the very way in which they are described in these works. They hold, that the words and the deeds attributed to Our Lord were actually uttered and performed by Him.[24]

Clearly this position (with its evident affinity to the biblical orientation of classic evangelical Protestantism) is no longer officially advocated or even required of the Roman Catholic theologian. New Shape Catholic biblical scholarship displays a very different alignment: with the historical-critical method which won the day among non-evangelical Protestant scholars during the Modernist era and which has continued as the operating methodology in those circles even to the post-Bultmannian present. Thus James M. Robinson, a leading figure in the Protestant "New Quest of the Historical Jesus," comments favorably on Bourke's midrash interpretation of Matthew 1-2:

> The main difference between Bourke and Renan on this point would seem to be that Renan lived at a time when this position was inadmissible within the Roman Catholic Church and Bourke is living in a time when it is admissible. Form criticism has made it possible for the Catholic scholar to assert that the literal sense of a given passage is not to present a true story but rather a story conveying truth.[25]

In the same vein, Robinson approvingly cites Raymond E. Brown's dissertation, *The Sensus Plenior of Sacred Scripture* (1955), which in the last decade has shifted the attention of Roman Catholic exegetes from the *sensus literalis* to a "fuller sense" allegedly conveyed by the biblical text:

> The interest in *sensus plenior* has some affinities with Gerhard von Rad's interest in the successive reinterpretation of the Old Testament *Heilsgeschichte* within the successive oral and written layers of the Old Testament itself, or with Rudolf Bultmann's detection that the Christology implicit in Jesus' mission becomes explicit in the Christological titles attributed to him after Easter.[26]

From Trent and Pius X to von Rand and Bultmann is a leap of staggering proportions. Let us now attempt to understand how it happened and to draw forth its implications for a contemporary evangelical theology of the Word.

THE RATIONALE OF REVOLUTION

The historian can easily remind us of shifts in the twentieth-century theological climate which make the Roman Catholic acceptance of radical biblical scholarship seem more understandable. For example, by the 1940's when *Divino afflante Spiritu* was promulgated, the less theologically radical Protestant Neo-Orthodoxy had sufficiently replaced Protestant Modernism that a more liberal approach to the Bible no longer appeared to pose any direct threat to the Church. But such considerations only scratch the surface of a revolution so radical that, without any change of traditional terminology ("inerrancy," "dictation by the Holy Ghost," etc.) a Church which once set itself unequivocally against literary dismembering of biblical books and against errors of any kind in their inspired contents, now allows these very positions to be held by her scholars.

Protestants are frequently bewildered by such changes in the face of the supposedly unchanging Rome. Not too many years ago a Roman Catholic priest in Boston was excommunicated for maintaining strictly the medieval position, hallowed by a famous bull of Boniface VIII, that salvation absolutely necessitates submission to the Roman pontiff; in holding that non-Catholics would not be saved, the priest violated the conviction of present-day Catholic theology that non-Catholics will be judged by the "natural law" known to them. The priest in question was bewildered; but even more so were Protestants who observed what appeared to be a blatant inconsistency in a Church claiming to be utterly consistent.

More recently, Father Hans Küng of Tübingen University electrified the theological world with his book, *Justification: The Doctrine of Karl Barth and a Catholic Reflection*, in which he argues in all seriousness that the Canons and Decrees of Trent, which were written in large part as an answer to the Reformer's central principle of Sola Gratia, are fully compatible with Barth's exposition of the historic Protestant doctrine of justification. Barth, in his Preface to Küng's book, wryly comments:

> All I can say is this: If what you have presented in Part Two of this book is actually the teaching of the Roman Catholic Church, then I must certainly admit that my view of justification agrees with the Roman Catholic view; if only for the reason that the Roman Catholic teaching would then be most strikingly in accord with mine! Of course, the problem is whether what you have presented here really represents the teaching of your Church.[27]

Here Barth betrays his Protestant mind-set: he questions whether Küng's reinterpretation of Trent can be squared with "the teaching" of the Roman Church. This is how a Protestant operates, to be sure; he assumes a permanent and perspicuous revelatory teaching in Holy Scripture, and then evaluates current theological interpretations against that standard. But this is not the way Rome does business theologically. Küng's activity looks bizarre to a Protestant, and *is* bizarre from the standpoint of Protestant theological methodology; but, when viewed from within the Roman Catholic understanding of theological truth, Küng's work is, in principle (wholly apart from the question of scholarly soundness), quite legitimate.

Rome's ultimate standard of religious truth is Rome itself: and by "Rome" is not meant a static body of historical creeds which impose their objective authority upon later generations, but rather a living organism which, as the extension of Christ's incarnation in time and as the vehicle of God's Holy Spirit, can creatively reshape its past. Listen to one of the greatest modern exponents of "the spirit of Catholicism," Karl Adam:

> In reality Christianity is an intimate organic unity, a vital unity, which unfolds itself indeed to its fulness progressively, and yet in all the stages of its unfolding is a unity and a whole, the Christianity of Christ. Just as I first appreciate the totality of the potential life which

is in the acorn when I see before me the mature oak, fully developed in all its grandeur, in a way that no mere study of the embryology of the acorn can enable me to realize it, so I can first discern the width and depth of Christ's Gospel, the whole vast richness of His mind and His message, His "fulness," when I have before me the fully-developed Christianity, and then only in the measure in which I appreciate its inner unity. . . . So there is in Catholic Christianity a unitary lifestream, a life of unity in fulness, a single mighty life. And if I would determine the content of the original cell of this life, the content of the Christianity of Christ, I must not approach the tree of Christianity with the knife of the critic and mutilate it in order to discover this original cell. On the contrary I must accept the Christian life as a whole and appraise it as a whole. Unlimited criticism, faulty and sterile historical or philological research: these things do not conduct us to the mystery of Christ. But we attain to Him by steeping ourselves lovingly in the abundance of life which has gone forth from Him.[28]

Once one understands the organic conception of truth at the heart of the Roman Church, one can see how ill-conceived was the excitement of many Protestant theologians and Vatican II observers when the Council did not incorporate into its Constitution on Divine Revelation the "two-source" theory (revelation is contained partly—*partim*—in Scripture and partly in the traditions) but stressed the unity of revelation: *Sola Scriptura in ore ecclesiae.* In point of fact, however one defines the source of revelation, the living Magisterium of the Church is the dynamic interpreter of it, shaping the Church's belief from age to age. Thus Adam describes the relation between Scripture and Magisterium:

Christianity is not a religion of dead documents and fragmentary records, but a life in the Holy Spirit preserved from generation to generation by the apostolical succession of commissioned preachers. . . . The surging life of the Christian present flows over the dead records of primitive documents, or rather, these documents are themselves nothing but that life grown stiff and numb, nothing but a deposit of the holy and supernatural life which still enfolds us in the present. Therefore those documents can be fully deciphered and yield their true revealed sense only in the light of this life.[29]

In precisely the same vein, R. A. F. MacKenzie summarizes the viewpoint of Vatican II's Constitution on Divine Revelation:

A written record is a dead letter, needing constant interpretation and commentary in succeeding ages. It cannot of itself answer new questions, or explain what was
once clear and has now become obscure. But the writings transmitted in a living community, from one generation to another, are accompanied by a continuous tradition of understanding and explanation which preserves
and re-expresses their meaning, and which applies them,
from time to time, to the solving of new problems. If
this tradition were only human, it would be liable to
grave error. But such a consequence is avoided by the
Church's magisterium.[30]

This approach to the foundational documents of the Roman
Church (the Holy Scriptures) is of course applied to the subsequent documentary history of that body: all of its past records are subject to perennial "decipherment" and "re-expression" by the living Magisterium. Thus the about-face on *Extra
ecclesiam nullus salus*; thus the possibility of a re-reading of
Trent in terms of Sola Gratia; and thus the totally new understanding of biblical inerrancy.

It is vital to note that from the Roman Catholic viewpoint,
no changes in doctrine actually take place in such cases. Once
the Magisterium reinterprets a teaching (e.g., the meaning of
biblical authority), then all previous authoritative expressions
of the teaching are held to have this meaning. The powerful
role of casuistry in Roman Catholic moral theology parallels
and encourages the casuistical re-expression of documentary
meaning in the Church's dogmatic theology. To the non-Catholic,
this procedure invariably suggests the Marxist rewriting of history and George Orwell's apocalyptic novel, *1984*, where Winston,
the hapless victim of a totalitarianism so complete that it continually redefines truth, searches in vain for a way to convince
his persecutor, O'Brien, that the state has fallen into the worst
epistemological hell of all, solipsism.[31]

Whether or not Roman Catholicism's organic view of theological truth amounts to solipsism is too large a question for
us to answer here.[32] But we do need to see that in its reinterpretation of the concept of biblical inspiration and inerrancy, the Church has in fact sapped all significant meaning
out of these doctrines. Any assertion—religious or otherwise—
which is compatible with anything and everything says precisely nothing.[33] If I claim that my wife is an excellent driver,
and yet cheerfully admit that she has a serious accident weekly,
which is invariably her fault, then my original claim (though
I may continue to voice it) is nonsense. By the same token,

when Roman Catholicism continues to insist that the Holy Scriptures were dictated by the Holy Ghost and are inerrant, while at the same time allowing internal contradictions through source conflation, external contradictions with known fact, employment of Midrash fictions, etc., the Church speaks nonsense. The argument that Scripture is in any case inerrant *theologically* is of no help at all, since the biblical writers make no distinction whatever between "theological" and "secular" fact, and indeed ground heavenly truth in earthly reality ("If I have told you earthly things, and ye believe not, how shall ye believe, if I tell you of heavenly things?"—John 3:12). [34] And the redefinition of biblical truthfulness in personalistic, existential categories ("I-Thou") by such Roman Catholic writers as John L. McKenzie only begs the question, for "encounters" are not self-authenticating,[35] and the Scripture itself makes truth-as-encounter dependent upon truth-as-factual reality ("If I do not the works of my Father, believe me not"—John 1:37). In New Shape Roman Catholic biblical theology, the words "authority," "infallibility," and "inerrancy" have been suffering what R. M. Hare has called the "death by a thousand qualifications": they have been qualified again and again—to such a point that they mean little or nothing. This is particularly evident from the fact that Roman Catholic biblical scholars now accept many of the radically critical arguments espoused by Protestant exegetes such as von Rad and Bultmann, who use these very arguments to support their *rejection* of theopneustic biblical authority.

To be sure, for Roman Catholics this problem is not particularly acute. The final authority is the living Magisterium, which, a priori, stands above criticism. Words, documents, and entire epochs of Church history have suffered the death of a thousand qualifications, and Rome still remains; ever-changing, ever the same. But what about the Protestant evangelical who, without a Magisterium, contemplates the path taken by his Roman Catholic counterpart?

THE EVANGELICAL SINE QUA NON: BIBLICAL AUTHORITY DEFINED HERMENEUTICALLY

In some quarters today, evangelical Protestants are apparently of the opinion that, like the Church of Rome, they can use the general terminology of biblical authority ("infallibility," "inerrancy," and the like) without committing themselves to any view of biblical truthfulness in the particulars. Thus a recent news item reported: "Canadian representatives of the Missouri Synod, The American Lutheran Church, and the Lutheran Church in America have agreed that a 'discrepancy' or an 'error of fact' can't affect the inerrancy of the Bible, according to a Canadian Lutheran Council report." [36] To which the present essayist replied:

> Whenever we reach the point of affirming on the one hand that the Bible is infallible or inerrant and admitting on the other hand to internal contradictions or factual inaccuracies within it, we not only make a farce of language, promoting ambiguity, confusion, and perhaps even deception in the church; more reprehensible than even these things, we in fact deny the plenary inspiration and authority of Scripture, regardless of the theological formulae we may insist on retaining. . . . I must—if only on the basis of common sense—protest the idea that "error can't affect inerrancy." This is like saying that the presence of corners can't affect a circle.[37]

My strong reply was an effort to remind my fellow churchmen of the centrality of unqualified biblical authority in their heritage. The Reformation irrevocably stated its theological claims upon a totally reliable, perspicuous Bible; it explicitly denied the notion of a living Magisterium as interpreter of Scripture. Indeed, the Reformers categorically refused to allow any human writing or teacher to stand above Holy Writ; they recognized full well that if God's Word were not entirely trustworthy, then man would be forever incapable of distinguishing its truth from its non-truth and even the salvatory Gospel would be imperiled.

During the heyday of Protestant Modernism, evangelicals were especially sensitive to the erosion of theological vocabulary among their Liberal opponents. They were well aware that without an infallible Magisterium the redefinition of terms such as "atonement" and "miracle" through pressure from the non-revelatory human situation would cause the Gospel—the material principle of the Reformation—to die the death of a thousand qualifications. Now, I submit, the same danger faces the formal principle—Scriptural authority.

And how are we to avoid this deleterious state of affairs? By a realistic recognition that *our statements of biblical inspiration, whatever their terminology*—whether positive ("entire trustworthiness") or negative ("infallibility," "inerrancy") —*having been derived from the general pronouncements of Scripture itself on the subject and particularly from the attitude of Christ and His chosen Apostles toward Scripture, must yield concrete hermeneutic guidelines for treating specific exegetical difficulties.* A doctrine of inspiration imposed upon the Bible from without is a denial of inspiration; a doctrine of limited biblical authority derived from passages manifesting difficulties is as false an induction and as flagrant a denial of the analogy of Scripture as is a morally imperfect Christology derived from questionable acts on Jesus' part (in both cases, proper induction requires that we go to the express teaching on the subject and allow this to create the inductively-derived *Gestalt* or pattern for treating particular problems); [38] and any doctrine of biblical authority without express hermeneutic application is already in the throes of the death by a thousand qualifications.

Quite obviously it would go beyond the scope of this paper to set forth a full-orbed doctrine of biblical authority governed by these criteria. But some suggestions can and ought to be made. When one observes the teaching and example of Christ and His chosen Apostles[39] on the subject of scriptural authority, one is overwhelmingly impressed by the attitude of *total trust* involved; nowhere, in no particular, and on no subject is Scripture subjected to criticism. Passages are quoted authoritatively from the most obscure corner of the Old Testament; individual words are forced to bear the weight of heavy doctrinal teaching; passages from diverse periods and from the pens of many authors are quoted together and sometimes conflated, obviously implying their consistency and common Divine authorship; no attempt is made to distinguish truth "in faith and practice" from veracity in historical and secular matters; and we are told that man lives ἐπὶ παντὶ ῥήματι ἐκπορευμένῳ διὰ στόματος θεοῦ. (Matt. 4:4, quoting Deut. 8:3).

A scripturally grounded doctrine of biblical authority thus implicates (in the strictest sense) an inerrant, non-contradictory Bible, and qualitatively distinguishes Scripture from all extra-biblical materials, such that none of them can be used to judge or criticize Holy Writ. If it is objected that we are implicitly importing a standard of consistency into our doctrine of scriptural authority, we can only reply that man is incapable of comprehending anything apart from the law of contradiction (as Emerson said to Brahma, "When me they fly, I am the wings"), so a "revelation" involving contradiction reveals nothing at all. Moreover, from a contradiction anything follows, so that the presence of any contradictions in God's Word would require the immediate testing of all its alleged truths—an impossible task in the very matters most vital to salvation. Thus the popular analogy breaks down between the Scripture and a sermon ("Can't a sermon reveal truth even with mistakes in it?"): the only way one knows that a sermon *does* reveal truth is by comparison of its teachings with Scripture; but there is no Bible-to-the-second-power by which to test the veracity of the *Bible's* salvatory teachings. And (to repeat the warning Jesus gave to Nicodemus when He preached the Gospel to him): "If I have told you earthly things, and ye believe not, how shall ye believe, if I tell you of heavenly things?"

In conclusion, then, let us set forth the basic hermeneutic implications of this evangelical view of biblical authority, thereby preserving it from the death of a thousand qualifications to which New Shape Roman Catholic inspiration doctrine is unhappily subject. Though other hermeneutic guidelines could doubtless be added, the following six principles should make clear the over-all interpretive implications of biblical authority for our day:

1. A passage of Holy Writ must be taken as veracious in its natural sense (*sensus literalis*) unless the context of the passage itself dictates otherwise, or unless an article of faith established elsewhere in Scripture requires a broader understanding of the text.

2. The prime article of faith applicable to the hermeneutic task is the attitude of Christ and His Apostles toward the Scriptures: their utter trust in Scripture—in all it teaches or touches—must govern the exegete's practice, thus eliminating in principle any interpretation which sees the biblical texts as erroneous or contradictory in fulfilling their natural intent.

3. Harmonization of scriptural difficulties should be pursued within reasonable limits, and when harmonization would pass beyond such bounds, the exegete must leave the problem open rather than, by assuming surd error, impugn the absolute truthfulness of the God who inspires all Holy Scripture for our learning.

4. Extra-biblical linguistic and cultural considerations must be employed ministerially, never magisterially, in the interpretation of a text; and any use of extra-biblical material to arrive at an interpretation inconsistent with the veracity of the scriptural passage is to be regarded as magisterial and therefore illegitimate. Extra-biblical data can and should put questions to a text, but only Scripture itself can in the last analysis legitimately answer questions about itself.

5. Not all literary forms are consistent with scriptural revelation; the exegete must not appeal to literary forms (such as the midrash) which cast doubt on the truthfulness or the morality of the Divine author of Scripture.[40]

6. The exegete should employ all scholarly research tools that do not involve rationalistic commitments. Rationalistic methodologies are identifiable by their presuppositions,

which either (like Bultmann's demythologizing) do violence
to articles of faith, or (like certain documentary theories)
oppose the perspicuity of the received biblical texts and
the facticity of the events recorded in them, or (like the
"circularity principle" of the so-called "New Hermeneutic")
give to the sinful cultural milieu, past and present, a constitutive role in the formulation of biblical teaching.[41]
These and other rationalistic techniques are to be scrupu-
lously avoided in carrying out the hermeneutic task.

But to conclude an essay on the perfection of Scripture with
less than the perfect number of principles seems woefully in-
appropriate; and to terminate an essay focusing on the Roman
Church without quoting one of her greatest saints would be
indeed ungracious. So let us hear again from St. Augustine,
who will provide our seventh and foundational principle for the
reading of that Sacred Book which brought him, and by God's
grace brings each of us, into the presence of the saving Christ:

7. In an authority so high, admit but one officious lie, and there
will not remain a single passage of those apparently difficult
to practise or to believe, which on the same most pernicious
rule may not be explained as a lie uttered by the author
willfully and to serve some higher end.[42]

NOTES

[1] Cf. Montgomery, "The Fourth Gospel Yesterday and Today; An Analysis of Two Reformation and Two 20th-Century Commentaries on the Gospel According to St. John," *Concordia
Theological Monthly*, XXXIV (April, 1963), pp. 197-222 (containing an examination of Lagrange's
Evagile selon Saint Jean). This essay has been reprinted in Montgomery, *The Suicide of Christian Theology* (Minneapolis: Bethany Fellowship, 1970).

[2] *The Documents of Vatican II*, ed. Walter M. Abbott (New York: Guild Press, America
Press, Association Press, 1966), p. 107.

[3] Denzinger, 783; *Canons and Decrees of the Council of Trent*, ed. H. J. Schroeder (St.
Louis, Mo.: Herder, 1941), pp. 17, 296. It is not our purpose here to discuss the exact force
of the word "dictatae"; surely it did not represent, even for Roman Catholics of the sixteenth
century, a "mechanical" inspiration theory that cancelled out the personalities of the human
authors of Scripture; but at the same time it leaves no room whatever for a biblical inspiration
of limited or partial scope (cf. Montgomery, "Sixtus of Siena and Roman Catholic Biblical
Scholarship in the Reformation Period," *Archiv fuer Reformationsgeschichte*, LIV/2 [1963],
214-34; reprinted in *Ecumenicity, Evangelicals and Rome* [Grand Rapids, Mich.: Zondervan,
1969], pp. 45-60).

[4] See the numerous documents collected in *Rome and the Study of Scripture*, ed. C. Louis
(7th ed.; St. Meinrad, Indiana: Abbey Press, 1964).

[5] Here Pius X quotes the "Constitutio dogmatica de fide catholicae," c. 2 ("De revelatione"),
approved at Session III of Vatican I (24 April 1870), which in turn cites the Tridentine decree
quoted earlier; see Denzinger, 1787.

280 / *God's Inerrant Word*

Augustine, Epist. 28, c. 3, in Migne's *Patrologiae cursus completus . . . series latina*, XXXIII (August, ii), pp. 112, 3.

[7] Denzinger, 2100, 2102.

[8] *Ibid.*, 2186-2188.

[9] So Lindbeck, an official observer at Vatican II, stated in a course of lectures on contemporary Roman Catholic theology which he delivered at the Chicago Lutheran Theological Seminary (Maywood, Illinois) during the summer of 1961.

[10] Paris-Louvain: Desclée de Brouwer, 1958.

[11] Levie, *The Bible, Word of God in Words of Men*, trans. S. H. Treman (New York: P. J. Kenedy, 1961), pp. 216-17.

[12] *Ibid.*, pp. 221-22.

[13] *Ibid.*, pp. 222, 225.

[14] *Ibid.*, pp. 226-27.

[15] *Ibid.*, pp. 228-29.

[16] R. A. F. MacKenzie, *Faith and History in the Old Testament* (New York: Macmillan, 1963), pp. 80-81. Even more extreme expressions of this viewpoint coupled with the judgment that "an excessive preoccupation with inerrancy can stultify exegesis" (p. 328), mark Spanish Jesuit Luis Alonso Schökel's *The Inspired Word; Scripture in the Light of Language and Literature*, trans. Francis Martin (New York: Herder, 1965); for my review of it see *Ecumenicity, Evangelicals, and Rome (op. cit.* in note 3 above), pp. 104-105.

[17] John L. McKenzie, *Myths and Realities: Studies in Biblical Theology* (Milwaukee: Bruce Publishing Co., 1963), p. 200. In line with his general existential orientation, McKenzie, as banquet speaker at the 7th Annual Meeting of the American Society of Christian Ethics (Seabury-Western Theological Seminary, Evanston, Illinois, January 22, 1966) severely criticized the traditional code morality of his Church and claimed that the New Testament requires only the *agape* ethic of responsible, personal decision in the situational context.

[18] *Catholic Biblical Quarterly*, XXII (1960), pp. 160-75.

[19] If it is argued that the Encyclical *Humani generis* (1950) seems to restrict the liberty permitted by *Divino afflante Spiritu*, one need only consider Jesuit Gustave Lambert's well-received interpretation that *Humani generis* does not function in this manner; this is likewise the conclusion of Count Begouen, the eminent French anthropologist (see James M. Connolly, *The Voices of France; a Survey of Contemporary Theology in France* [New York: Macmillan, 1961], pp. 189-90).

[20] Joseph A. Fitzmyer, S. J. (ed.), *The Historical Truth of the Gospels (The 1964 Instruction of the Biblical Commission) with Commentary* (Glen Rock, N.J.: Paulist Press, 1964), p. 14; Fitzmyer's edition of the Instruction appeared first in *Theological Studies*, XXV (September, 1964), pp. 386-408.

[21] *The Documents of Vatican II (op. cit.*, in note 2 above), p. 119.

[22] *Ibid.*

[23] Fitzmyer, *op. cit.*, p. 18, n. 19.

[24] J. C. Fenton, "Father Moran's Prediction," *American Ecclesiastical Review*, CXLVI (1962), pp. 194-95.

[25] James M. Robinson, "Interpretation of Scripture in Biblical Studies Today," in *Ecumenical Dialogue at Harvard: The Roman Catholic-Protestant Colloquium*, ed. Samuel H. Miller and G. Ernest Wright (Cambridge, Mass.: Belknap Press of Harvard University Press, 1964), p. 102.

[26] *Ibid.*, p. 105. Cf. the Protestant and Roman Catholic contributions to *Scripture and Ecumenism: Protestant, Catholic, Orthodox and Jewish*, ed. Leonard J. Swidler ("Duquesne Studies. Theological Series," 3; Pittsburgh, Pa.: Duquesne University Press, 1965).

[27] Barth, "A Letter to the Author," in Küng's *Justification*, trans. Collins, Tolk, and Granskou (New York: Thomas Nelson, 1964). For my review of Küng's book, see *Ecumenicity, Evangelicals, and Rome (op. cit.* in note 3 above), pp. 103-104.

[28] Karl Adam, *The Spirit of Catholicism*, trans. Justin McCann (rev. ed.; Garden City, N.Y.: Doubleday Image Books, 1954), pp. 62-63.

[29] *Ibid.*, p. 232.

[30] *The Documents of Vatican II (op. cit.* in note 2 above), p. 109.

[31] On Marxist historiography and Orwell's *1984*, see Montgomery, *The Shape of the Past: An Introduction to Philosophical Historiography* (Ann Arbor, Mich.: Edwards Brothers, 1963), pp. 8-9, 74-75, 80-81, 217-56, 275-77.

[32] For further discussion on the subject, see my article, "Evangelical Unity in the Light of Contemporary Orthodox Eastern-Roman Catholic-Protestant Ecumenicity," *The Spring-*

fielder, XXX (Autumn, 1965), pp. 8-30 (published in shorter form under the title "Evangelical Unity and Contemporary Ecumenicity," in *The Gordon Review*, IX [Winter, 1966], pp. 69-90, and reprinted in *Ecumenicity, Evangelicals, and Rome* [*op. cit.* in note 3 above], pp. 13-44).

[33] Cf. Montgomery, *The 'Is-God-Dead?' Controversy* (Grand Rapids, Mich.: Zondervan, 1966), *passim*, and *The Suicide of Christian Theology* (*op. cit.* in note 1 above), *passim*.

[34] I have developed this point at some length in my article, "Inspiration and Inerrancy: A New Departure," *Evangelical Theological Society Bulletin*, VIII (Spring, 1965), pp. 45-75. This essay appears in revised form in my books, *The Suicide of Christian Theology*, and *Crisis in Lutheran Theology* (2 vols.; 2d ed.; Minneapolis: Bethany Fellowship, 1973), I, pp. 15-44.

[35] See Frederick Ferré, *Language, Logic and God* (New York: Harper, 1961), chap. viii ("The Logic of Encounter"), pp. 94-104; C. B. Martin, "A Religious Way of Knowing," in *New Essays in Philosophical Theology*, ed. Antony Flew and Alasdair MacIntyre (London: SCM Press, 1955), pp. 76-95; and Kai Nielsen, "Can Faith Validate God-Talk?" in *New Theology No. 1*, ed. Martin E. Marty and Dean G. Peerman (New York: Macmillan Paperbacks, 1964).

[36] *Lutheran Witness Reporter: Great Lakes Edition*, May 8, 1966, p. 1.

[37] *Lutheran Witness Reporter: Great Lakes Edition*, May 22, 1966, p. 7. Cf. Montgomery, "Lutheran Hermeneutics and Hermeneutics Today " in *Aspects of Biblical Hermeneutics* ("Concordia Theological Monthly. Occasional Papers," No. 1; St. Louis, Mo., 1966), pp. 78-108 (reprinted in my *Crisis in Lutheran Theology* [*op. cit.*], I, pp. 45-77, and *In Defense of Martin Luther* [Milwaukee: Northwestern Publishing House, 1970], pp. 40-85).

[38] A non-biblical example may help here. In understanding modern stream-of-consciousness writing (e.g., portions of James Joyce's *A Portrait of the Artist As a Young Man;* his *Ulysses*; parts of Faulkner's *The Sound and the Fury;* Salinger's *Catcher in the Rye*; the reader is hopelessly led astray by the *indicia* until he discovers, through the express teaching of the novel, the actual age of the character involved. Having learned this, he has an inductively derived *Gestalt* for understanding the particulars of the stream-of-consciousness narration; to reverse the procedure would be to lose all hope of meaningful interpretation.

[39] Christ gave His Apostles a special gift of the Holy Spirit which we today would probably term "total recall" (see John 14:26-27; 16:12-15; cf. Acts 1:21-16); this is the basis of the scriptural authority of the New Testament writings, which were produced in Apostolic circles. On this and the status of Paul as an Apostle, see my *Shape of the Past* (*op. cit.* in note 31 above), pp. 138-39, 171-72.

[40] A point well made by Augustin Cardinal Bea in his valuable syllabus, *De inspiratione et inerrantia Sacrae Scripturae; notae historicae et dogmaticae quas in usum privatum auditorum composuit* (new ed.; Rome: Pontificium Institutum Biblicum, 1954), pp. 44-45, but unfortunately ignored by most representatives of New Shape Roman Catholic biblical scholarship. See also Bea's excellent work, *The Study of The Synoptic Gospels; New Approaches and Outlooks*, ed. Joseph A. Fitzmyer (New York: Harper, 1965).

[41] On the incompatibility between the "New Hermeneutic" (represented by Ebeling, Fuchs, Ott, Conzelmann, G. Bornkamm, *et al.*) and the hermeneutic of the Reformation, see my essay, "Lutheran Hermeneutics and Hermeneutics Today" (cited above in note 37).

[42] See above, note 6 and corresponding text.

CONTRIBUTORS

JOHN H. FRAME—A. B., Princeton University; B.D., Westminster Theological Seminary; M.A., Yale University; M.Phil., Yale University. Assistant Professor of Systematic Theology at Westminster Theological Seminary; M.Th., Westminster Theological Seminary, Philadelphia (1968-).

JOHN H. GERSTNER—B.A., Westminster College; B.Th., Westminster Theological Seminary; Ph.D., Harvard University; D.D., Tarkio College. Professor of Church History, Pittsburgh Theological Seminary (1950-).

PETER R. JONES—B.A., University of Wales, Cardiff; B.D., Gordon Divinity School; Th.M., Harvard; Ph.D., Princeton Theological Seminary. Professor-elect of New Testament at the Faculté Libre de Théologie Réformée of the University of Marseille in Aix-en-Provence (1973-).

JOHN WARWICK MONTGOMERY—A.B. with distinction in philosophy, Cornell University, B.L.S. and M.A., University of California at Berkeley; B.D. and Master of Sacred Theology, Wittenberg University; Ph.D., University of Chicago; Docteur de l'Université, mention Théologie Protestante, University of Strasbourg, France. Professor and Chairman, Division of Church History and History of Christian Thought, Trinity Evangelical Divinity School, Illinois (1964-1974); Director of the Seminary's European Program at University of Strasbourg, France (1966-1974); Professor-elect of Law and Theology, International School of Law, Washington, D. C. (1974-).

J. I. PACKER—B.A., Oxford (1st cl Classics, 2nd cl Literae Humaniores, 1st cl Theology); D.Phil., Oxford. Associate Principal, Trinity College, Bristol, England (1972-).

CLARK H. PINNOCK—B.A., University of Toronto; Ph.D., University of Manchester. Professor of Systematic Theology, Trinity Evangelical Divinity School, Illinois (1969-1974); Associate Professor-elect of Systematic Theology, Regents College, Vancouver, British Columbia (1974-).

ROBERT C. SPROUL—B.A., Westminster College; B.D., Pittsburgh Theological Seminary; Drs., Free University of Amsterdam. Staff Theologian for Ligonier Valley Study Center (1971-) and Visiting Professor of Apologetics at Gordon-Conwell Seminary (1972-).

INDEX

A

Abbott, Walter M.—279
Abraham—29, 73, 74, 106, 147, 183, 184, 202
Abel—202
Abimilech—127
Adam—100, 171, 172, 254
Adam, Karl—272, 273, 280
Aesop—135
Philo—230, 231, 235
Albright, William Foxwell—249, 260
Aldrich, Virgil C.—30, 41
Alexander, Archibald—115, 118, 128, 129, 131, 138
Altenburg—94
Althans, Paul—70, 92, 127
Amalek—185
Annas—82
Apollos—226
Aquinas, Thomas—64, 93, 113, 252
Arberry, A. J.—34, 42
Aristotle—14, 48
Arndt, W. F.—13, 92
Aubert, Roger—269
Augustine (St.)—34, 45, 61, 64, 68, 90, 108, 113, 121, 123, 125, 135, 140, 141, 142, 143, 144, 154, 266, 279, 280
Ayer, A. J.—175

B

Bach, Johann Sebastian—64
Bachmann, E. Theodore—92
Bacon, Francis—128
Bainton, Roland H.—61, 89
Baird, William—226, 237, 238
Balaam—127
Bakker, J. T.—260
Bardtke, H.—240
Barr, James—50, 53, 54, 58, 59, 62
Barrett, Cyril K.—176, 218, 235, 236, 260
Barth, Karl—18, 46, 57, 58, 60, 62, 123, 127, 128, 135, 164, 165, 166, 167, 172, 173, 174, 175, 194, 195, 196, 197, 200, 244, 255, 260, 261, 272, 280
Barzun, Jacques—25, 41
Battles, F. L.—99, 112, 113
Bauke, H.—96, 113
Baum, N. W.—112
Bavnick, H.—152, 158, 261

Baxter, Richard—126
Bea, Augustin—281
Beardsley—30
Beattie, F. R.—121, 123, 135, 140
Beegle, Dewey M.—13, 62, 151, 158
Begouen (Count)—280
Behannon, W.—132
Bellarmine—61
Benedictus XV—260, 266
Benoit, P.—240
Bentzen, Aage—240
Berger, Pete—17, 40
Berger, Samuel—93
Berkhof, H.—243, 244, 245, 260
Berkhof, Louis—55
Berkouwer, G. C.—20, 243, 244, 245, 258, 260
Bertrangs, A.—238
Betz, O.—239, 240
Beveridge, Henry—260
Beyerhaus, Pekr—62
Bigg, Charles—235
Bizer, E.—142
Black, Matthew—240
Blanke, Fritz—93
Bliss, Henry Evelyn—26, 41
Bloch, Renée—240
Bloesch, Donald—85, 86, 93
Bodamer, W.—92
Boniface VIII—271
Bornkamm, G.—237, 281
Bornkamm, Heinrich—67, 76, 90, 91
Bourke, Myles M.—269, 270
Bowden, John—261
Braaten, Carl E.—261
Brahma—277
Brand, Hennig—38
Briggs, Charles A.—97, 113, 116, 136
Bromiley, G. W.—176, 200, 218, 261
Brown, Jerry Wayne—93
Brown, R. E.—218, 271
Brown, W. A.—132, 140
Brownlee, W. H.—240
Bruce, F. F.—20, 234, 236, 238, 240, 260
Brunner, Emil—69, 92, 116, 194, 199, 200, 253, 254, 260
Brunotte, H.—93
Buber, Martin—165, 176, 268
Bucer, Martin—112
Bultmann, Rudolf—57, 62, 148, 154, 281, 237, 259, 261, 271, 275, 279

Burtchaell, James T.—21, 40, 41
Buswell, J. Oliver—141
Butler, Joseph—113, 116

C

Callahan, Daniel—18, 40
Callahan, D. J.—61
Calvin, John—46, 47, 48, 52, 53, 54, 55, 59, 60, 61, 62, 64, 95-114, 123, 124, 125, 134, 139, 236, 251, 260
Campbell, Robert—18, 40
Canisius—61
Cano, Melchior—61
Carlstadt, Bodenstein von—82, 93
Carlyle, Thomas—64
Carnell, E. J.—148, 157
Carter, Douglas—92
Cartwright, Thomas—56
Cassern, N. H.—157
Cazelles, H.—240
Cerfaux, L.—238
Chesterton, G. R.—135
Cicero—36, 48
Clark, Gordon—42, 175
Clement—200
Cocceius—137, 142
Cohen, A.—236
Coleridge, Samuel Taylor—135
Collange, J.-F.—237, 238, 239
Connolly, James M.—280
Conzelmann, H.—236, 241, 281
Cordatus—91
Cornelius, David K.—41
Costello, Charles Joseph—91, 157
Counts, W. M.—132
Craig, Samuel G.—42, 140, 198
Croll, P. C.—91, 93
Cross, F. M. Jr.—239
Cullmann, O.—58, 236, 240
Cunitz, E.—112

D

Daniel—205, 254
Dantine, W.—218
Daruma—42
Daube, David—209, 218
David, (King)—103, 202, 203, 205
Davidson, Robert—157
Davies, Rupert E.—97, 107, 113, 114
Davies, W. D.—218, 239
de Jongste—198
Delcor, M.—240
Demosthenes—48
Denis, O.—237
Denzinger, Heinrich—260, 265, 279, 280
De Vries, J. H.—198
Dewart, Leslie—18
Dewey, John—41
Dibelius, Martin—236, 241

Dodd, C. H.—218, 235, 252, 254, 260
Dooeyweerd, H.—248
Doumergue—97, 107, 113, 123
Dowey—97, 123
Drummond, Henry—20
Dupont-Sommer, André—240

E

Ebling, Gerhard—69, 92, 93, 281
Eccles (Rev. Mr.)—15
Eck, Johann von—44, 61, 68, 93
Edwards, Jonathan—122, 124, 126
Einstein, Albert—65
Eisenhower, Dwight D.—39
Emerson, Ralph Waldo—277
Engelder, Theodore—13, 69, 92
Erasmus, Desiderius—51, 52, 146
Erichson, A.—112
Euclid—33
Eusebius—81
Evans, Christopher—58, 62
Eve—171, 172

F

Farrer, Austin—226, 237
Faulkner, William—281
Fearnside, W. Ward—260
Fenton, J. C.—280
Ferré, Frederick—281
Ficker, J.—42, 91
Fitzgerald, K. L.—238
Fitzmyer, Joseph A.—280, 281
Flew, Anthony—161, 162, 163, 165, 166, 169, 171, 172, 175, 176, 281
Forestell, J.—157
Frame, John—254
France, R. T.—211, 218
Freed, E. D.—218
Fuchs, E.—281
Fuller, Daniel—20, 24, 29, 31, 37, 38, 41, 42, 132, 147, 148, 157
Fuller, R. H.—240

G

Gabriel—34
de Gaiffier, Baudouin—93
Gale, Theophilus—126
Gasque, W. Ward—234
Gaussen, Louis—20, 40, 180, 198
Gaussen, Ulysse—40
Gechan, E. R.—140
Geiselmann, J. R.—61
Geldenhys, N.—218
Georgi, Dieter—235, 237
Gerhardsson, B.—238
Gerrish, B. A.—61
Gerstner, John—180
Giblet, J.—238
Gillespie, George—117
Glasson, T. F.—239
Goguel, M.—217

Gollwitzer, Helmut—260
Gordon, C. H.—154, 158
Gorer, Geoffrey—16, 40
Green—131
Grant, F. C.—200
Gregory I.—252
Gritsch, E. W. and R. C.—91
Grosheide—236
Gruhn, Victor I.—91
Güttgemann, E.—235
Gunkel, H.—268
Gustavus Adolphus—94

H
Hadden, Jeffrey K.—22, 40, 41
Hahn, F.—240
Haire, J. L. M.—176
Haley, J. W.—158
Hamilton, Sir William—121
Hanson, R. P. C.—61
Haran—74
Harbison, E. Harris—91
Hare, R. M.—275
Harnack, Adolf von—69, 92, 219, 234
Harris, J. R.—235
Harrison, R. K.—148, 158
Harrold, Charles Fredrick—41
Hase, Karl von—212
Hastings—122
Haupt, E.—219, 234
Hay, Charles E.—91
Henderson, Ian—16, 40
Henry VIII—61
Henry, Carl F. H.—41, 198, 236
Heppe, H.—136, 142
Herod (King)—28, 82
Hershberger, Guy F.—93
Hill, Samuel S. Jr.—93
Hillerbrand, Hans—94
Hodge, A. A.—119, 136, 142
Hoether, William B.—260
Hodge, Charles—55, 115, 116, 117, 118, 121, 122, 126, 128, 129, 131, 137, 138, 157
Hoenecke, Adolf—83, 93
Hoenecke, W. and O.—93
Hoffecker, W. A.—115, 129, 138, 140, 141, 142
Holden, William—146
Holl, Karl—88
Holtz, Traugott—238
Hoogstra, J. T.—112, 142
Hooke, S. H.—93
Hooker, Richard—56
Hooper, Walter—158
Hosea—75
Houtin, Albert—41
Hughes, P. E.—237, 239

I
Iranaeus—235, 259

Isaac—202
Isaacs, W. H.—237
Isaiah—75, 76, 205, 254

J
Jacob—106, 202
Jacobs, Charles M.—92, 93
James (St.)—78, 79, 80, 83, 256
Jensen, John M.—94
Jeremiah—75, 106, 221, 254
Jeremias, Gert—231, 240
Jeremias, Joachim—202, 218, 241, 254, 260
Jerome (St.)—68, 81, 91
Jethro—127
Jewett, Paul King—92, 260
John (the Baptist)—206, 212
John (St.)—46, 67, 80, 217
Johnston, O. R.—62
Johnston, W. B.—176
Jonah—67, 203, 208
Jones, Henry—236
Josephus—230, 238, 239
Joshua—185, 188
Joyce, James—281
Judas Iscariot—82

K
Kähler, Martin—257, 261
Käsemann, E.—236, 239, 241
Kant, Emmanuel—57
Kantzer, Kenneth S.—96, 103, 110, 112, 113, 114, 148, 158, 218
Kaufman, G. D.—157, 218
Kierkegaard, Søren—166
Kelly, J. N. D.—241
Kelsey, D. H.—157
Kepler, Johannes—64
Kerrigan, A.—238
Keyes, Clinton W.—238
Kidd, B. J.—112
Kik, J. W.—198
Kirk, K. E.—237
Kitchen, K. A.—158
Kittel, G.—218, 259, 261
Kline, Meredith G.—180, 186, 198, 199, 236, 241
Klug, Eugene F. A.—74, 92
Knaske, J. C. F.—61
Knight, Harold—200
Knudsen (Prof.)—27
Köberle, Adolf—86, 93
Koester, Helmut—241
Kooiman, Willem Jan—66, 88-90
Köstlin, Julius—66, 73, 74, 91, 92, 124
Kraus, C. Norman—120, 121, 132, 140
Krentz, Edgar—92, 93
Küng, Hans—18, 40, 151, 157, 259, 261, 272, 280
Kuitert, H. M.—260

Kuyper, Abraham—9, 119, 121, 124, 125, 126, 140, 180, 198, 245, 248

L

Ladd, G. E.—218, 236, 237
Lagrange, Marie-Joseph—263, 279
Lamb, Rev. Basil—16
Lambert, Gustave—280
Langevin, P.-E.—238
Leaney, A. R. C.—157
Lehmann, Helmut T.—91
Leibniz, Wilhelm—121
Leitch, James W.—260
Lelong, Maurice—19, 40
Leo XIII—260
Lessing, G. E.—38, 93
Levie, Jean—266, 267, 268, 280
Lewis, C. S.—150, 154, 158
Liddell, H. G.—236
Lightfoot, J. B.—234
Lightner, R. P.—217
Lindbeck, George—266, 280
Lindsay, T. M.—132
Livingston, William D.—132, 140, 141
Litton, E. A.—55
Lobstein, P.—97, 112, 113
Locke, John—121, 131
Loetscher, L. A.—142
Lohse, Eduard—239
Loisy, Alfred—26, 27, 41, 265, 266, 269
Louis, C.—279
Luke (St.)—136, 148, 204, 235
Luther, Hans—64
Luther, Martin—20, 42, 43, 44, 45, 46, 51, 52, 54, 56, 61, 62, 63-94, 124, 135, 144, 152, 257

M

McCann, Justin—280
McDonald, John—240
Machen, J. Gresham—126, 131, 140, 141
MacIntyre, Alasdair—175, 176, 281
MacKay, John R.—115, 140
Mackenzie, R. A. F.—263, 268, 273, 280
McKenzie, John L.—268, 275, 280
McNeile, A. H.—218
McNeill, J. T.—112
McPherson, Thomas—165, 176
Manichaeus—142
Mann, C. S.—249, 260
Marcel, Pierre—41
Mark (St.)—114, 254
Markarian, J. J.—116, 123, 133, 139, 140, 141
Martin, C. B.—281
Martin, Francis—280
Martin, James—260
Martin, R. P.—234

Martini, C. M.—157, 238
Marty, Martin E.—281
Masters, Donald C.—20, 40
Matthew (St.)—147
Mavrodes, George I.—37, 38, 42
Meeks, Wayne A.—239
Meeter—140
Melanchthon—43, 112, 125
Melchizedek—127
Metzger, Bruce M.—20, 238
Meuleman, G. E.—260
Michelangelo—64
Migne—280
Miller, Samuel H.—280
Mitchell, Edwin Knox—92
Moffatt, J.—236
Mohammed—34
Monod, Théodore—88, 94
Montgomery, John Warwick—14, 40, 41, 42, 91, 92, 93, 151, 157, 158, 180, 279, 281
Morris, L.—218, 236
Moses—67, 73, 74, 185, 186, 188, 189, 198, 199, 200, 205, 220, 224, 225, 226, 227, 228, 229, 230, 231, 232, 233, 234, 237, 238, 239, 240, 241, 253, 256
Mueller, J. Theodore—92
Müntzer, Thomas—87, 94
Muggeridge, Malcolm—16, 40
Mulhaupt, E.—112
Munck, J.—233, 235, 236, 240
Murphy, R. E.—157
Murray, John—106, 113, 114, 180, 198, 200, 254

N

Nakamura, Julia V.—42
Nash, Ronald H.—42
Needham, H.—198
Newman, John Henry—25, 41, 146
Nicodemus—29, 278
Nicole, Rodger—156, 158, 254
Nielsen, Kai—280
Nineham, D. E.—52, 58, 62
Noah—198, 203, 267

O

Obermann, H. A.—61
O'Brien—274
Ockenga, Harold John—263
Oethius, James H.—261
O'Hanlan, D. U.—61
Oostendorp, D. W.—239
Origen—113
Orr, James—20, 116, 253, 254, 260
Orwell, George—80, 274
Ott, Heinrich—281
Otto, Rudolph—165

P

Pache, René—180, 198

Packer, J. I.—62, 148, 157, 158, 180, 208, 215, 218, 254, 260
Paine, Thomas—93
Painter, F. V. N.—91
Pannier, J.—97, 113
Parker, T. H. L.—52, 62, 96, 105, 112, 113, 114, 160, 176
Pascal, Blasé—64
Patton, Francis Lindey—116, 132, 140, 141
Pauck, Wilhelm—92, 94
Paul (St.)—46, 53, 78, 79, 80, 82, 83, 102, 103, 114, 136, 148, 150, 162, 163, 190, 191, 200, 217, 219-241, 256, 281
Pease, Robert—27, 41
Peerman, Dean G.—281
Pelikan, Jaroslav—91, 92
Peter (St.)—65, 82, 103, 190, 192, 200
Peter, C. J.—157
Pfürtner, Stephanus—93
Pharaoh—127
Phillips, J. B.—158
Pieper, Francis—55, 93, 158
Piepkorn, Arthur Carl—143, 157
Pilate, Pontius—28, 82
Pinnock, Clark H.—37, 41, 133, 180, 198, 217, 241, 254
Pius IX—265
Pius X—265, 271, 279
Plato—36, 48
Plummer, A.—236, 237
Polman, A. D. R.—98, 112, 113, 114
Pope, W. B.—55
Poulat, Emile—41
Prenter, Regin—61, 94
Preus, Robert D.—157

Q

Quenstedt, Johann Andreas—149
Quinn, Edward—40, 93, 261

R

Rabelais, F.—31
Ramm, Bernard—126
Reid, J. K. S.—66, 91, 113
Reid, Thomas—120
Reitschel—66
Remensnyder, Junius B.—91
Renan—270
Rengstorf, K. H.—238
Renwick, A. M.—61
Reu, M.—69, 84, 91, 93
Reuss, E.—112
Rhees, Rush—176
Richardson, Cyril C.—261
Richardson, Ernest Cushing—26, 41
Ridderbos, H.—180, 198
Rieff, Philip—92
Robertson, A.—236

Robinson, James R.—270, 271
Rogers, Jack—117, 129, 133, 140
Roloff, Jurgen—221, 235, 238
Runia, Klaas—123, 158, 260
Russell, C. A.—126

S

St. Vincent, Edwin—41
Salinger, J. D.—281
Sanday, W.—130
Sandeen, Ernest R.—117, 118, 119, 136, 140, 142
Sartiaux, Félix—41
Sarah—74, 183
Sass, G.—238
Satan—89, 188
Scaer, David P.—236
Schadow—66
Schippers, R.—260
Schleiermacher, Friedrich—97, 128, 249
Schmidt, John—88
Schmidthals, Walter—219, 234, 235
Schnakenburg, Rudolf—219, 234
Schökels, Luis Alonso—280
Schroeder, H. J.—279
Schultz, Robert C.—92
Scott, D. D.—198
Scott, Robert—236
Searle, Ronald—16, 40
Seeberg, R.—69, 97, 113
Seely—141
Segal, M. H.—153
Shakespeare, William—36
Shelley, Bruce—93
Sixtus of Siena—279
Smart, J. D.—157
Smith, Charles Merrill—17, 40
Smith, G. B.—132, 140
Smythies, Yorick—176
Snow, C. P.—25
Solomon—203, 208
Southey, Robert—64
Spitz, Lewis W. Sr.—202
Sproul, R. C.—9
Spurgeon, C. H.—202
Stanely, D. M.—238, 239
Steely, John E.—235
Stegner, W. R.—239
Stephen (St.)—73, 74, 147, 148
Stephenson, A. M. G.—237
Stonehouse, N. R.—198, 214, 236, 241
Stott, John R. W.—218
Strachen, R. H.—237
Strong, A. H.—55
Surburg, Raymond F.—158
Swete, H. B.—218
Swidler, Leonard J.—280

T

Tasker, R. V. G.—215, 218, 239

Tatian—52
Tavard, G.—61
Taylor, James—176
Teeple, H. M.—240
Tenney, M. C.—241
Terence—25, 41
Tertullian—140, 141, 142
Thomas, W. H. Griffith—55
Thomson, G. T.—142, 176, 200
Tilden, E. E.—218
Timothy—191, 237
Torrance, D. W.—112
Torrance, T. F.—112, 116, 140, 176, 200, 207, 218
Travers, Walter—56
Treman, S. H.—280
Trites—132

U
Updike, John—15
Urquhart, Thomas—31

V
Vander Woude, A. S.—240, 260
Van Til, Cornelius—62, 116, 119, 123, 140, 198, 244, 245, 246, 248, 260
van Unnik, W. C.—238
Vawter, Bruce—42, 157, 218
Vermès, G.—240
Von Rad, G.—240, 271, 275
Vorgrimmler, H.—157
Vos, G.—131

W
Walther, Wilhelm—83, 93
Walvoord, John F.—92, 112, 217, 260

Warfield, B. B.—20, 37, 38, 42, 46, 53, 61, 62, 97, 103, 112, 113, 114, 115-142, 151, 152, 155, 157, 158, 180, 189, 198, 199, 200, 207, 217, 248, 254, 258
Watson, Philip—66, 91
Waugh, Evelyn—16
Weber, O.—94
Wells, David F.—157, 158
Wells, H. G.—161
Wenham, J. W.—180, 198, 212, 213, 214, 217, 218
Wesley, John—64, 80
Westermann, Claus—240
Whitgift, Johnathan—56
Wieder, N.—240
Wilson—131
Wimsatt—30
Winkworth, Catherine—94
Winston—274
Winter, Ralph—62
Wittgenstein, Ludwig—176
Wright, G. Ernest—280
Wood, Arthur Skevington—44, 45, 61, 62, 73, 92
Woolley, P.—198
Wyon, Olive—92, 199, 260

Y
Yamauchi, Edwin—153, 158
Yoder, J. H.—218
Young, E. J.—180, 198, 254, 258, 259, 261

Z
Zechariah—67
Zerafa, P.—157
Zwingli, Huldrich—68, 125
Zylstra, Bernard—257